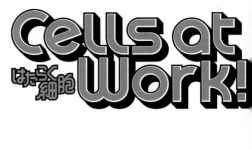

Cells at Work!

はたらく細胞

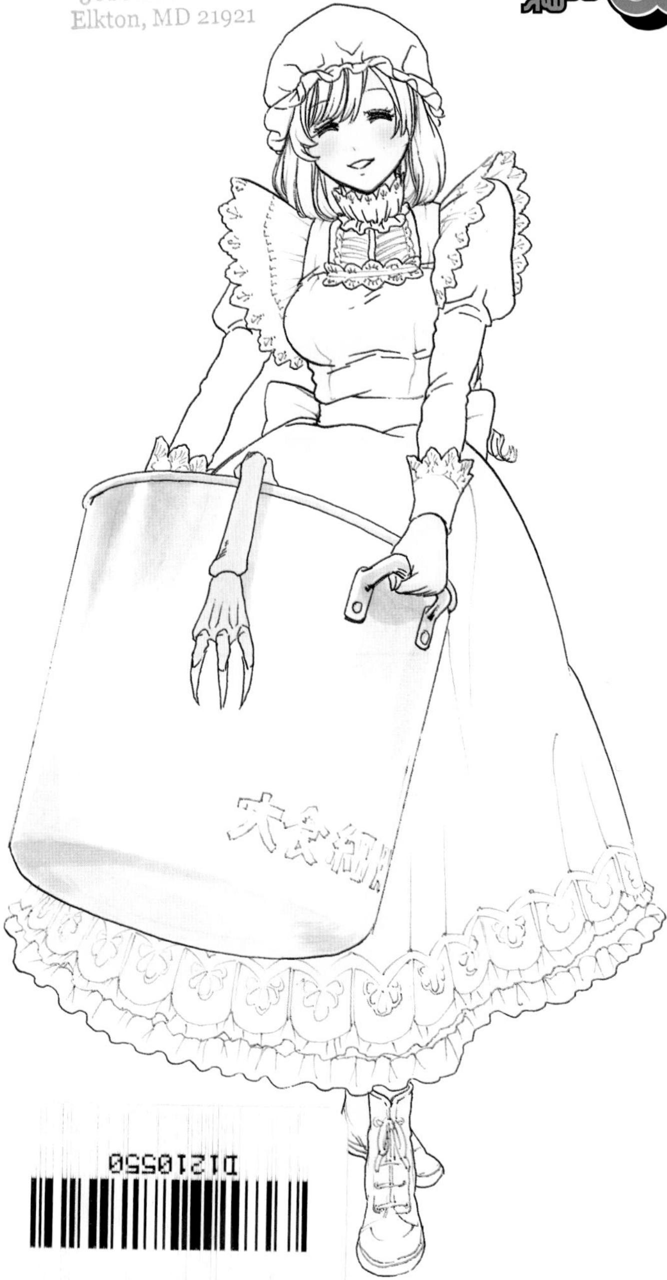

04

AKANE SHIMIZU

CONTENTS

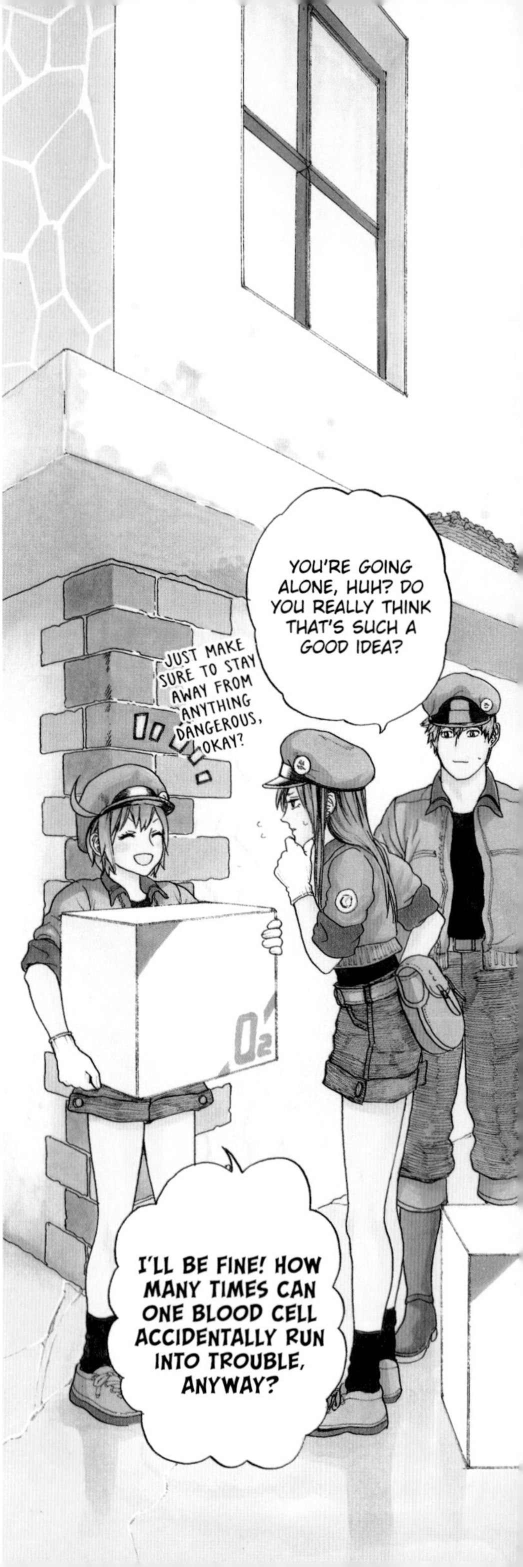

YOU'RE GOING ALONE, HUH? DO YOU REALLY THINK THAT'S SUCH A GOOD IDEA?
JUST MAKE SURE TO STAY AWAY FROM ANYTHING DANGEROUS, OKAY?
I'LL BE FINE! HOW MANY TIMES CAN ONE BLOOD CELL ACCIDENTALLY RUN INTO TROUBLE, ANYWAY?

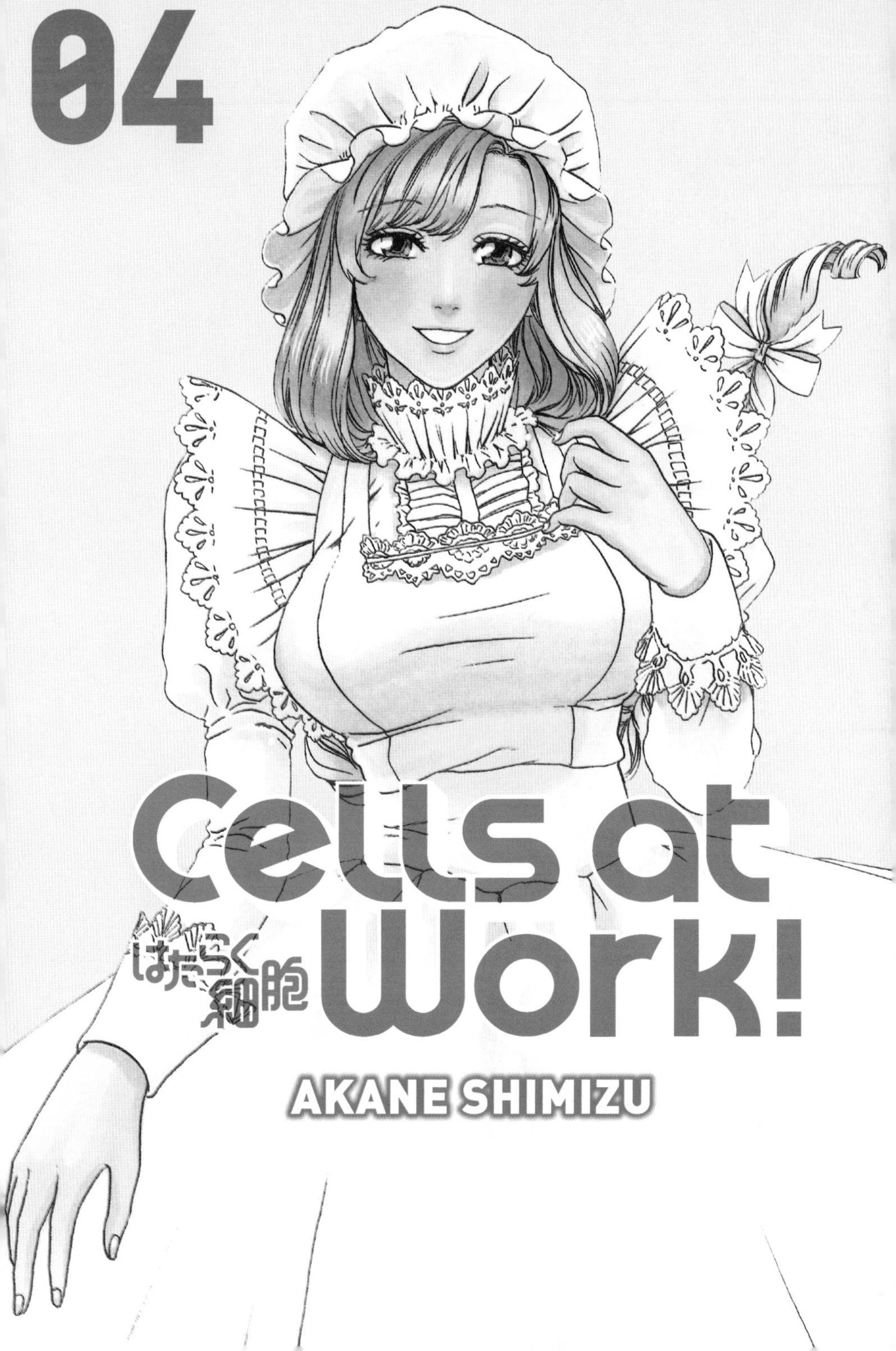

04

Cells at Work!

はたらく細胞

AKANE SHIMIZU

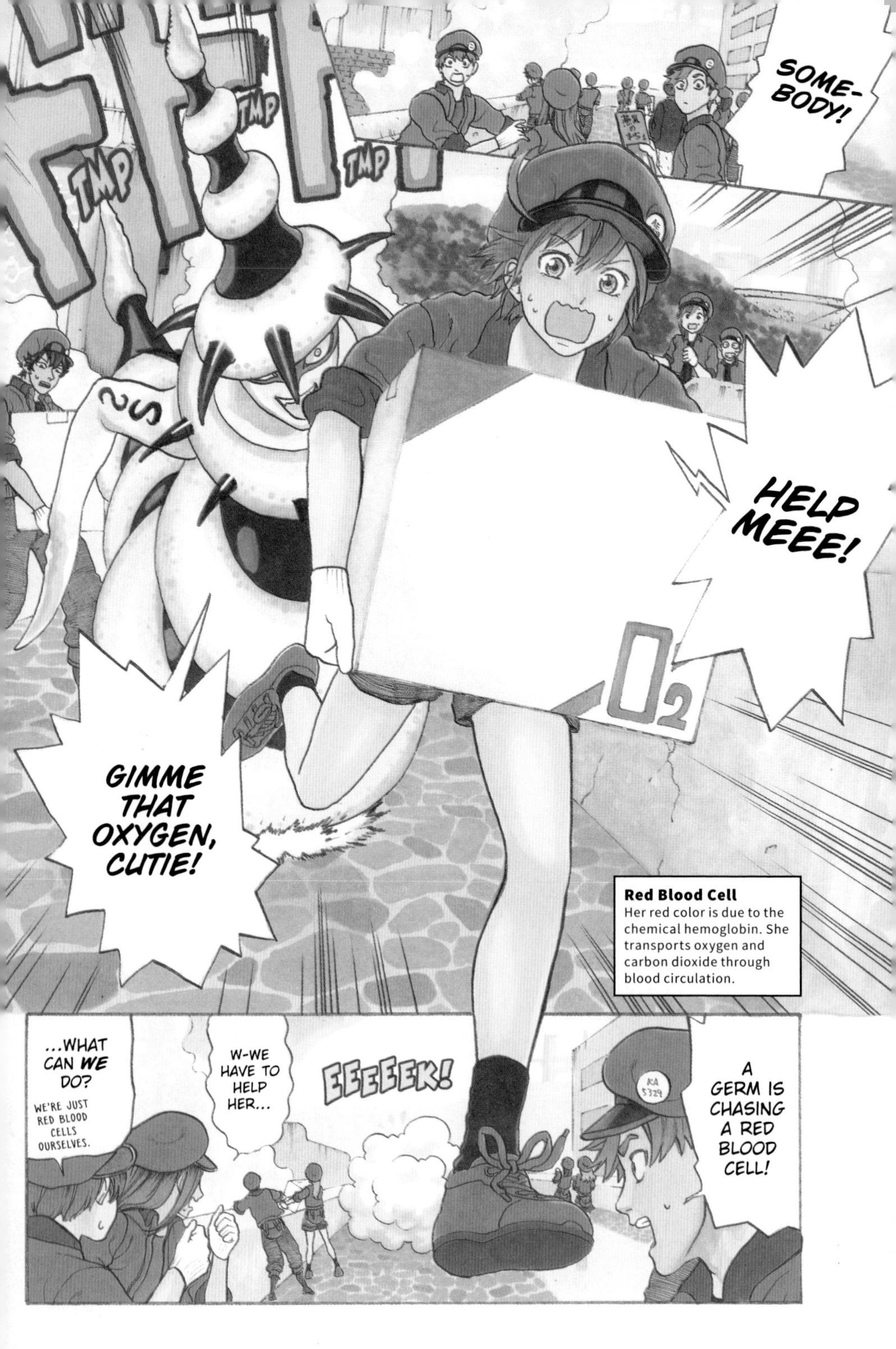
TMP TMP TMP
SOME-BODY!
HELP MEEE!
GIMME THAT OXYGEN, CUTIE!
O_2
Red Blood Cell
Her red color is due to the chemical hemoglobin. She transports oxygen and carbon dioxide through blood circulation.
A GERM IS CHASING A RED BLOOD CELL!
EEEEEK!
W-WE HAVE TO HELP HER...
...WHAT CAN WE DO?
WE'RE JUST RED BLOOD CELLS OURSELVES.

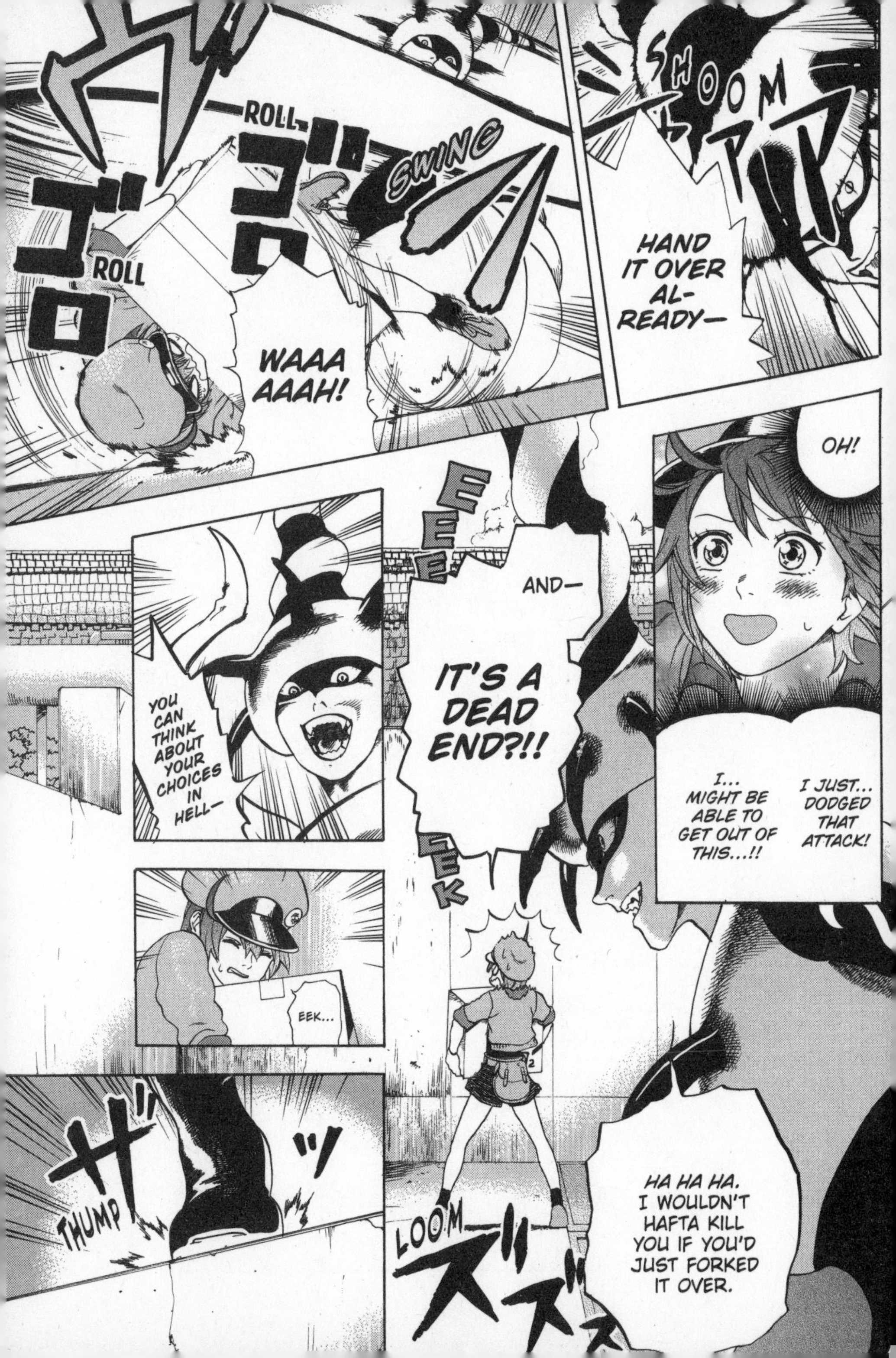
SHOOM
HAND IT OVER AL- READY—
ROLL
ROLL
SWING
WAAAAAAH!
OH!
I JUST... DODGED THAT ATTACK!
I... MIGHT BE ABLE TO GET OUT OF THIS...!!
EEEEEK
AND—
IT'S A DEAD END?!!
YOU CAN THINK ABOUT YOUR CHOICES IN HELL—
EEK...
HA HA HA. I WOULDN'T HAFTA KILL YOU IF YOU'D JUST FORKED IT OVER.
LOOM
THUMP

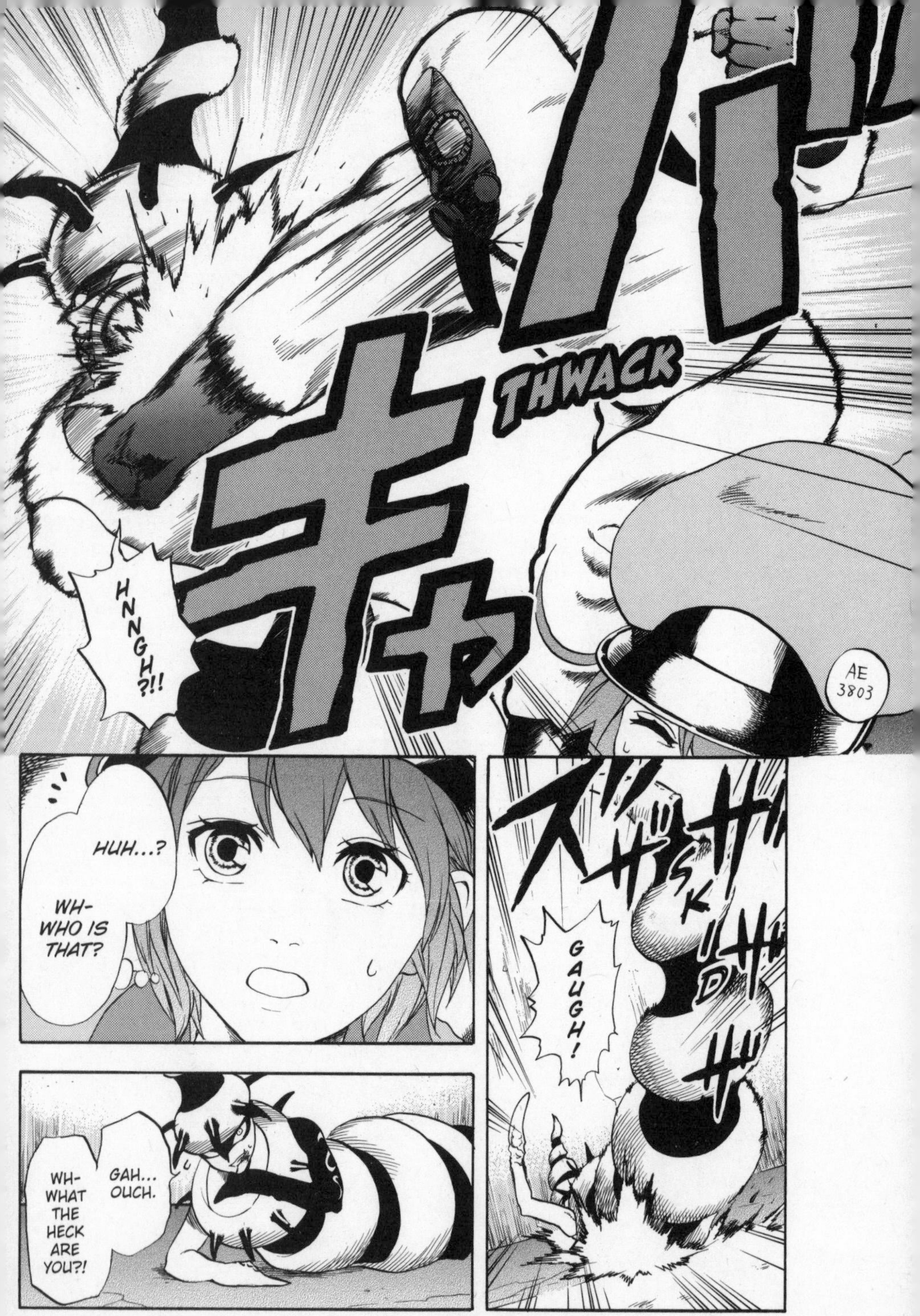

AE 3803
THWACK
HNNGH?!!
SKID
GAUGH!
HUH...?
WH- WHO IS THAT?
GAH... OUCH.
WH- WHAT THE HECK ARE YOU?!

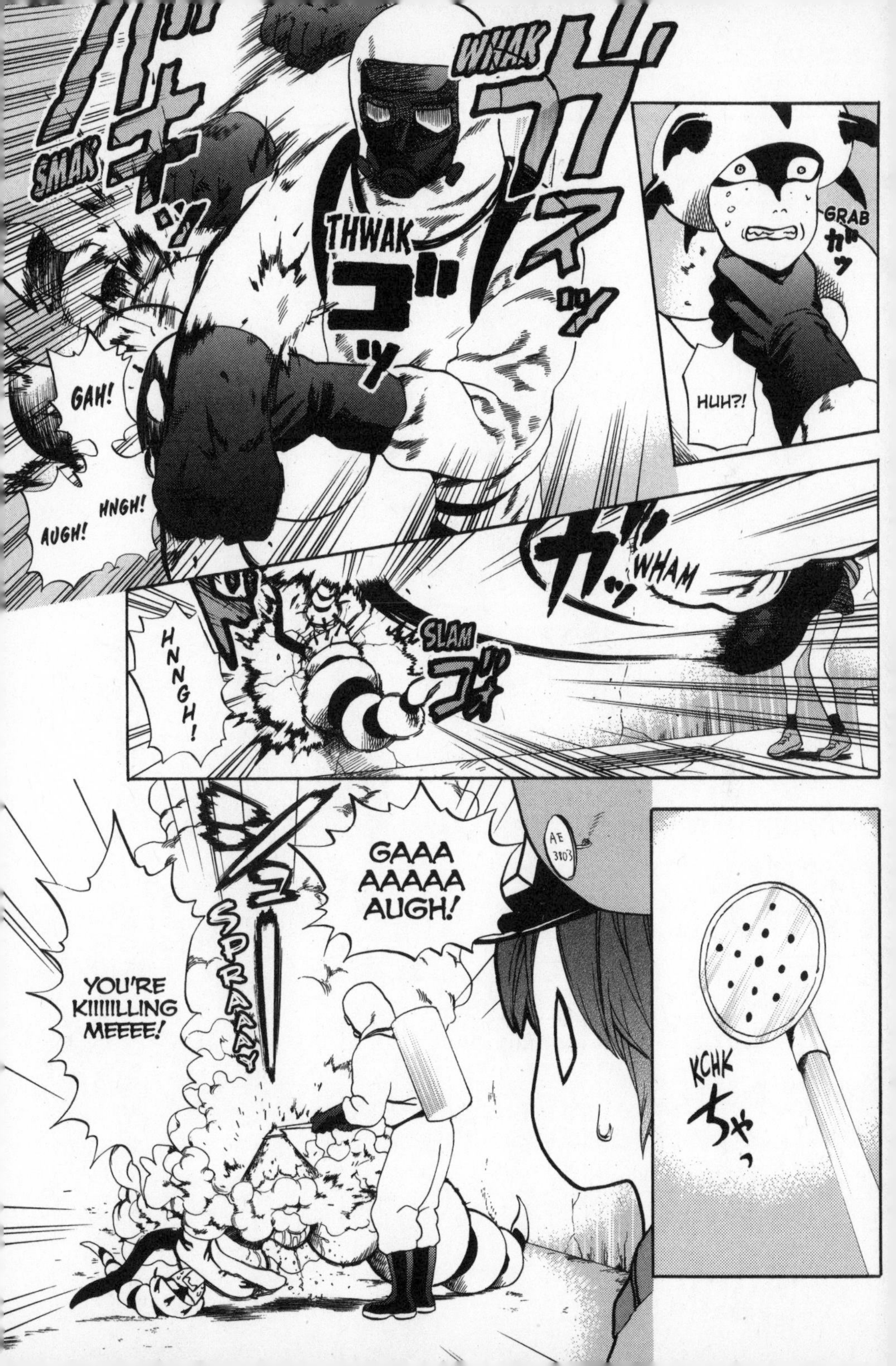
GRAB
HUH?!
WHAK
THWAK
SMAK
GAH!
HNGH!
AUGH!
WHAM
SLAM
HNNGH!
KCHK
GAAA AAAAA AUGH!
SPRAAAY
YOU'RE KIIIIILLING MEEEE!

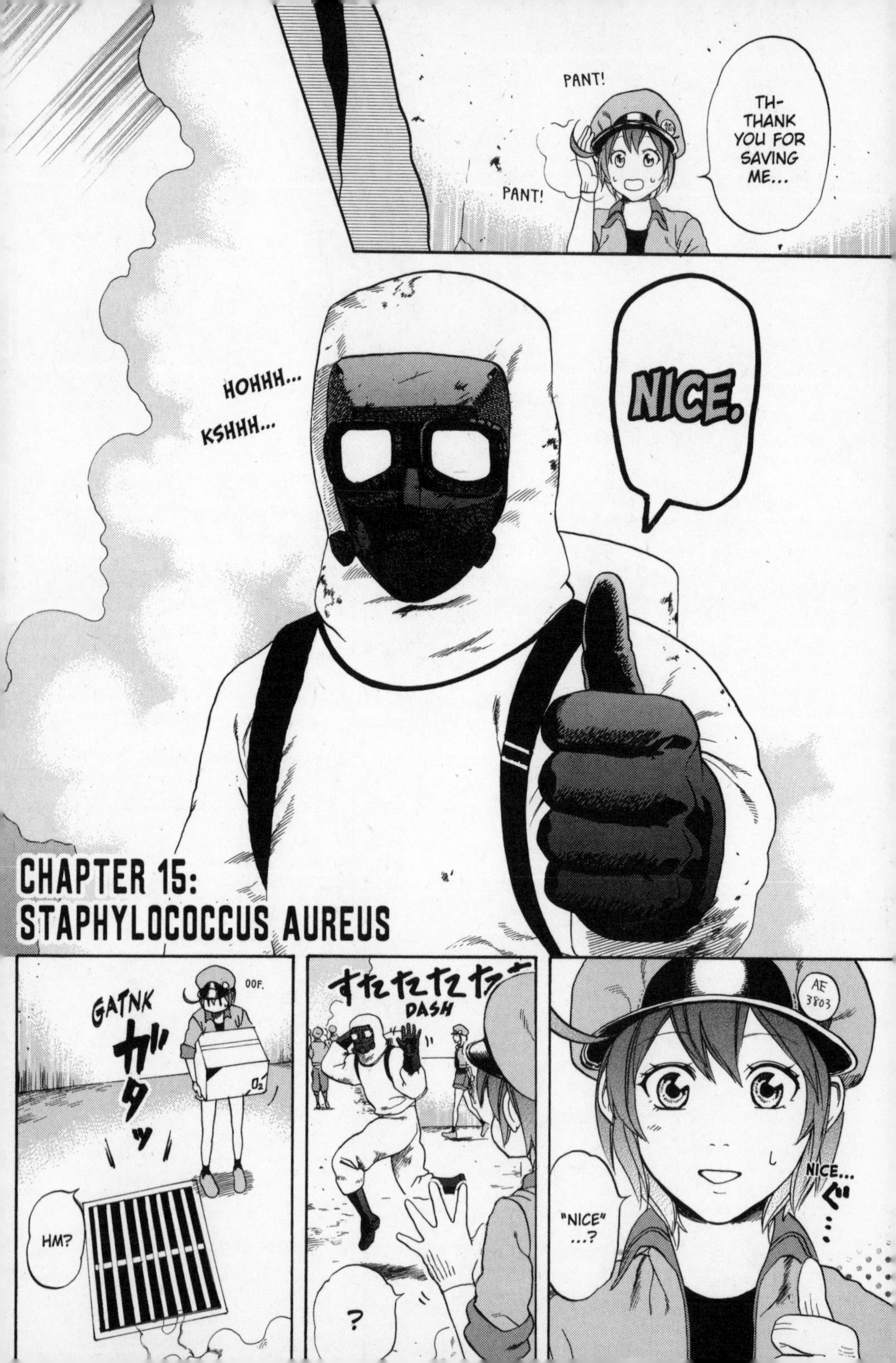

PANT!
TH-THANK YOU FOR SAVING ME...
PANT!
NICE.
HOHHH...
KSHHH...
CHAPTER 15: STAPHYLOCOCCUS AUREUS
AE 3803
NICE...
ぐ…
"NICE" ...?
すたたたた
DASH
?
OOF.
GATNK
ガタッ
HM?

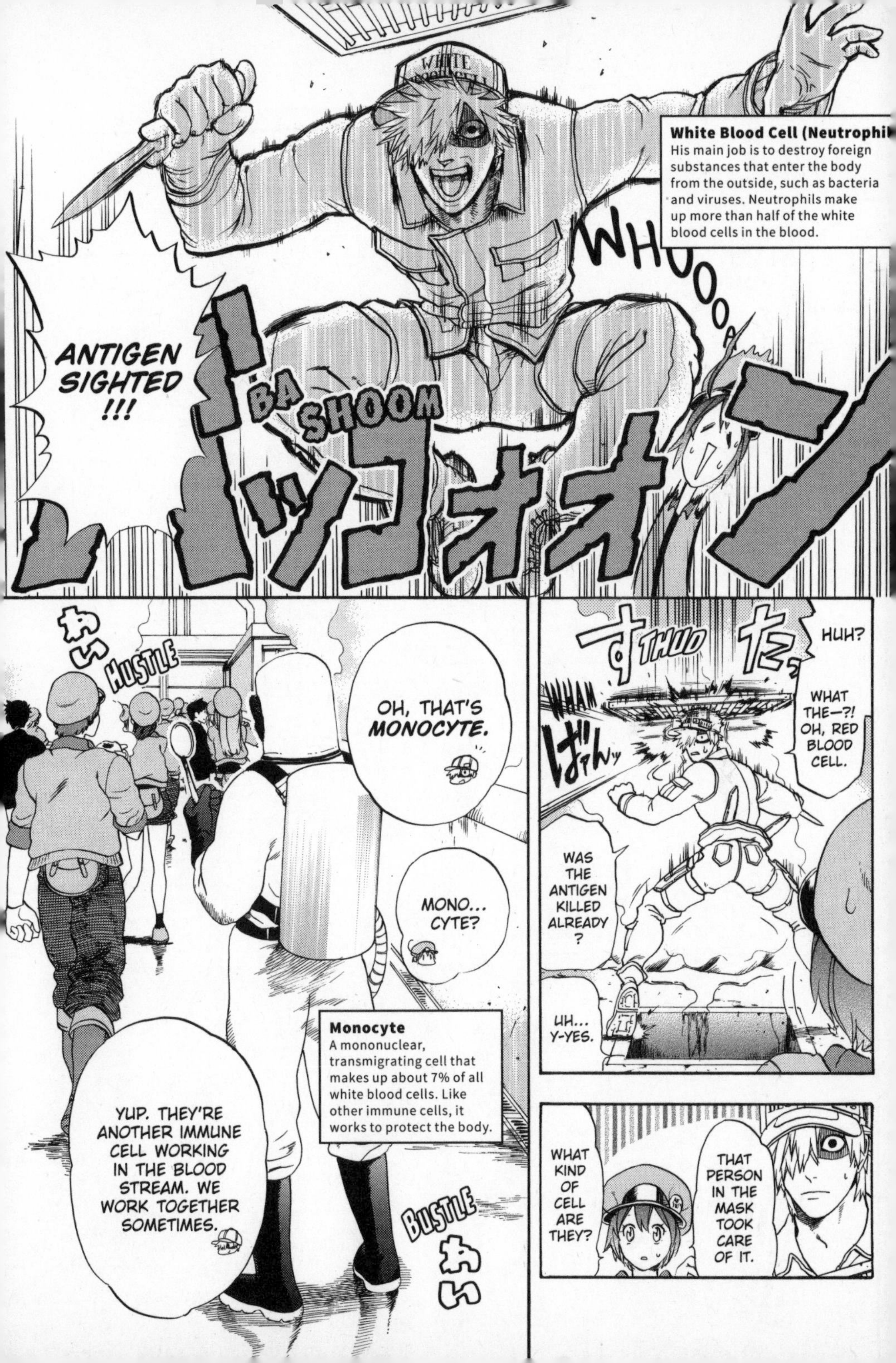

White Blood Cell (Neutrophil
His main job is to destroy foreign substances that enter the body from the outside, such as bacteria and viruses. Neutrophils make up more than half of the white blood cells in the blood.
WHOOOOA
ANTIGEN SIGHTED !!!
BA SHOOM
HUH?
WHAT THE—?! OH, RED BLOOD CELL.
す THUD たっ
WHAM
ばぁんッ
WAS THE ANTIGEN KILLED ALREADY ?
UH... Y-YES.
THAT PERSON IN THE MASK TOOK CARE OF IT.
WHAT KIND OF CELL ARE THEY?
OH, THAT'S *MONOCYTE.*
MONO... CYTE?
わい
HUSTLE
Monocyte
A mononuclear, transmigrating cell that makes up about 7% of all white blood cells. Like other immune cells, it works to protect the body.
YUP. THEY'RE ANOTHER IMMUNE CELL WORKING IN THE BLOOD STREAM. WE WORK TOGETHER SOMETIMES.
BUSTLE
わい

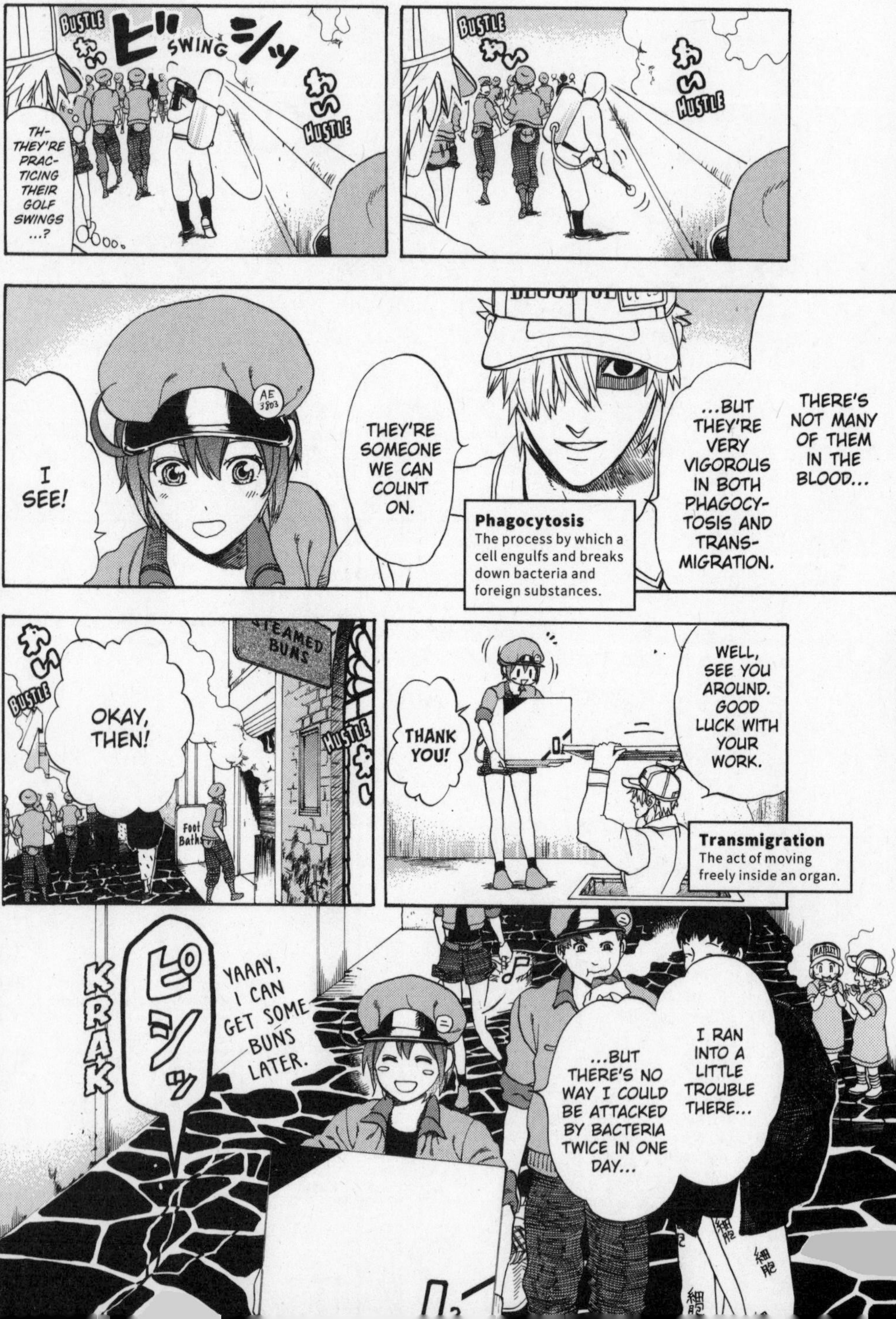
BUSTLE
わい
わい
HUSTLE
BUSTLE
わい
SWING
シッ
わい
HUSTLE
TH-THEY'RE PRACTICING THEIR GOLF SWINGS...?
THERE'S NOT MANY OF THEM IN THE BLOOD...
...BUT THEY'RE VERY VIGOROUS IN BOTH PHAGOCYTOSIS AND TRANSMIGRATION.
Phagocytosis
The process by which a cell engulfs and breaks down bacteria and foreign substances.
THEY'RE SOMEONE WE CAN COUNT ON.
AE 3803
I SEE!
WELL, SEE YOU AROUND. GOOD LUCK WITH YOUR WORK.
THANK YOU!
Transmigration
The act of moving freely inside an organ.
STEAMED BUNS
HUSTLE
わい
OKAY, THEN!
BUSTLE
わい
Foot Baths
I RAN INTO A LITTLE TROUBLE THERE...
...BUT THERE'S NO WAY I COULD BE ATTACKED BY BACTERIA TWICE IN ONE DAY...
YAAAY, I CAN GET SOME BUNS LATER.
ピシッ
KRAK

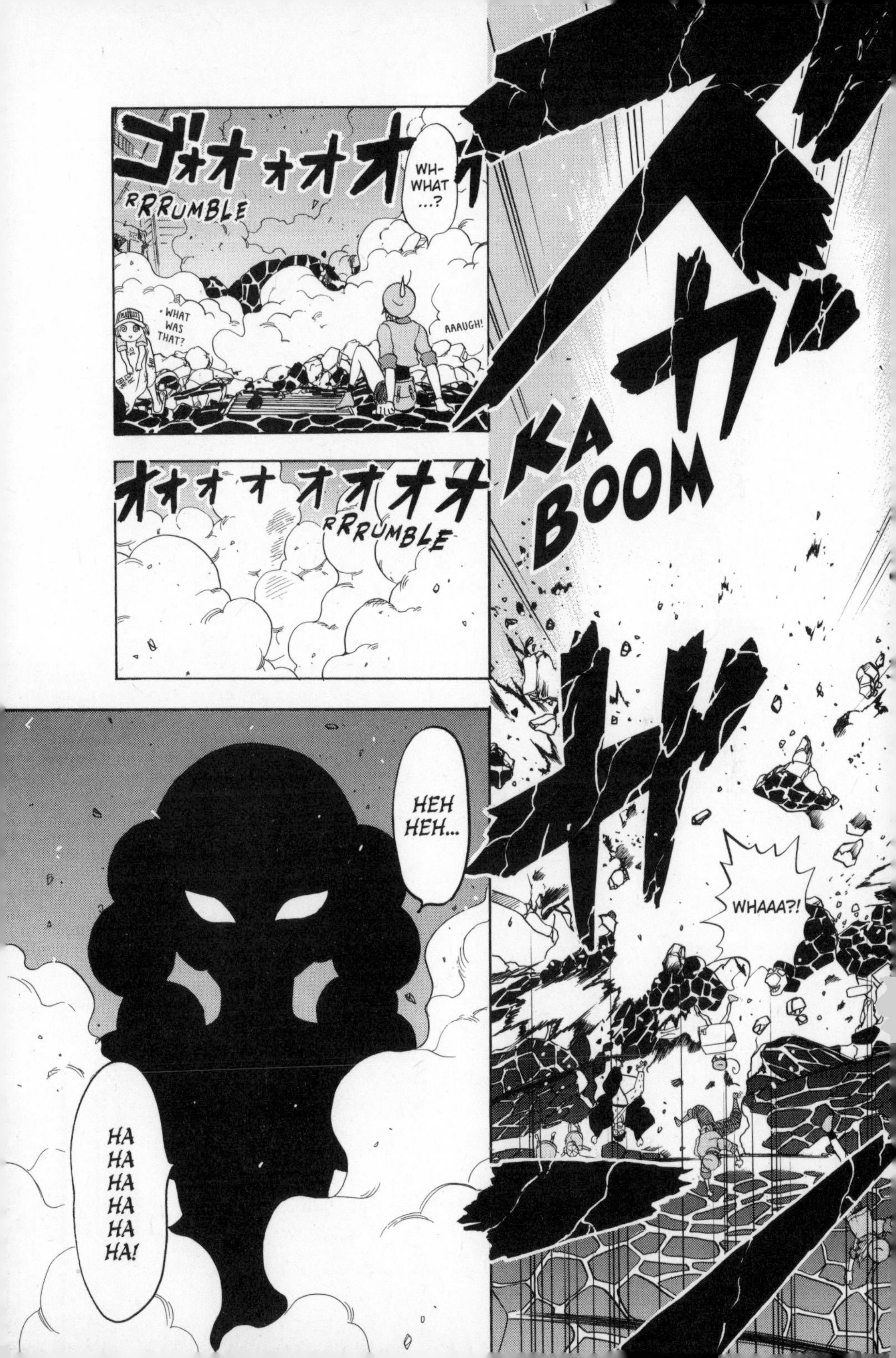
KA BOOM
WHAAA?!
RRRUMBLE
WH-WHAT ...?
AAAUGH!
WHAT WAS THAT?
RRRUMBLE
HEH HEH...
HA HA HA HA HA HA!

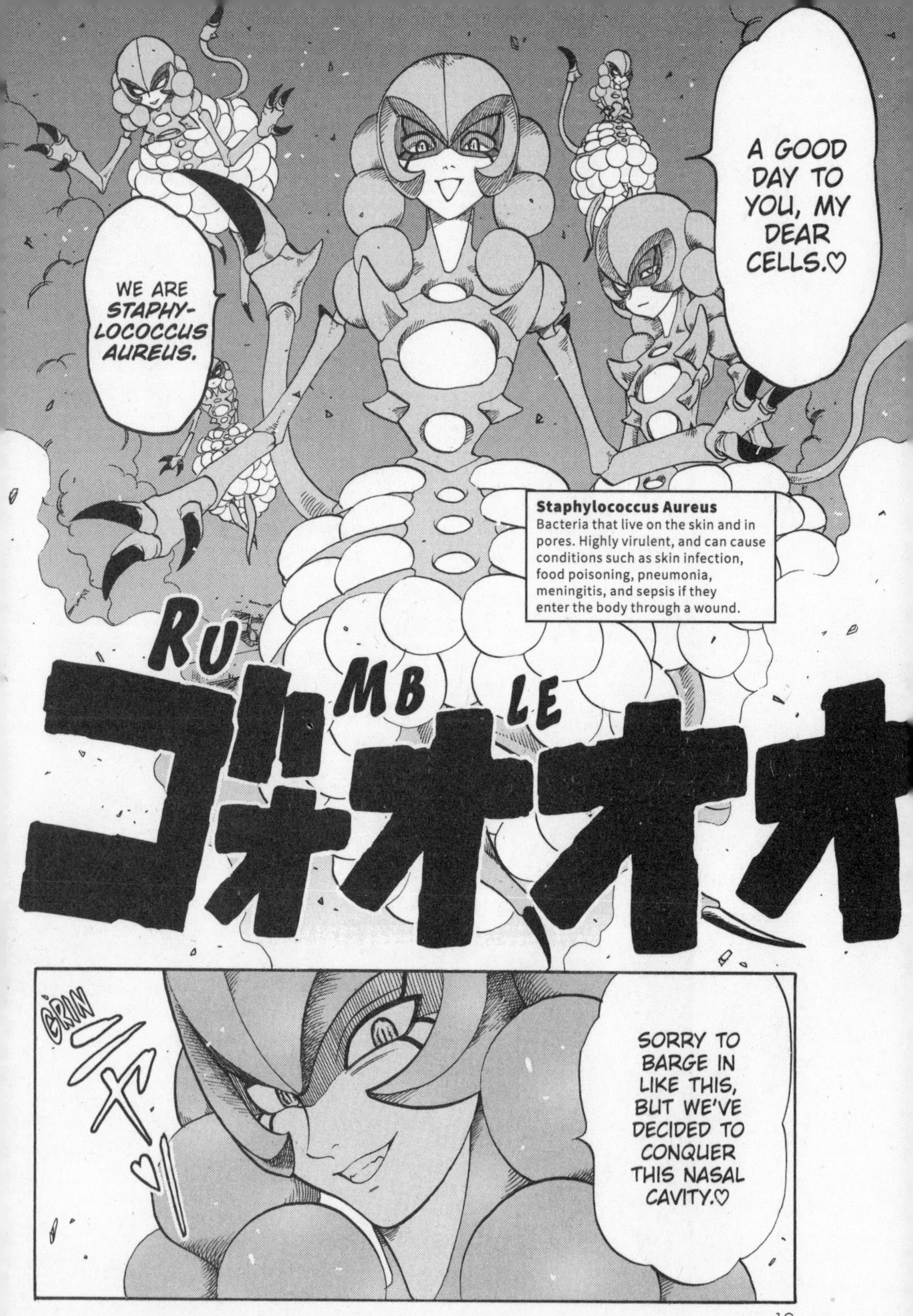
A GOOD DAY TO YOU, MY DEAR CELLS.♡
WE ARE STAPHYLOCOCCUS AUREUS.
Staphylococcus Aureus
Bacteria that live on the skin and in pores. Highly virulent, and can cause conditions such as skin infection, food poisoning, pneumonia, meningitis, and sepsis if they enter the body through a wound.
RUMBLE
SORRY TO BARGE IN LIKE THIS, BUT WE'VE DECIDED TO CONQUER THIS NASAL CAVITY.♡
GRIN

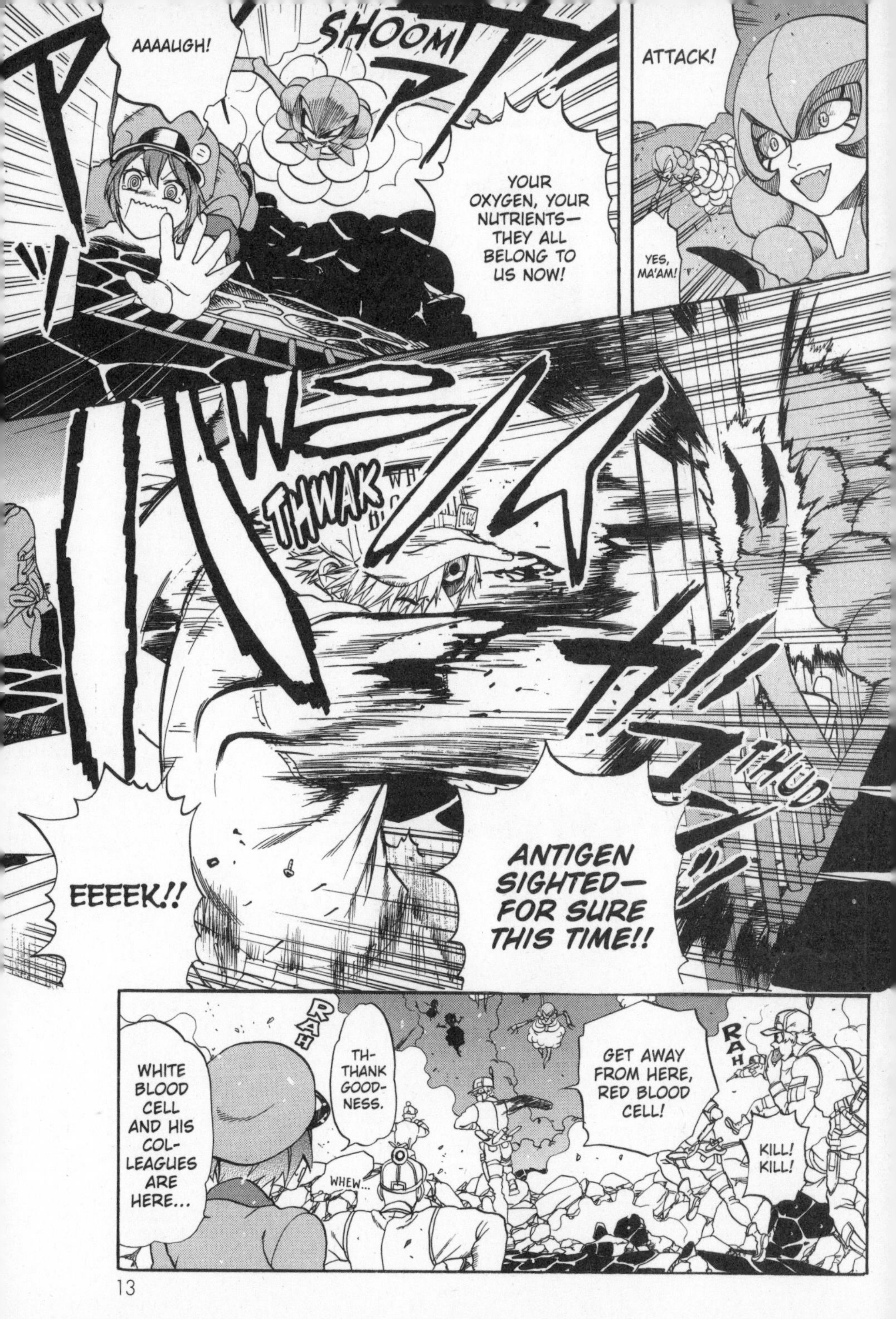
ATTACK!
YES, MA'AM!
SHOOM
AAAAUGH!
YOUR OXYGEN, YOUR NUTRIENTS—THEY ALL BELONG TO US NOW!
THWAK
THUD
ANTIGEN SIGHTED—FOR SURE THIS TIME!!
EEEEK!!
RAH
GET AWAY FROM HERE, RED BLOOD CELL!
KILL! KILL!
TH-THANK GOOD-NESS.
WHEW...
RAH
WHITE BLOOD CELL AND HIS COL-LEAGUES ARE HERE...

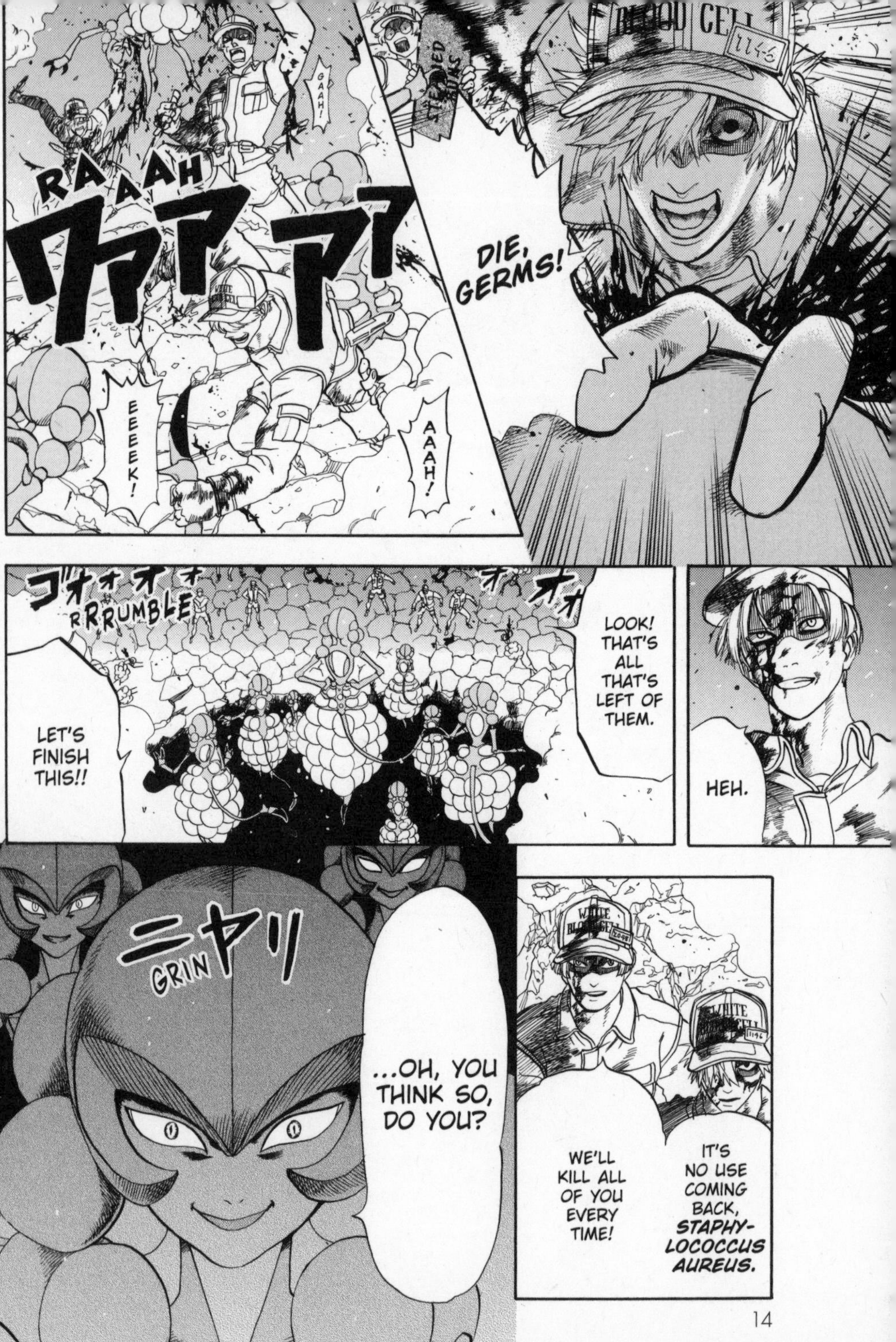
DIE, GERMS!
GAAH!
RAAAH
ワァァァ
EEEEEK!
AAAH!
HEH.
LOOK! THAT'S ALL THAT'S LEFT OF THEM.
ゴォォォォォ
RRRUMBLE
LET'S FINISH THIS!!
IT'S NO USE COMING BACK, STAPHYLOCOCCUS AUREUS.
WE'LL KILL ALL OF YOU EVERY TIME!
ニヤリ
GRIN
...OH, YOU THINK SO, DO YOU?

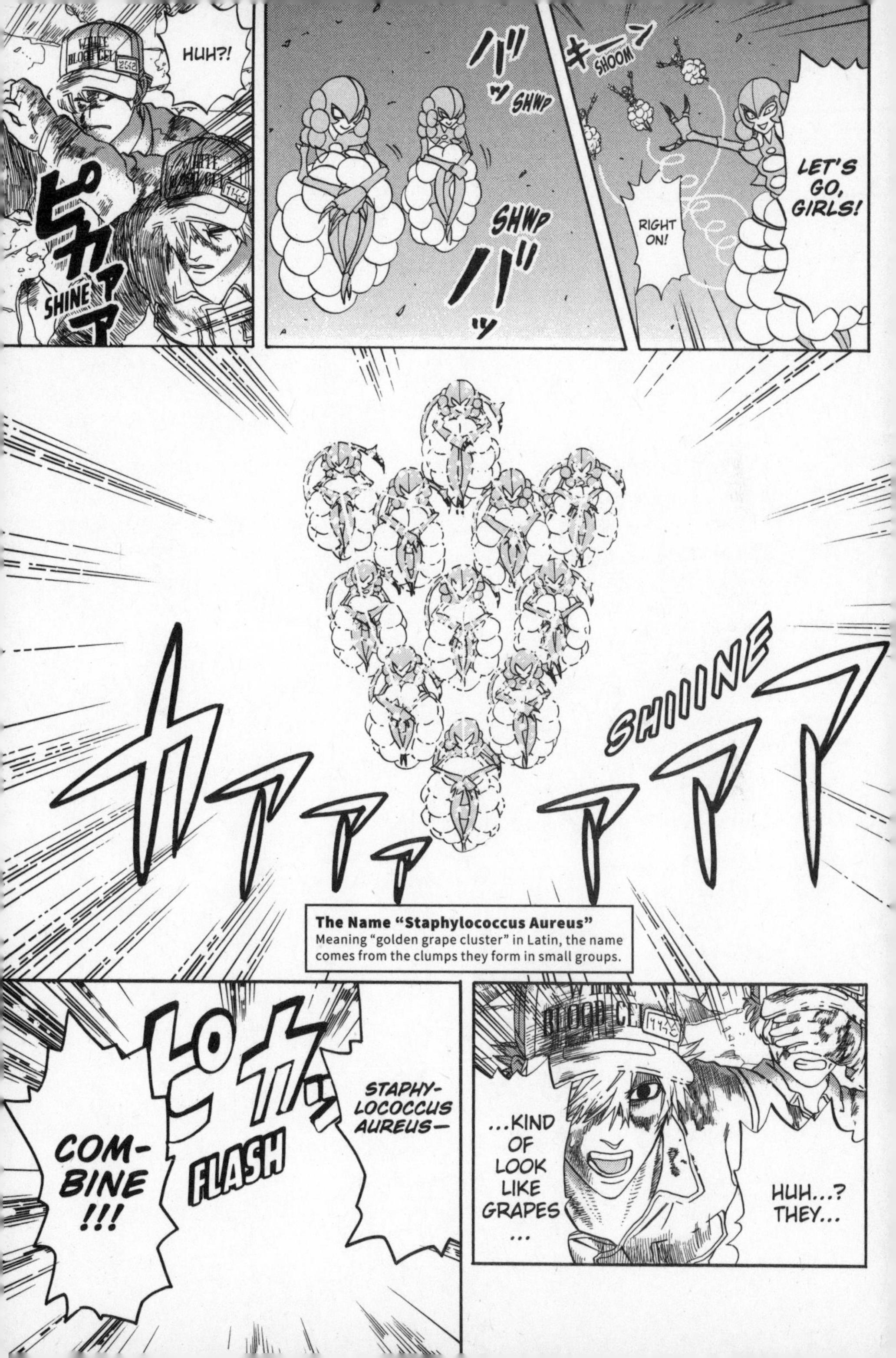
SHOOM
LET'S GO, GIRLS!
RIGHT ON!
SHWP
SHWP
HUH?!
SHINE
SHIIINE
The Name "Staphylococcus Aureus"
Meaning "golden grape cluster" in Latin, the name comes from the clumps they form in small groups.
HUH...? THEY...
...KIND OF LOOK LIKE GRAPES...
STAPHY-LOCOCCUS AUREUS—
FLASH
COM-BINE!!!

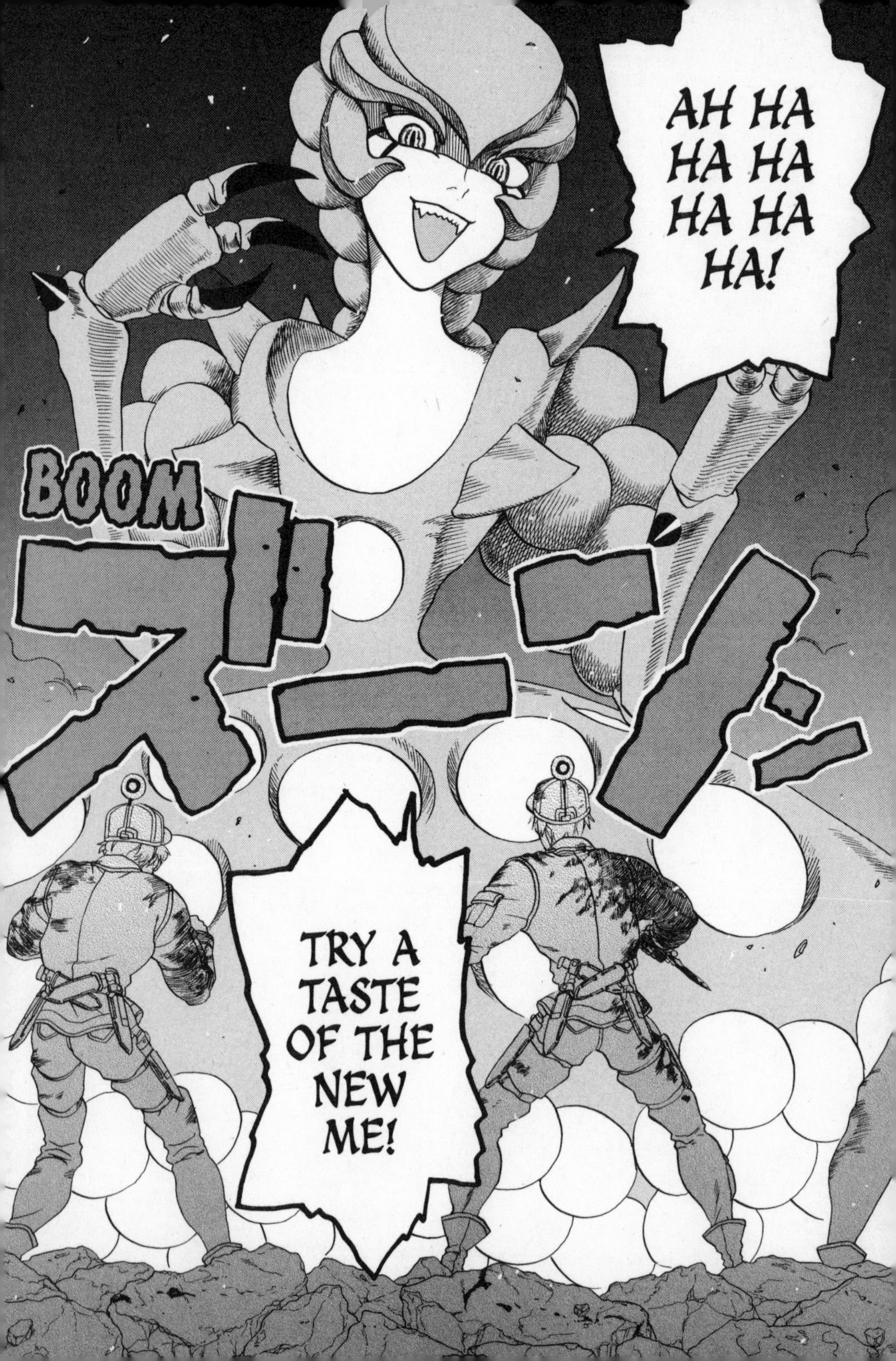
AH HA HA HA HA HA HA!
BOOM
ズーン
TRY A TASTE OF THE NEW ME!

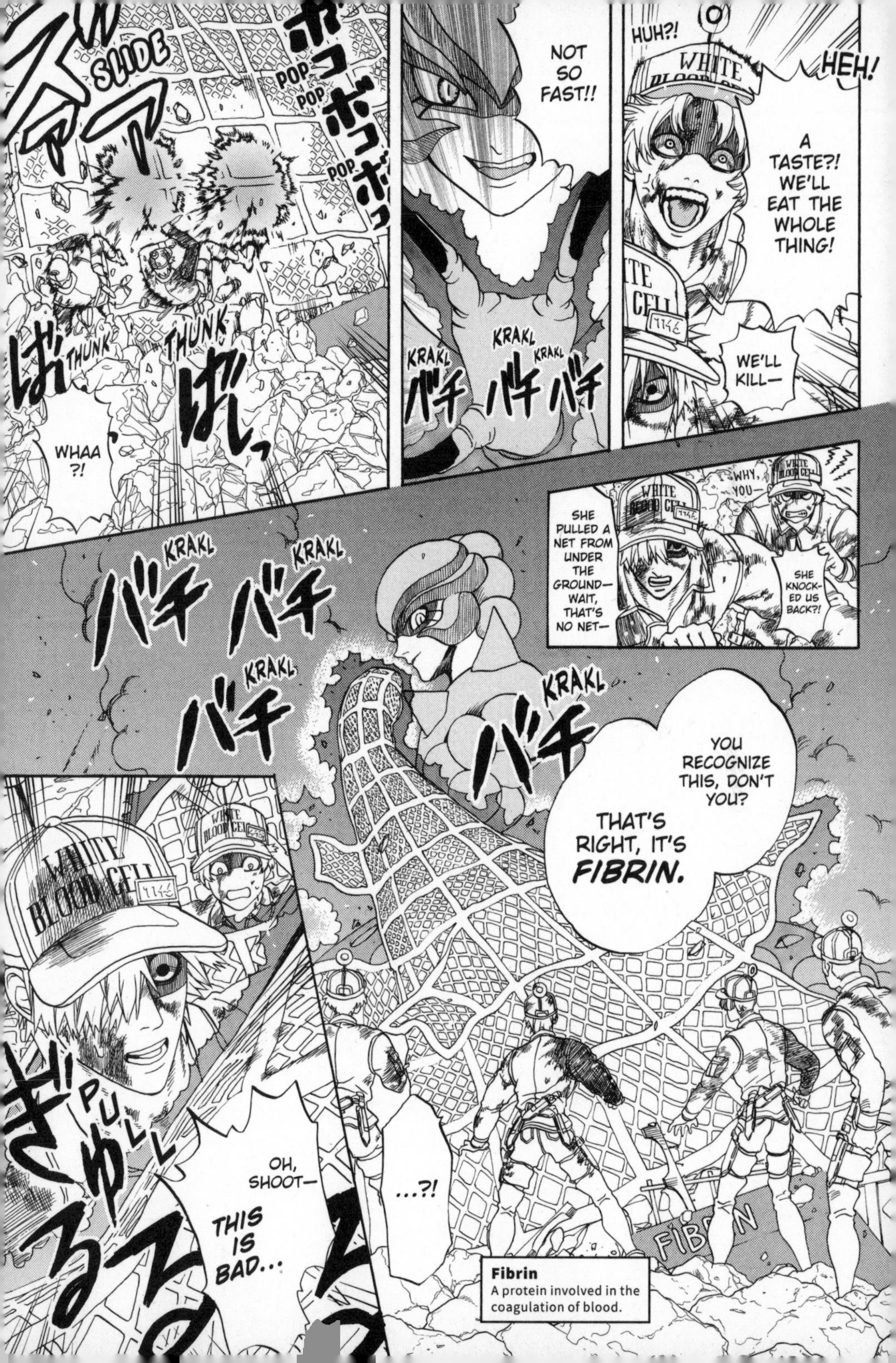
HUH?!
HEH!
A TASTE?! WE'LL EAT THE WHOLE THING!
WE'LL KILL—
NOT SO FAST!!
KRAKL
KRAKL
KRAKL
SLIDE
POP POP POP
THUNK
THUNK
WHAA ?!
WHY, YOU—
SHE KNOCKED US BACK?!
SHE PULLED A NET FROM UNDER THE GROUND—WAIT, THAT'S NO NET—
KRAKL
KRAKL
KRAKL
KRAKL
YOU RECOGNIZE THIS, DON'T YOU?
THAT'S RIGHT, IT'S **FIBRIN.**
...?!
FIBRIN
Fibrin
A protein involved in the coagulation of blood.
PULL
OH, SHOOT—
THIS IS BAD...

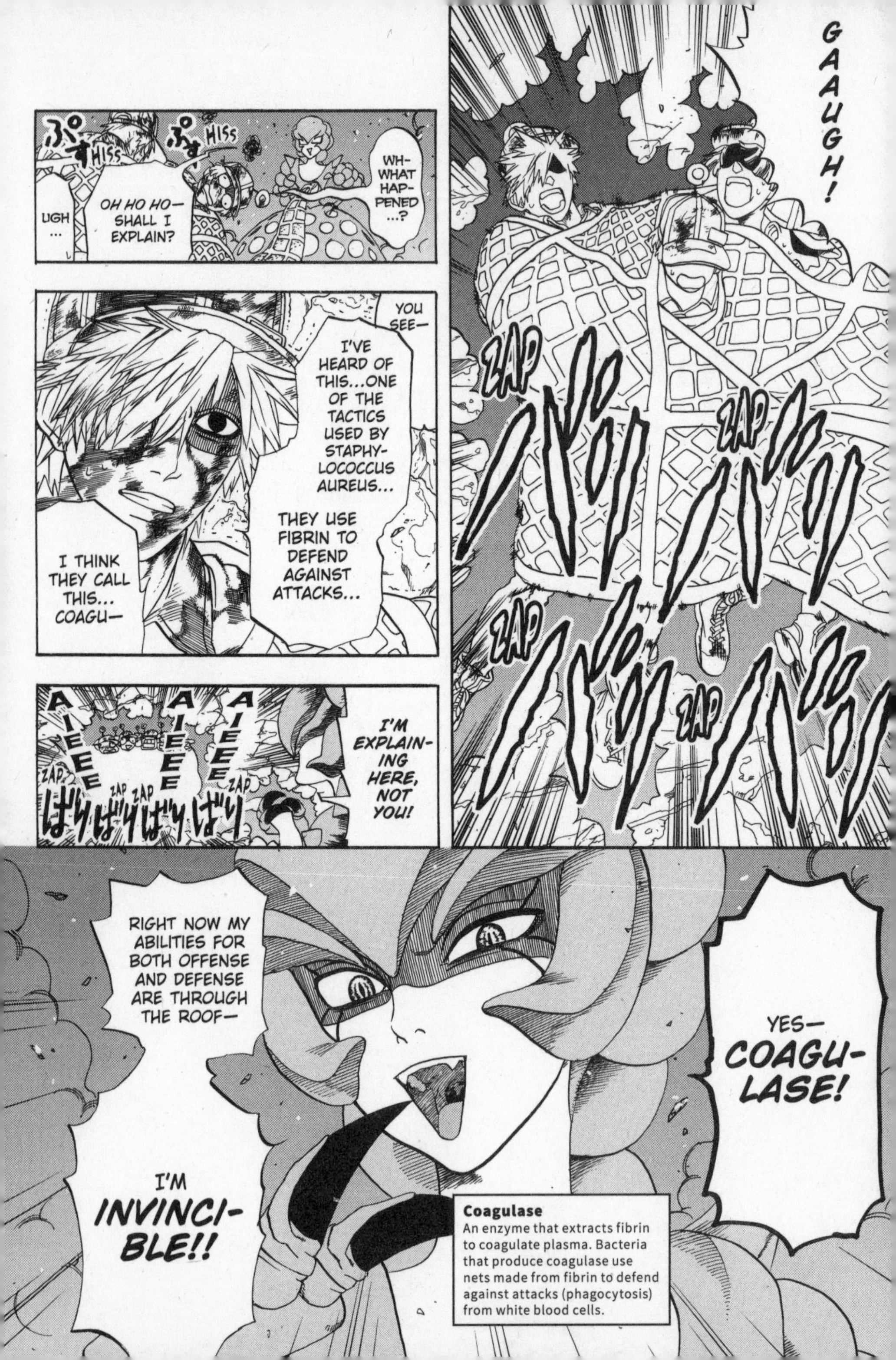
GAAUGH!
ZAP
ZAP
ZAP
ZAP
WH-WHAT HAPPENED...?
OH HO HO— SHALL I EXPLAIN?
UGH...
HISS
HISS
HISS
ぷす
ぷす
YOU SEE—
I'VE HEARD OF THIS...ONE OF THE TACTICS USED BY STAPHYLOCOCCUS AUREUS...
THEY USE FIBRIN TO DEFEND AGAINST ATTACKS...
I THINK THEY CALL THIS... COAGU—
I'M EXPLAINING HERE, NOT YOU!
AIEEE
AIEEE
AIEEE
AIEEE
ZAP
ZAP
ZAP
ZAP
ばりばりばりばり
YES— COAGULASE!
RIGHT NOW MY ABILITIES FOR BOTH OFFENSE AND DEFENSE ARE THROUGH THE ROOF—
I'M INVINCIBLE!!

Coagulase
An enzyme that extracts fibrin to coagulate plasma. Bacteria that produce coagulase use nets made from fibrin to defend against attacks (phagocytosis) from white blood cells.

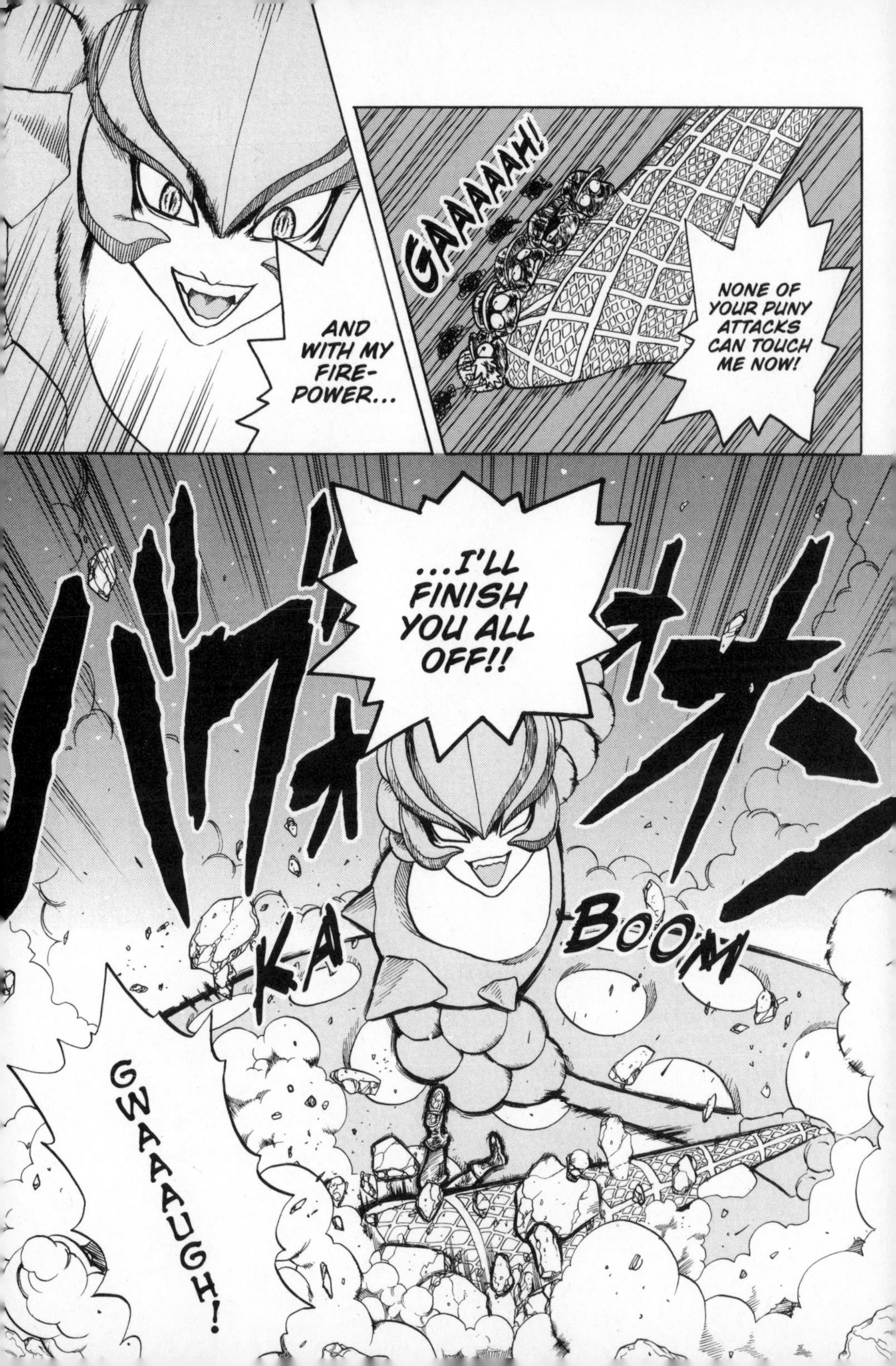
GAAAAH!
NONE OF YOUR PUNY ATTACKS CAN TOUCH ME NOW!
AND WITH MY FIRE-POWER...
...I'LL FINISH YOU ALL OFF!!
KA-BOOM
GWAAAUGH!

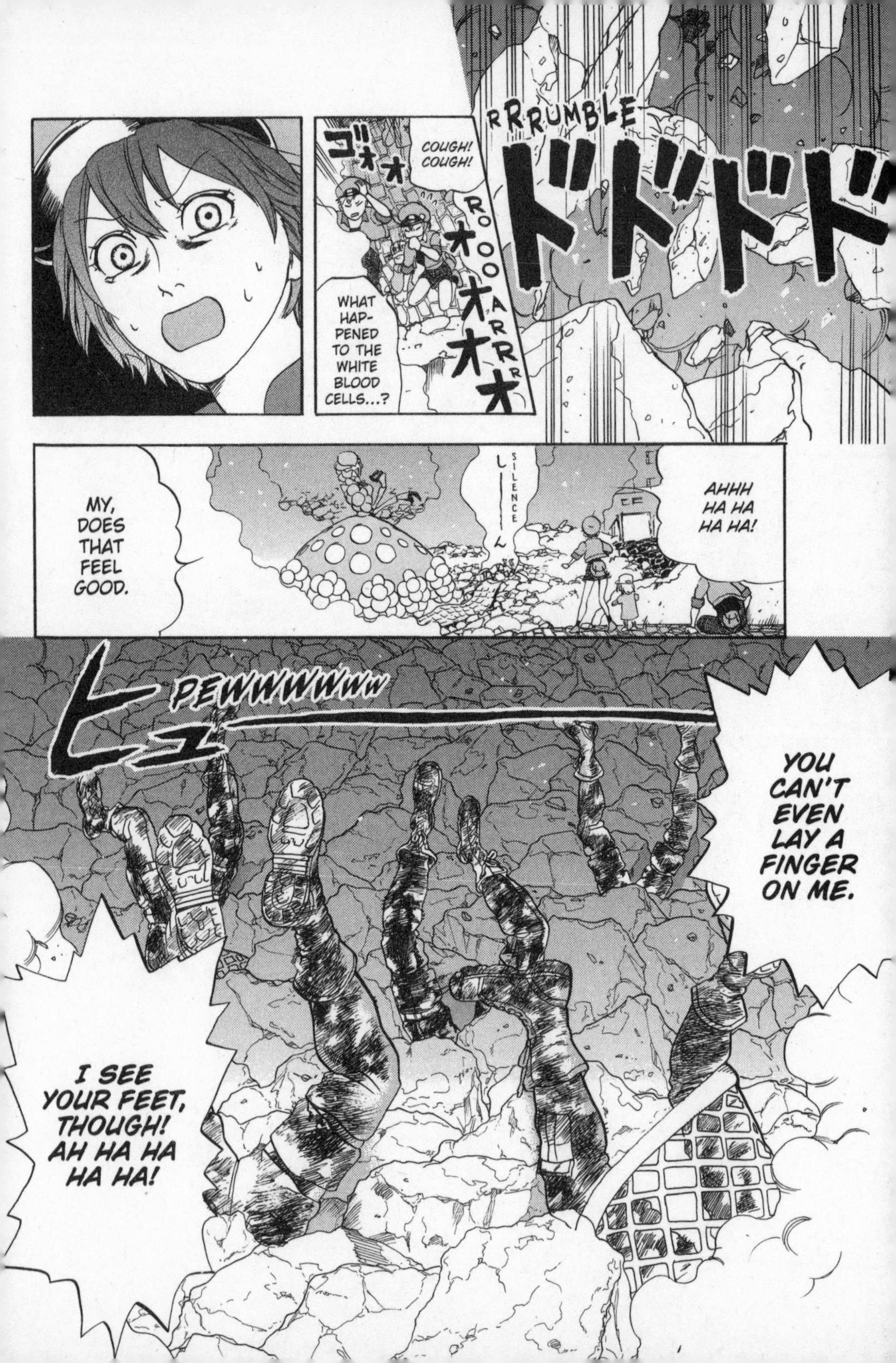
RRRUMBLE
ドドドドド
ゴォオ
COUGH! COUGH!
ROOOARRRR
オオオオオ
WHAT HAP-PENED TO THE WHITE BLOOD CELLS...?
AHHH HA HA HA HA!
SILENCE
MY, DOES THAT FEEL GOOD.
ヒュー
PEWWWWWWW
YOU CAN'T EVEN LAY A FINGER ON ME.
I SEE YOUR FEET, THOUGH! AH HA HA HA HA!

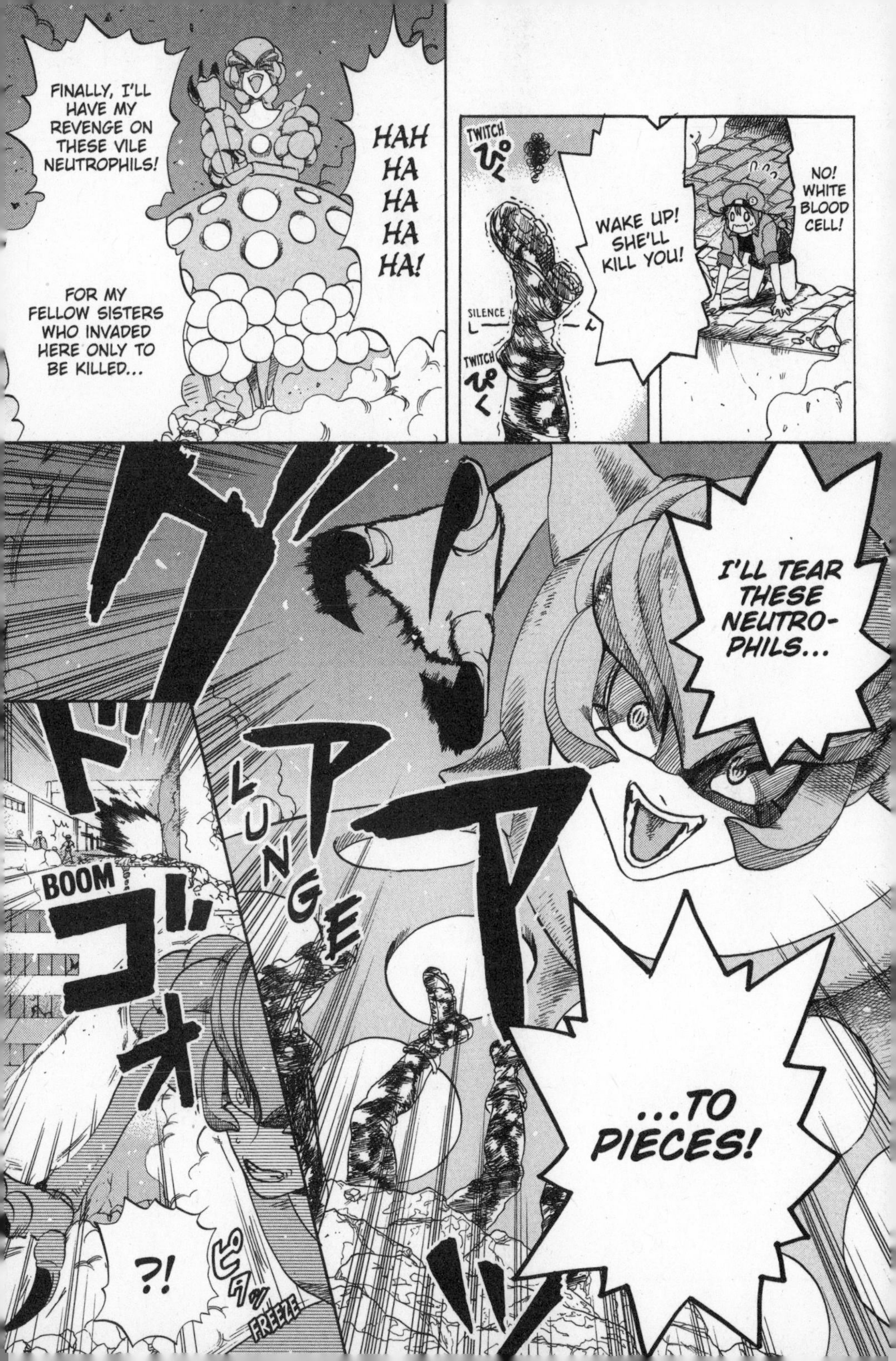
NO! WHITE BLOOD CELL!
TWITCH
ぴく
WAKE UP! SHE'LL KILL YOU!
SILENCE
TWITCH
ぴく
FINALLY, I'LL HAVE MY REVENGE ON THESE VILE NEUTROPHILS!
HAH HA HA HA HA!
FOR MY FELLOW SISTERS WHO INVADED HERE ONLY TO BE KILLED...
I'LL TEAR THESE NEUTRO-PHILS...
LUNGE
...TO PIECES!
BOOM
?!
FREEZE

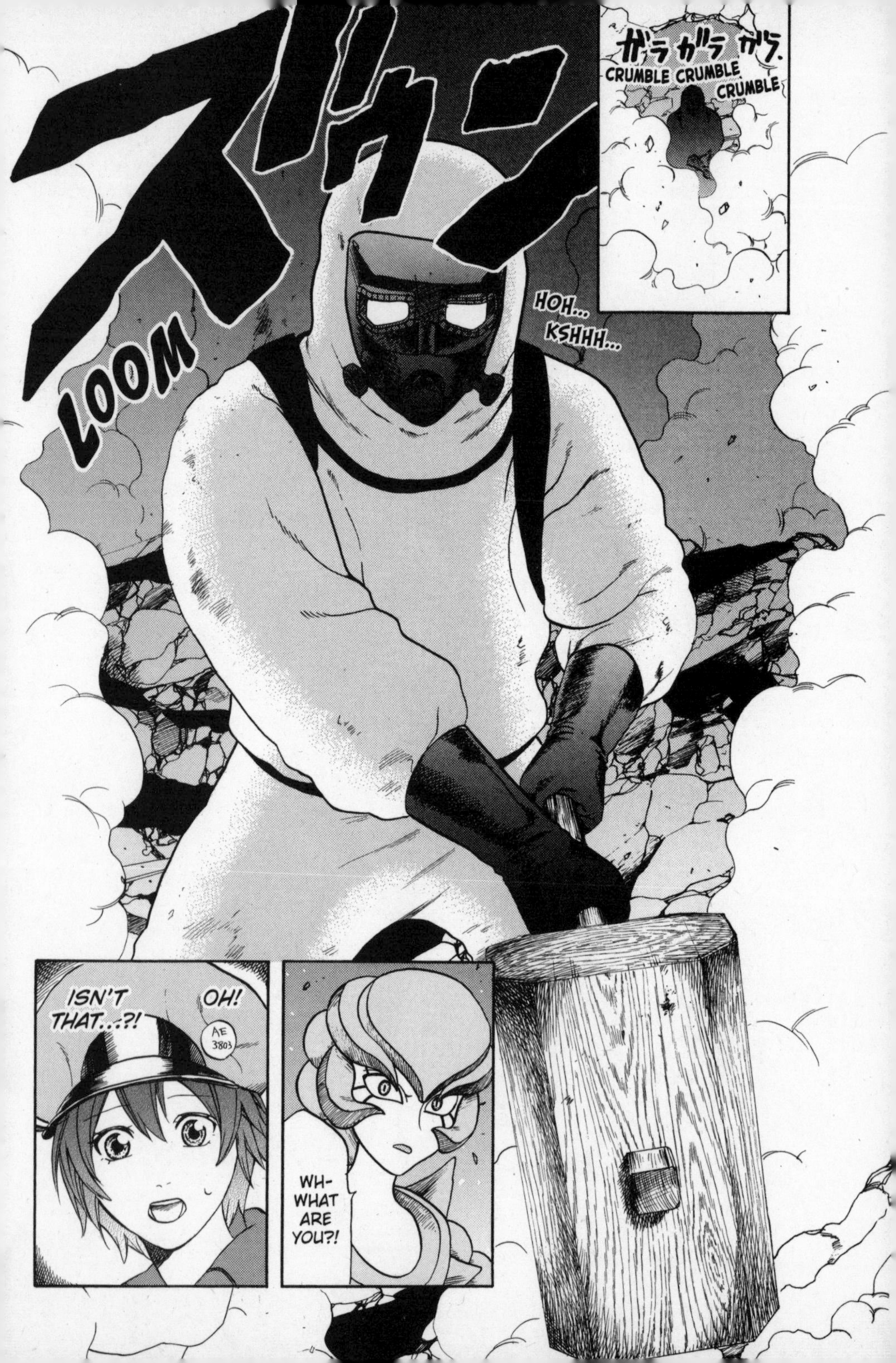
ガラガラガラ
CRUMBLE CRUMBLE CRUMBLE
LOOM
HOH... KSHHH...
WH- WHAT ARE YOU?!
OH!
AE 3803
ISN'T THAT...?!

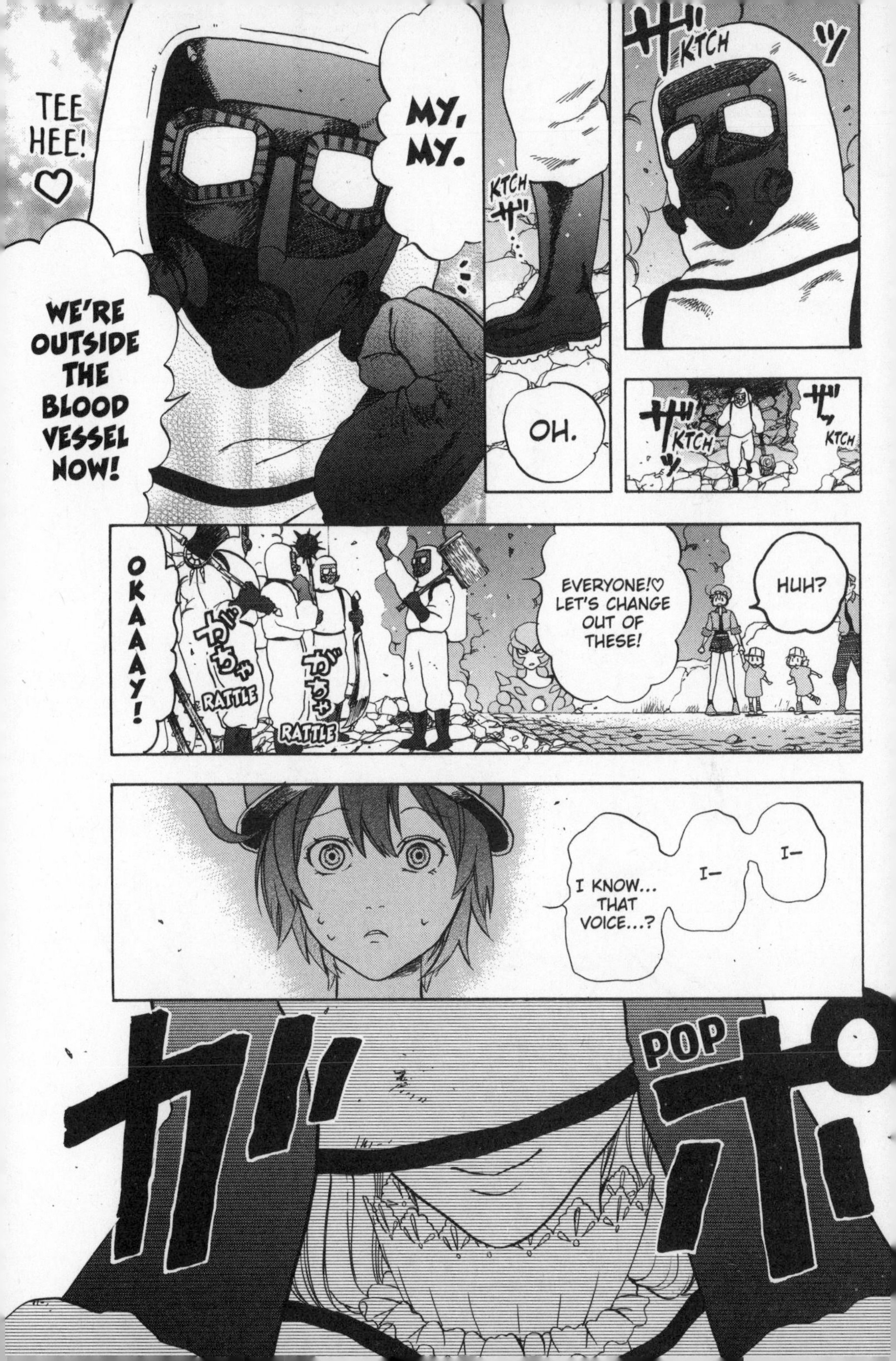
KTCH
KTCH
KTCH
KTCH
OH.
MY, MY.
TEE HEE! ♡
WE'RE OUTSIDE THE BLOOD VESSEL NOW!
HUH?
EVERYONE!♡ LET'S CHANGE OUT OF THESE!
OKAAAAY!
RATTLE
RATTLE
I—
I—
I KNOW... THAT VOICE...?
POP

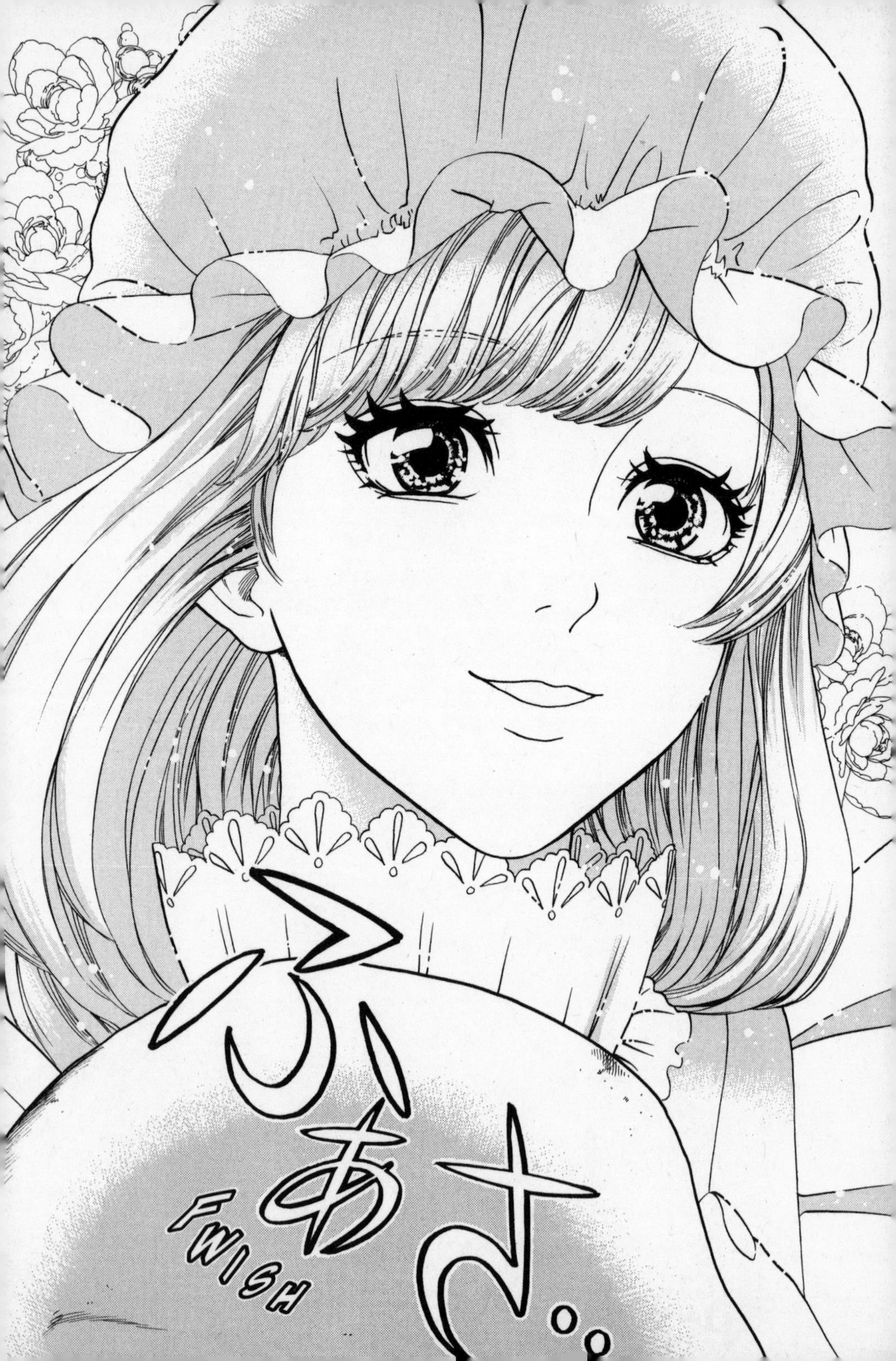
ふあさ。。
FWISH

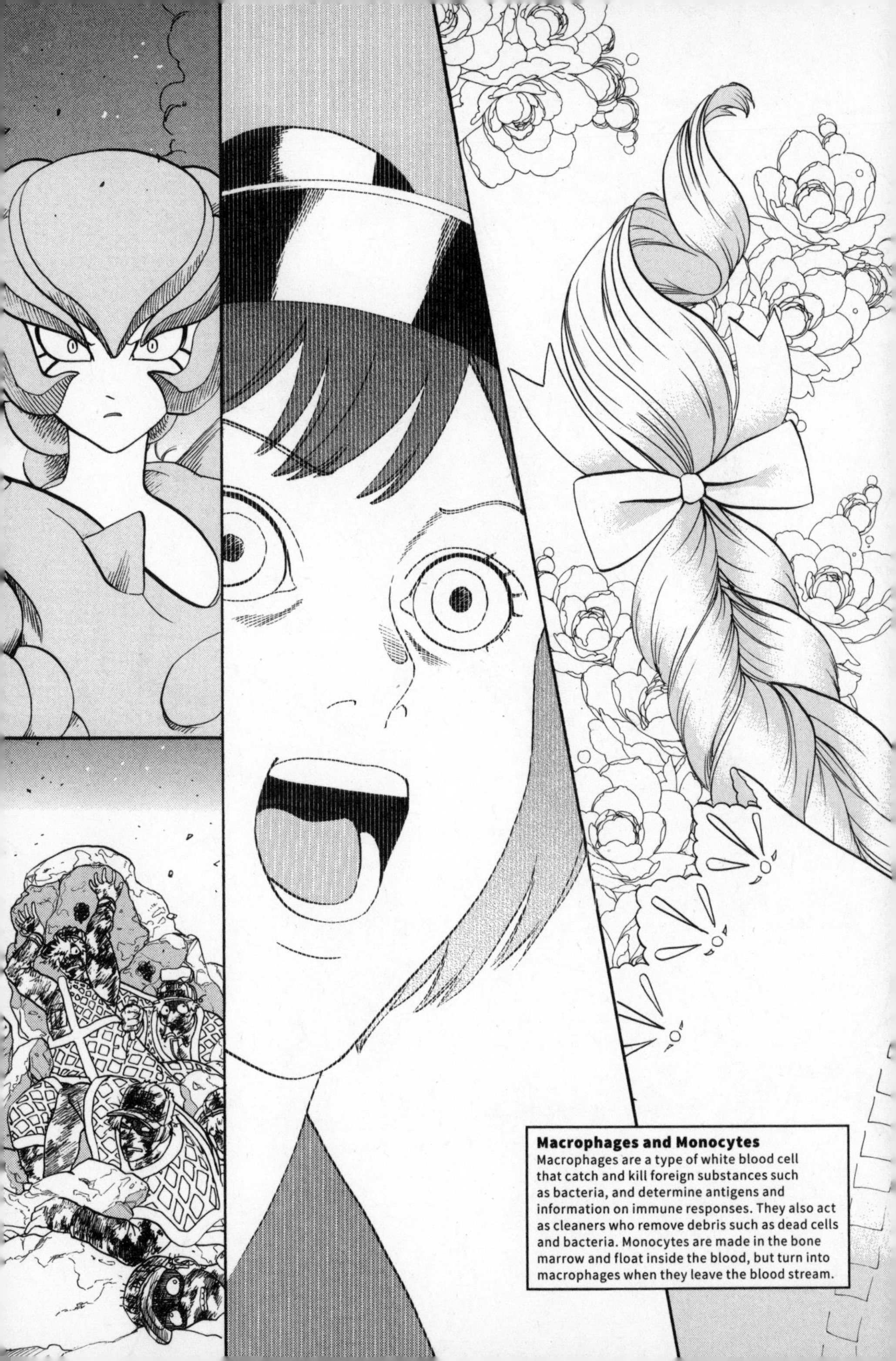
Macrophages and Monocytes
Macrophages are a type of white blood cell that catch and kill foreign substances such as bacteria, and determine antigens and information on immune responses. They also act as cleaners who remove debris such as dead cells and bacteria. Monocytes are made in the bone marrow and float inside the blood, but turn into macrophages when they leave the blood stream.

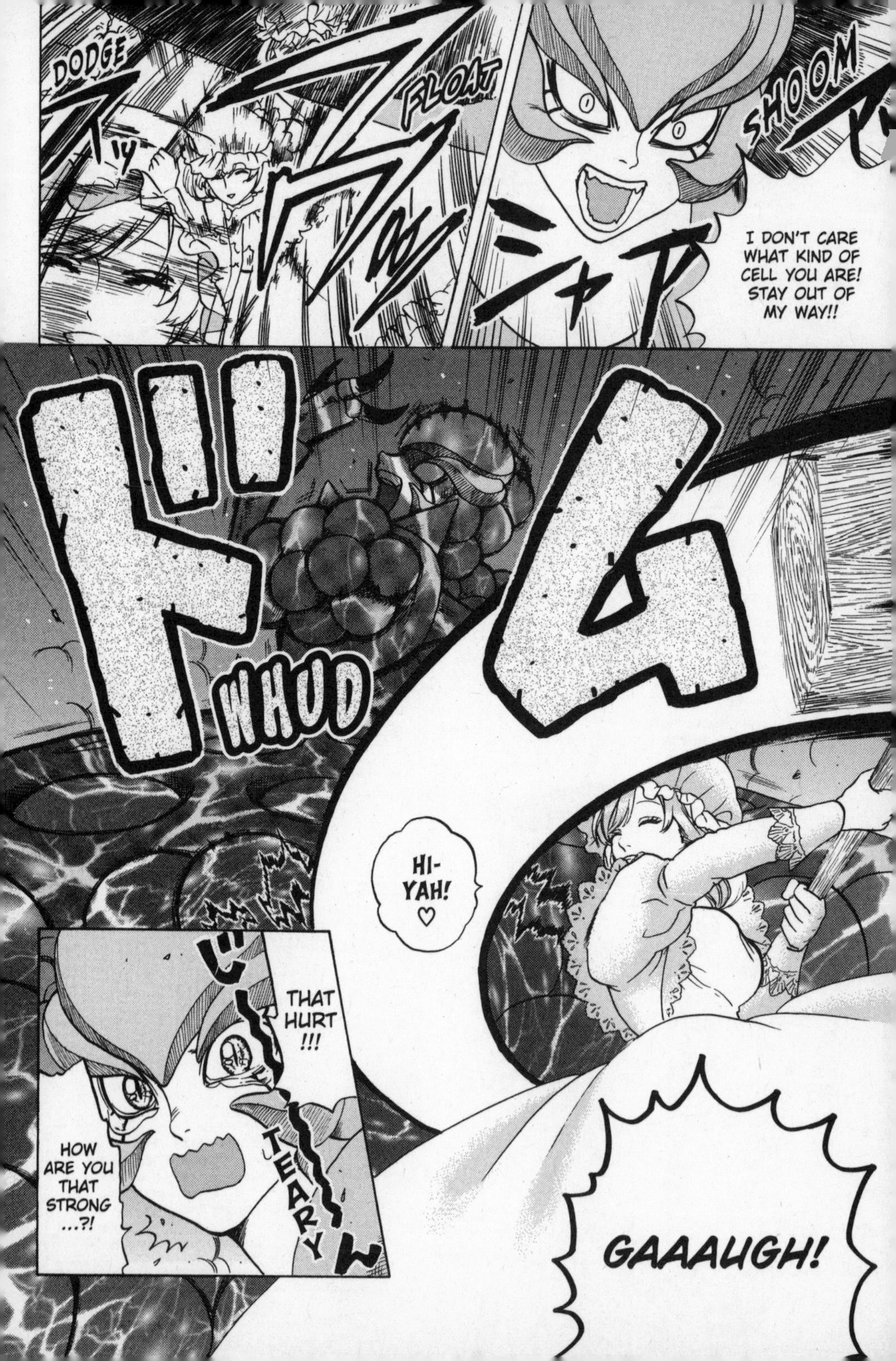
SHOOM
I DON'T CARE WHAT KIND OF CELL YOU ARE! STAY OUT OF MY WAY!!
FLOAT
DODGE
WHUD
HI-YAH! ♡
GAAAUGH!
THAT HURT !!!
TEARY
HOW ARE YOU THAT STRONG ...?!

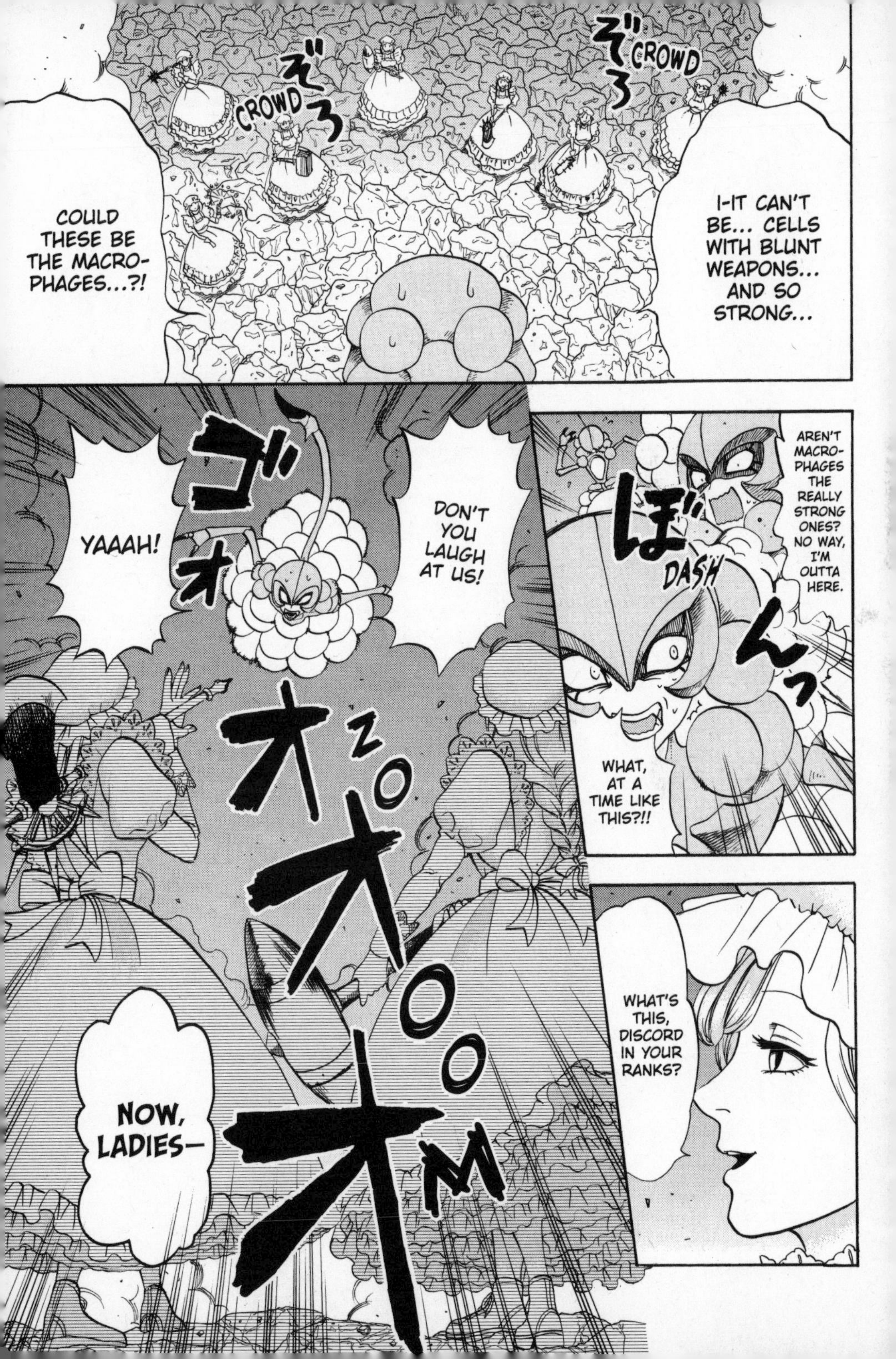
ぞろ
CROWD
ぞろ
CROWD
I-IT CAN'T BE... CELLS WITH BLUNT WEAPONS... AND SO STRONG...
COULD THESE BE THE MACRO-PHAGES...?!
AREN'T MACRO-PHAGES THE REALLY STRONG ONES? NO WAY, I'M OUTTA HERE.
ぼん
DASH
WHAT, AT A TIME LIKE THIS?!!
WHAT'S THIS, DISCORD IN YOUR RANKS?
DON'T YOU LAUGH AT US!
YAAAH!
ゴオ
オオオ
ZOOOOM
NOW, LADIES—

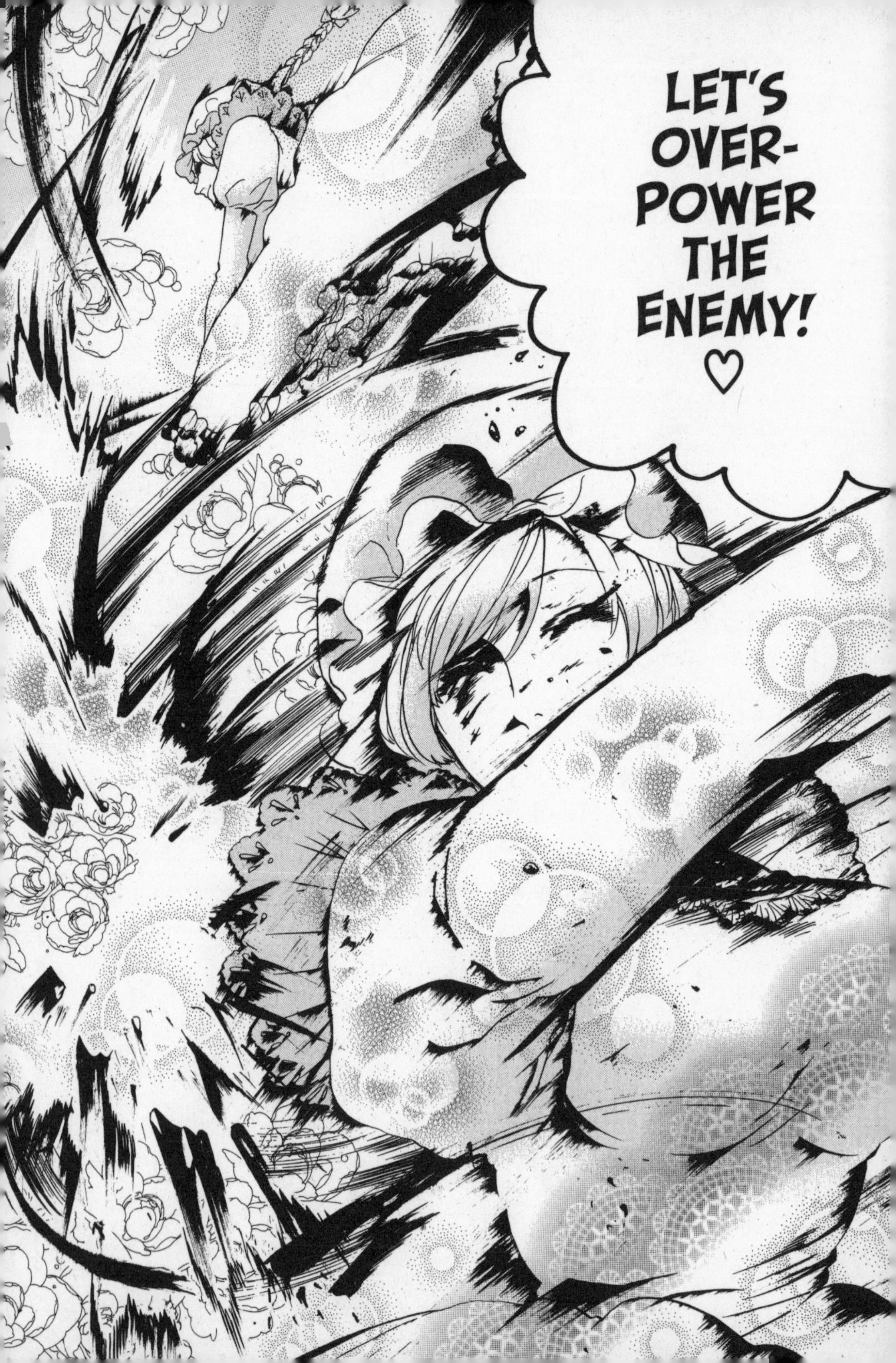
LET'S OVER-POWER THE ENEMY! ♡

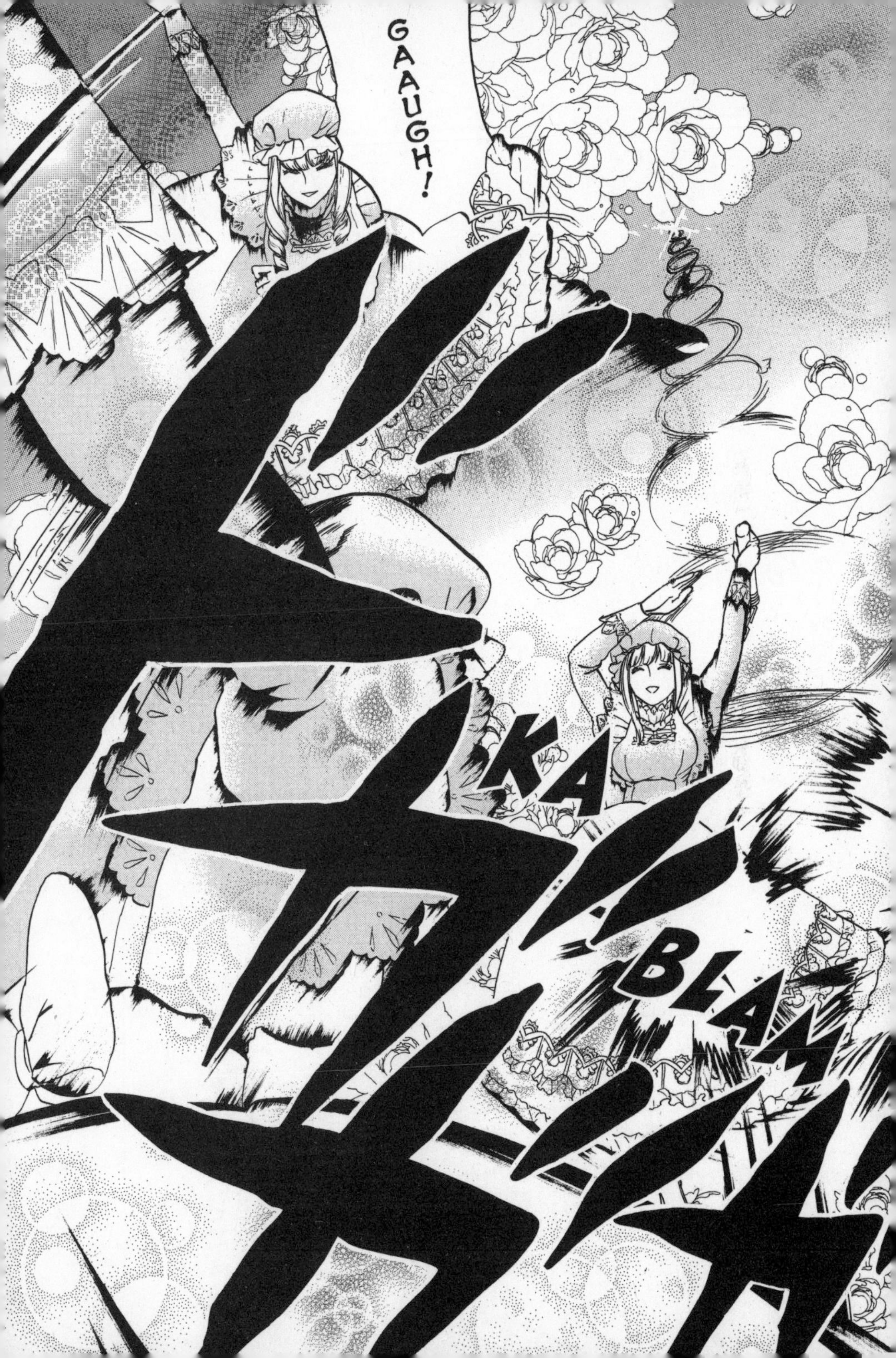
GAAUGH!
KA-BLAM

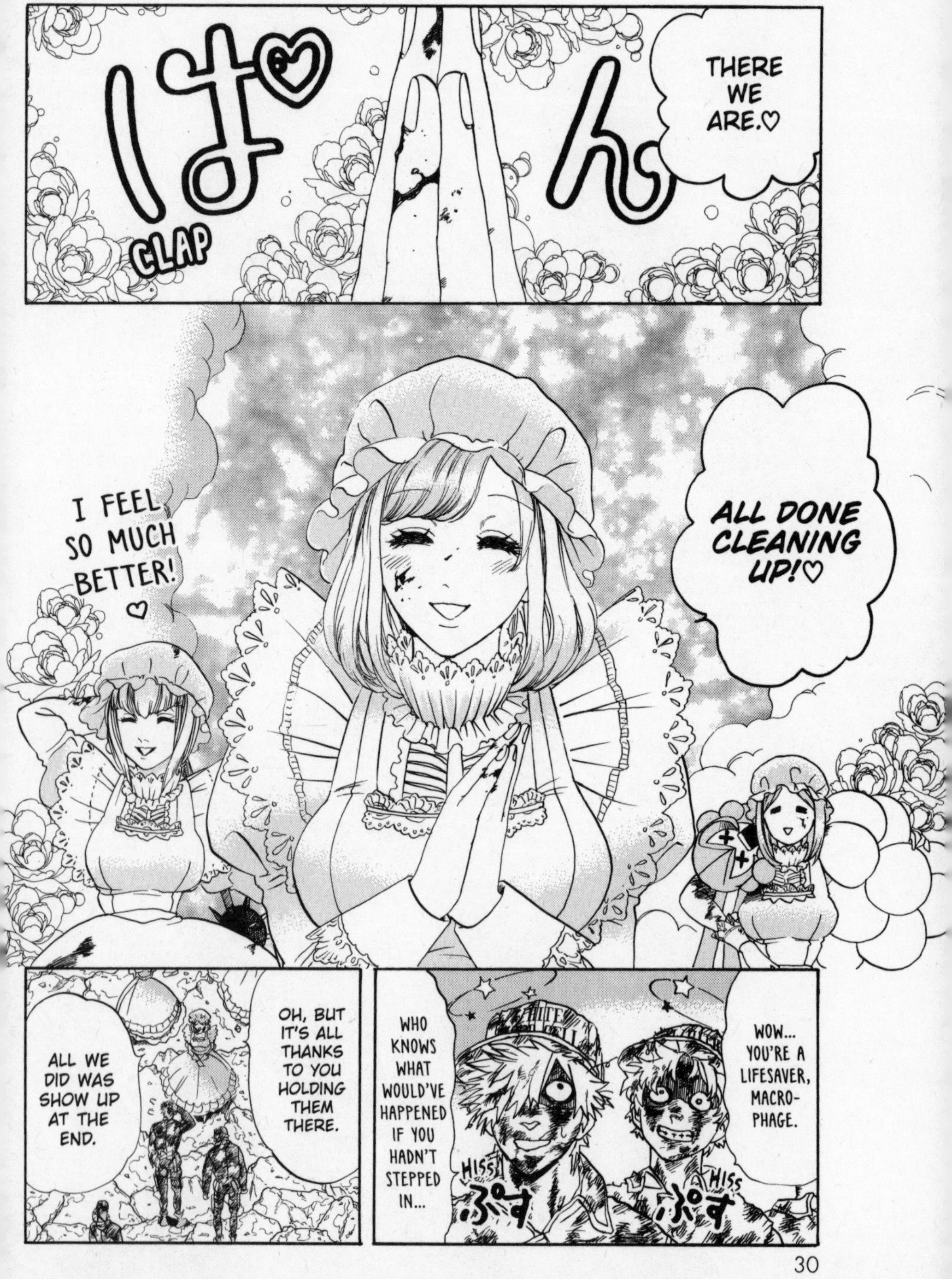

ぱ♡ん
THERE WE ARE.♡
CLAP
ALL DONE CLEANING UP!♡
I FEEL SO MUCH BETTER! ♡
WOW... YOU'RE A LIFESAVER, MACRO-PHAGE.
HISS
ぷす
WHO KNOWS WHAT WOULD'VE HAPPENED IF YOU HADN'T STEPPED IN...
HISS
ぷす
OH, BUT IT'S ALL THANKS TO YOU HOLDING THEM THERE.
ALL WE DID WAS SHOW UP AT THE END.

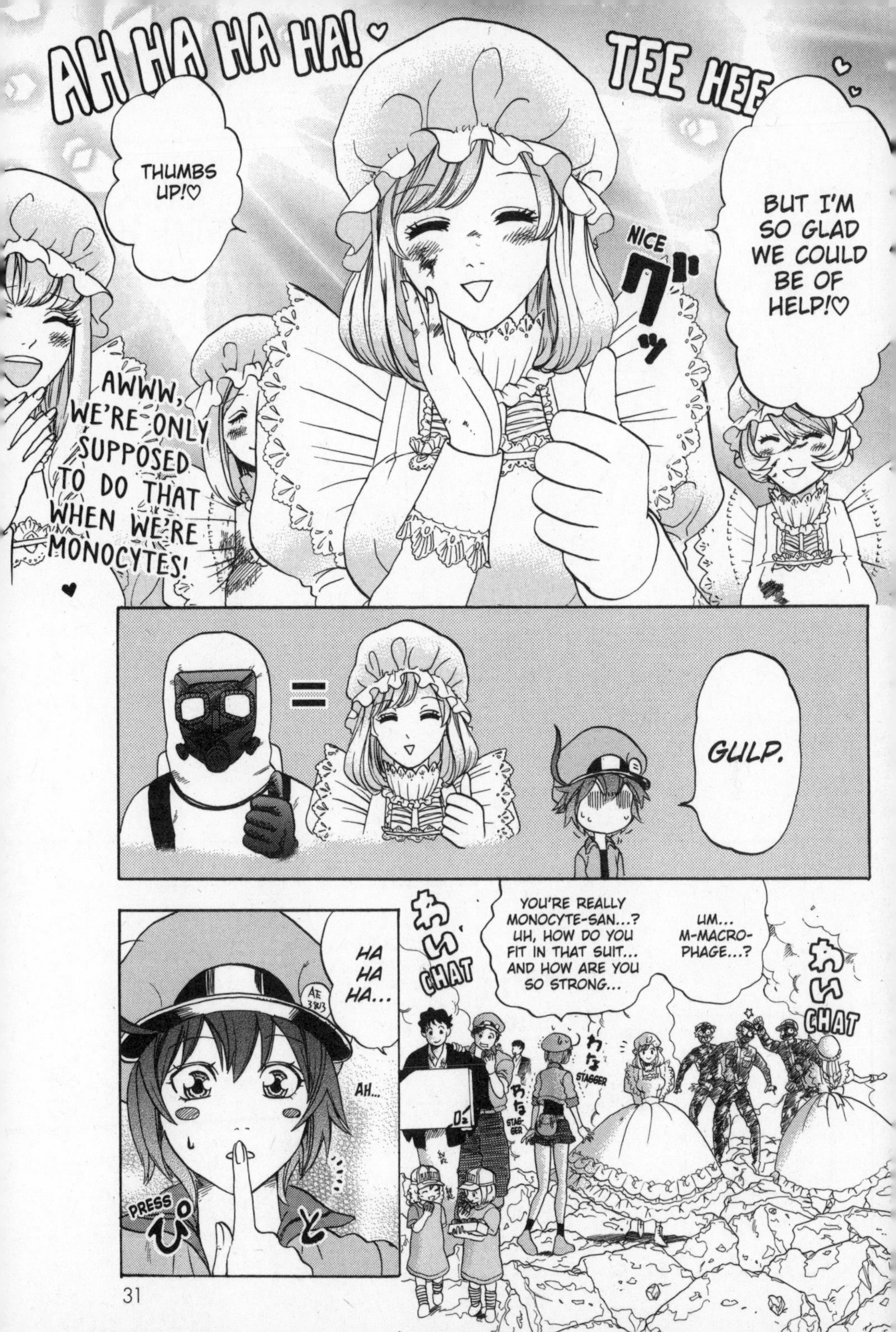
TEE HEE
BUT I'M SO GLAD WE COULD BE OF HELP!♡
NICE
AH HA HA HA!♡
THUMBS UP!♡
AWWW, WE'RE ONLY SUPPOSED TO DO THAT WHEN WE'RE MONOCYTES!
GULP.
UM... M-MACRO-PHAGE...?
CHAT
YOU'RE REALLY MONOCYTE-SAN...? UH, HOW DO YOU FIT IN THAT SUIT... AND HOW ARE YOU SO STRONG...
CHAT
STAGGER
STAGGER
HA HA HA...
AE 3803
AH...
PRESS

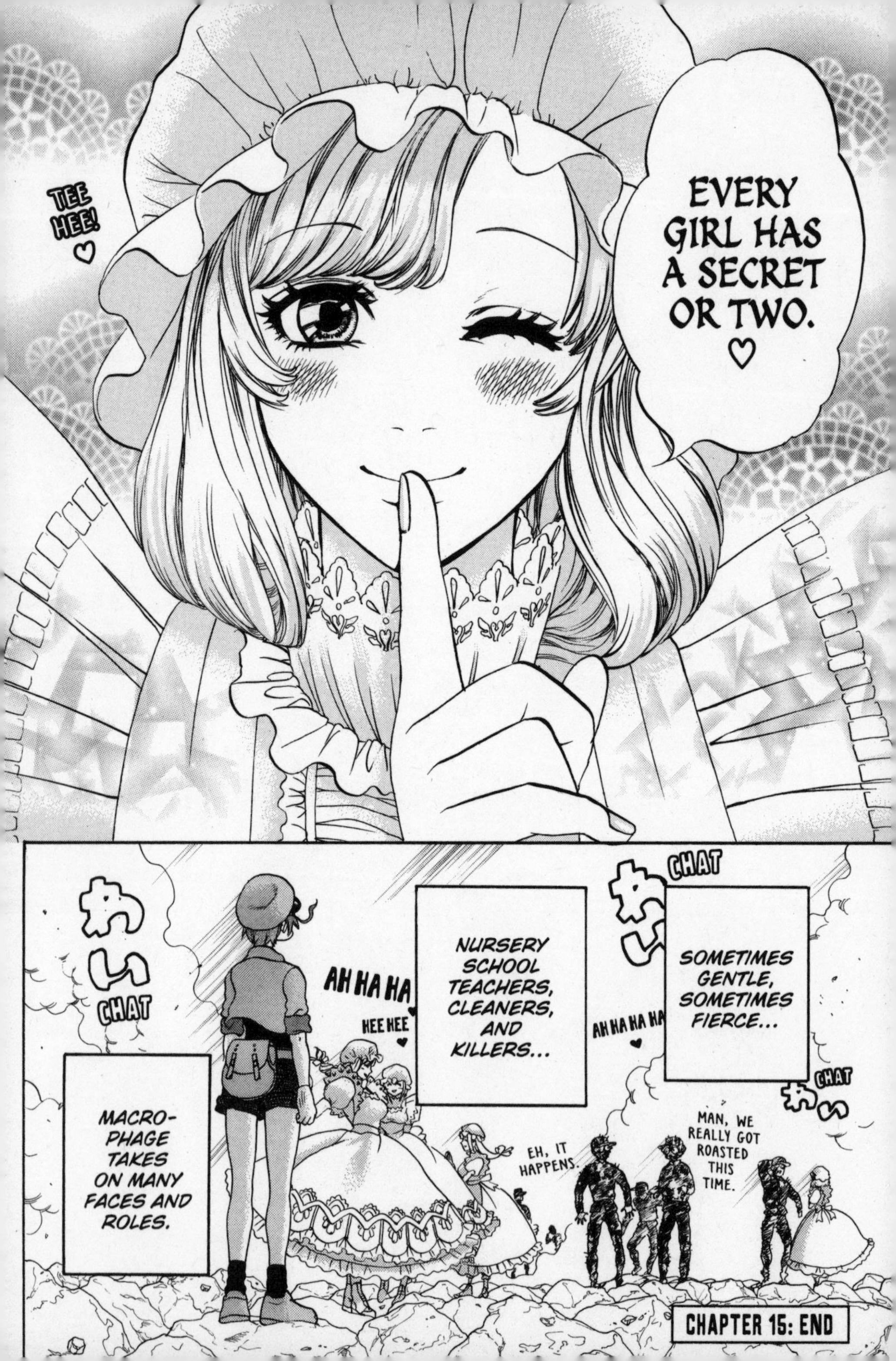
EVERY GIRL HAS A SECRET OR TWO. ♡
TEE HEE! ♡
SOMETIMES GENTLE, SOMETIMES FIERCE...
わい CHAT
わい CHAT
MAN, WE REALLY GOT ROASTED THIS TIME.
EH, IT HAPPENS.
AH HA HA HA ♥
NURSERY SCHOOL TEACHERS, CLEANERS, AND KILLERS...
AH HA HA ♥
HEE HEE ♥
わい CHAT
MACRO-PHAGE TAKES ON MANY FACES AND ROLES.
CHAPTER 15: END

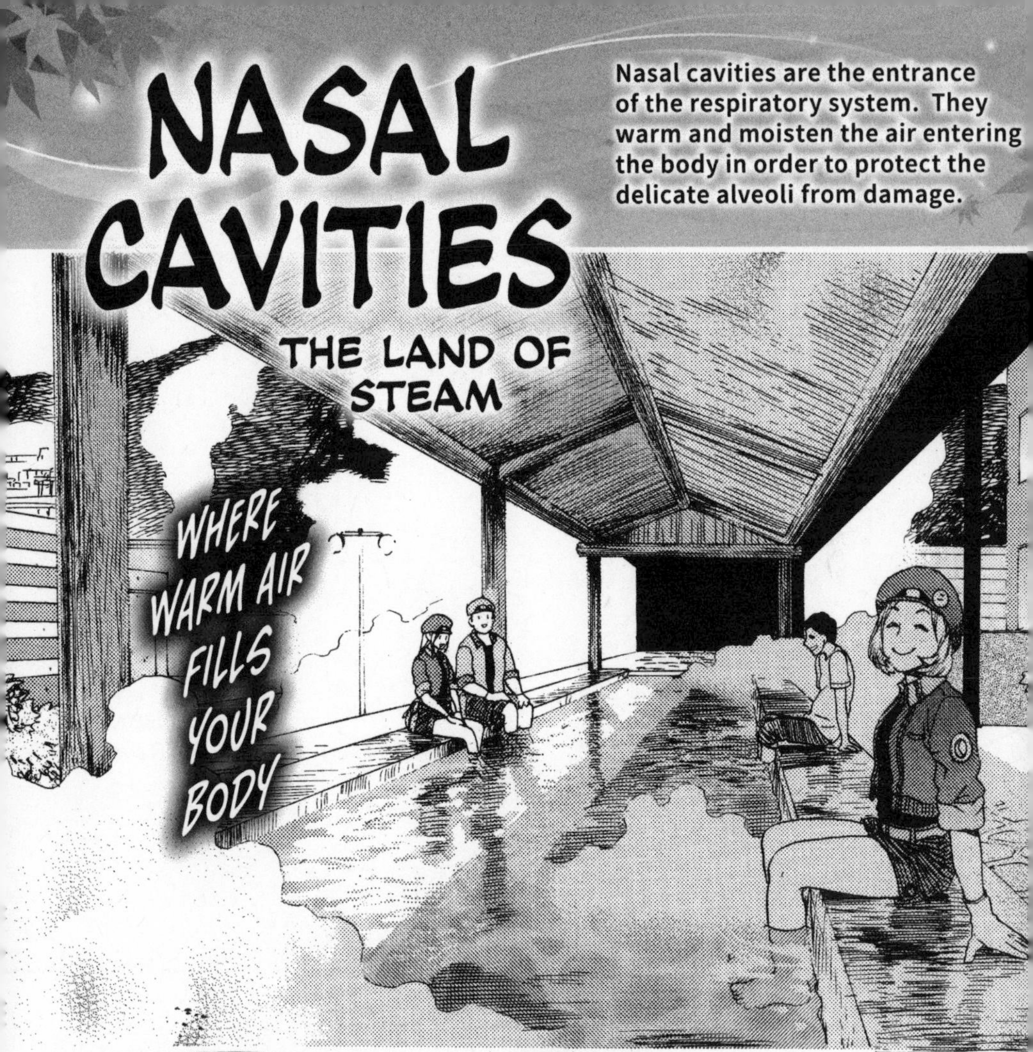
NASAL CAVITIES
Nasal cavities are the entrance of the respiratory system. They warm and moisten the air entering the body in order to protect the delicate alveoli from damage.
THE LAND OF STEAM
WHERE WARM AIR FILLS YOUR BODY

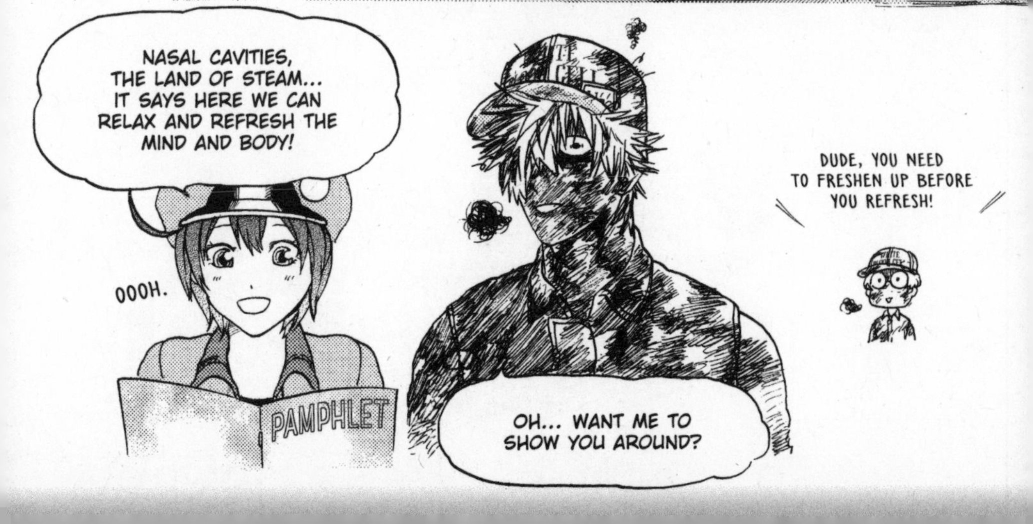
NASAL CAVITIES, THE LAND OF STEAM... IT SAYS HERE WE CAN RELAX AND REFRESH THE MIND AND BODY!
OOOH.
PAMPHLET
OH... WANT ME TO SHOW YOU AROUND?
DUDE, YOU NEED TO FRESHEN UP BEFORE YOU REFRESH!

Cells at Work!
はたらく細胞

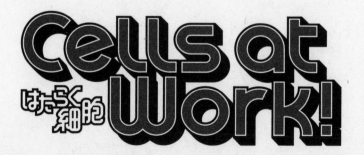

CHAPTER 16: DENGUE FEVER

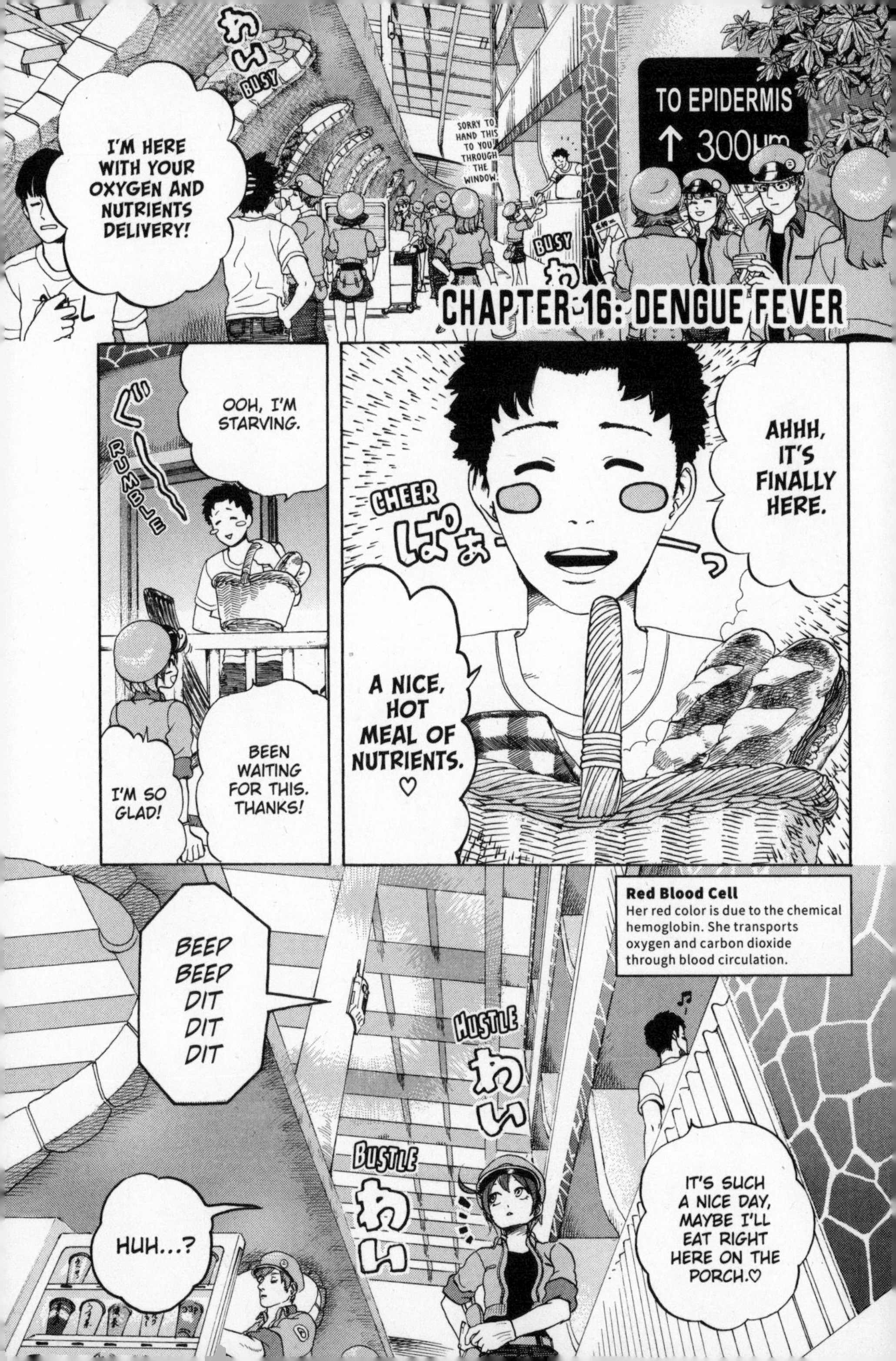
TO EPIDERMIS
↑ 300μm
SORRY TO HAND THIS TO YOU THROUGH THE WINDOW.
BUSY
I'M HERE WITH YOUR OXYGEN AND NUTRIENTS DELIVERY!
BUSY
AHHH, IT'S FINALLY HERE.
CHEER
A NICE, HOT MEAL OF NUTRIENTS. ♡
OOH, I'M STARVING.
RUMBLE
BEEN WAITING FOR THIS. THANKS!
I'M SO GLAD!
Red Blood Cell
Her red color is due to the chemical hemoglobin. She transports oxygen and carbon dioxide through blood circulation.
IT'S SUCH A NICE DAY, MAYBE I'LL EAT RIGHT HERE ON THE PORCH.♡
HUSTLE
BUSTLE
BEEP BEEP DIT DIT DIT
HUH...?

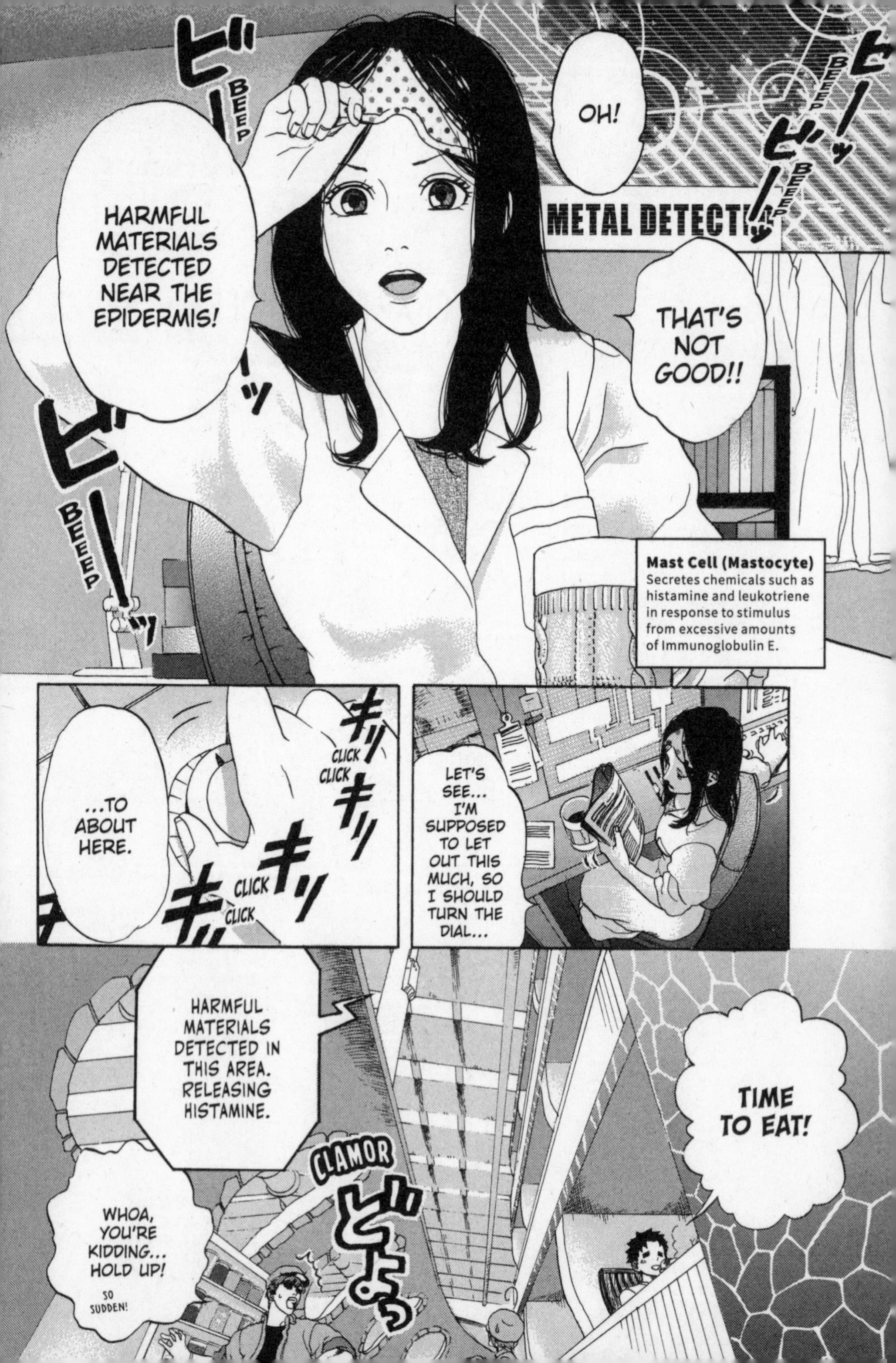
BEEP
BEEP
OH!
METAL DETECT
THAT'S NOT GOOD!!
BEEP
HARMFUL MATERIALS DETECTED NEAR THE EPIDERMIS!
BEEP
Mast Cell (Mastocyte)
Secretes chemicals such as histamine and leukotriene in response to stimulus from excessive amounts of Immunoglobulin E.
LET'S SEE... I'M SUPPOSED TO LET OUT THIS MUCH, SO I SHOULD TURN THE DIAL...
CLICK CLICK
CLICK CLICK
...TO ABOUT HERE.
TIME TO EAT!
HARMFUL MATERIALS DETECTED IN THIS AREA. RELEASING HISTAMINE.
CLAMOR
WHOA, YOU'RE KIDDING... HOLD UP!
SO SUDDEN!

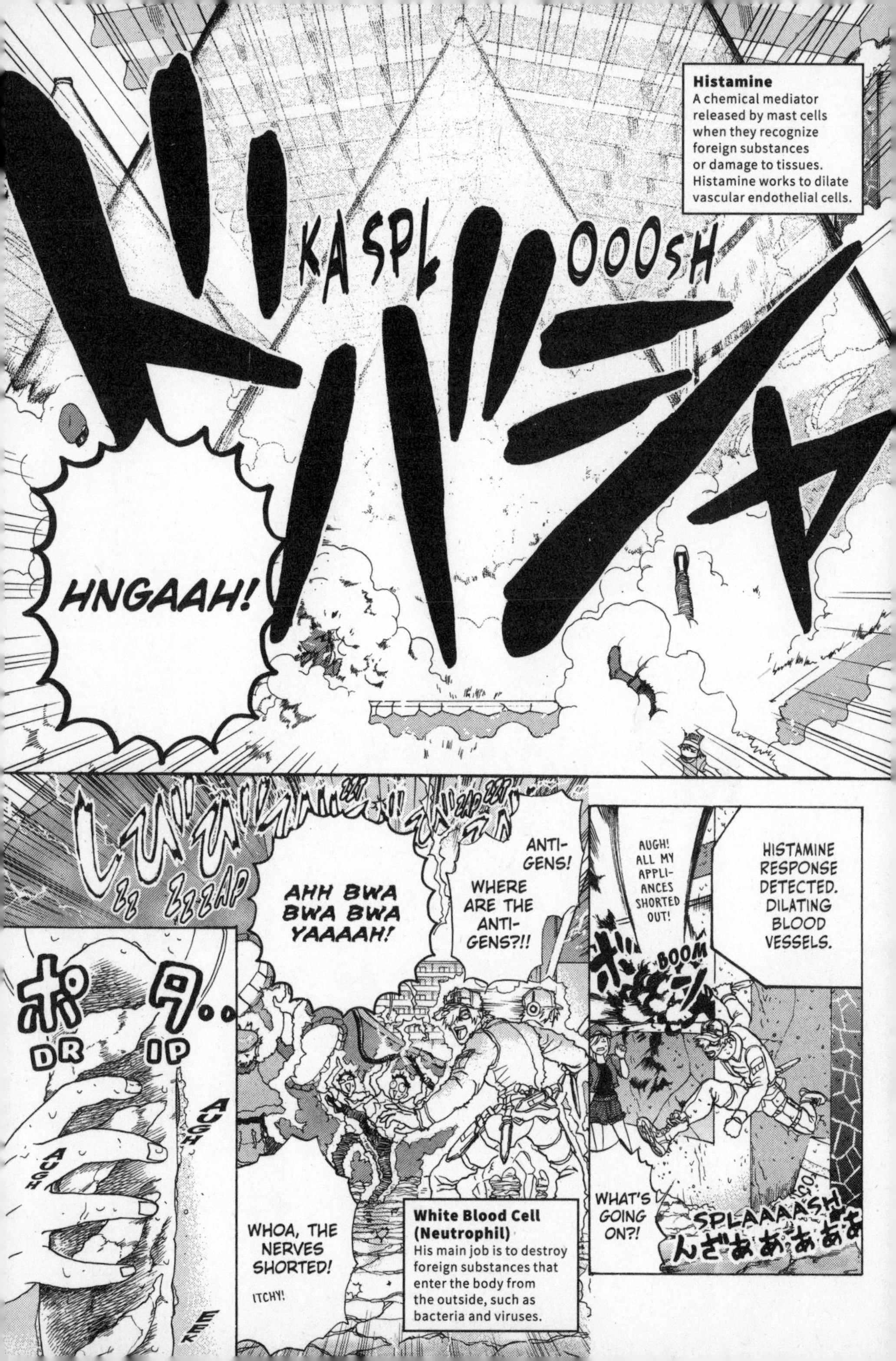
Histamine
A chemical mediator released by mast cells when they recognize foreign substances or damage to tissues. Histamine works to dilate vascular endothelial cells.
KASPLOOOOSH
HNGAAH!
HISTAMINE RESPONSE DETECTED. DILATING BLOOD VESSELS.
AUGH! ALL MY APPLIANCES SHORTED OUT!
BOOM
WHAT'S GOING ON?!
SPLAAAASH
ANTI-GENS!
WHERE ARE THE ANTI-GENS?!!
AHH BWA BWA BWA YAAAAH!
White Blood Cell (Neutrophil)
His main job is to destroy foreign substances that enter the body from the outside, such as bacteria and viruses.
WHOA, THE NERVES SHORTED!
ITCHY!
ZZ ZZZAP
DRIP
AUGH
AUGH
EEK

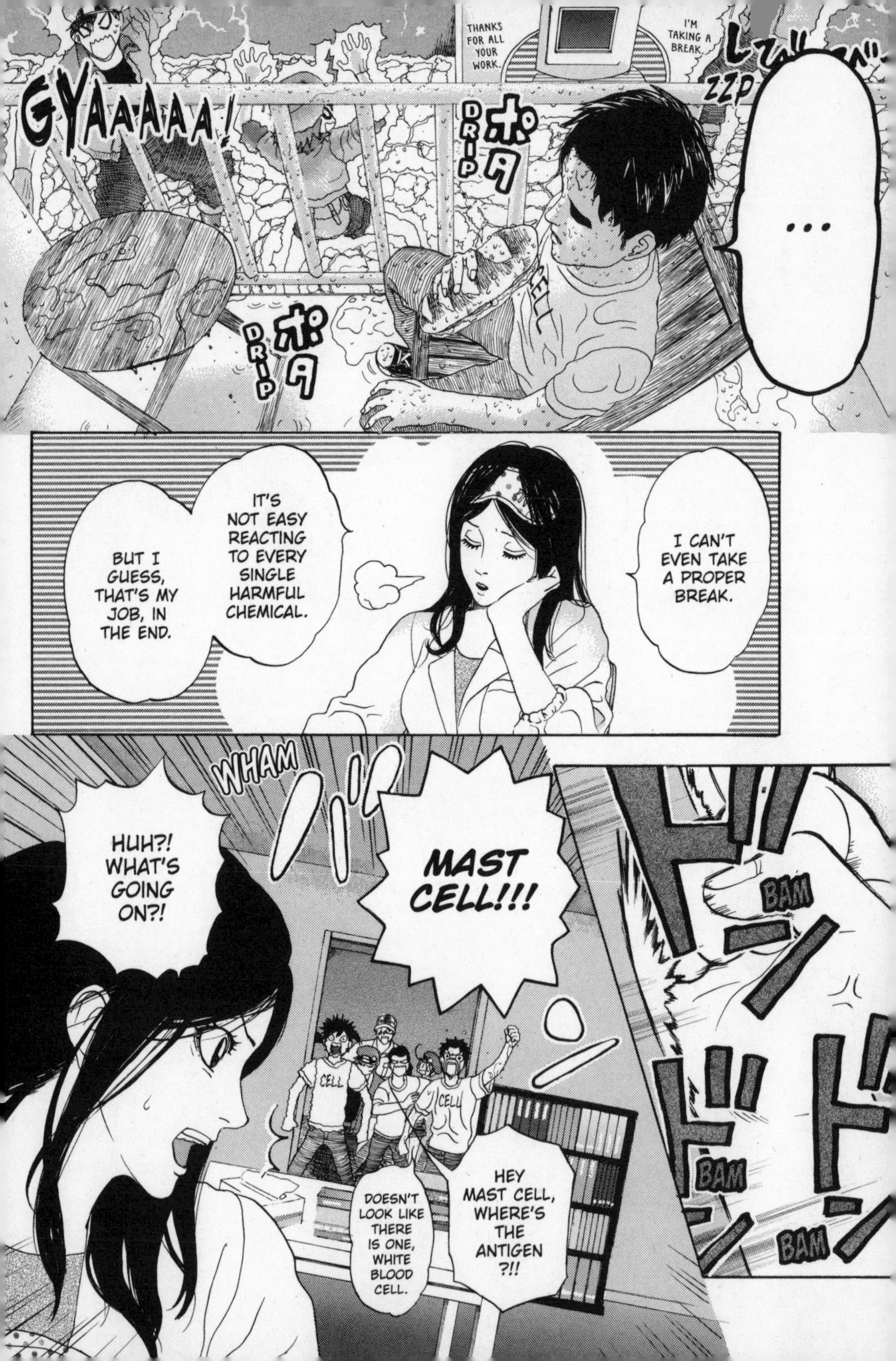
...
ZZP
I'M TAKING A BREAK.
THANKS FOR ALL YOUR WORK.
DRIP
DRIP
GYAAAAA!
I CAN'T EVEN TAKE A PROPER BREAK.
IT'S NOT EASY REACTING TO EVERY SINGLE HARMFUL CHEMICAL.
BUT I GUESS, THAT'S MY JOB, IN THE END.
BAM
BAM
BAM
WHAM
MAST CELL!!!
HUH?! WHAT'S GOING ON?!
HEY MAST CELL, WHERE'S THE ANTIGEN?!!
DOESN'T LOOK LIKE THERE IS ONE, WHITE BLOOD CELL.

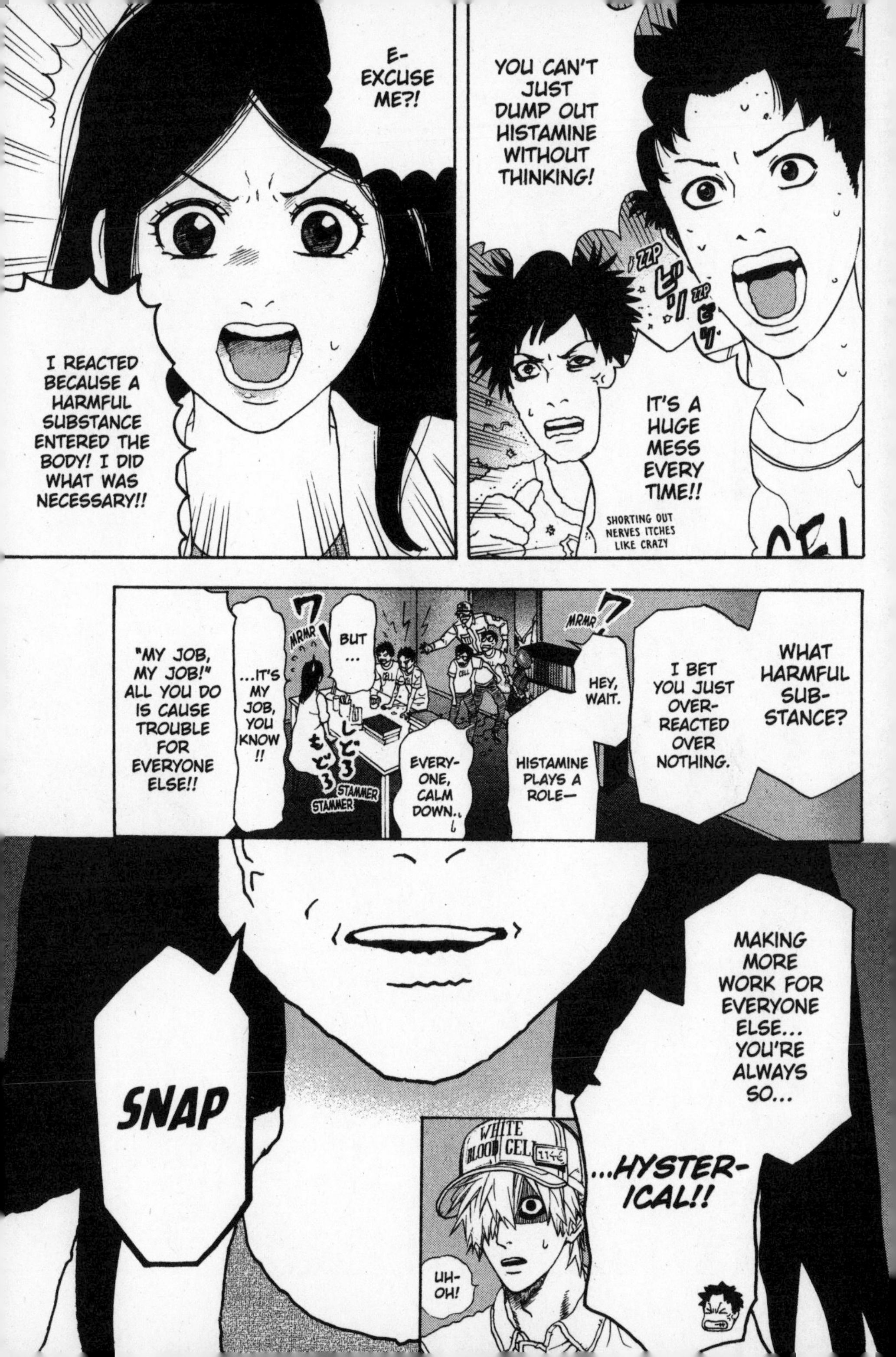

YOU CAN'T JUST DUMP OUT HISTAMINE WITHOUT THINKING!
ZZP
ZZP
IT'S A HUGE MESS EVERY TIME!!
SHORTING OUT NERVES ITCHES LIKE CRAZY
E-EXCUSE ME?!
I REACTED BECAUSE A HARMFUL SUBSTANCE ENTERED THE BODY! I DID WHAT WAS NECESSARY!!
WHAT HARMFUL SUB-STANCE?
I BET YOU JUST OVER-REACTED OVER NOTHING.
MRMR
HEY, WAIT.
HISTAMINE PLAYS A ROLE—
EVERY-ONE, CALM DOWN..
BUT ...
MRMR
STAMMER
STAMMER
...IT'S MY JOB, YOU KNOW!!
"MY JOB, MY JOB!" ALL YOU DO IS CAUSE TROUBLE FOR EVERYONE ELSE!!
MAKING MORE WORK FOR EVERYONE ELSE... YOU'RE ALWAYS SO...
...HYSTER-ICAL!!
UH-OH!
SNAP

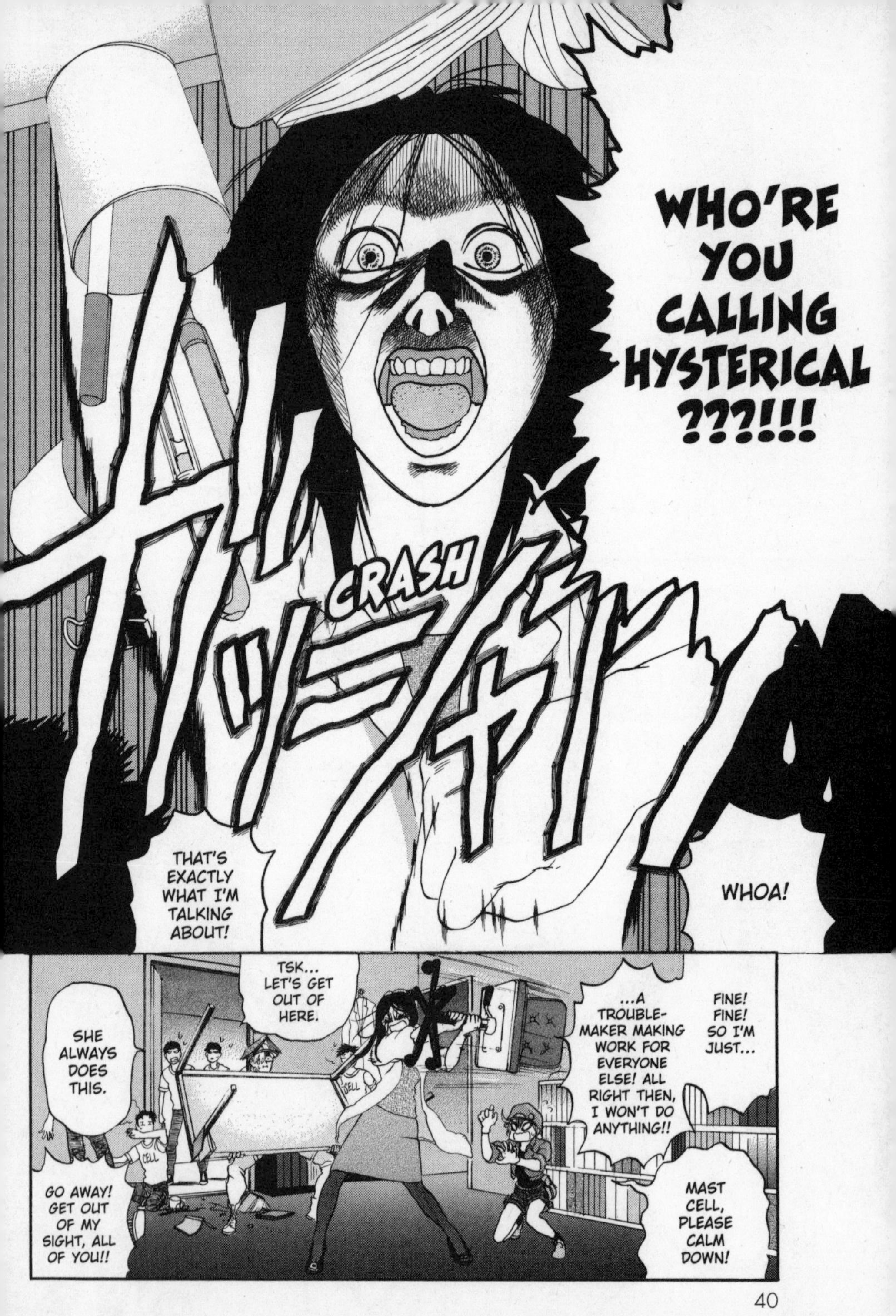
WHO'RE YOU CALLING HYSTERICAL???!!!
CRASH
WHOA!
THAT'S EXACTLY WHAT I'M TALKING ABOUT!
FINE! FINE! SO I'M JUST...
...A TROUBLE-MAKER MAKING WORK FOR EVERYONE ELSE! ALL RIGHT THEN, I WON'T DO ANYTHING!!
TSK... LET'S GET OUT OF HERE.
SHE ALWAYS DOES THIS.
MAST CELL, PLEASE CALM DOWN!
GO AWAY! GET OUT OF MY SIGHT, ALL OF YOU!!

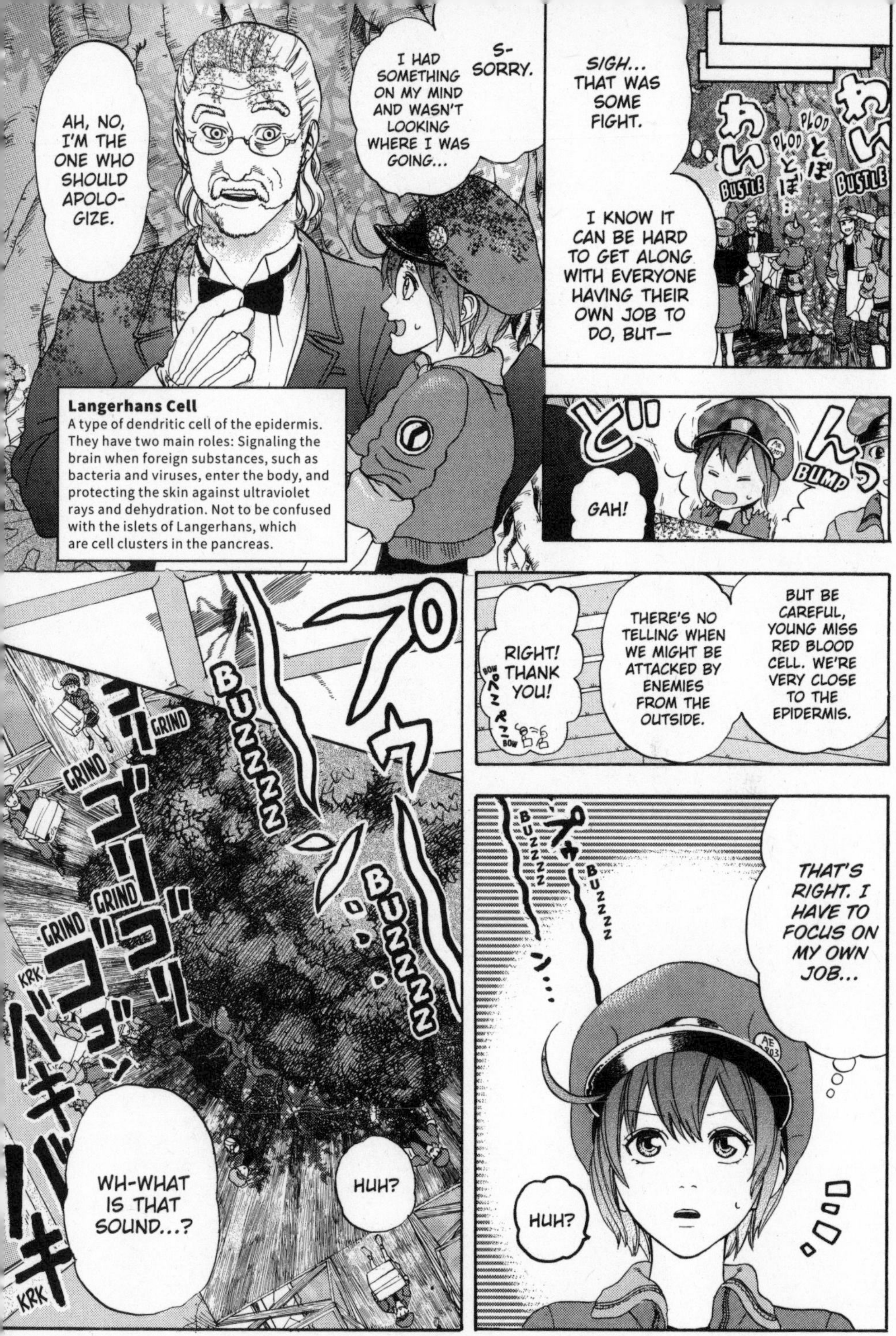
SIGH... THAT WAS SOME FIGHT.
BUSTLE
PLOD PLOD
BUSTLE
I KNOW IT CAN BE HARD TO GET ALONG WITH EVERYONE HAVING THEIR OWN JOB TO DO, BUT—
BUMP
GAH!
S-SORRY.
I HAD SOMETHING ON MY MIND AND WASN'T LOOKING WHERE I WAS GOING...
AH, NO, I'M THE ONE WHO SHOULD APOLOGIZE.
Langerhans Cell
A type of dendritic cell of the epidermis. They have two main roles: Signaling the brain when foreign substances, such as bacteria and viruses, enter the body, and protecting the skin against ultraviolet rays and dehydration. Not to be confused with the islets of Langerhans, which are cell clusters in the pancreas.
BUT BE CAREFUL, YOUNG MISS RED BLOOD CELL. WE'RE VERY CLOSE TO THE EPIDERMIS.
THERE'S NO TELLING WHEN WE MIGHT BE ATTACKED BY ENEMIES FROM THE OUTSIDE.
RIGHT! THANK YOU!
BOW BOW
THAT'S RIGHT. I HAVE TO FOCUS ON MY OWN JOB...
BUZZZZ
BUZZZZ
HUH?
BUZZZZZ
BUZZZZZ
GRIND
GRIND
GRIND
GRIND
KRK
KRK
HUH?
WH-WHAT IS THAT SOUND...?

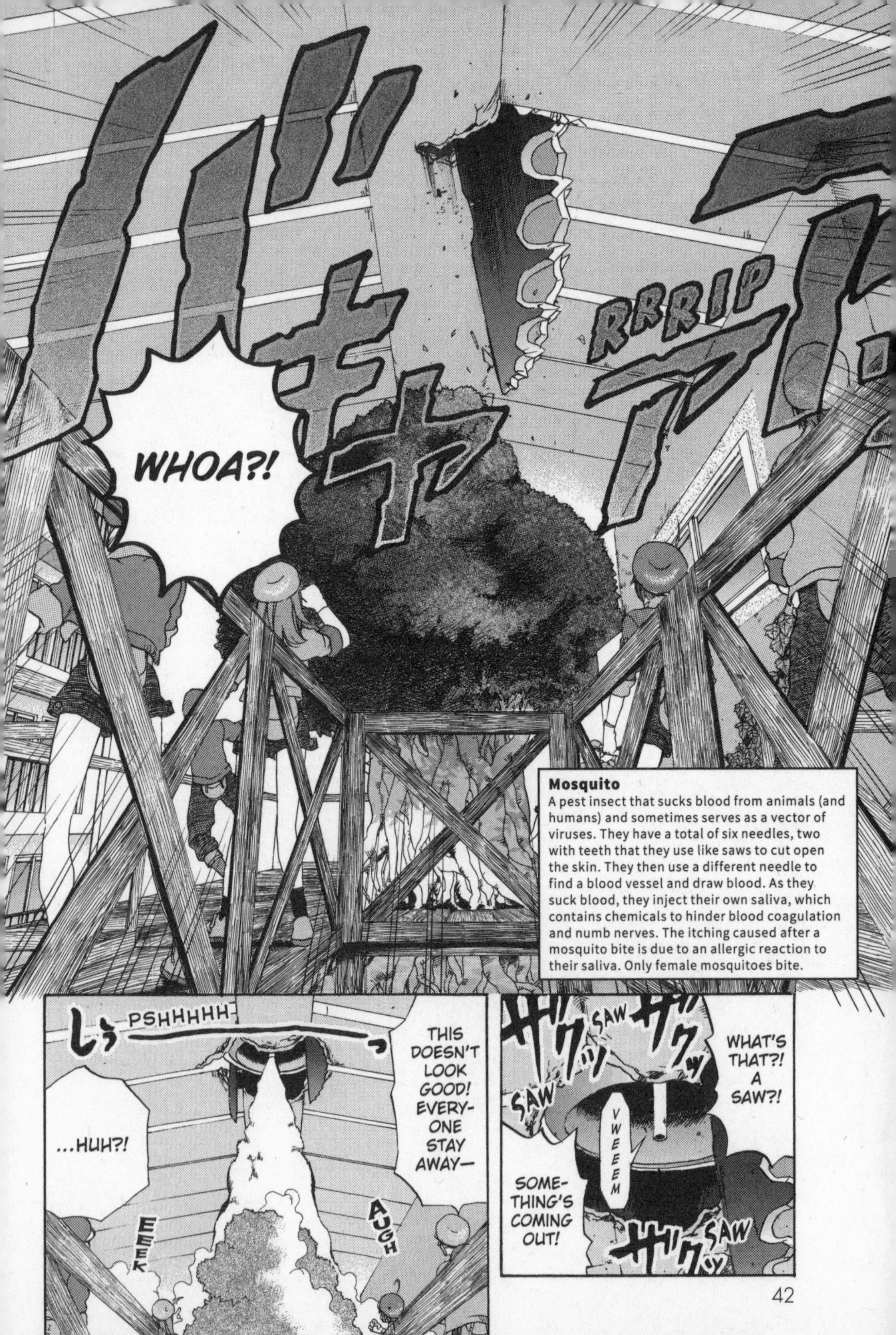
RRRIP
WHOA?!
SAW
SAW
WHAT'S THAT?! A SAW?!
VWEEEEM
SOME-THING'S COMING OUT!
SAW
PSHHHHH
THIS DOESN'T LOOK GOOD! EVERY-ONE STAY AWAY—
...HUH?!
AUGH
EEEK

Mosquito
A pest insect that sucks blood from animals (and humans) and sometimes serves as a vector of viruses. They have a total of six needles, two with teeth that they use like saws to cut open the skin. They then use a different needle to find a blood vessel and draw blood. As they suck blood, they inject their own saliva, which contains chemicals to hinder blood coagulation and numb nerves. The itching caused after a mosquito bite is due to an allergic reaction to their saliva. Only female mosquitoes bite.

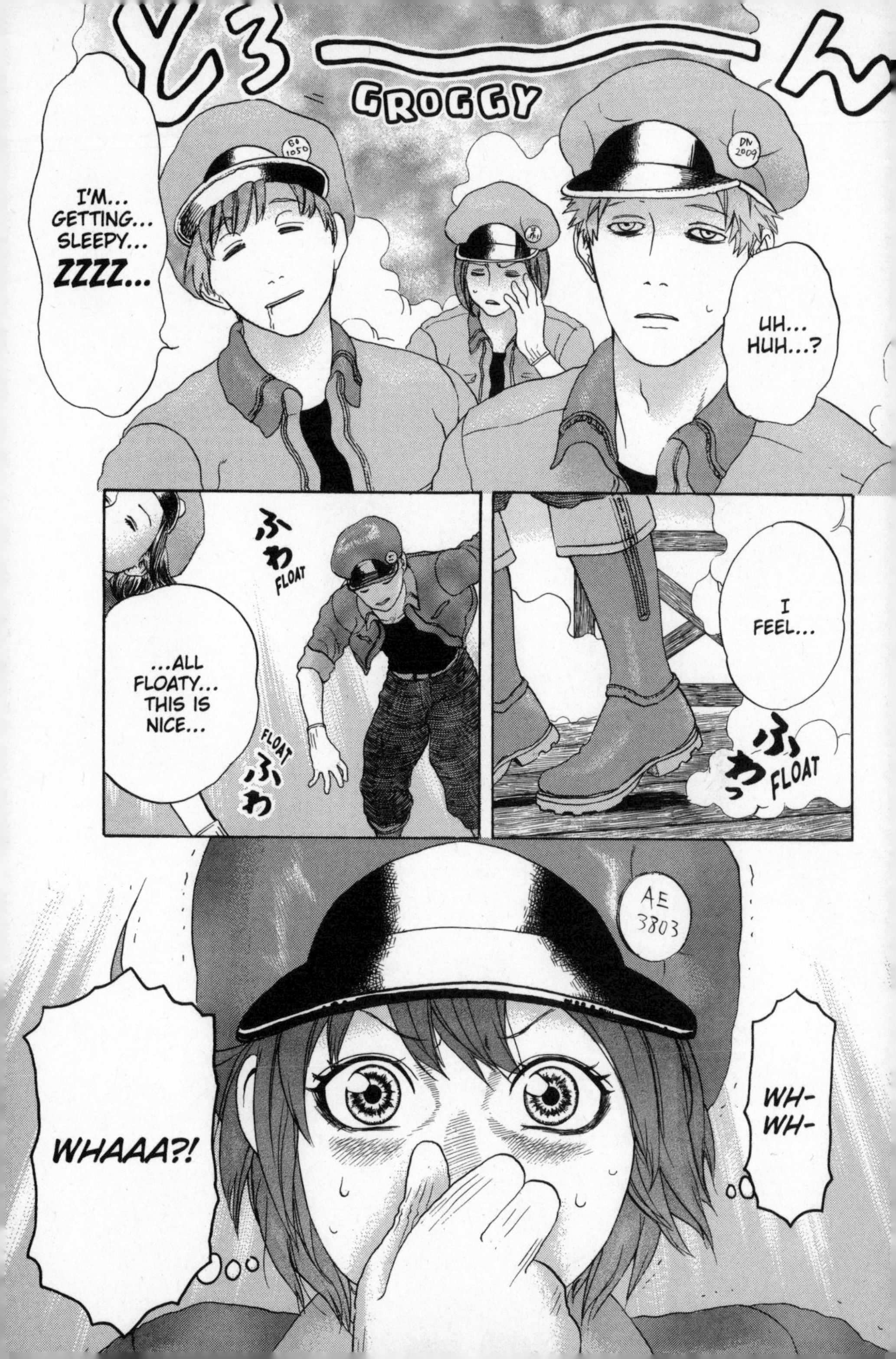
GROGGY
DN 2009
UH... HUH...?
BO 1050
I'M... GETTING... SLEEPY... ZZZZ...
I FEEL...
ふわっ FLOAT
ふわ FLOAT
...ALL FLOATY... THIS IS NICE...
FLOAT ふわ
AE 3803
WH- WH-
WHAAA?!

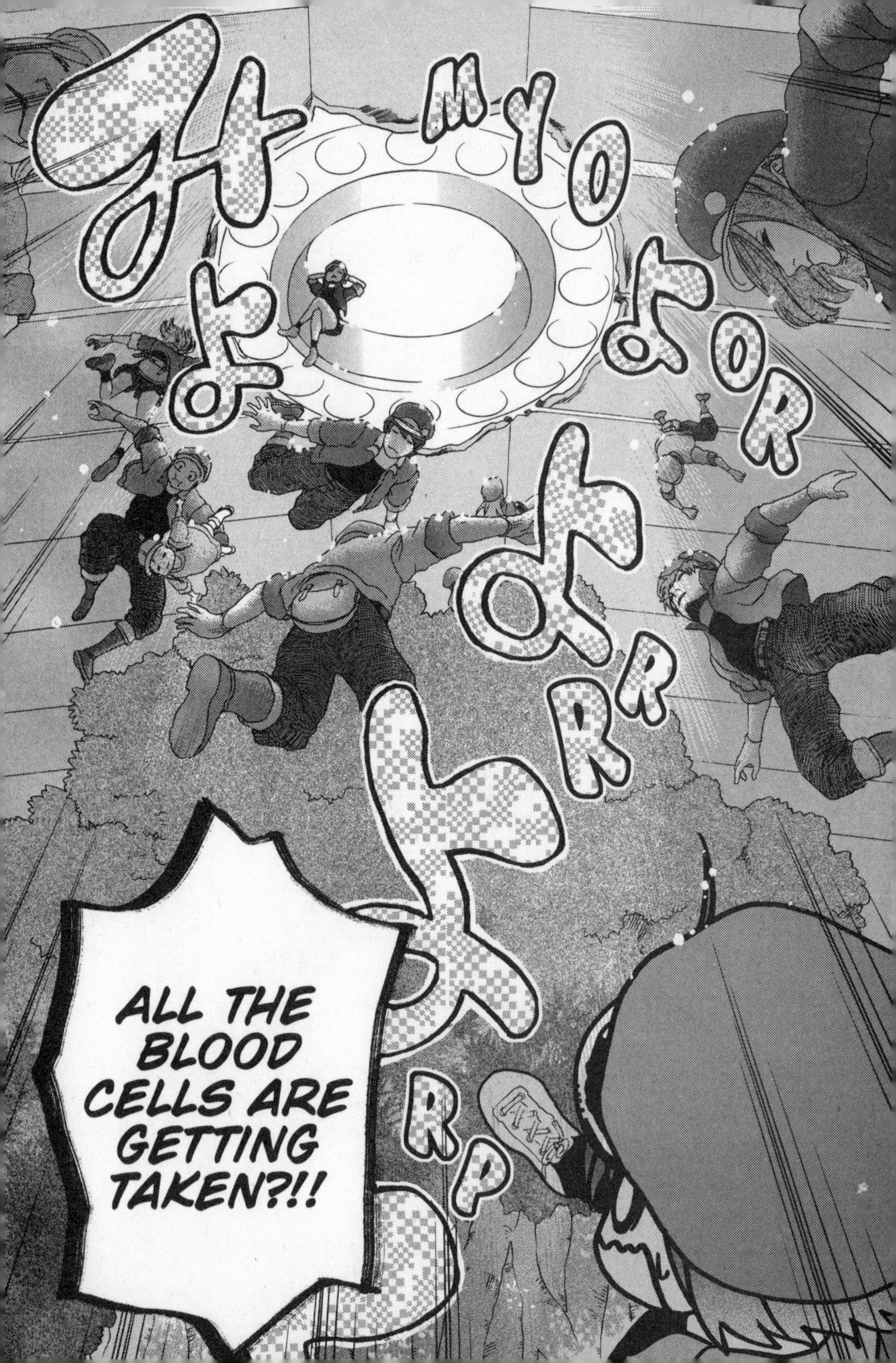
ALL THE BLOOD CELLS ARE GETTING TAKEN?!!

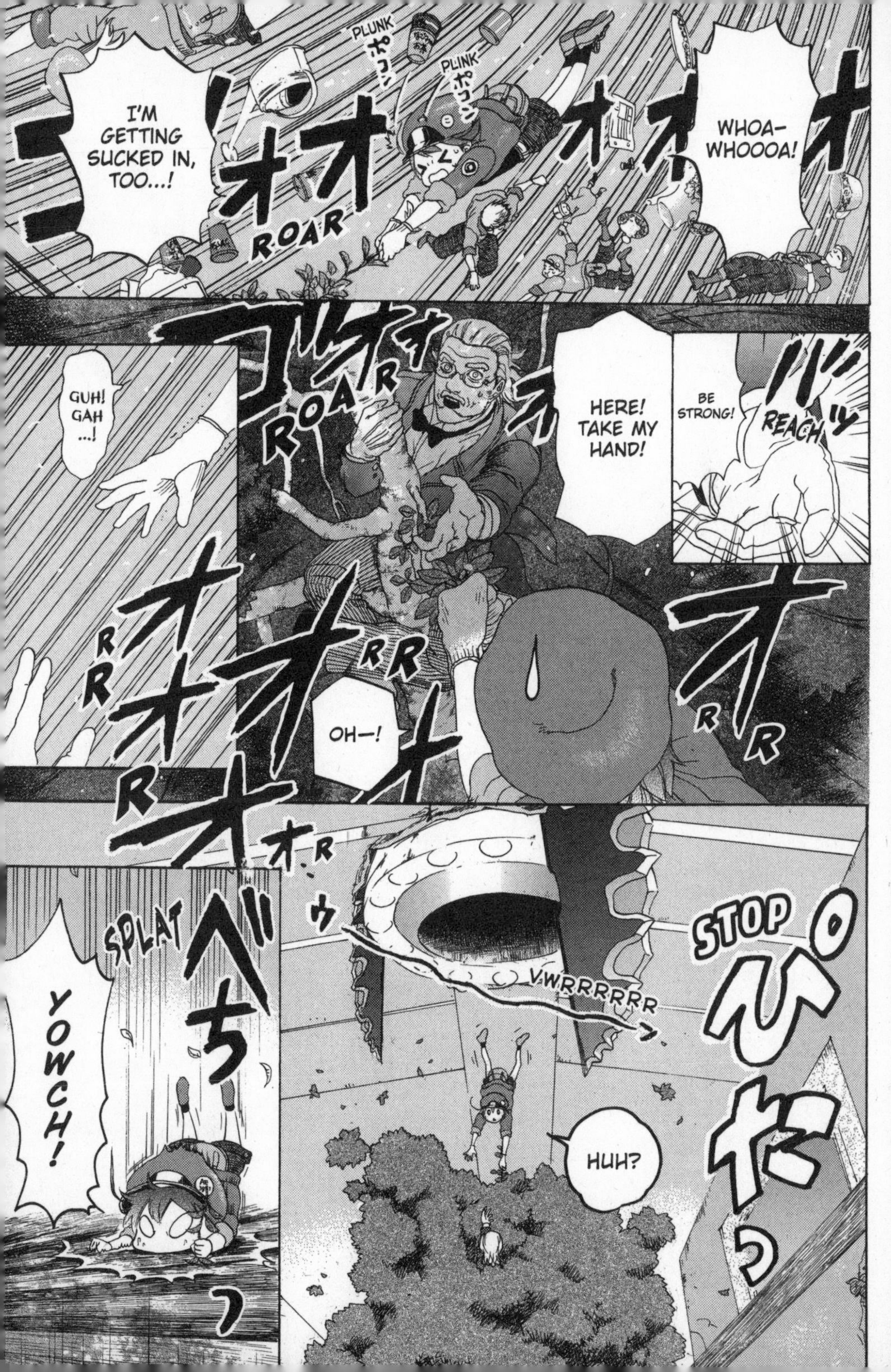

WHOA-WHOOOA!
PLINK
PLINK
I'M GETTING SUCKED IN, TOO...!
ROAR
BE STRONG!
REACH
HERE! TAKE MY HAND!
ROAR
OH—!
RRR
RRR
GUH! GAH ...!
STOP
VWRRRRRRR
HUH?
SPLAT
YOWCH!

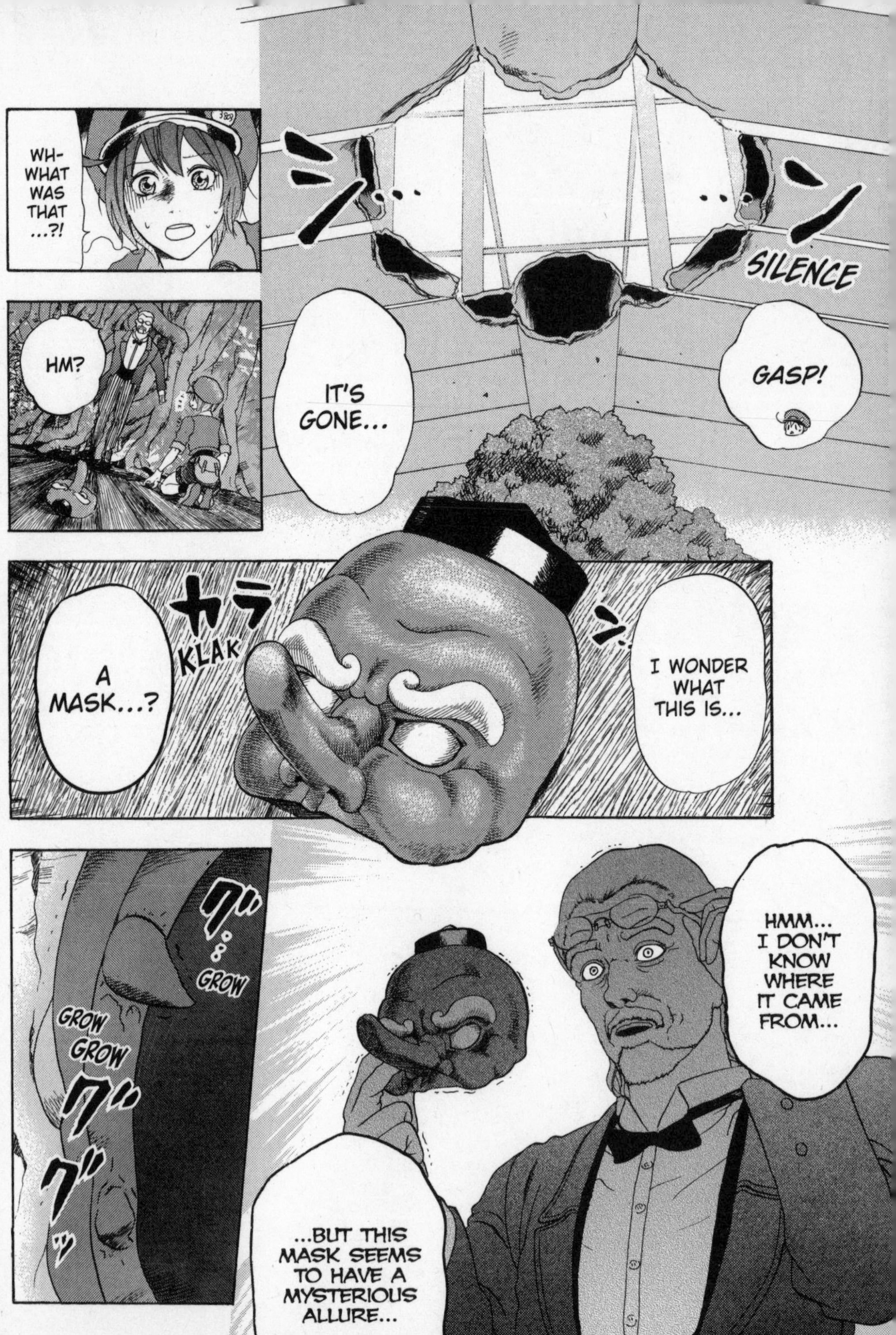
SILENCE
GASP!
IT'S GONE...
WH-WHAT WAS THAT...?!
HM?
I WONDER WHAT THIS IS...
KLAK
A MASK...?
HMM... I DON'T KNOW WHERE IT CAME FROM...
...BUT THIS MASK SEEMS TO HAVE A MYSTERIOUS ALLURE...
GROW
GROW GROW

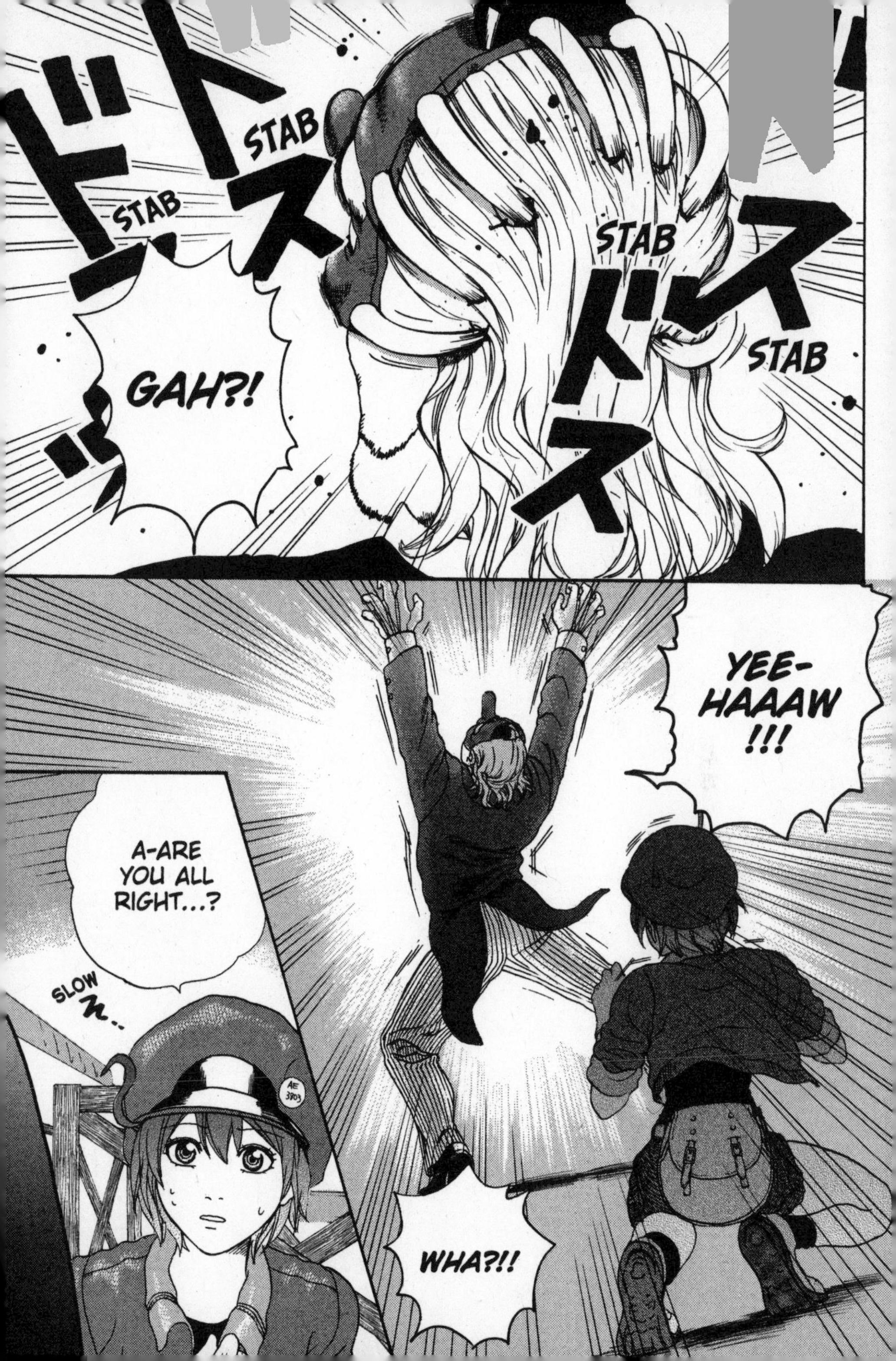

STAB
STAB
GAH?!
STAB
STAB
YEE-HAAAW!!!
WHA?!!
A-ARE YOU ALL RIGHT...?
SLOW
AE 3803

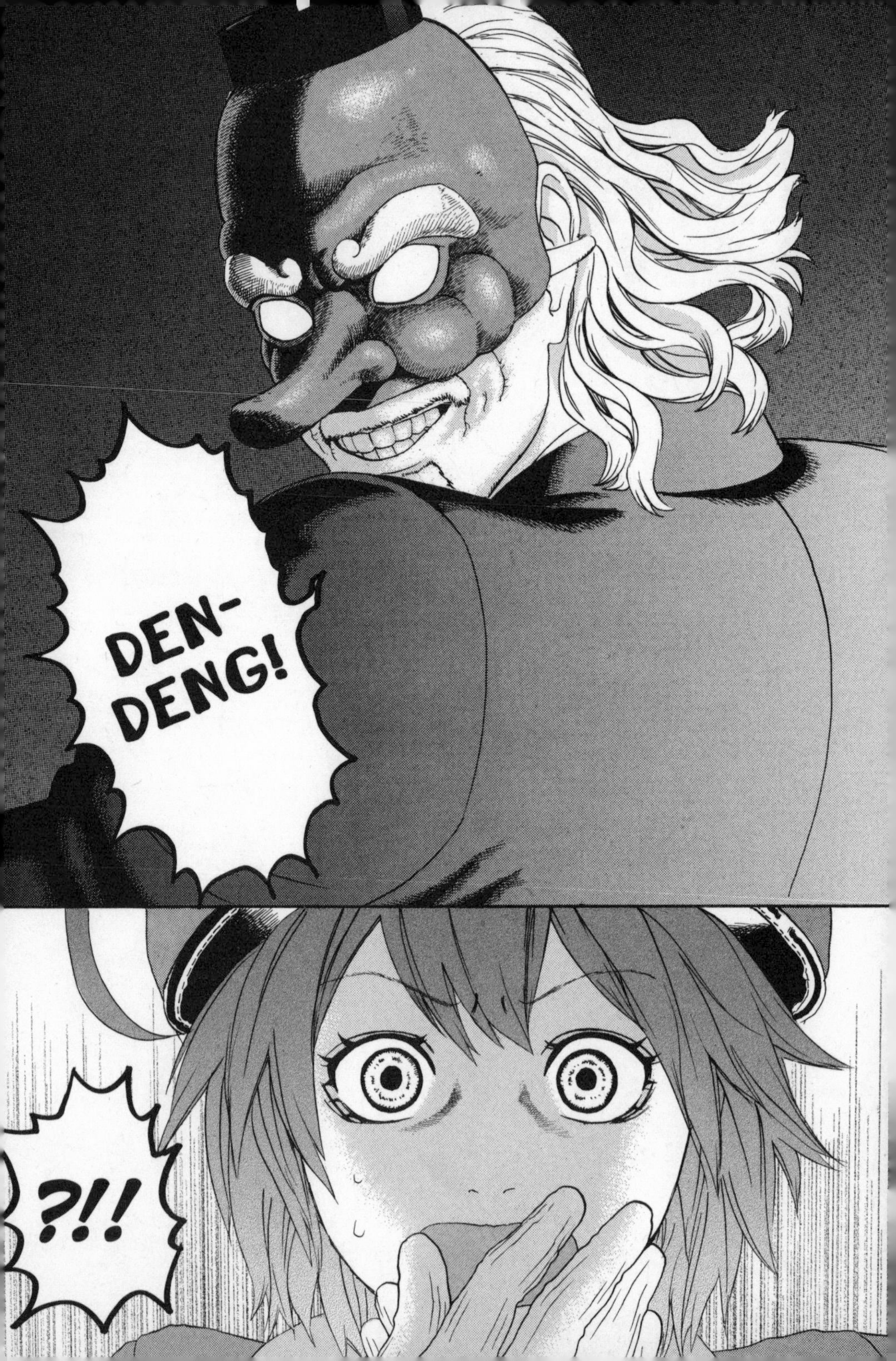
DEN-
DENG!
?!!

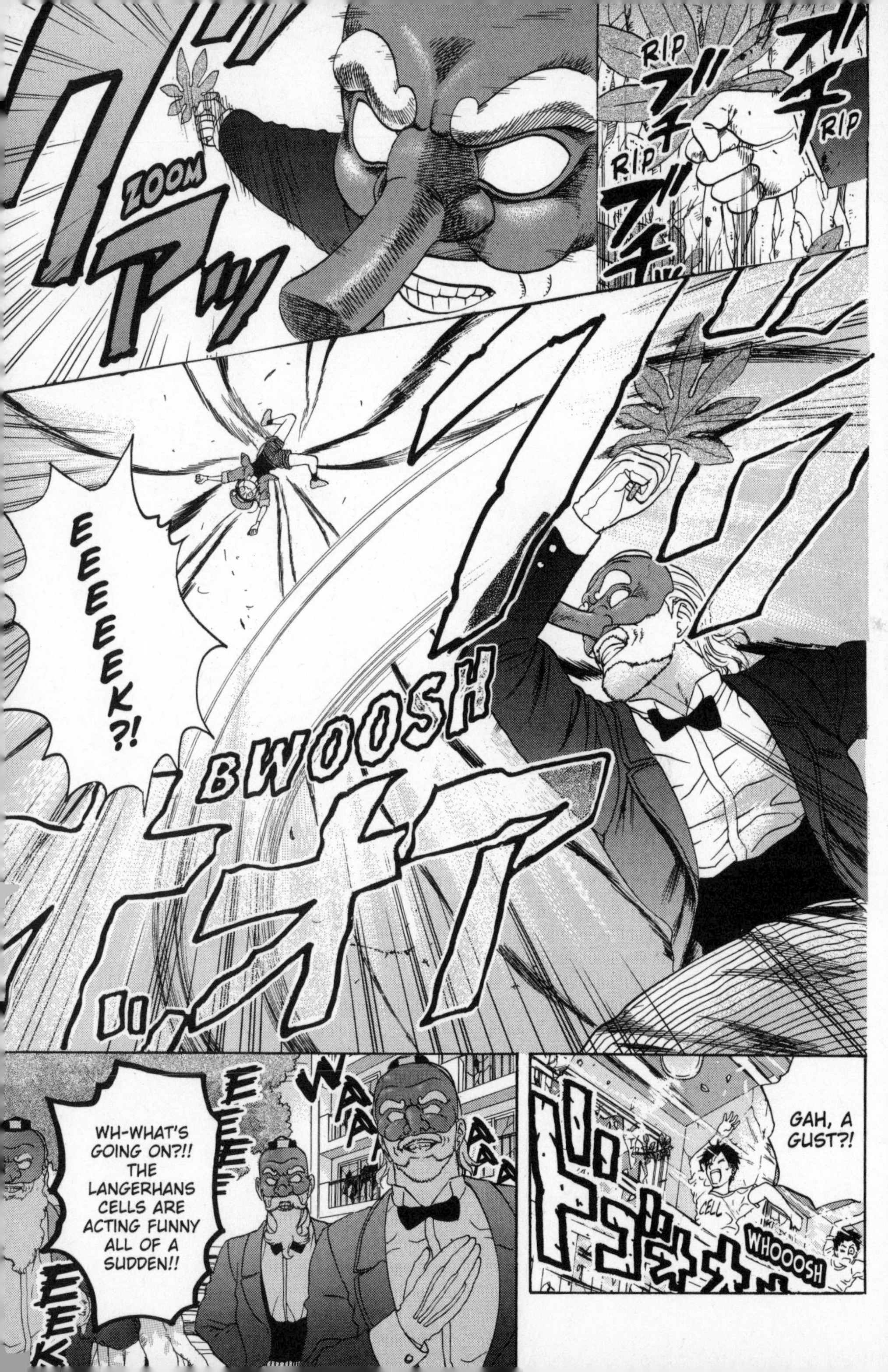
RIP
RIP
RIP
ZOOM
EEEEEEEK?!
BWOOSH
GAH, A GUST?!
WHOOOSH
WH-WHAT'S GOING ON?!! THE LANGERHANS CELLS ARE ACTING FUNNY ALL OF A SUDDEN!!
EEEE
WAAAAA
EEEK

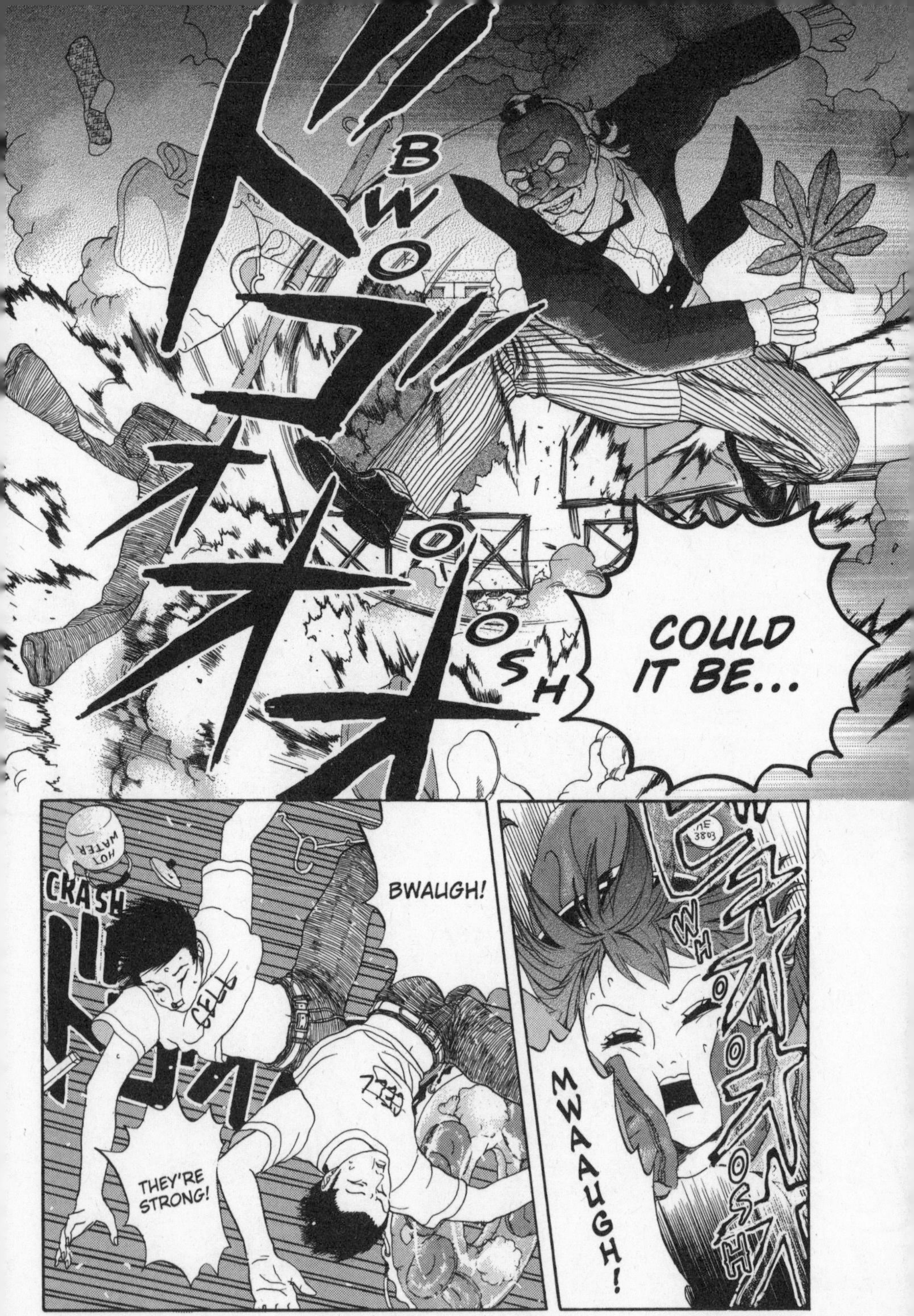
BWOOOOSH
COULD IT BE...
WHOOOOSH
MWAAUGH!
CRASH
BWAUGH!
THEY'RE STRONG!

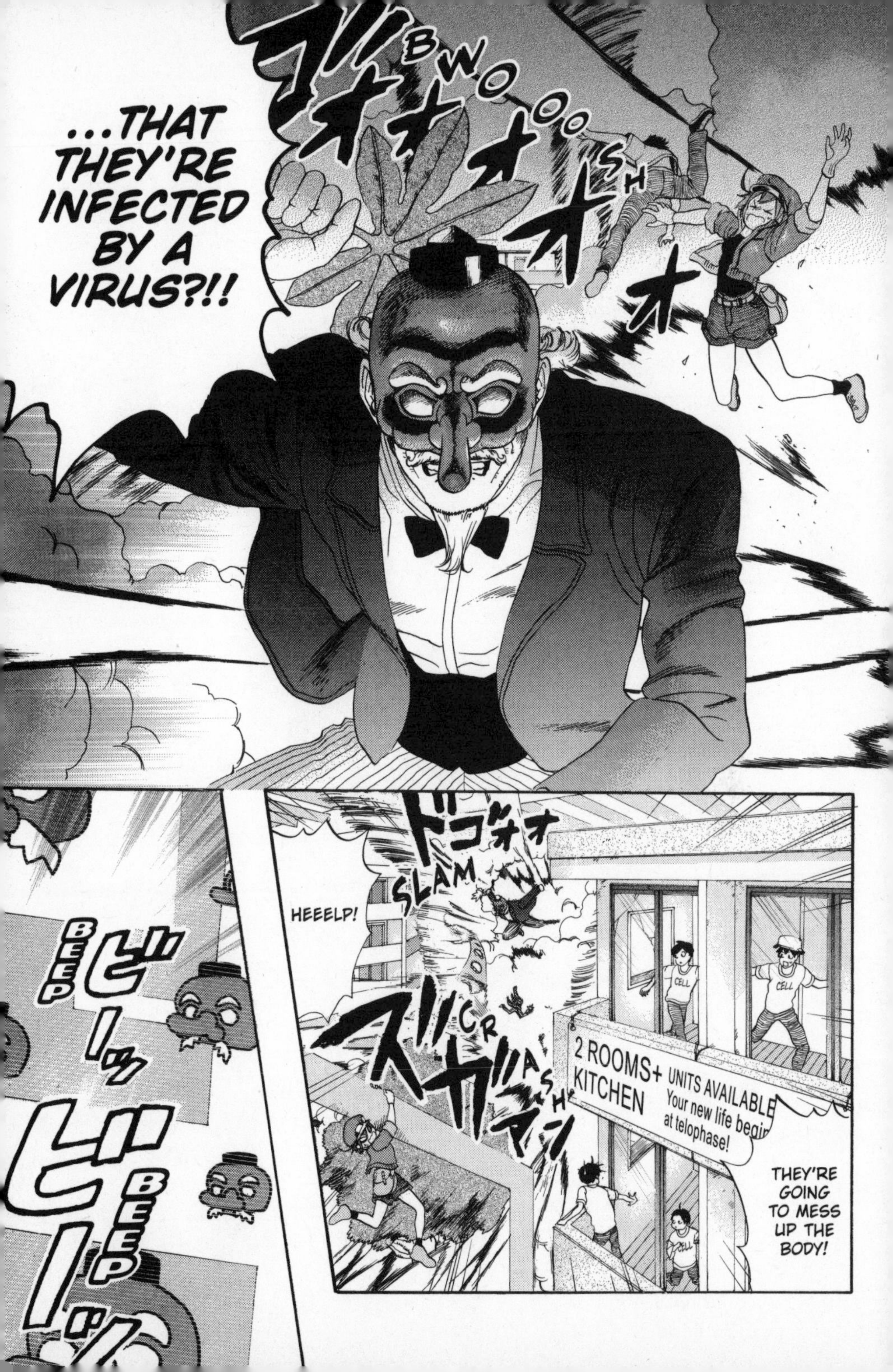
BWOOOOSH
...THAT THEY'RE INFECTED BY A VIRUS?!!
SLAM
HEEELP!
CRASH
CELL
CELL
2 ROOMS+ KITCHEN
UNITS AVAILABLE
Your new life begin
at telophase!
CELL
THEY'RE GOING TO MESS UP THE BODY!
BEEP
BEEP

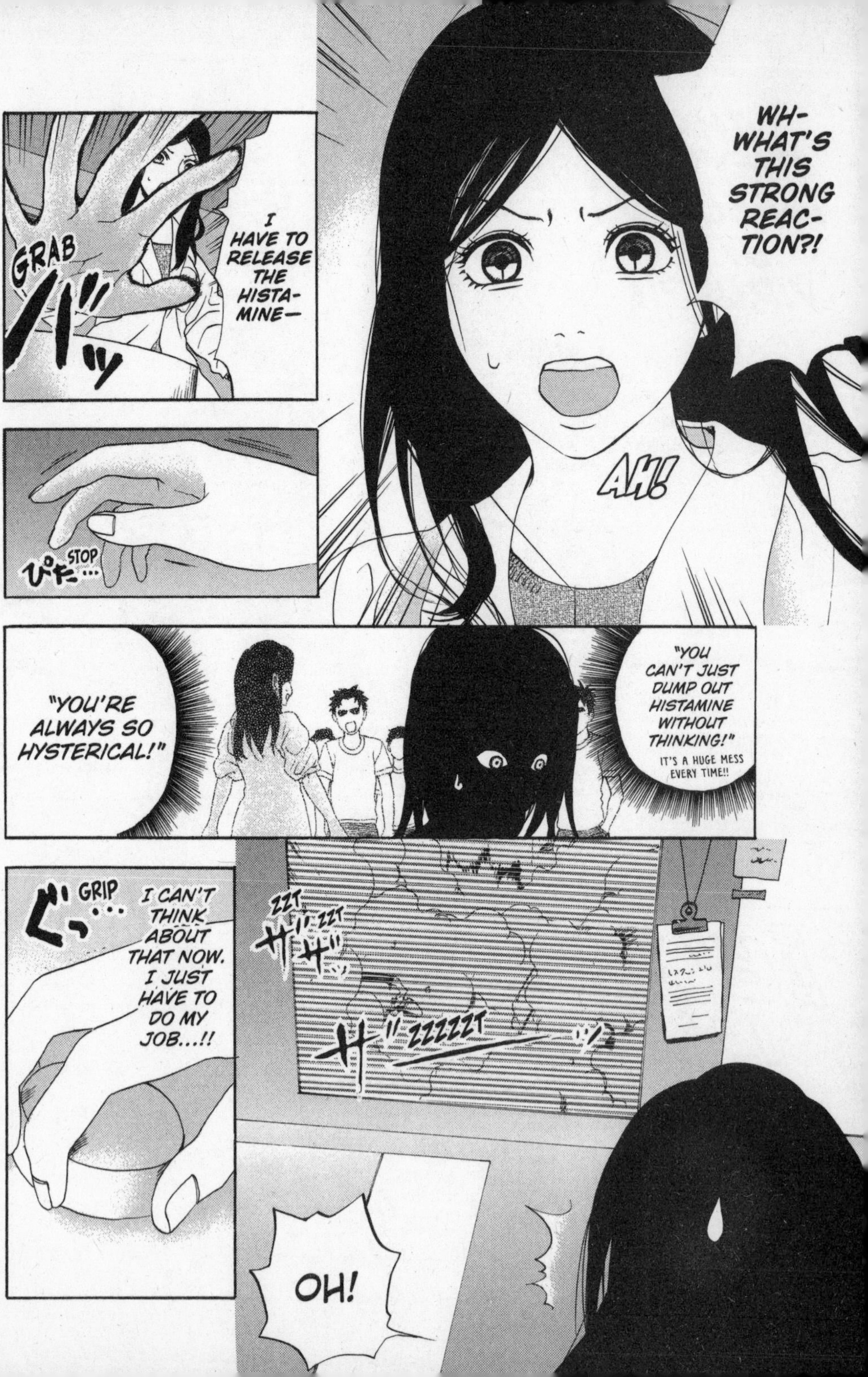

WH- WHAT'S THIS STRONG REAC- TION?!
AH!
GRAB
I HAVE TO RELEASE THE HISTA- MINE—
ぴた… STOP
"YOU CAN'T JUST DUMP OUT HISTAMINE WITHOUT THINKING!"
IT'S A HUGE MESS EVERY TIME!!
"YOU'RE ALWAYS SO HYSTERICAL!"
ZZT
ZZT
ZZZZZT
OH!
ぐっ… GRIP
I CAN'T THINK ABOUT THAT NOW. I JUST HAVE TO DO MY JOB...!!

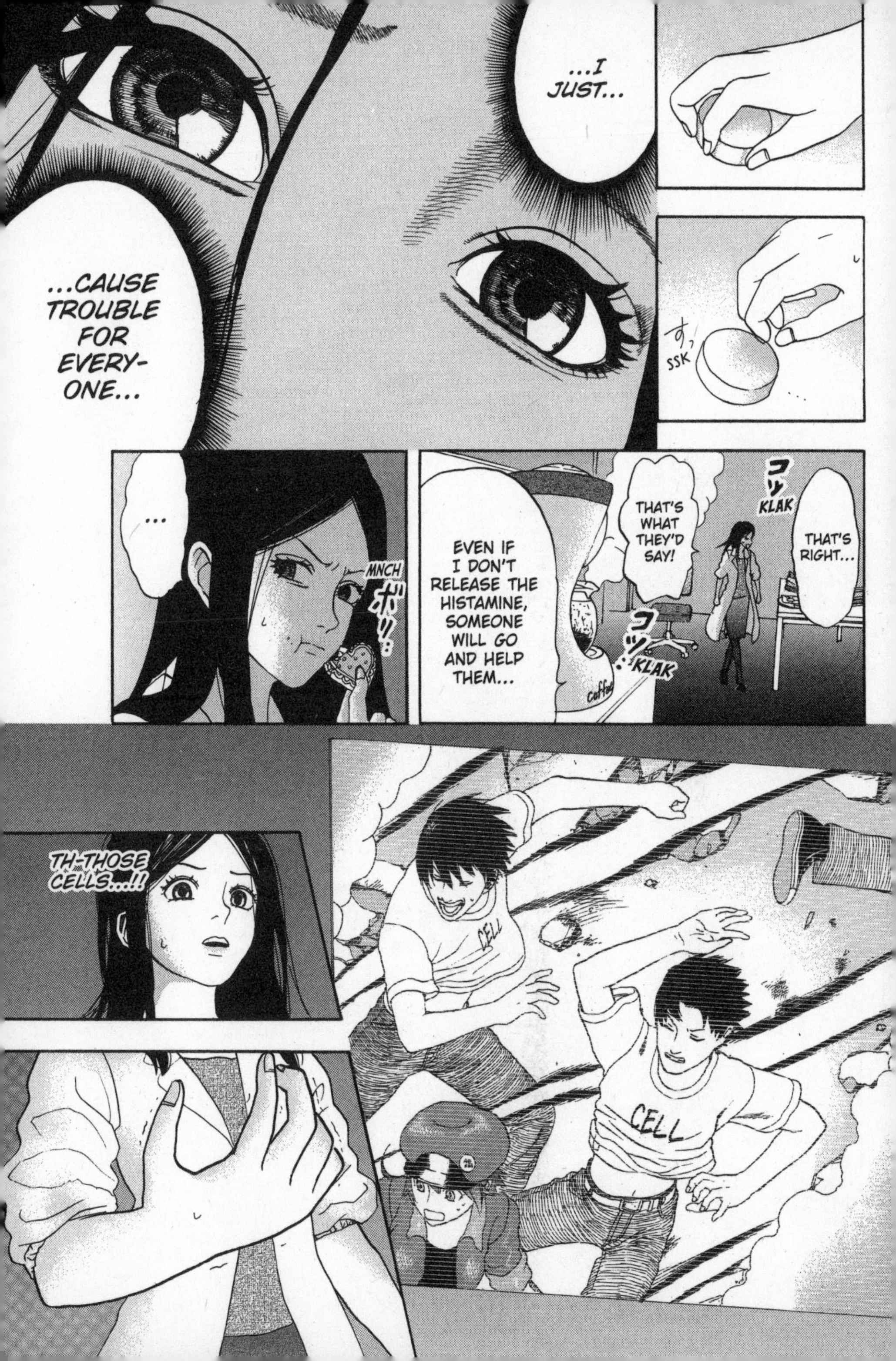

すっ
SSK
...I JUST...
...CAUSE TROUBLE FOR EVERY-ONE...
THAT'S RIGHT...
コツ
KLAK
THAT'S WHAT THEY'D SAY!
EVEN IF I DON'T RELEASE THE HISTAMINE, SOMEONE WILL GO AND HELP THEM...
コツ
KLAK
MNCH
ポリ
...
CELL
CELL
TH-THOSE CELLS...!!

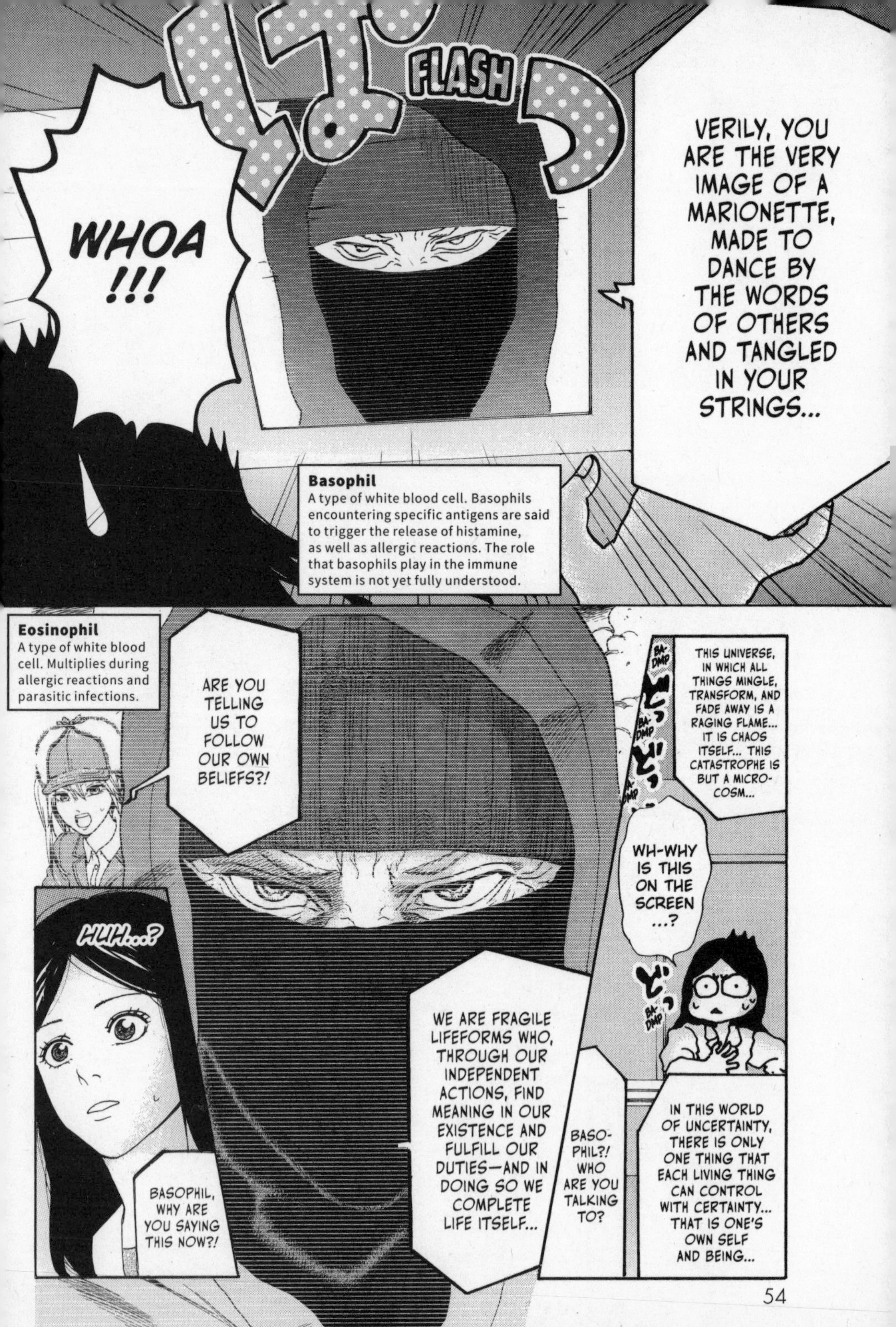
FLASH
VERILY, YOU ARE THE VERY IMAGE OF A MARIONETTE, MADE TO DANCE BY THE WORDS OF OTHERS AND TANGLED IN YOUR STRINGS...
WHOA !!!
Basophil
A type of white blood cell. Basophils encountering specific antigens are said to trigger the release of histamine, as well as allergic reactions. The role that basophils play in the immune system is not yet fully understood.
BA-DMP
THIS UNIVERSE, IN WHICH ALL THINGS MINGLE, TRANSFORM, AND FADE AWAY IS A RAGING FLAME... IT IS CHAOS ITSELF... THIS CATASTROPHE IS BUT A MICRO-COSM...
BA-DMP
WH-WHY IS THIS ON THE SCREEN ...?
BA-DMP
IN THIS WORLD OF UNCERTAINTY, THERE IS ONLY ONE THING THAT EACH LIVING THING CAN CONTROL WITH CERTAINTY... THAT IS ONE'S OWN SELF AND BEING...
BASO-PHIL?! WHO ARE YOU TALKING TO?
WE ARE FRAGILE LIFEFORMS WHO, THROUGH OUR INDEPENDENT ACTIONS, FIND MEANING IN OUR EXISTENCE AND FULFILL OUR DUTIES—AND IN DOING SO WE COMPLETE LIFE ITSELF...
Eosinophil
A type of white blood cell. Multiplies during allergic reactions and parasitic infections.
ARE YOU TELLING US TO FOLLOW OUR OWN BELIEFS?!
HUH...?
BASOPHIL, WHY ARE YOU SAYING THIS NOW?!

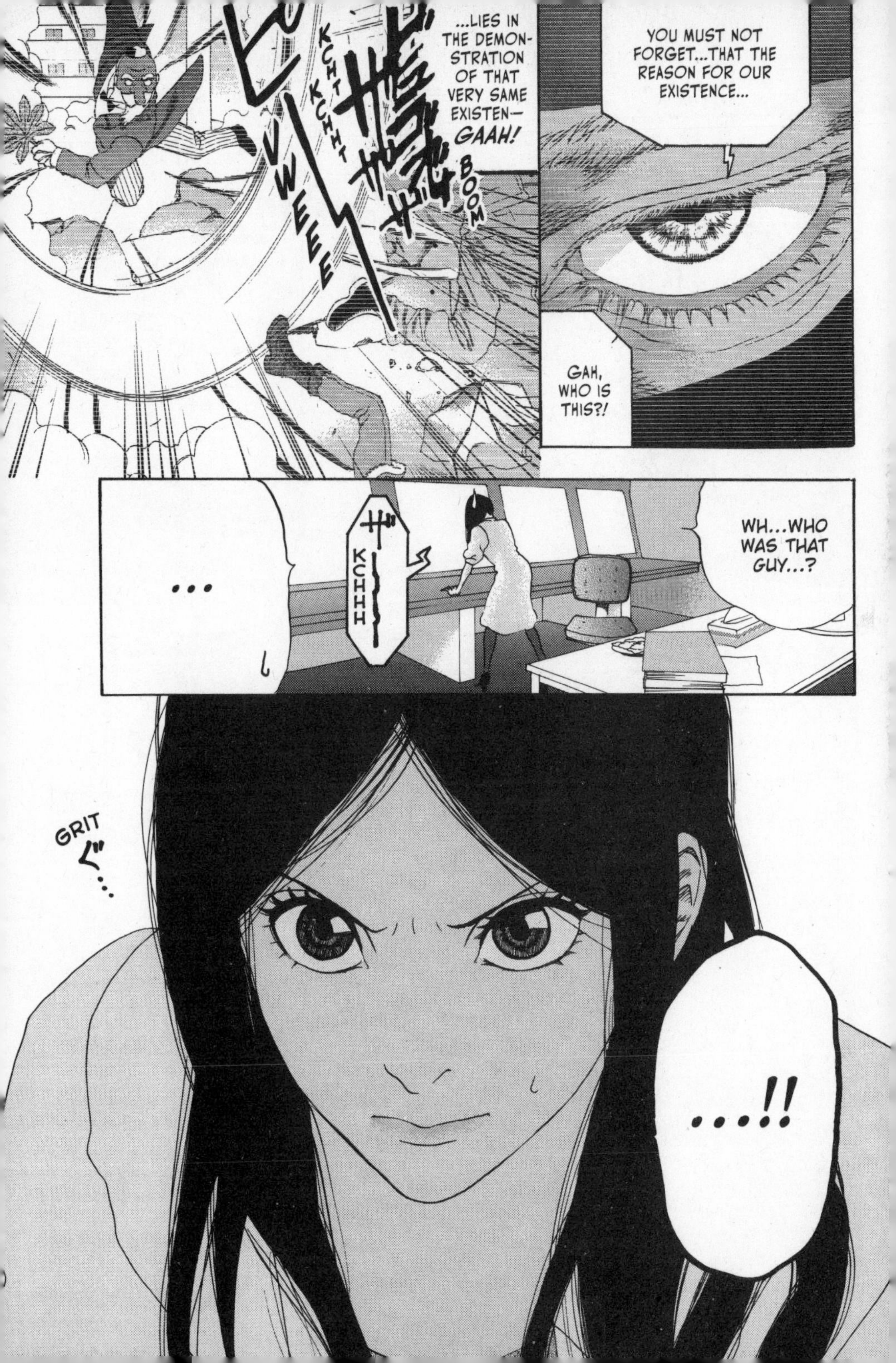
YOU MUST NOT FORGET...THAT THE REASON FOR OUR EXISTENCE...
GAH, WHO IS THIS?!
...LIES IN THE DEMONSTRATION OF THAT VERY SAME EXISTEN—GAAH!
KCHT KCHHT
BOOM
VWEEE
WH...WHO WAS THAT GUY...?
KCHHH
...
...!!
GRIT
ぐ…

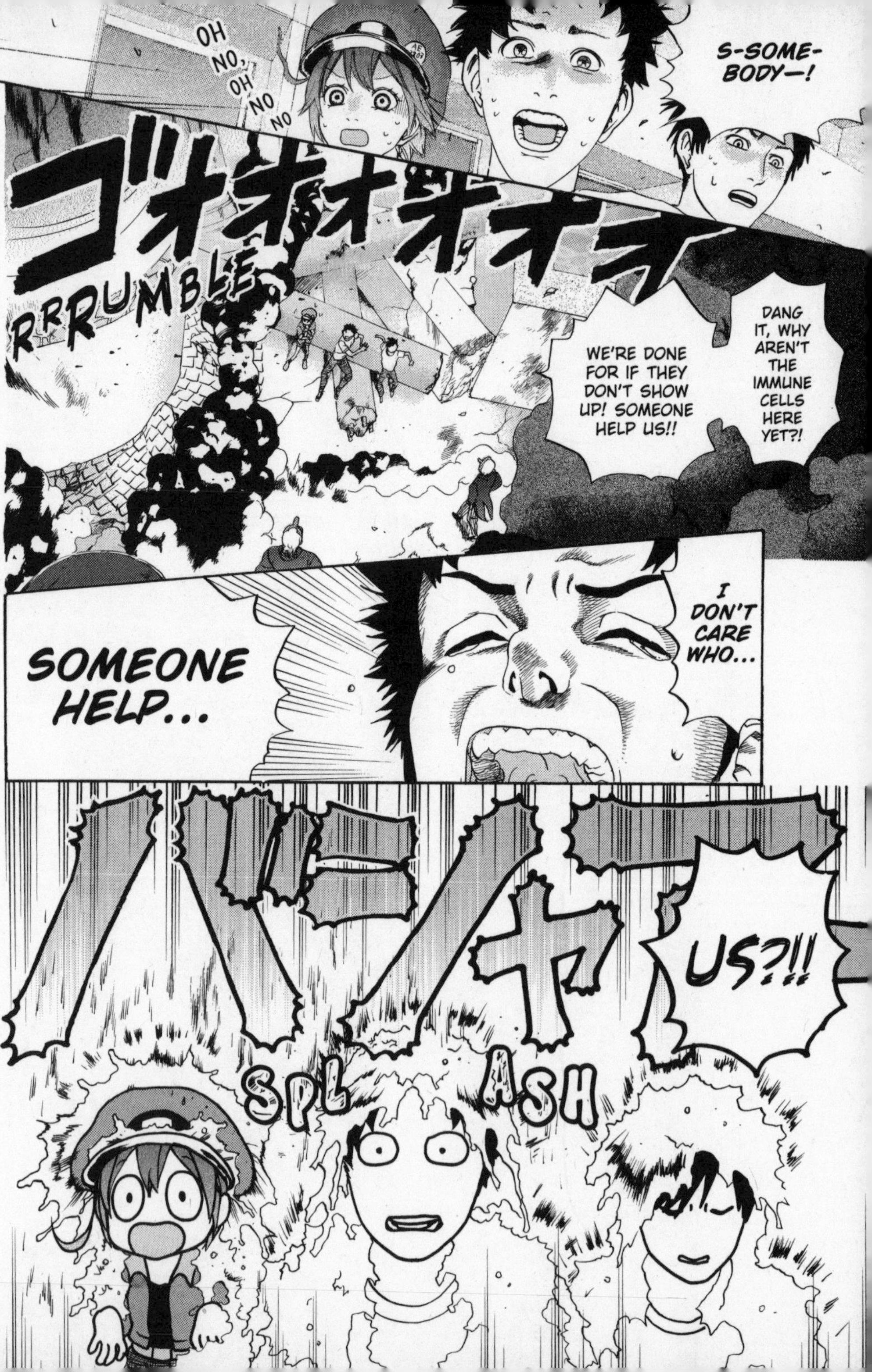
S-SOME-BODY—!
OH NO, OH NO NO
RRRUMBLE
DANG IT, WHY AREN'T THE IMMUNE CELLS HERE YET?!
WE'RE DONE FOR IF THEY DON'T SHOW UP! SOMEONE HELP US!!
I DON'T CARE WHO...
SOMEONE HELP...
US?!!
SPLASH

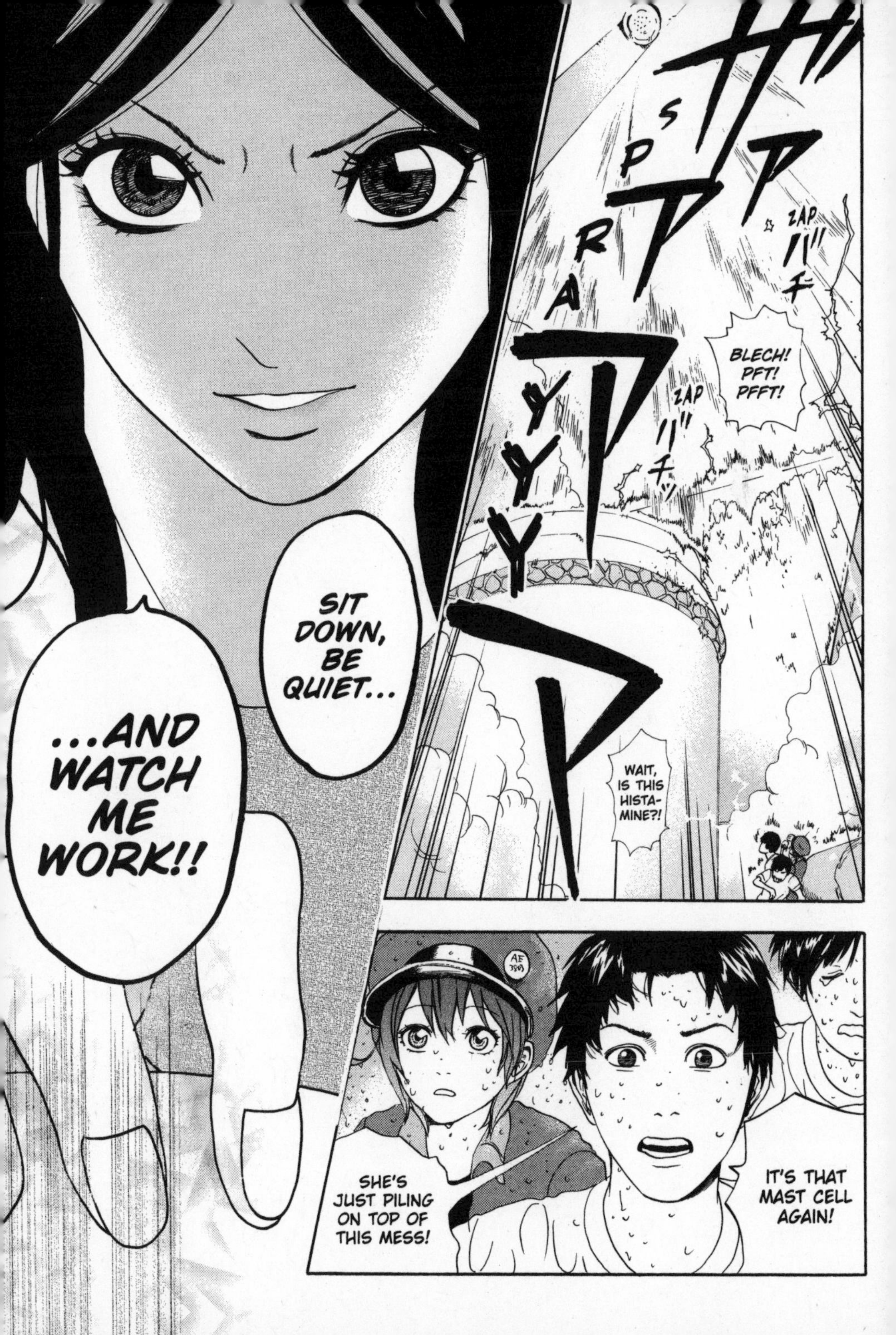
SPRAYYYY
ZAP
BLECH! PFT! PFFT!
ZAP
WAIT, IS THIS HISTA-MINE?!
IT'S THAT MAST CELL AGAIN!
SHE'S JUST PILING ON TOP OF THIS MESS!
SIT DOWN, BE QUIET...
...AND WATCH ME WORK!!

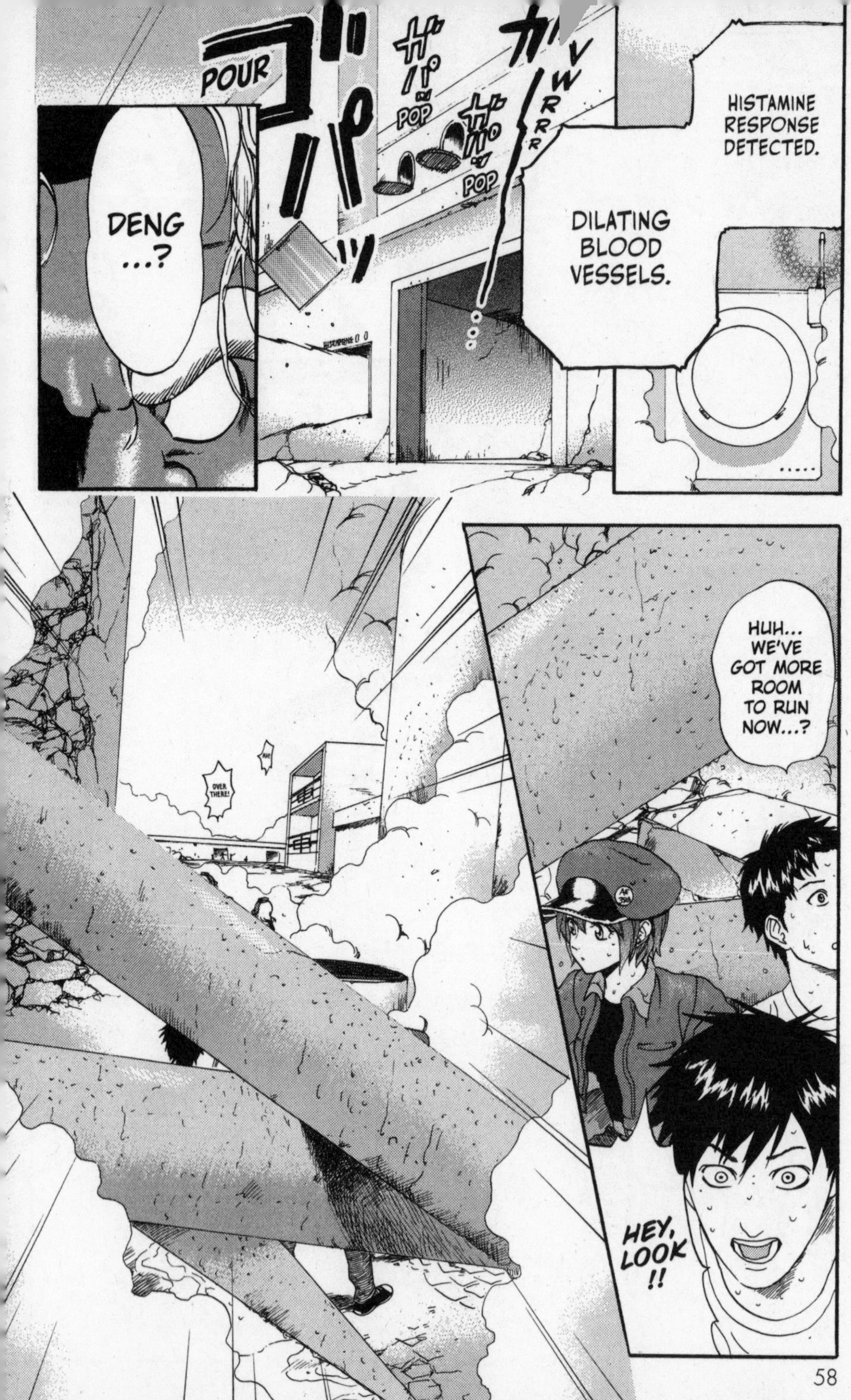
HISTAMINE RESPONSE DETECTED.
DILATING BLOOD VESSELS.
.....
VWRRR
POP
POP
POUR
DENG ...?
HUH... WE'VE GOT MORE ROOM TO RUN NOW...?
HEY, LOOK !!
AH!
OVER THERE!

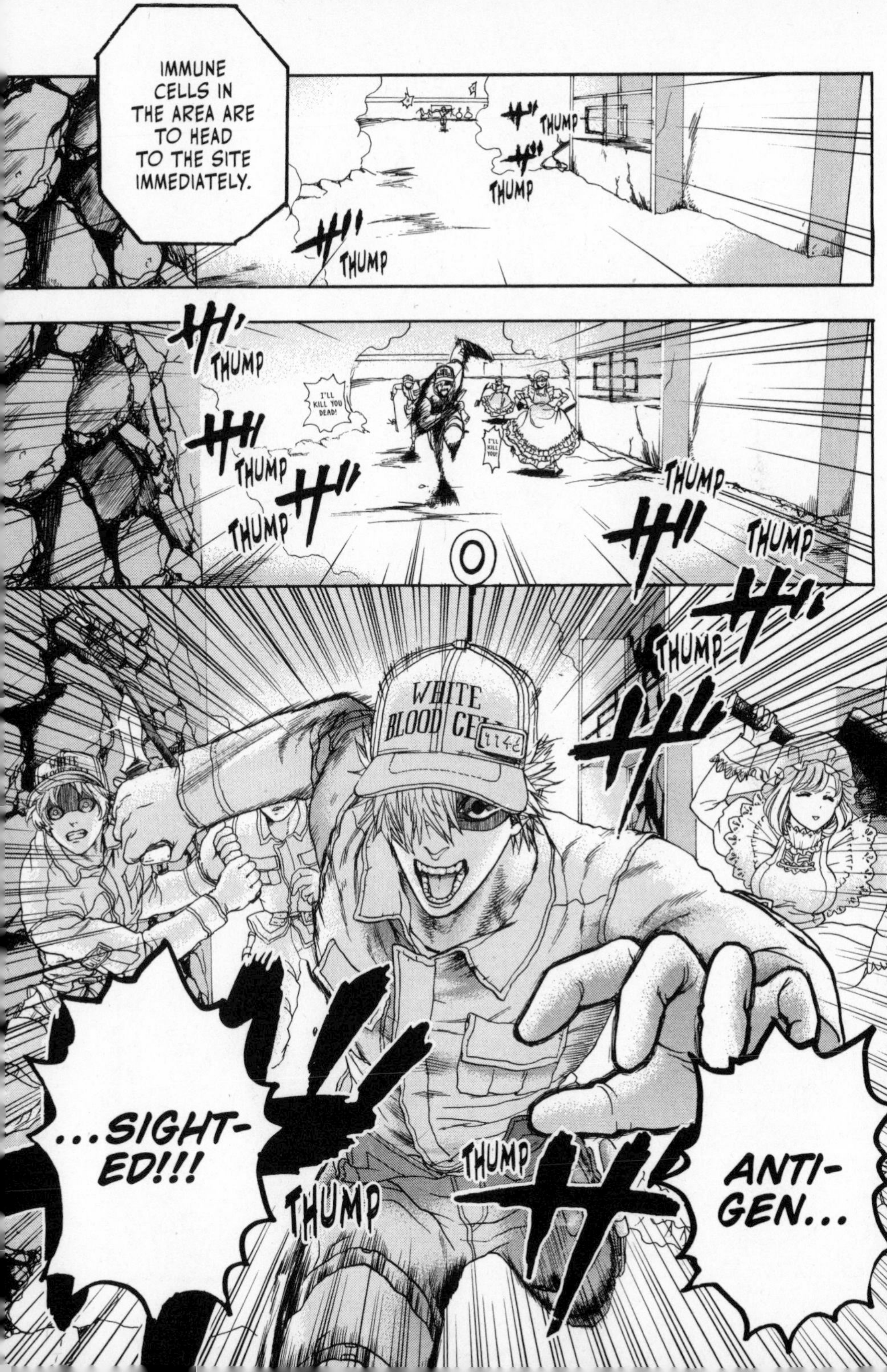
IMMUNE CELLS IN THE AREA ARE TO HEAD TO THE SITE IMMEDIATELY.
THUMP
THUMP
THUMP
THUMP
THUMP
I'LL KILL YOU!
I'LL KILL YOU DEAD!
THUMP
THUMP
THUMP
THUMP
ANTI-GEN...
THUMP
THUMP
...SIGHT-ED!!!

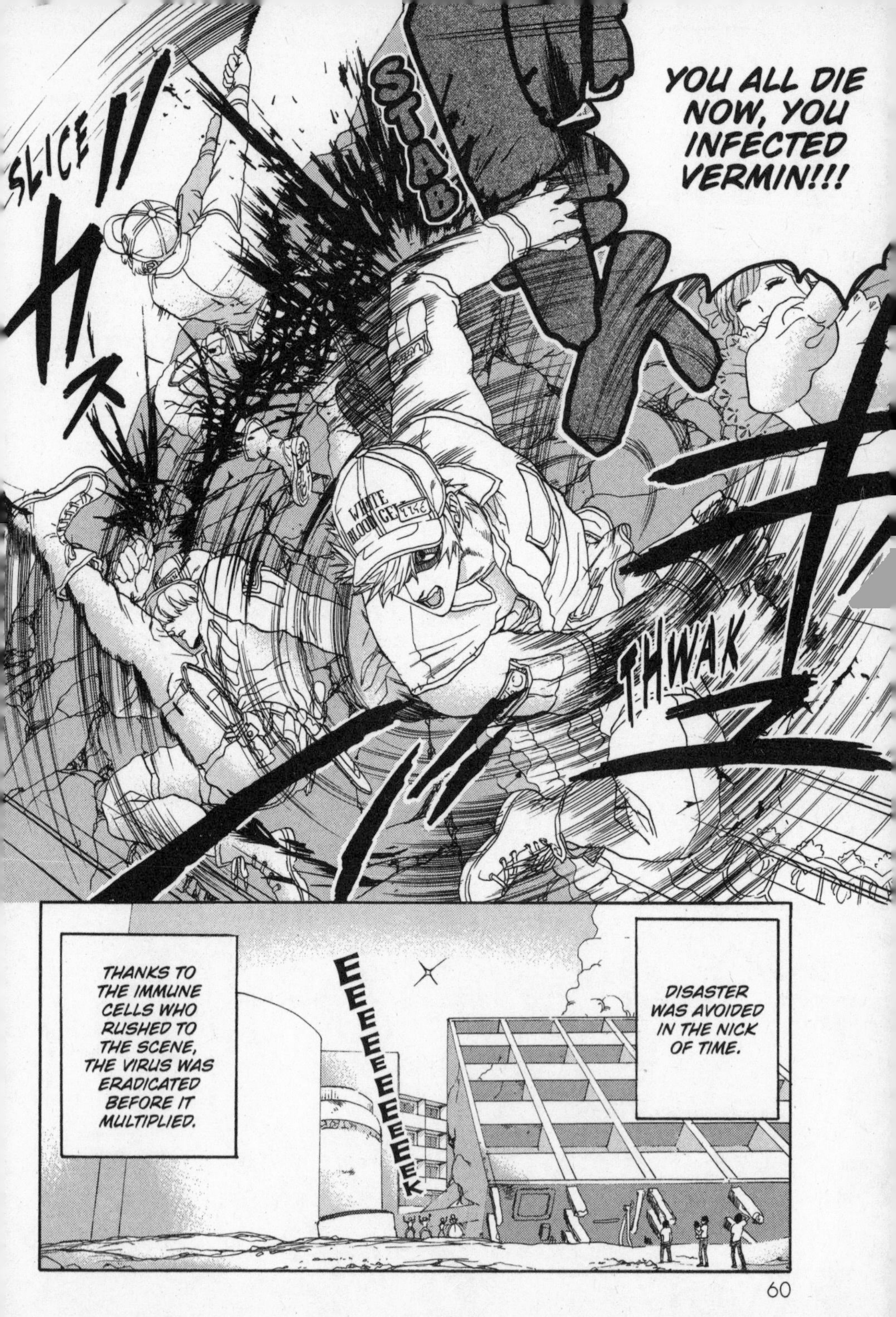
YOU ALL DIE NOW, YOU INFECTED VERMIN!!!
STAB
THWAK
SLICE
DISASTER WAS AVOIDED IN THE NICK OF TIME.
EEEEEEEEEEK
THANKS TO THE IMMUNE CELLS WHO RUSHED TO THE SCENE, THE VIRUS WAS ERADICATED BEFORE IT MULTIPLIED.

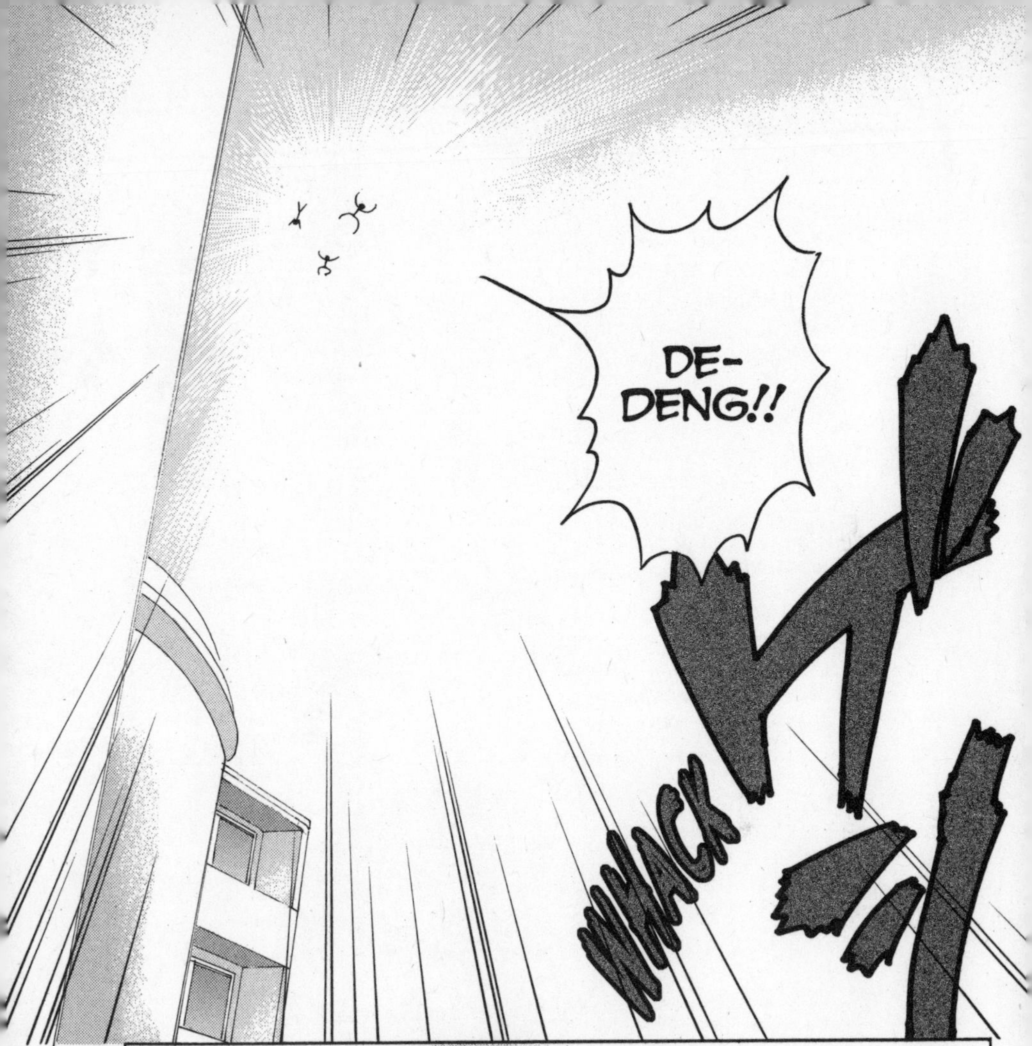
DE-
DENG!!
WHACK

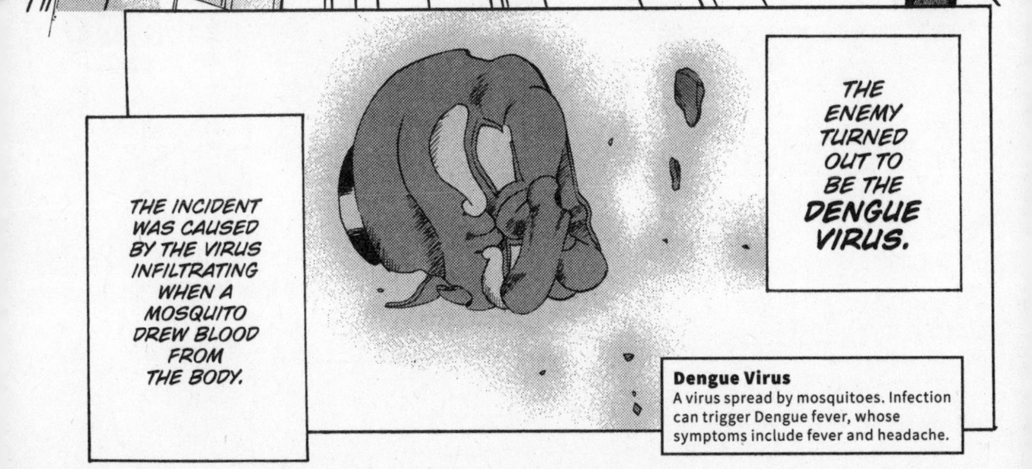
THE ENEMY TURNED OUT TO BE THE DENGUE VIRUS.
THE INCIDENT WAS CAUSED BY THE VIRUS INFILTRATING WHEN A MOSQUITO DREW BLOOD FROM THE BODY.

Dengue Virus
A virus spread by mosquitoes. Infection can trigger Dengue fever, whose symptoms include fever and headache.

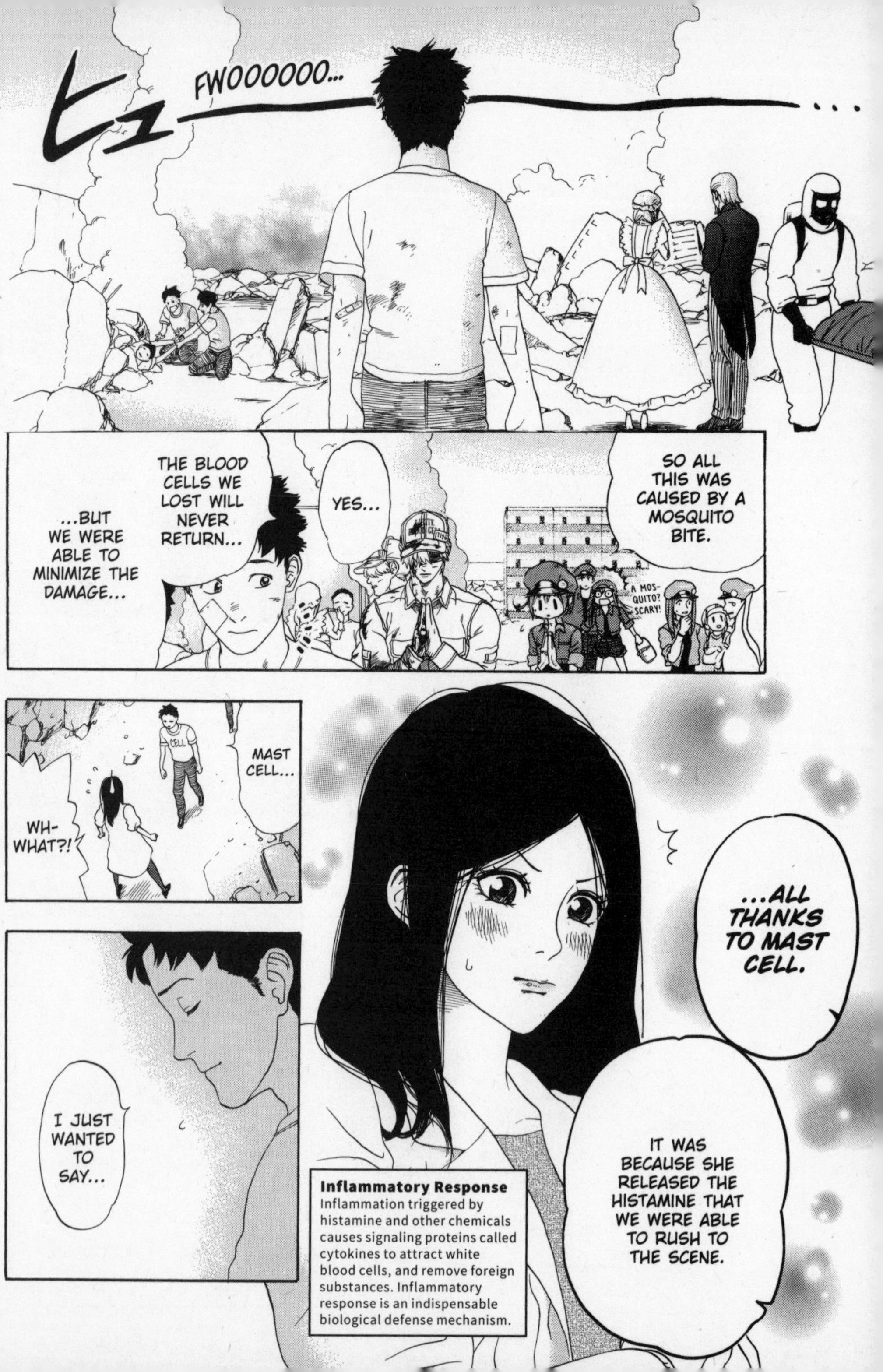
ヒュ
FWOOOOOO...
SO ALL THIS WAS CAUSED BY A MOSQUITO BITE.
A MOSQUITO? SCARY!
YES...
THE BLOOD CELLS WE LOST WILL NEVER RETURN...
...BUT WE WERE ABLE TO MINIMIZE THE DAMAGE...
...ALL THANKS TO MAST CELL.
IT WAS BECAUSE SHE RELEASED THE HISTAMINE THAT WE WERE ABLE TO RUSH TO THE SCENE.
Inflammatory Response
Inflammation triggered by histamine and other chemicals causes signaling proteins called cytokines to attract white blood cells, and remove foreign substances. Inflammatory response is an indispensable biological defense mechanism.
MAST CELL...
WH-WHAT?!
I JUST WANTED TO SAY...

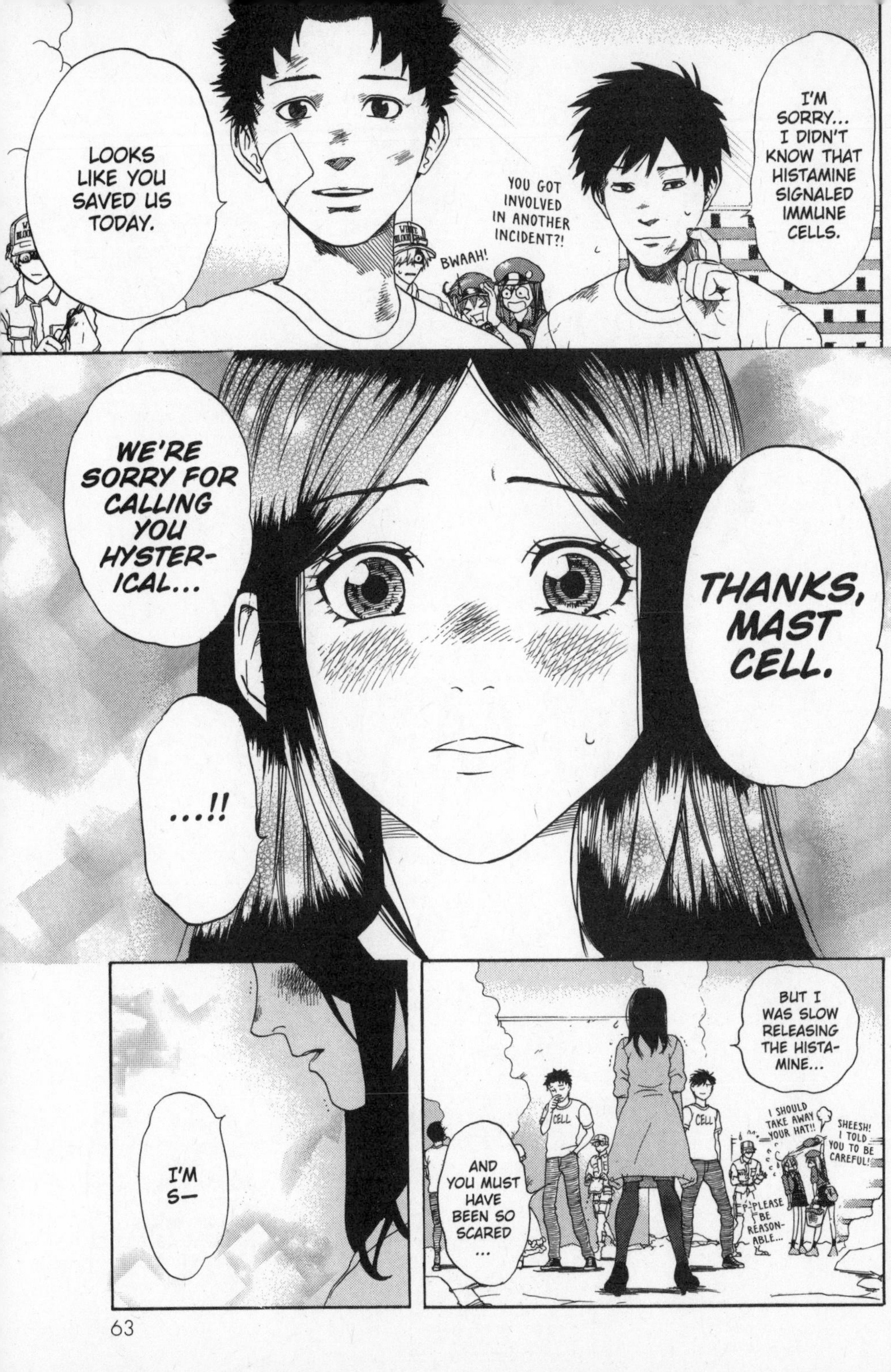

I'M SORRY... I DIDN'T KNOW THAT HISTAMINE SIGNALED IMMUNE CELLS.
YOU GOT INVOLVED IN ANOTHER INCIDENT?!
BWAAH!
LOOKS LIKE YOU SAVED US TODAY.
THANKS, MAST CELL.
WE'RE SORRY FOR CALLING YOU HYSTER-ICAL...
...!!
BUT I WAS SLOW RELEASING THE HISTA-MINE...
SHEESH! I TOLD YOU TO BE CAREFUL!
I SHOULD TAKE AWAY YOUR HAT!!
P-PLEASE BE REASON-ABLE...
AND YOU MUST HAVE BEEN SO SCARED ...
I'M S—

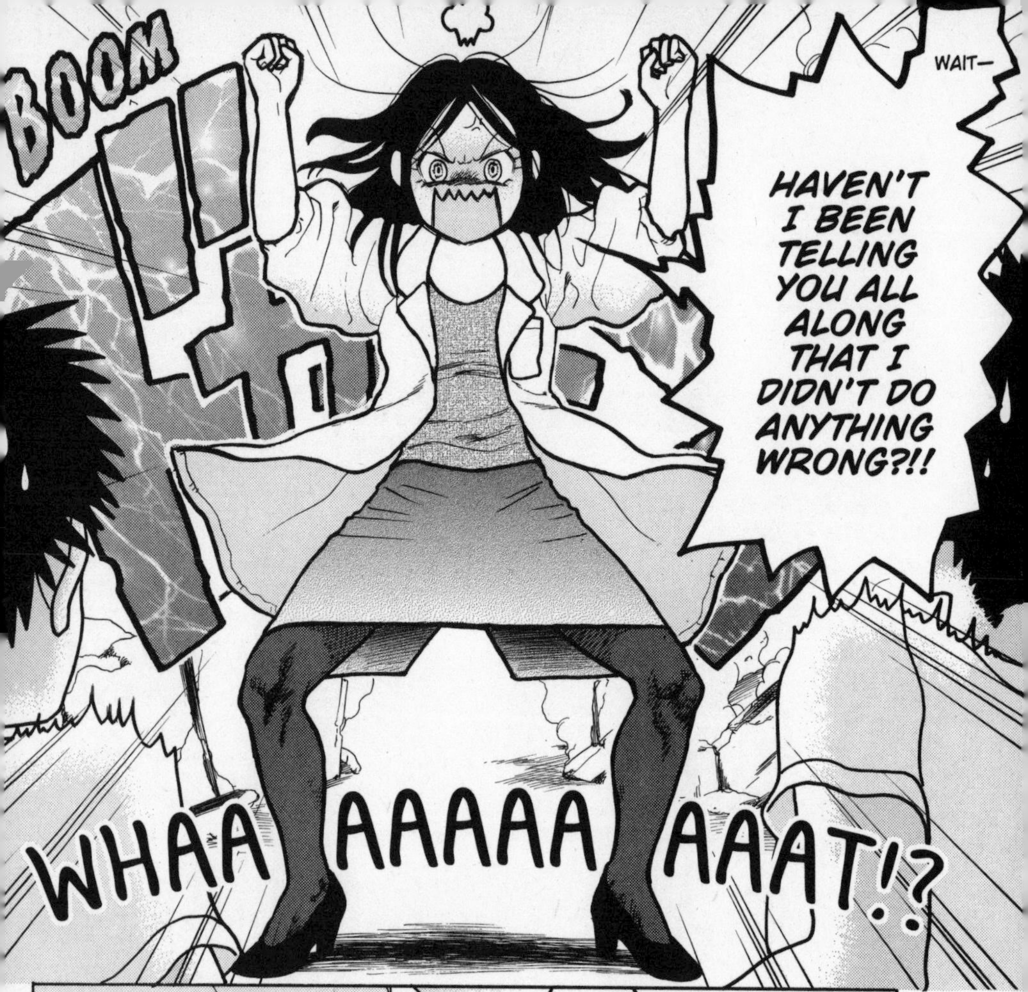
WAIT—
HAVEN'T I BEEN TELLING YOU ALL ALONG THAT I DIDN'T DO ANYTHING WRONG?!!
BOOM
WHAA AAAAA AAAT!?

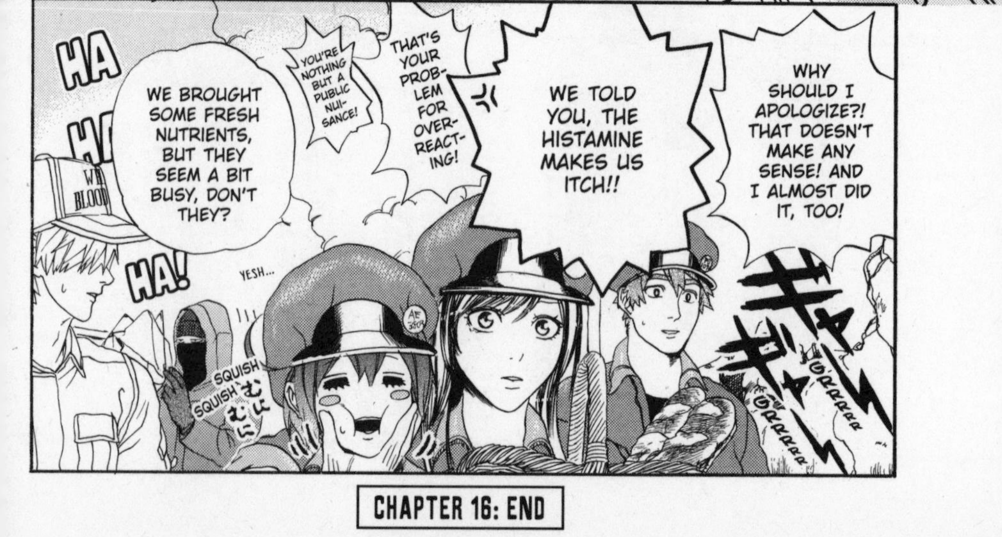
WHY SHOULD I APOLOGIZE?! THAT DOESN'T MAKE ANY SENSE! AND I ALMOST DID IT, TOO!
GRRRRRR
GRRRRRR
WE TOLD YOU, THE HISTAMINE MAKES US ITCH!!
THAT'S YOUR PROB-LEM FOR OVER-REACT-ING!
YOU'RE NOTHING BUT A PUBLIC NUI-SANCE!
WE BROUGHT SOME FRESH NUTRIENTS, BUT THEY SEEM A BIT BUSY, DON'T THEY?
HA HA HA!
YESH...
SQUISH SQUISH

CHAPTER 16: END

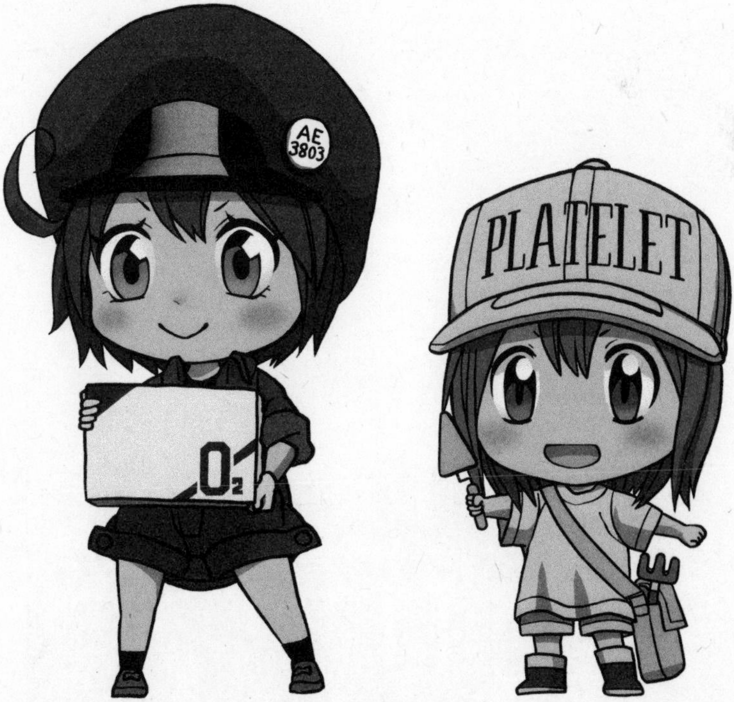
AE
3803
O2
PLATELET

Cells at Work!
はたらく細胞

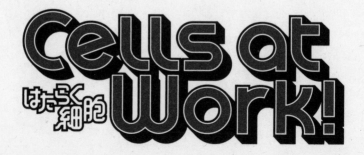

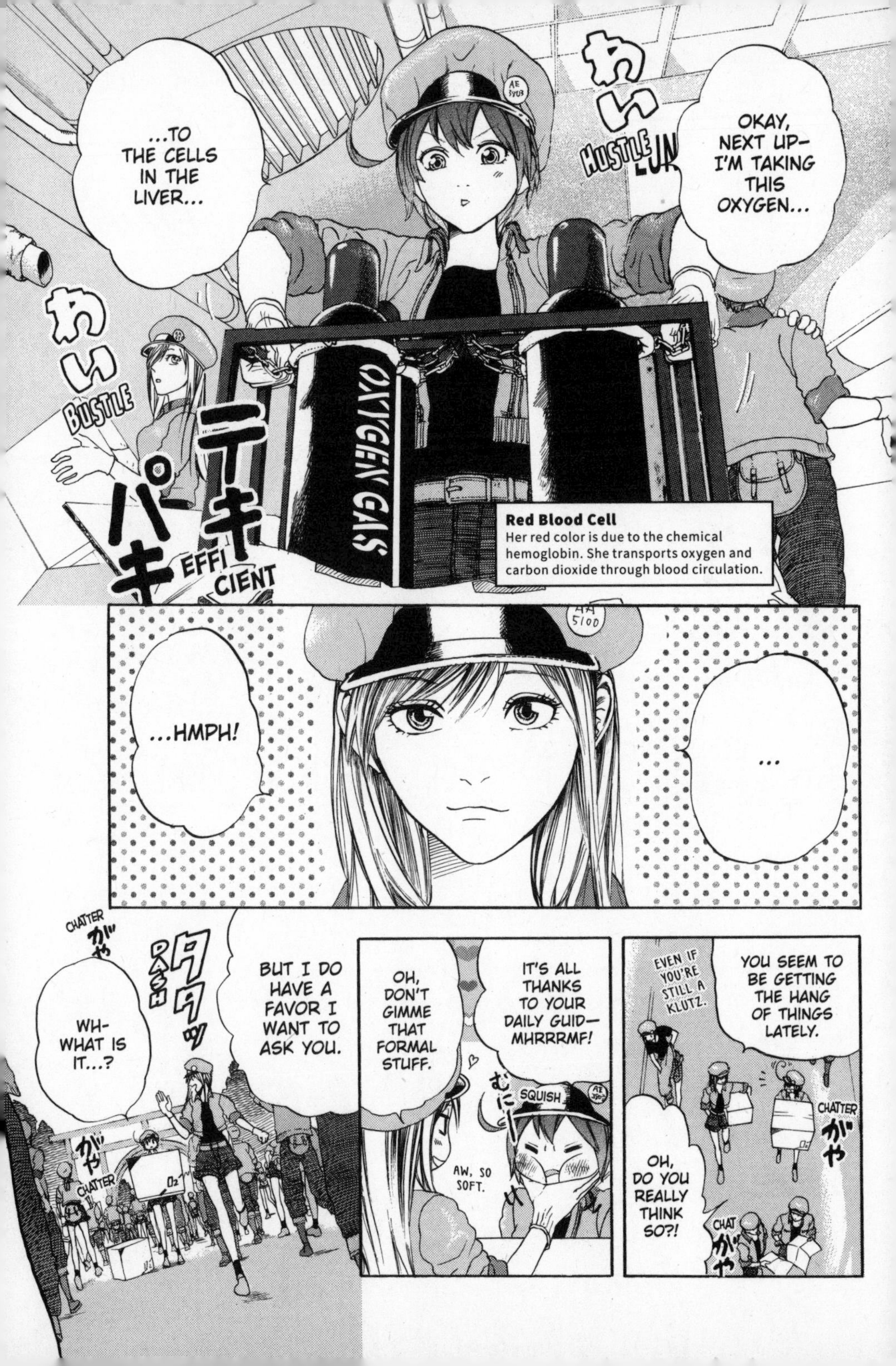
OKAY, NEXT UP— I'M TAKING THIS OXYGEN...
HUSTLE
...TO THE CELLS IN THE LIVER...
BUSTLE
EFFICIENT
OXYGEN GAS
Red Blood Cell
Her red color is due to the chemical hemoglobin. She transports oxygen and carbon dioxide through blood circulation.
...
...HMPH!
YOU SEEM TO BE GETTING THE HANG OF THINGS LATELY.
EVEN IF YOU'RE STILL A KLUTZ.
CHATTER
OH, DO YOU REALLY THINK SO?!
CHAT
IT'S ALL THANKS TO YOUR DAILY GUID—MHRRRMF!
SQUISH
OH, DON'T GIMME THAT FORMAL STUFF.
AW, SO SOFT.
BUT I DO HAVE A FAVOR I WANT TO ASK YOU.
DASH
CHATTER
WH-WHAT IS IT...?
CHATTER

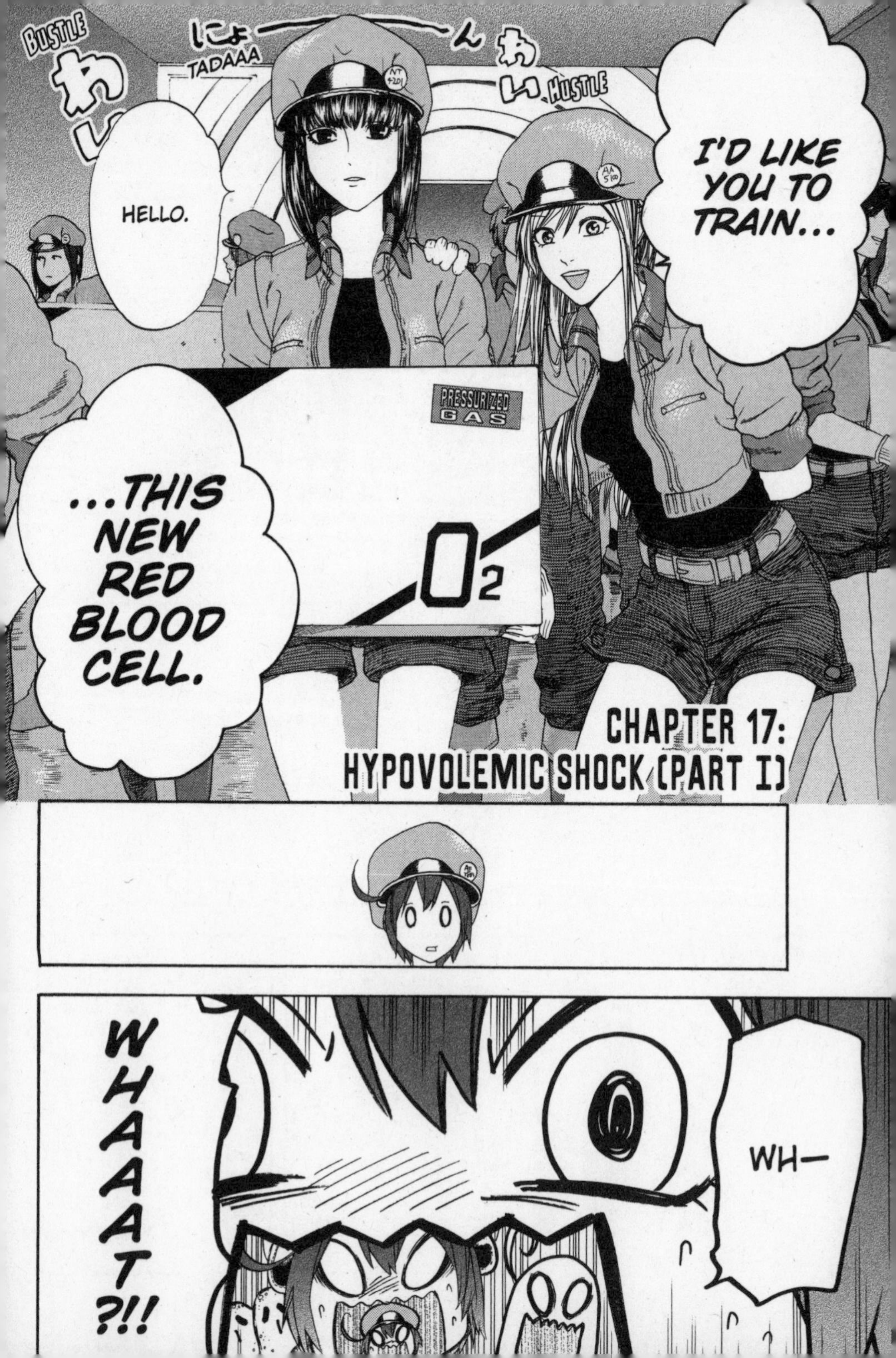
わい
HUSTLE
I'D LIKE YOU TO TRAIN...
にょーーーーんわ
TADAAA
HELLO.
わい
BUSTLE
PRESSURIZED GAS
O2
...THIS NEW RED BLOOD CELL.
CHAPTER 17: HYPOVOLEMIC SHOCK (PART I)
WH—
WHAAAAT?!!

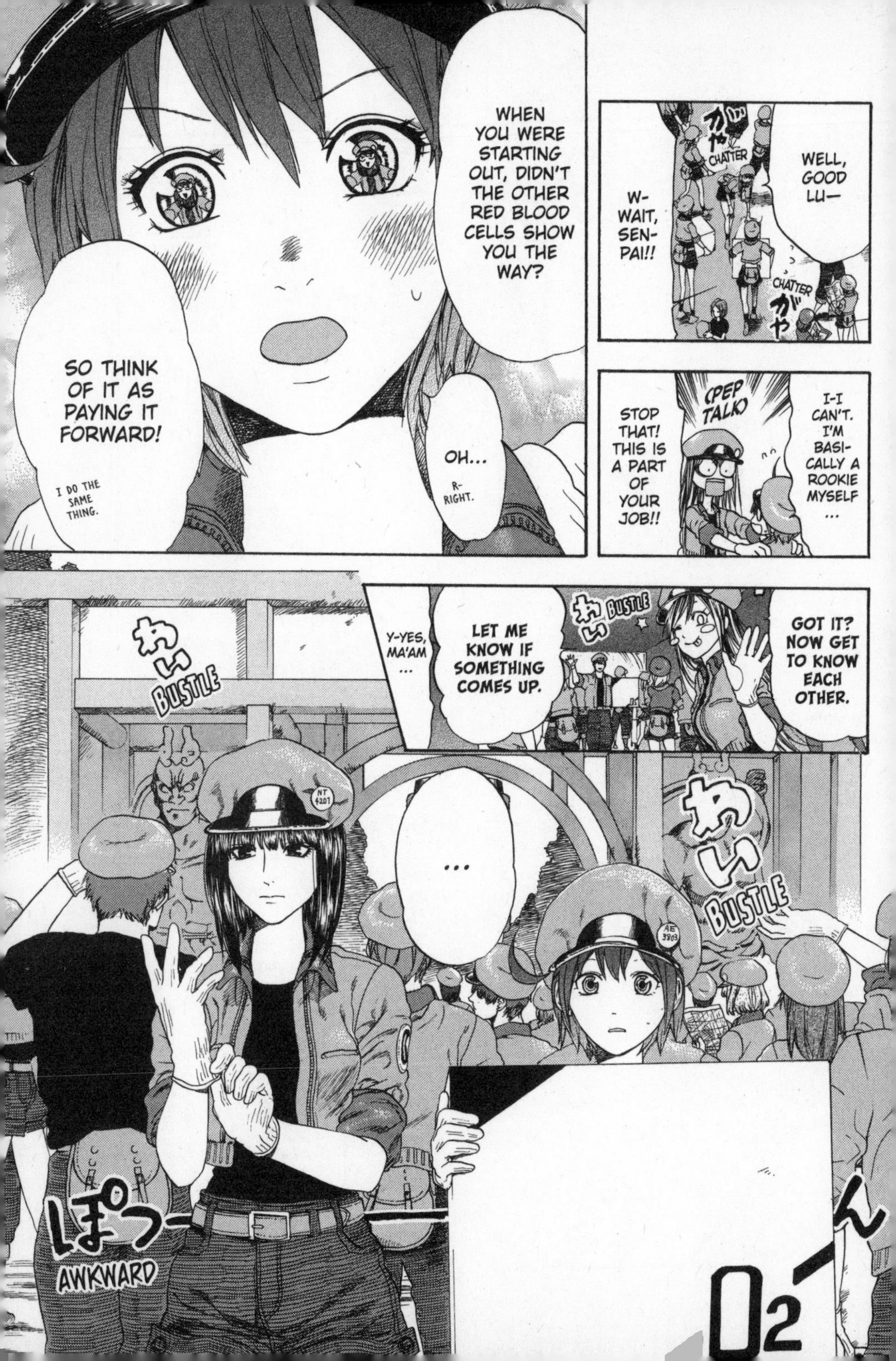

WELL, GOOD LU—
ガヤ
CHATTER
W-WAIT, SENPAI!!
ガヤ
CHATTER
I-I CAN'T. I'M BASICALLY A ROOKIE MYSELF ...
(PEP TALK)
STOP THAT! THIS IS A PART OF YOUR JOB!!
WHEN YOU WERE STARTING OUT, DIDN'T THE OTHER RED BLOOD CELLS SHOW YOU THE WAY?
OH... R-RIGHT.
SO THINK OF IT AS PAYING IT FORWARD!
I DO THE SAME THING.
GOT IT? NOW GET TO KNOW EACH OTHER.
わい
BUSTLE
LET ME KNOW IF SOMETHING COMES UP.
Y-YES, MA'AM ...
わい
BUSTLE
...
わい
BUSTLE
ぽつーーん
AWKWARD
O2

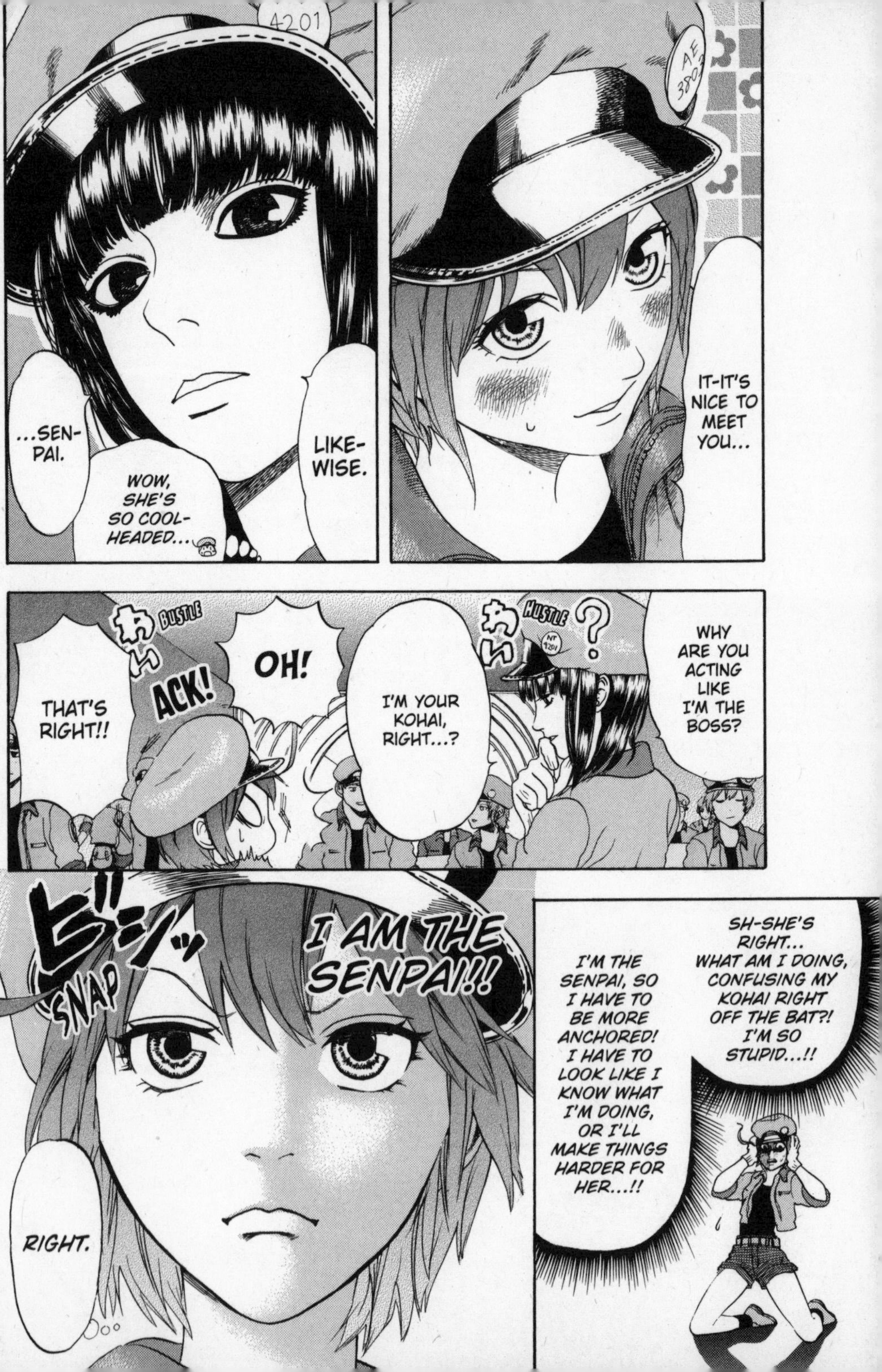
IT-IT'S NICE TO MEET YOU...
LIKE-WISE.
...SEN-PAI.
WOW, SHE'S SO COOL-HEADED...
WHY ARE YOU ACTING LIKE I'M THE BOSS?
?
HUSTLE
I'M YOUR KOHAI, RIGHT...?
OH!
ACK!
BUSTLE
THAT'S RIGHT!!
SH-SHE'S RIGHT... WHAT AM I DOING, CONFUSING MY KOHAI RIGHT OFF THE BAT?! I'M SO STUPID...!!
I'M THE SENPAI, SO I HAVE TO BE MORE ANCHORED! I HAVE TO LOOK LIKE I KNOW WHAT I'M DOING, OR I'LL MAKE THINGS HARDER FOR HER...!!
I AM THE SENPAI!!
SNAP
RIGHT.

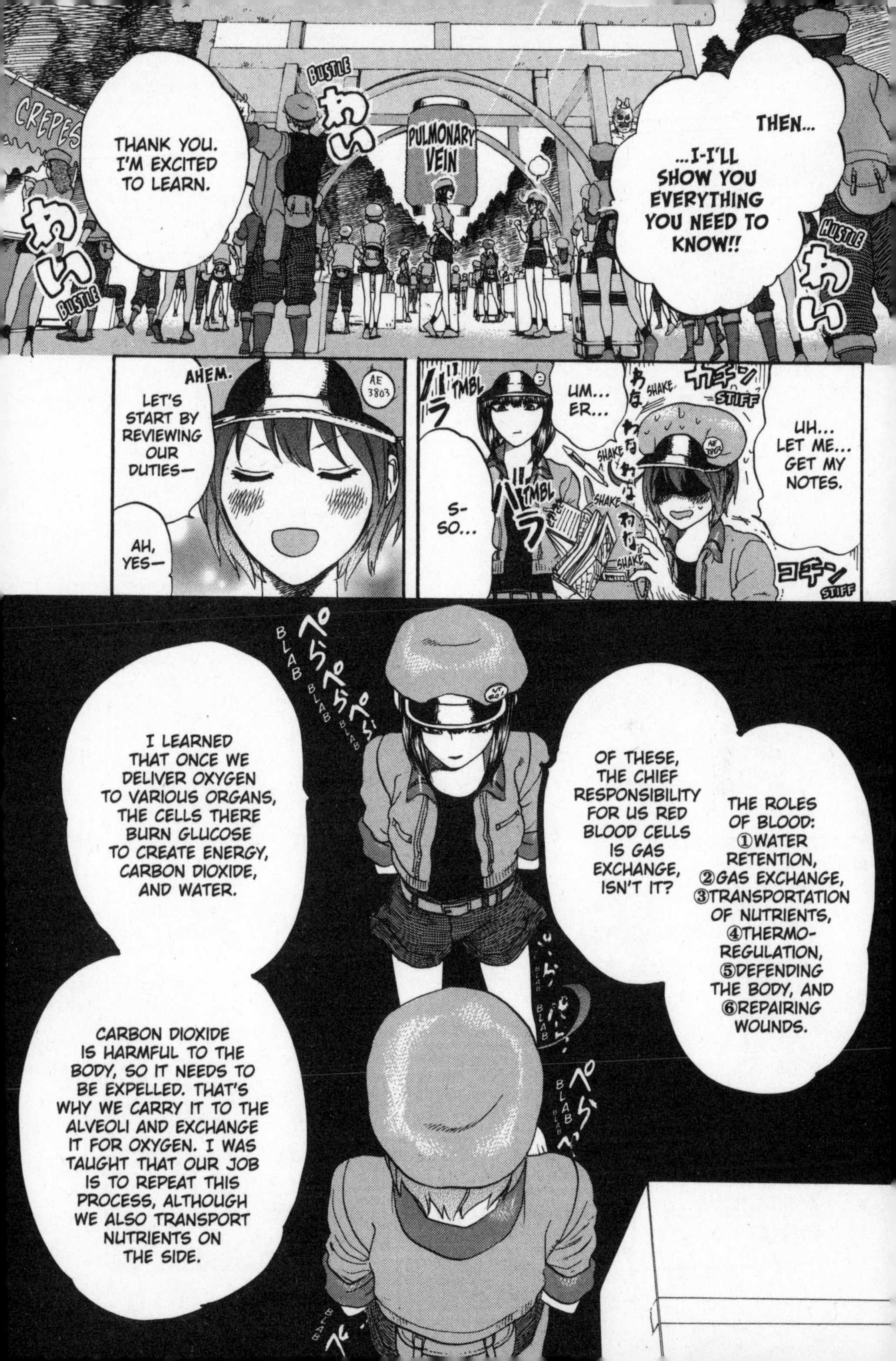
CREPES
PULMONARY VEIN
BUSTLE
HUSTLE
THEN...
...I-I'LL SHOW YOU EVERYTHING YOU NEED TO KNOW!!
THANK YOU. I'M EXCITED TO LEARN.
BUSTLE
STIFF
UH... LET ME... GET MY NOTES.
SHAKE
UM... ER...
TMBL
SHAKE
SHAKE
SHAKE
S- SO...
TMBL
STIFF
AE 3803
AHEM.
LET'S START BY REVIEWING OUR DUTIES—
AH, YES—
BLAB BLAB BLAB
THE ROLES OF BLOOD: ①WATER RETENTION, ②GAS EXCHANGE, ③TRANSPORTATION OF NUTRIENTS, ④THERMO-REGULATION, ⑤DEFENDING THE BODY, AND ⑥REPAIRING WOUNDS.
OF THESE, THE CHIEF RESPONSIBILITY FOR US RED BLOOD CELLS IS GAS EXCHANGE, ISN'T IT?
I LEARNED THAT ONCE WE DELIVER OXYGEN TO VARIOUS ORGANS, THE CELLS THERE BURN GLUCOSE TO CREATE ENERGY, CARBON DIOXIDE, AND WATER.
BLAB BLAB
BLAB BLAB
CARBON DIOXIDE IS HARMFUL TO THE BODY, SO IT NEEDS TO BE EXPELLED. THAT'S WHY WE CARRY IT TO THE ALVEOLI AND EXCHANGE IT FOR OXYGEN. I WAS TAUGHT THAT OUR JOB IS TO REPEAT THIS PROCESS, ALTHOUGH WE ALSO TRANSPORT NUTRIENTS ON THE SIDE.
BLAB

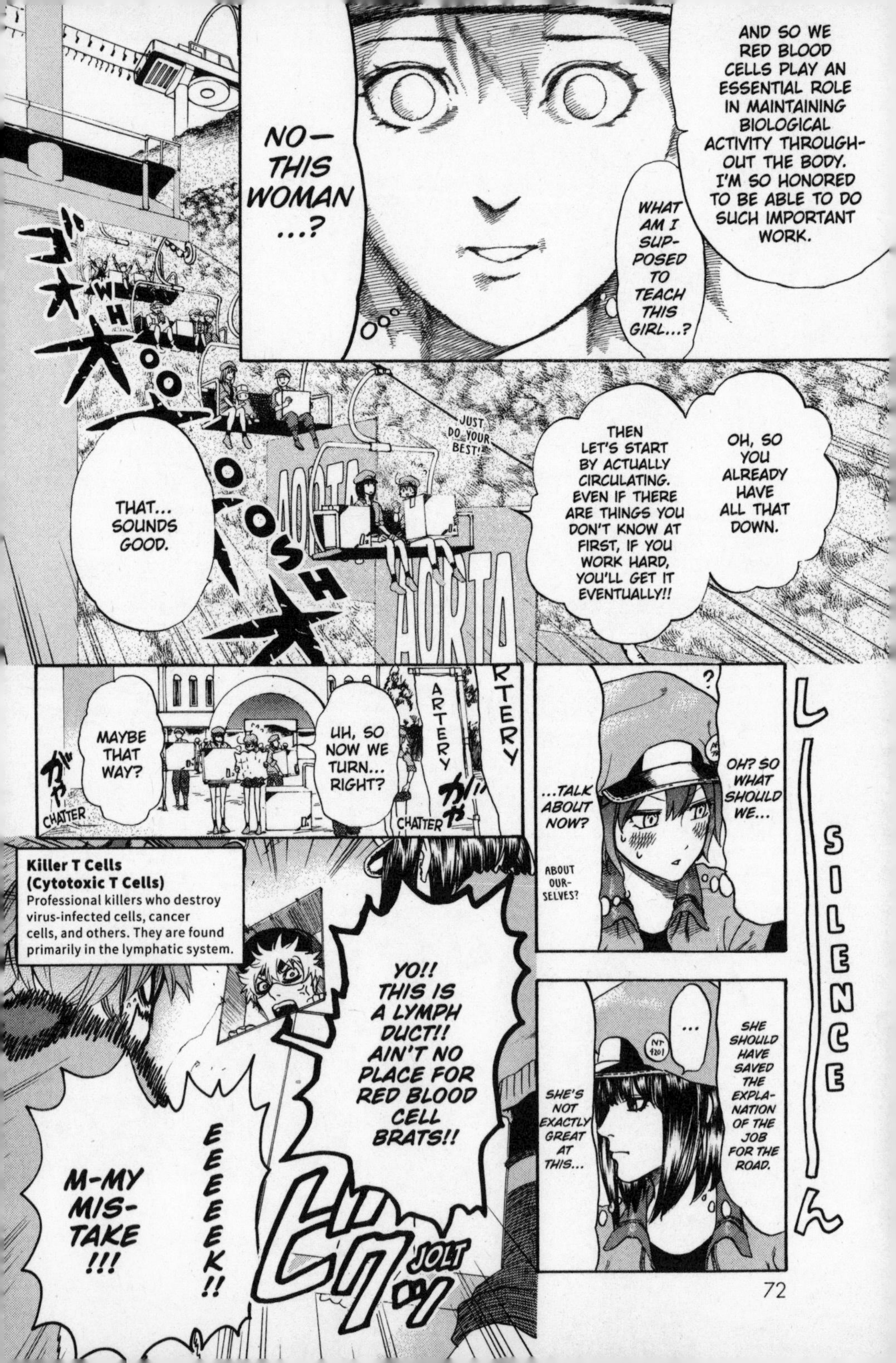
AND SO WE RED BLOOD CELLS PLAY AN ESSENTIAL ROLE IN MAINTAINING BIOLOGICAL ACTIVITY THROUGH-OUT THE BODY. I'M SO HONORED TO BE ABLE TO DO SUCH IMPORTANT WORK.
WHAT AM I SUP-POSED TO TEACH THIS GIRL...?
NO—THIS WOMAN...?
OH, SO YOU ALREADY HAVE ALL THAT DOWN.
THEN LET'S START BY ACTUALLY CIRCULATING. EVEN IF THERE ARE THINGS YOU DON'T KNOW AT FIRST, IF YOU WORK HARD, YOU'LL GET IT EVENTUALLY!!
JUST DO YOUR BEST!
AORTA
AORTA
THAT... SOUNDS GOOD.
AORTA
WHOOOSH
SILENCE
OH? SO WHAT SHOULD WE...
...TALK ABOUT NOW?
ABOUT OUR-SELVES?
?
...
SHE SHOULD HAVE SAVED THE EXPLA-NATION OF THE JOB FOR THE ROAD.
SHE'S NOT EXACTLY GREAT AT THIS...
ARTERY
ARTERY
UH, SO NOW WE TURN... RIGHT?
CHATTER
MAYBE THAT WAY?
CHATTER
Killer T Cells (Cytotoxic T Cells)
Professional killers who destroy virus-infected cells, cancer cells, and others. They are found primarily in the lymphatic system.
YO!! THIS IS A LYMPH DUCT!! AIN'T NO PLACE FOR RED BLOOD CELL BRATS!!
JOLT
EEEEEEK!!
M-MY MIS-TAKE!!!

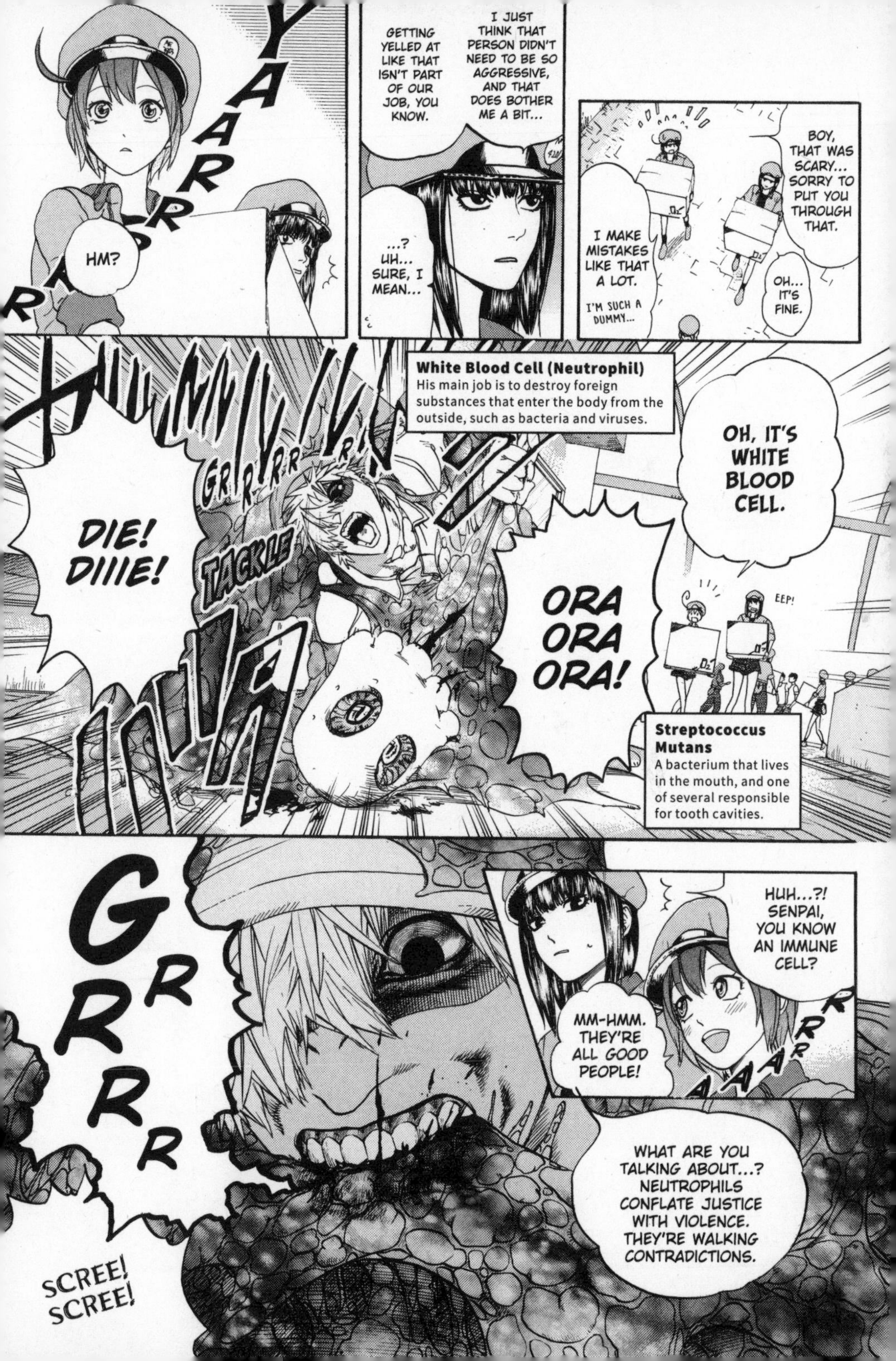
BOY, THAT WAS SCARY... SORRY TO PUT YOU THROUGH THAT.
OH... IT'S FINE.
I MAKE MISTAKES LIKE THAT A LOT.
I'M SUCH A DUMMY...
I JUST THINK THAT PERSON DIDN'T NEED TO BE SO AGGRESSIVE, AND THAT DOES BOTHER ME A BIT...
GETTING YELLED AT LIKE THAT ISN'T PART OF OUR JOB, YOU KNOW.
...? UH... SURE, I MEAN...
YAARRRR
HM?
OH, IT'S WHITE BLOOD CELL.
EEP!
White Blood Cell (Neutrophil)
His main job is to destroy foreign substances that enter the body from the outside, such as bacteria and viruses.
Streptococcus Mutans
A bacterium that lives in the mouth, and one of several responsible for tooth cavities.
ORA ORA ORA!
GRRRRR
TACKLE
DIE! DIIIE!
HUH...?! SENPAI, YOU KNOW AN IMMUNE CELL?
MM-HMM. THEY'RE ALL GOOD PEOPLE!
RRRAAA
WHAT ARE YOU TALKING ABOUT...? NEUTROPHILS CONFLATE JUSTICE WITH VIOLENCE. THEY'RE WALKING CONTRADICTIONS.
GRRRRR
SCREE! SCREE!

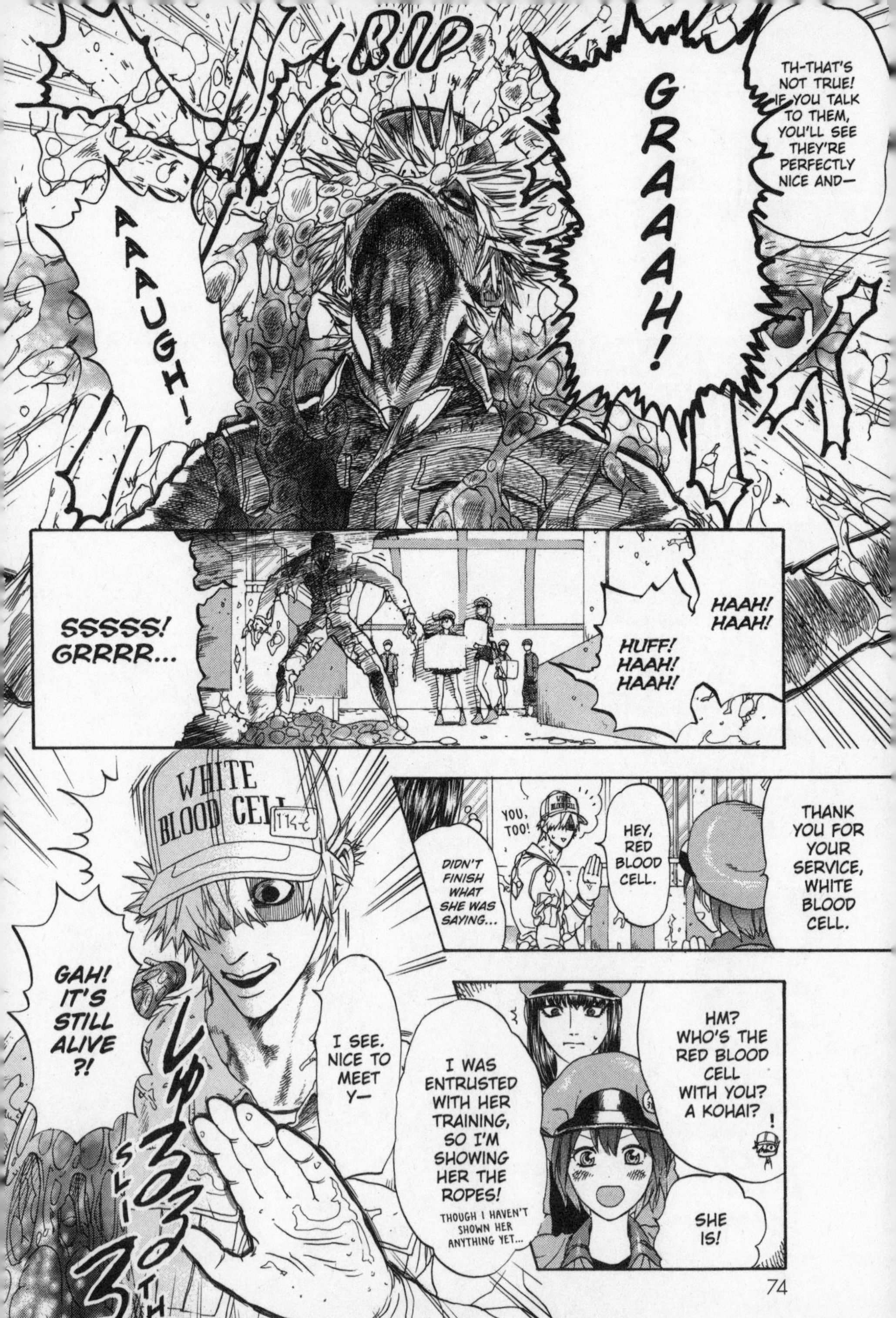
TH-THAT'S NOT TRUE! IF YOU TALK TO THEM, YOU'LL SEE THEY'RE PERFECTLY NICE AND—
GRAAAAH!
RIP
AAAUGH!
HAAH! HAAH!
HUFF! HAAH! HAAH!
SSSSS! GRRRR...
THANK YOU FOR YOUR SERVICE, WHITE BLOOD CELL.
HEY, RED BLOOD CELL.
YOU, TOO!
DIDN'T FINISH WHAT SHE WAS SAYING...
HM? WHO'S THE RED BLOOD CELL WITH YOU? A KOHAI?
!
SHE IS!
I WAS ENTRUSTED WITH HER TRAINING, SO I'M SHOWING HER THE ROPES!
THOUGH I HAVEN'T SHOWN HER ANYTHING YET...
I SEE. NICE TO MEET Y—
WHITE BLOOD CELL
1146
GAH! IT'S STILL ALIVE?!
SLI—
THR

SEE, THERE'RE ACTUALLY DIFFERENT KINDS OF WHITE BLOOD CELLS WORKING IN THE BLOOD VESSELS.
FLUSTER FLUSTER あせあせ
THERE'RE NEUTROPHILS, LIKE HIM, AND... DO YOU WANT TO TAKE THIS ONE, WHITE BLOOD CELL?
ROLL
HUH?! UH, SURE! THERE ARE SEVERAL KINDS OF US... GUH!
WHAM
WHAM
NEUTRO-PHILS, EOSINO-PHILS, BASO-PHILS... NGH, WHY YOU—
ROLL ゴロ
ROLL ゴロ
AND THEN THERE'RE MACROPH-GUH, DIE!! AND LYMPHO-CYTES—DIE!!
EVERYONE SEEMS SCARED OF WHITE BLOOD CELL HERE...
AE 3803
...BUT HE'S ACTUALLY A REALLY KIND PERSON!!
STAB
ORA!
STAB
STAB
WHAM
DIE, YOU GERM BAS-TARD!!
STAB STAB
EEEEEEEK
SO I HOPE YOU GET ALONG...
GRAARGH!
SPURT
SENPAI, THE BLOOD SPRAY! LOOK OUT!!

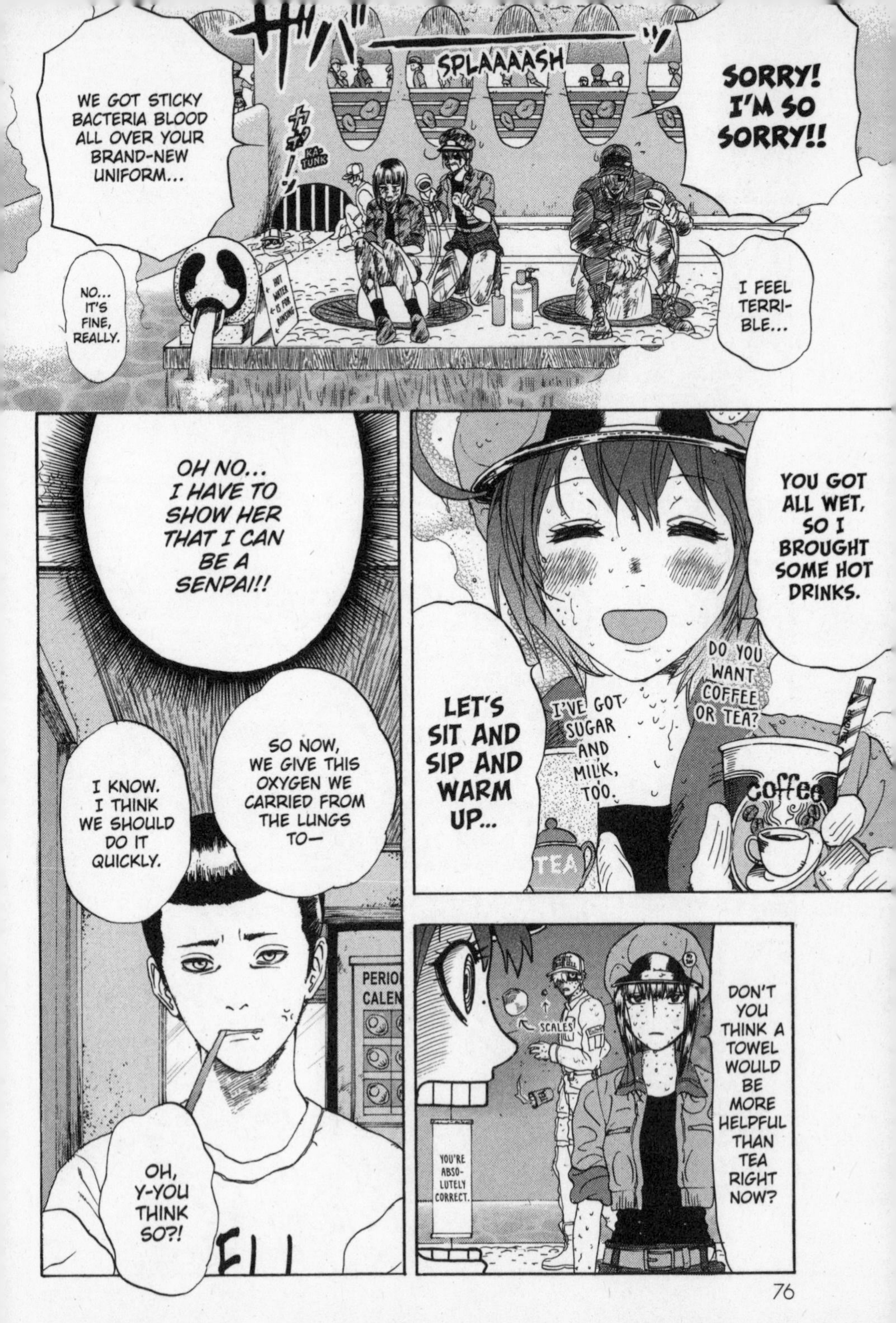
SPLAAAASH
SORRY! I'M SO SORRY!!
WE GOT STICKY BACTERIA BLOOD ALL OVER YOUR BRAND-NEW UNIFORM...
KA-TUNK
I FEEL TERRIBLE...
HOT WATER IS FOR RINSING
NO... IT'S FINE, REALLY.
YOU GOT ALL WET, SO I BROUGHT SOME HOT DRINKS.
DO YOU WANT COFFEE OR TEA?
Coffee
I'VE GOT SUGAR AND MILK, TOO.
LET'S SIT AND SIP AND WARM UP...
TEA
DON'T YOU THINK A TOWEL WOULD BE MORE HELPFUL THAN TEA RIGHT NOW?
SCALES
YOU'RE ABSOLUTELY CORRECT.
OH NO... I HAVE TO SHOW HER THAT I CAN BE A SENPAI!!
SO NOW, WE GIVE THIS OXYGEN WE CARRIED FROM THE LUNGS TO—
I KNOW. I THINK WE SHOULD DO IT QUICKLY.
OH, Y-YOU THINK SO?!

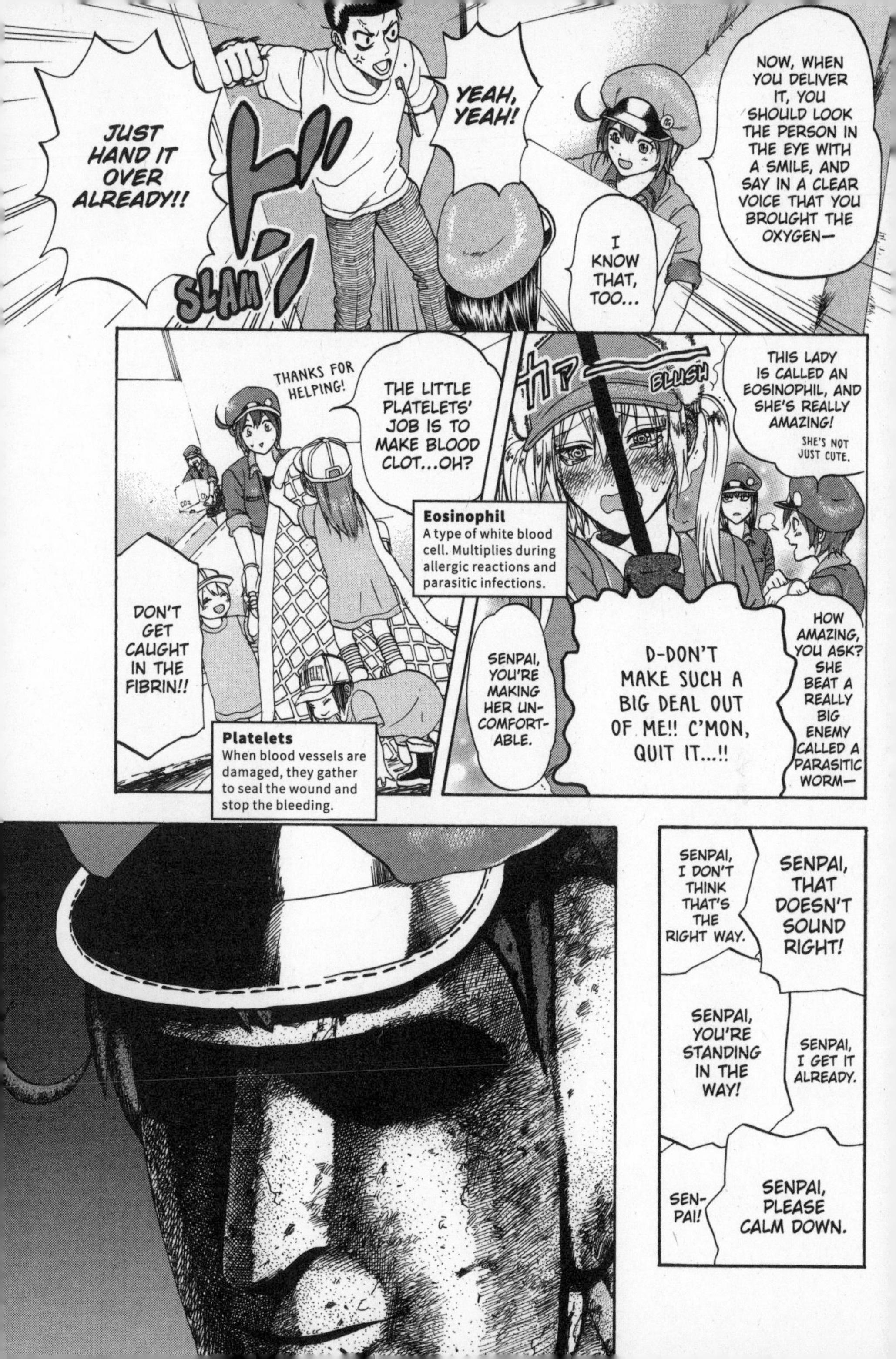
NOW, WHEN YOU DELIVER IT, YOU SHOULD LOOK THE PERSON IN THE EYE WITH A SMILE, AND SAY IN A CLEAR VOICE THAT YOU BROUGHT THE OXYGEN—
I KNOW THAT, TOO...
YEAH, YEAH!
JUST HAND IT OVER ALREADY!!
SLAM
THIS LADY IS CALLED AN EOSINOPHIL, AND SHE'S REALLY AMAZING!
SHE'S NOT JUST CUTE.
BLUSH
HOW AMAZING, YOU ASK? SHE BEAT A REALLY BIG ENEMY CALLED A PARASITIC WORM—
D-DON'T MAKE SUCH A BIG DEAL OUT OF ME!! C'MON, QUIT IT...!!
SENPAI, YOU'RE MAKING HER UN-COMFORT-ABLE.
Eosinophil
A type of white blood cell. Multiplies during allergic reactions and parasitic infections.
THE LITTLE PLATELETS' JOB IS TO MAKE BLOOD CLOT...OH?
THANKS FOR HELPING!
DON'T GET CAUGHT IN THE FIBRIN!!
Platelets
When blood vessels are damaged, they gather to seal the wound and stop the bleeding.
SENPAI, THAT DOESN'T SOUND RIGHT!
SENPAI, I DON'T THINK THAT'S THE RIGHT WAY.
SENPAI, I GET IT ALREADY.
SENPAI, YOU'RE STANDING IN THE WAY!
SENPAI, PLEASE CALM DOWN.
SEN-PAI!

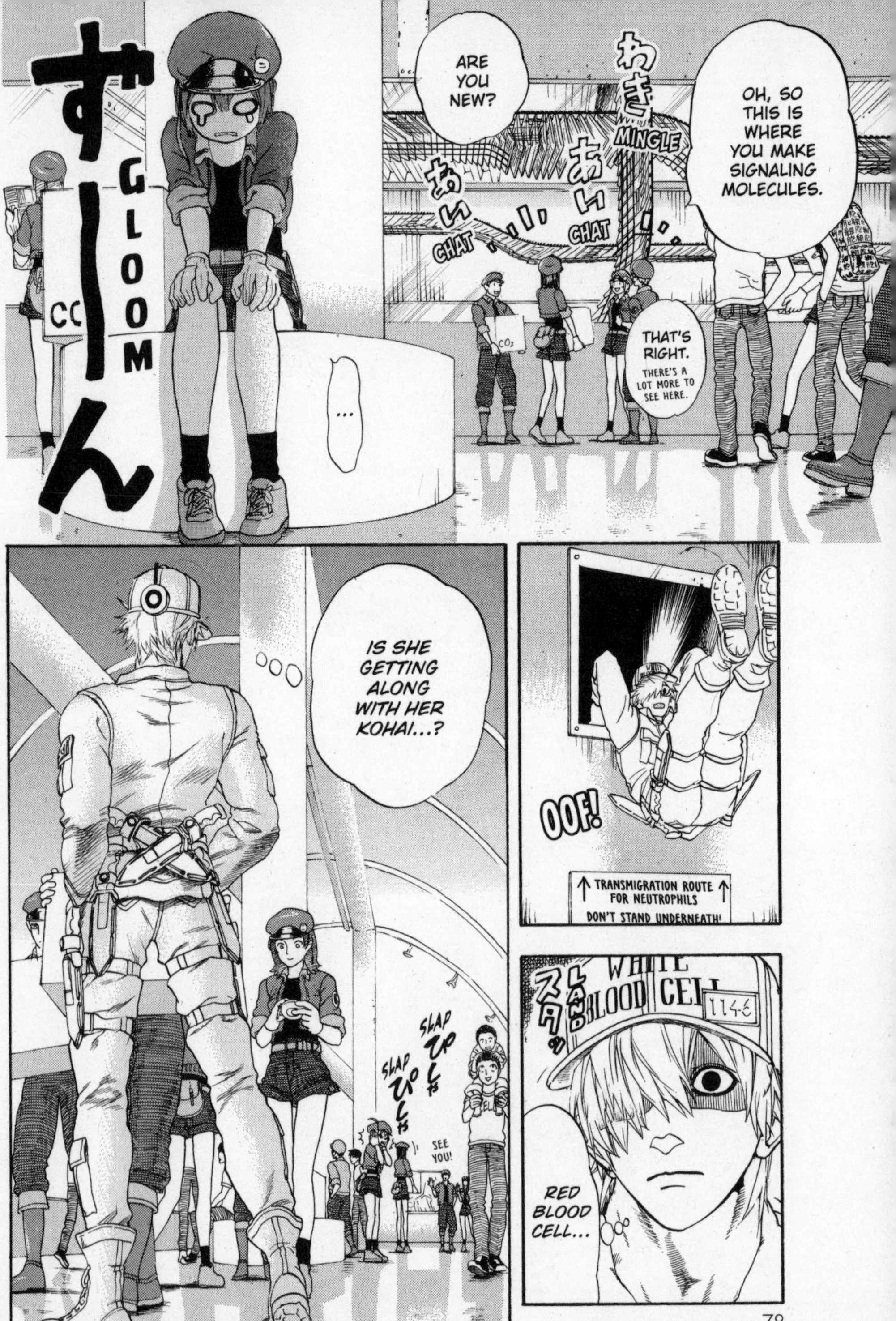
OH, SO THIS IS WHERE YOU MAKE SIGNALING MOLECULES.
わき
MINGLE
あい
CHAT
ARE YOU NEW?
あい
CHAT
THAT'S RIGHT.
THERE'S A LOT MORE TO SEE HERE.
ずーん
GLOOM
CO
...
OOF!
↑ TRANSMIGRATION ROUTE FOR NEUTROPHILS ↑
DON'T STAND UNDERNEATH!
スタ
LAND
WHITE BLOOD CELL
1146
RED BLOOD CELL...
IS SHE GETTING ALONG WITH HER KOHAI...?
SEE YOU!
ぴし
SLAP
ぴし
SLAP

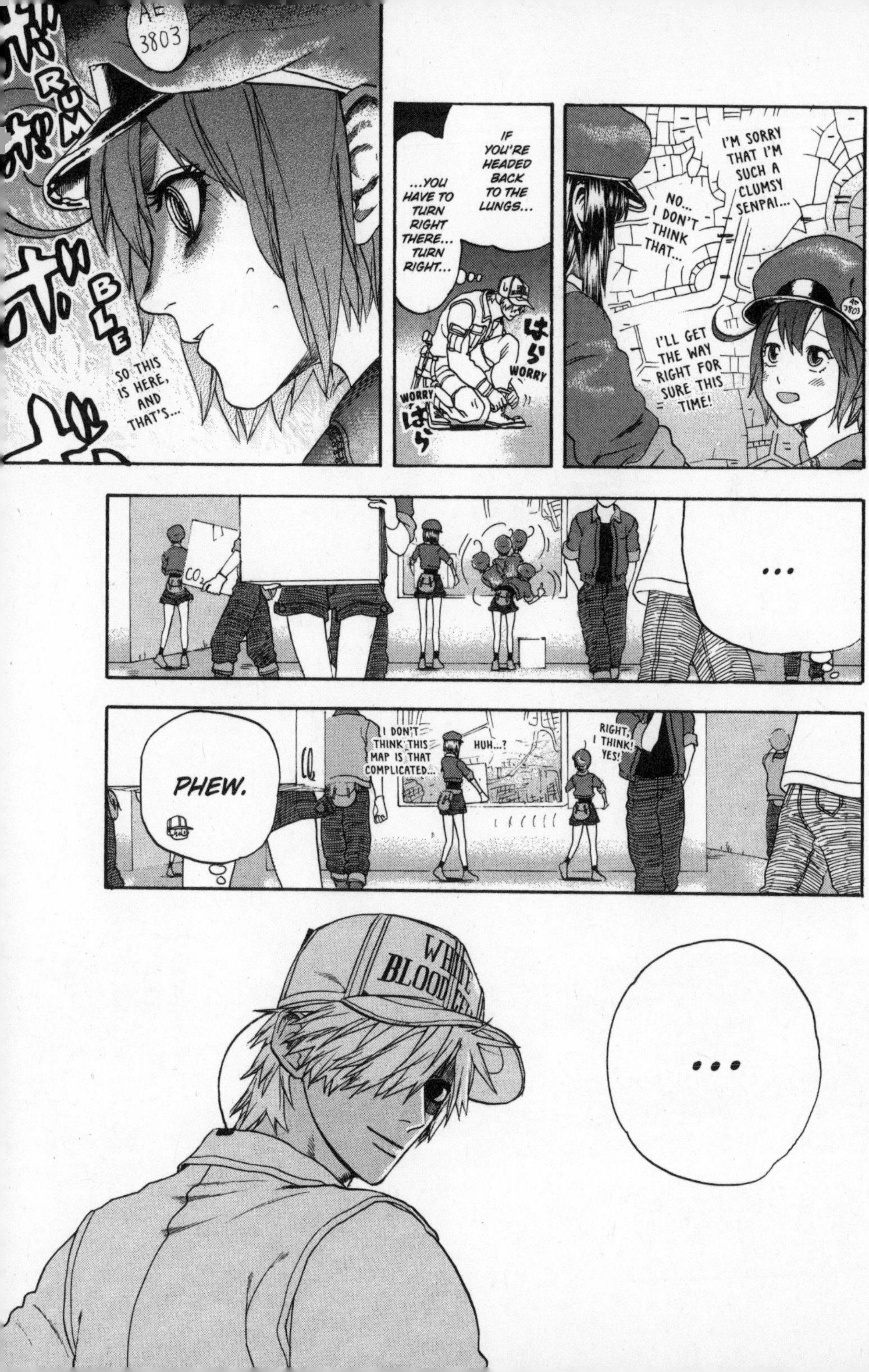
I'M SORRY THAT I'M SUCH A CLUMSY SENPAI...
NO... I DON'T THINK THAT...
I'LL GET THE WAY RIGHT FOR SURE THIS TIME!
AE 3803
IF YOU'RE HEADED BACK TO THE LUNGS...
...YOU HAVE TO TURN RIGHT THERE... TURN RIGHT...
WORRY
WORRY
AE 3803
RUMBLE
SO THIS IS HERE, AND THAT'S...
...
RIGHT, I THINK! YES!
HUH...?
I DON'T THINK THIS MAP IS THAT COMPLICATED...
PHEW.
...

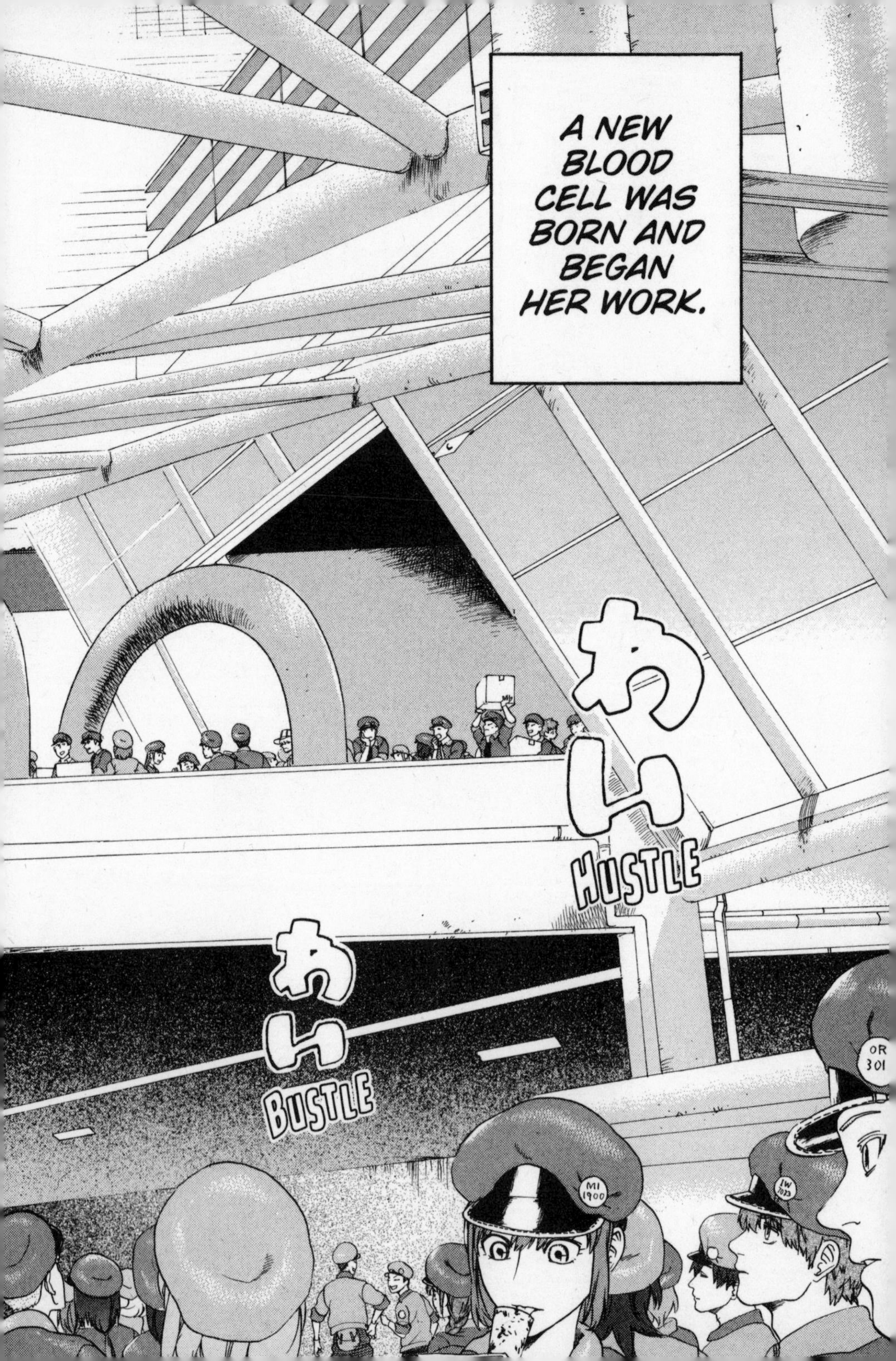
A NEW BLOOD CELL WAS BORN AND BEGAN HER WORK.
わい
HUSTLE
わい
BUSTLE
OR 301
MI 1900
IW 7023

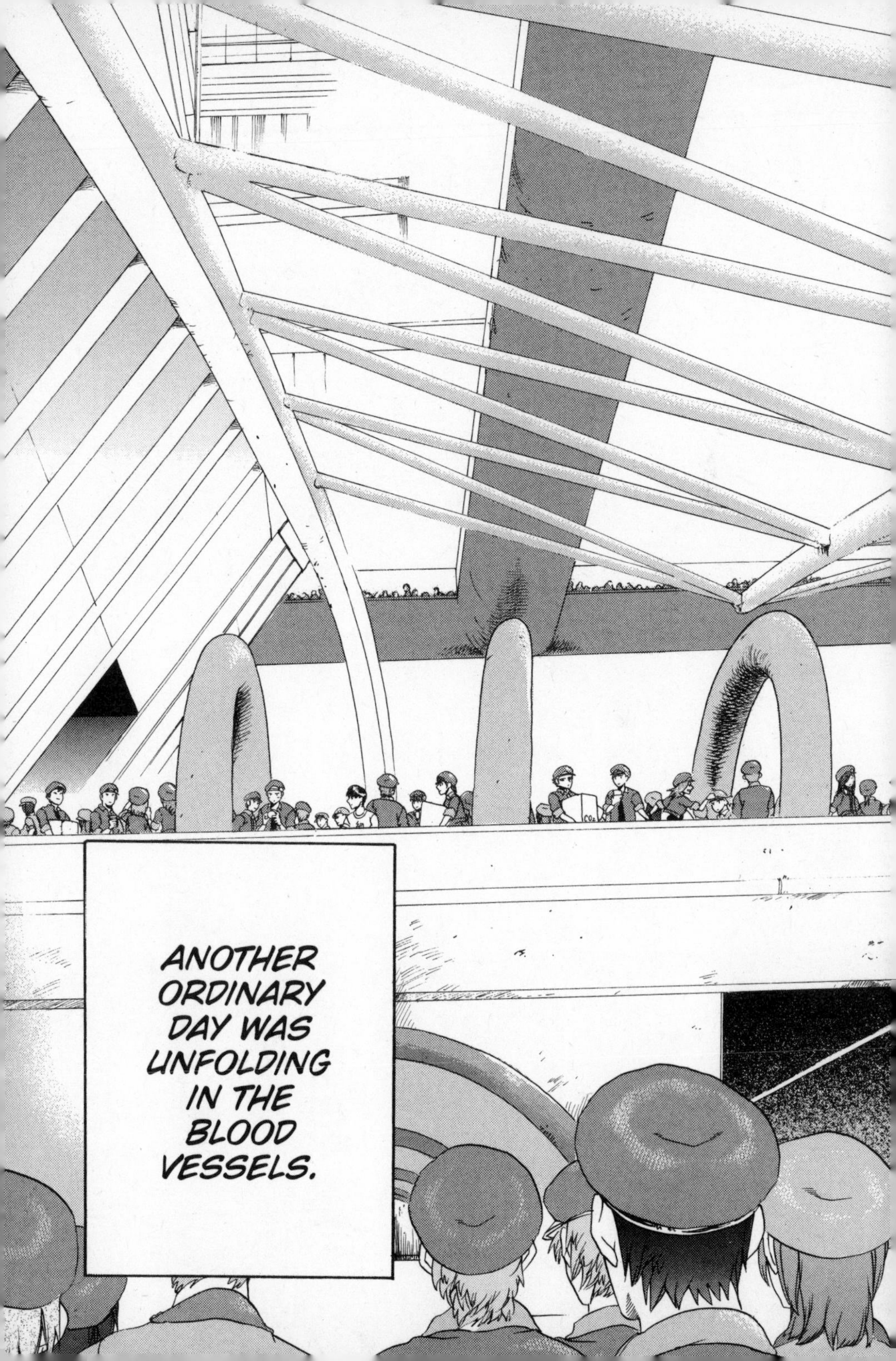
ANOTHER ORDINARY DAY WAS UNFOLDING IN THE BLOOD VESSELS.

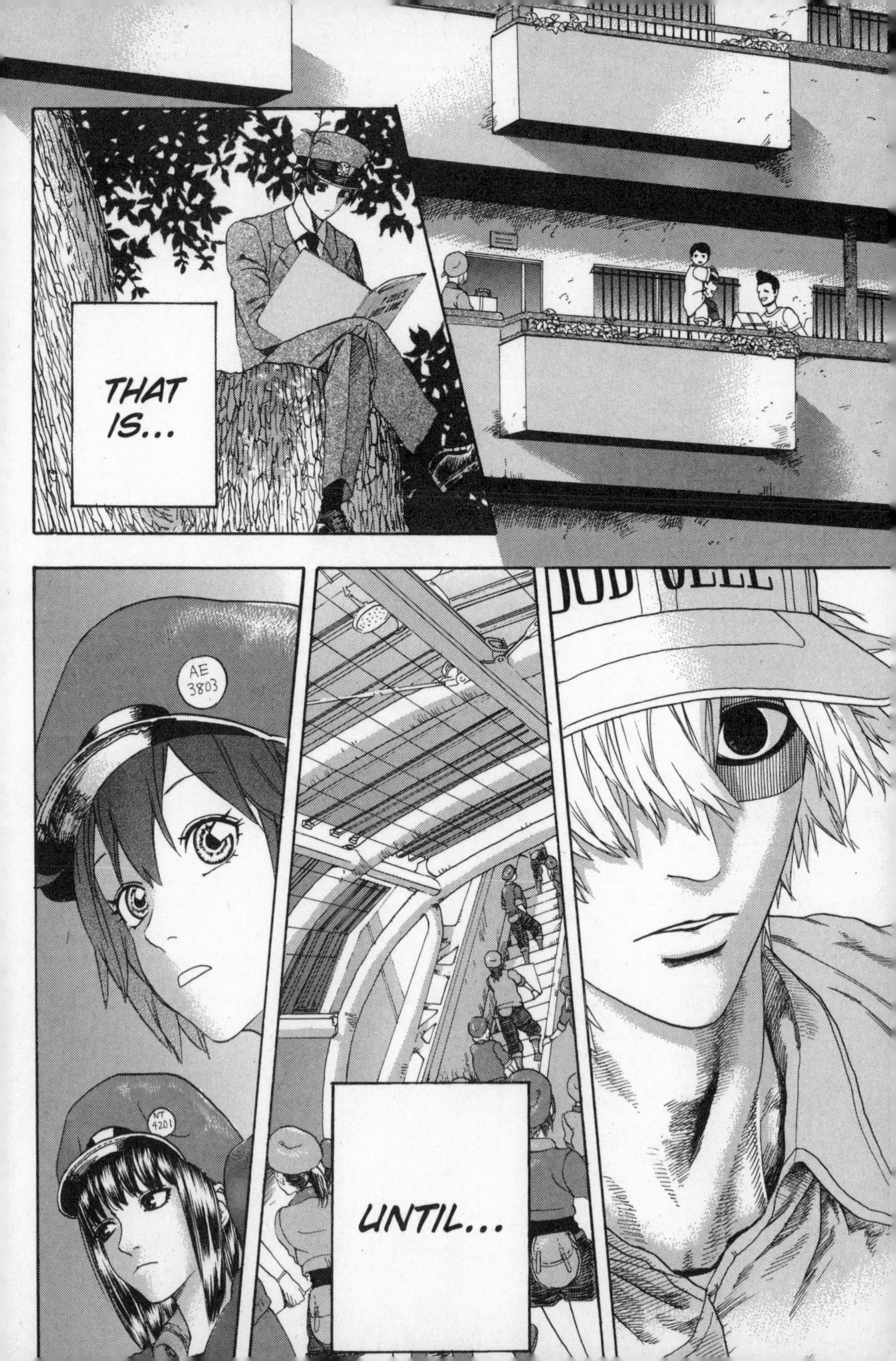
THAT IS...
UNTIL...
AE 3803
NT 4201

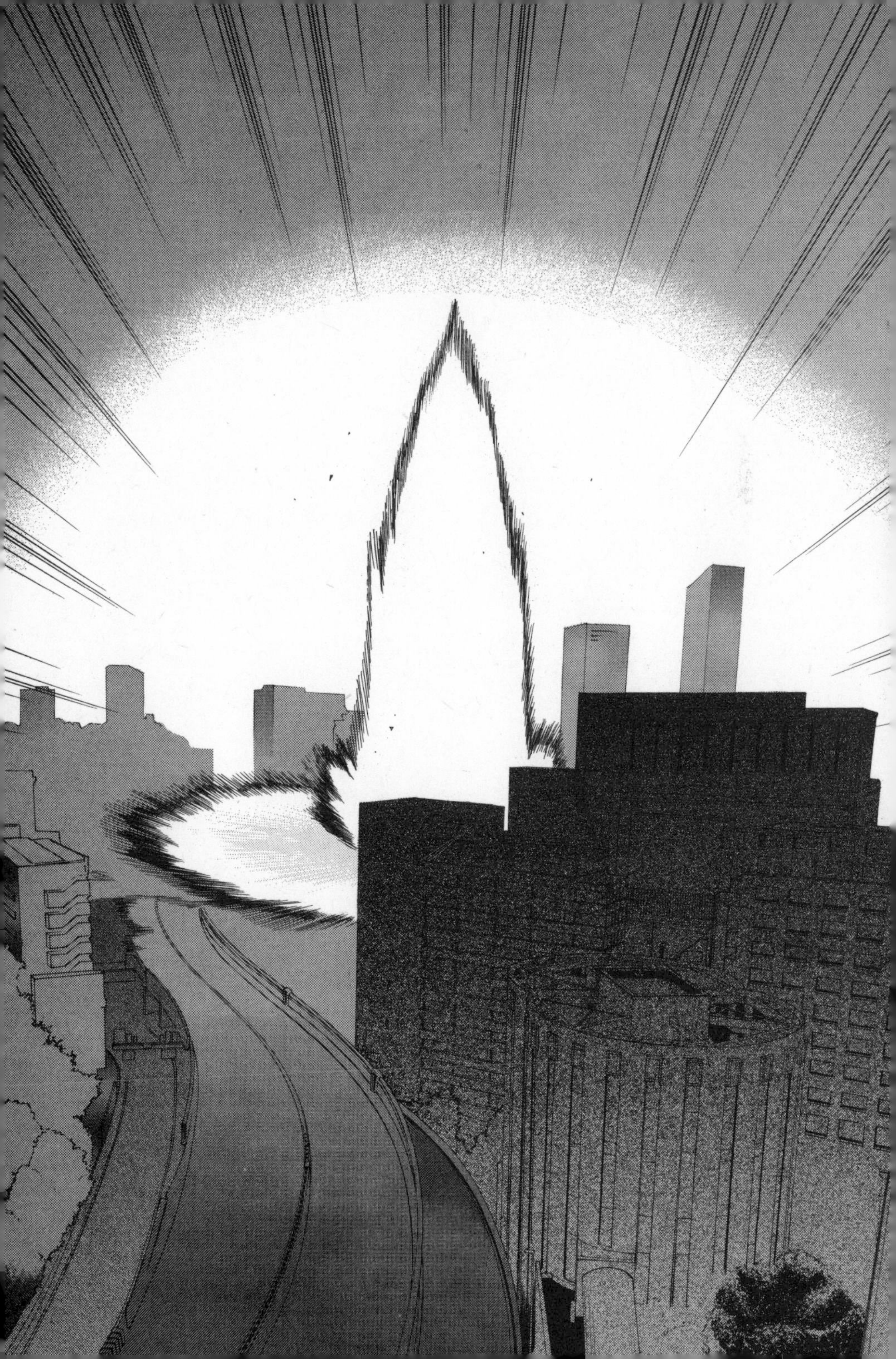

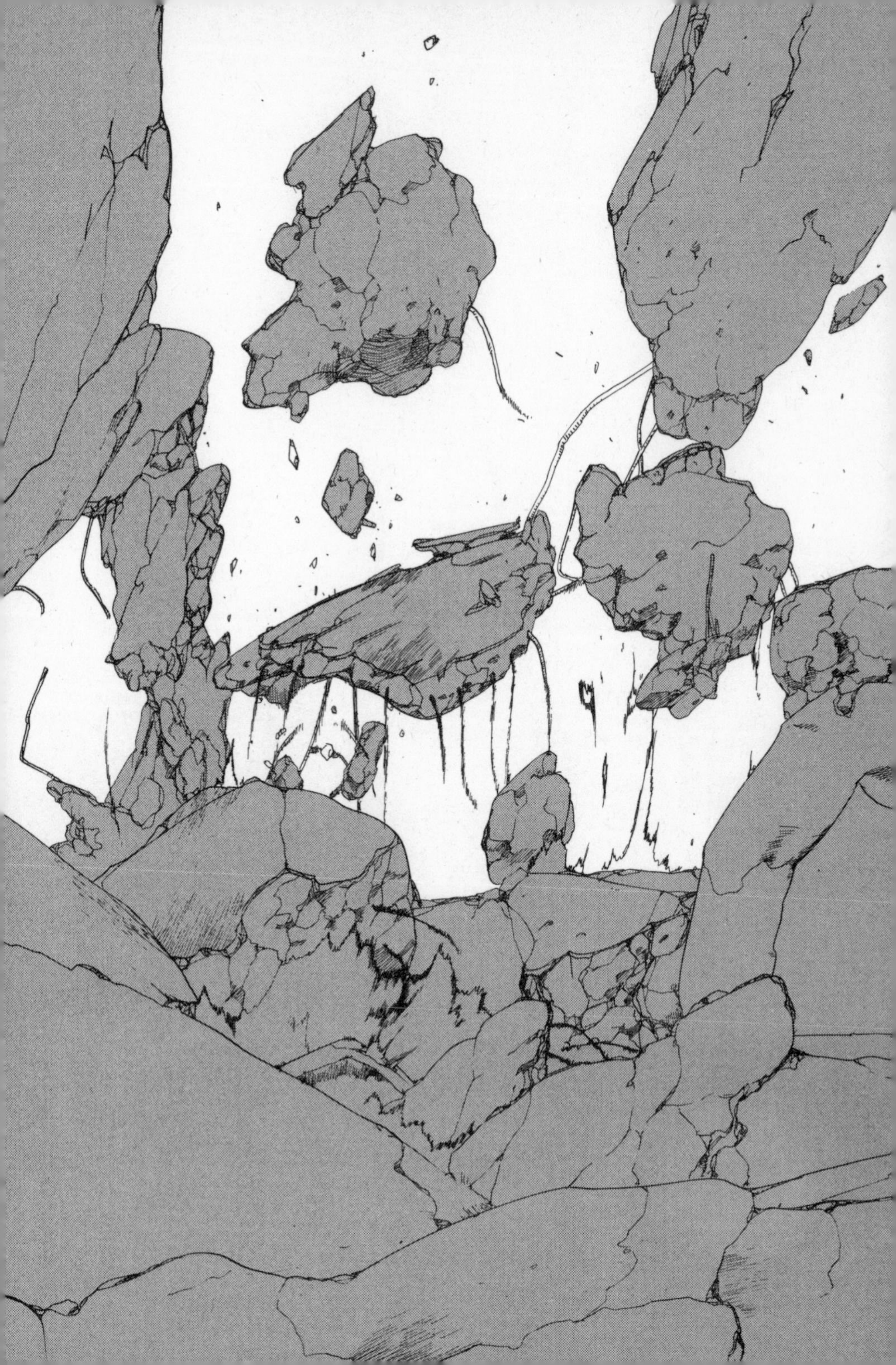

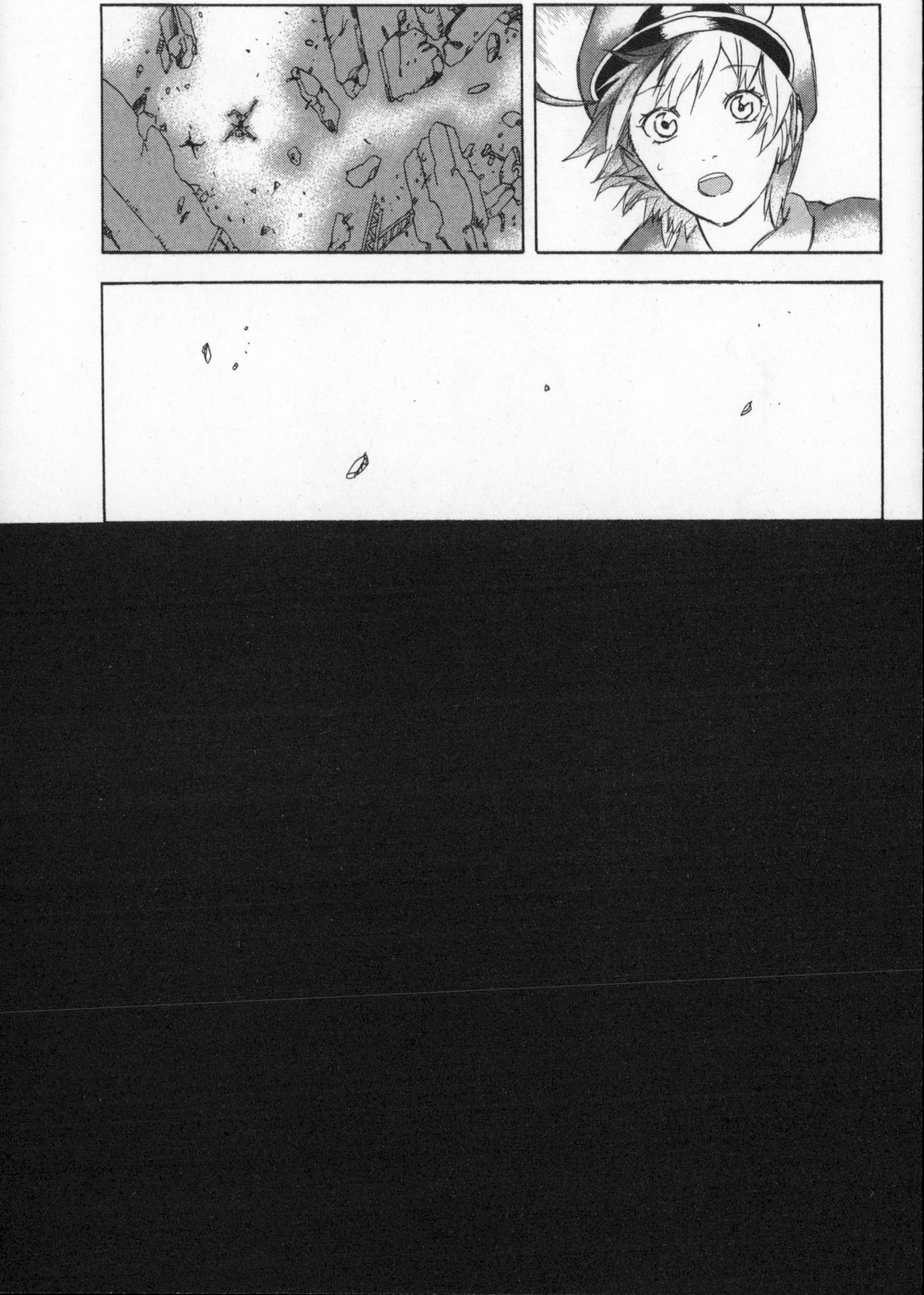

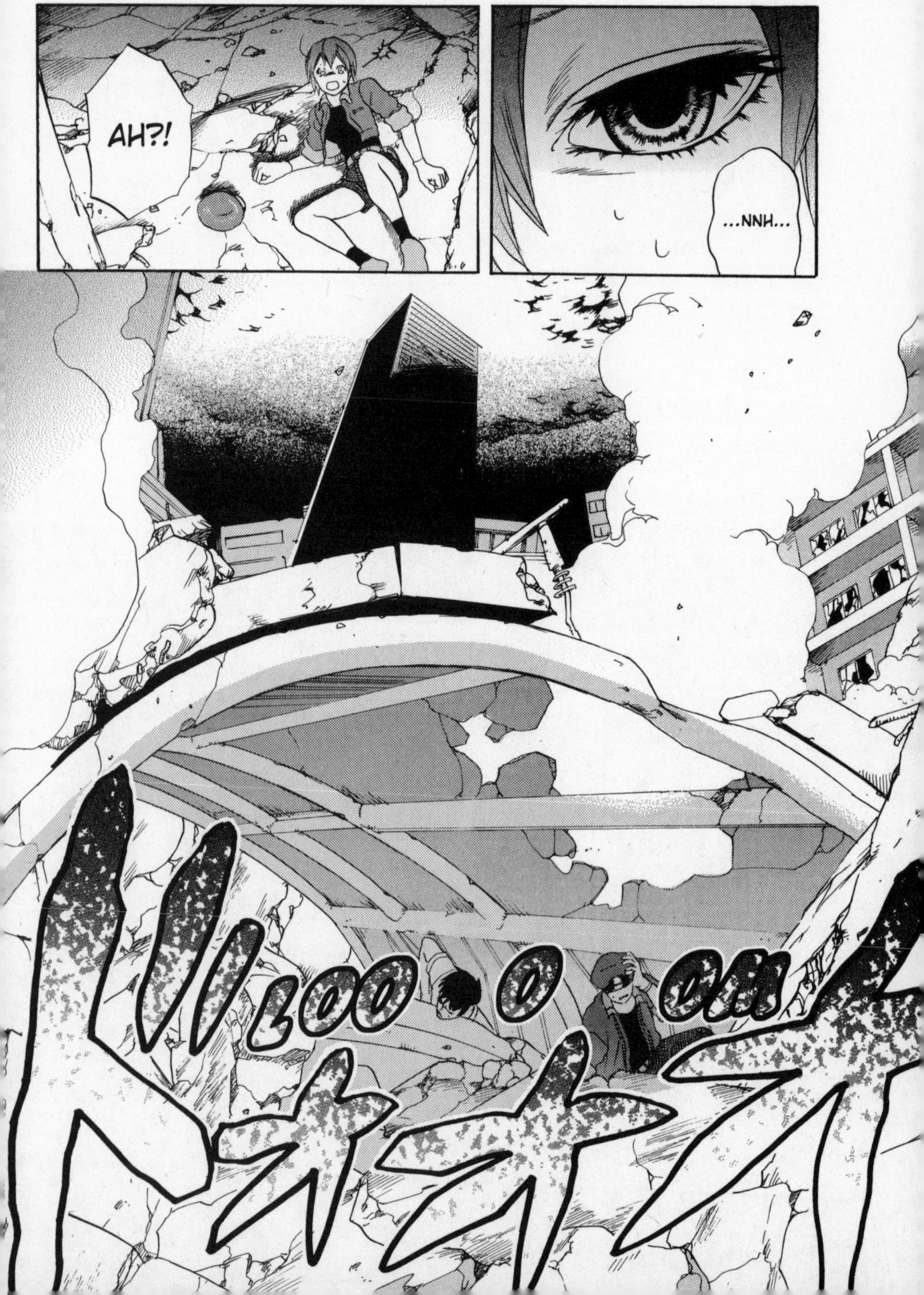
...NNH...
AH?!

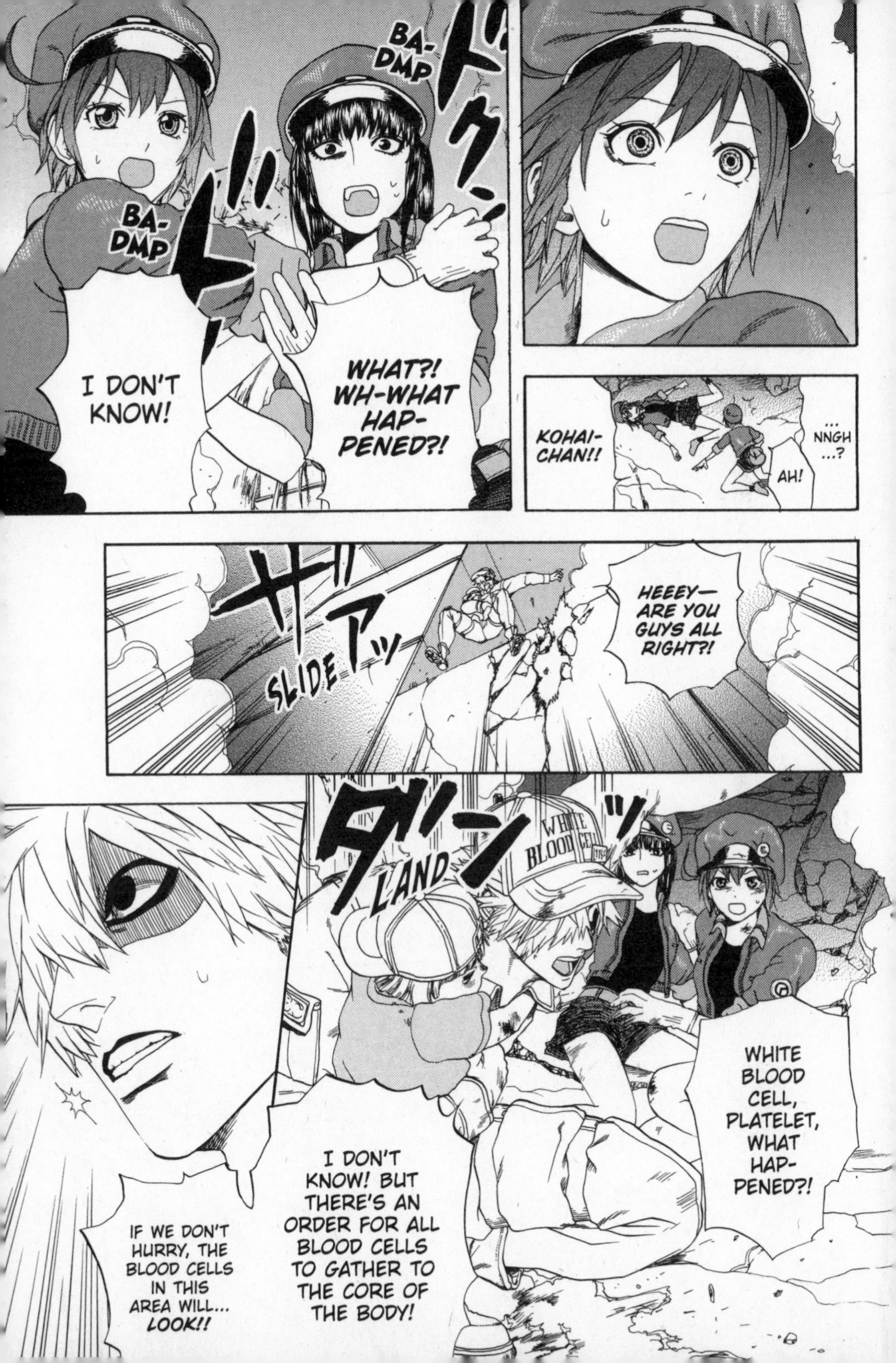
...NNGH...?
KOHAI-CHAN!!
AH!
BA-DMP
BA-DMP
WHAT?! WH-WHAT HAP-PENED?!
I DON'T KNOW!
SLIDE
HEEEY— ARE YOU GUYS ALL RIGHT?!
LAND
WHITE BLOOD CELL
WHITE BLOOD CELL, PLATELET, WHAT HAP-PENED?!
I DON'T KNOW! BUT THERE'S AN ORDER FOR ALL BLOOD CELLS TO GATHER TO THE CORE OF THE BODY!
IF WE DON'T HURRY, THE BLOOD CELLS IN THIS AREA WILL... LOOK!!

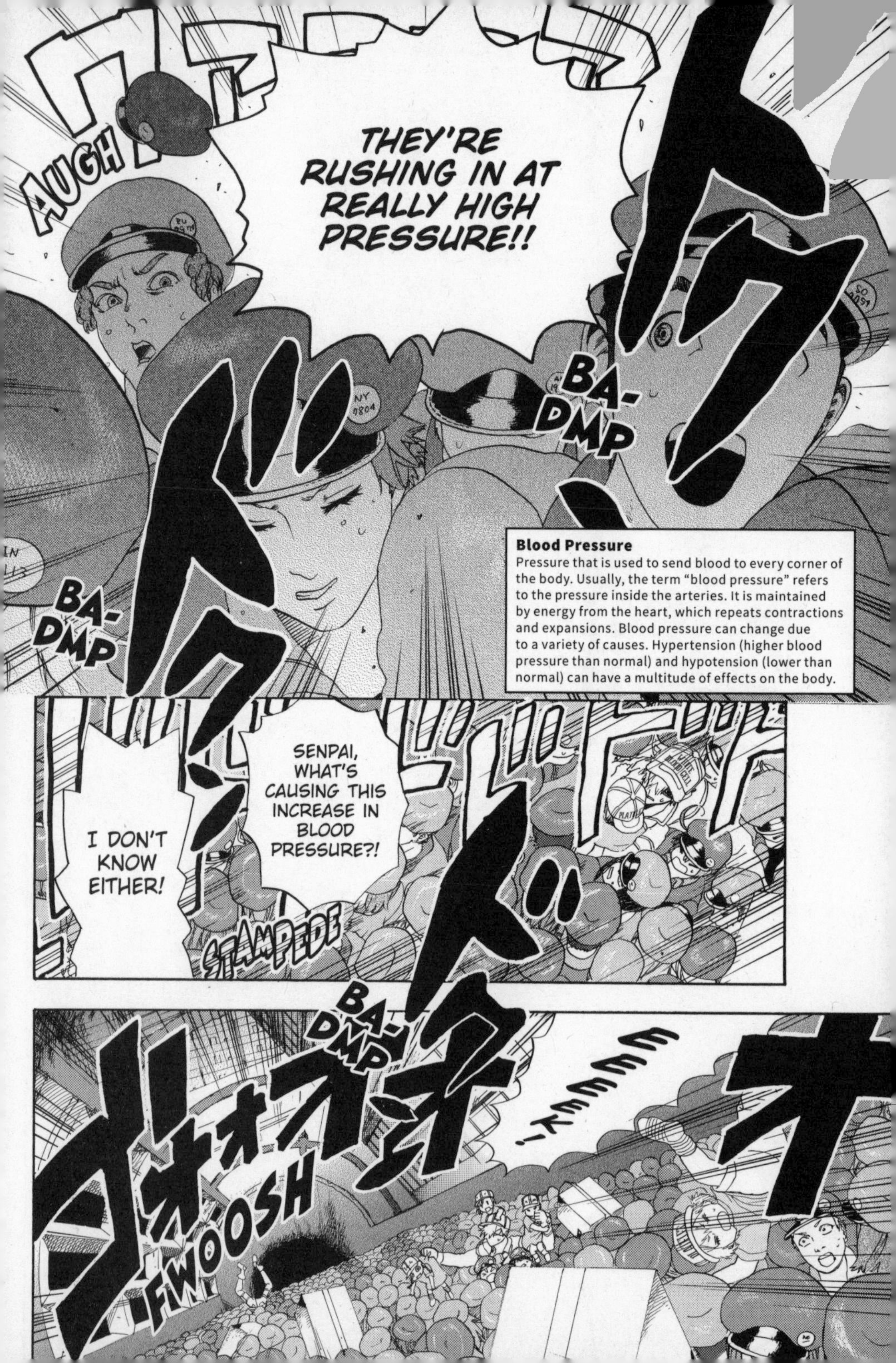

AUGH
THEY'RE RUSHING IN AT REALLY HIGH PRESSURE!!
BA-DMP
BA-DMP
Blood Pressure
Pressure that is used to send blood to every corner of the body. Usually, the term "blood pressure" refers to the pressure inside the arteries. It is maintained by energy from the heart, which repeats contractions and expansions. Blood pressure can change due to a variety of causes. Hypertension (higher blood pressure than normal) and hypotension (lower than normal) can have a multitude of effects on the body.
SENPAI, WHAT'S CAUSING THIS INCREASE IN BLOOD PRESSURE?!
I DON'T KNOW EITHER!
STAMPEDE
BA-DMP
EEEEEK!
FWOOSH

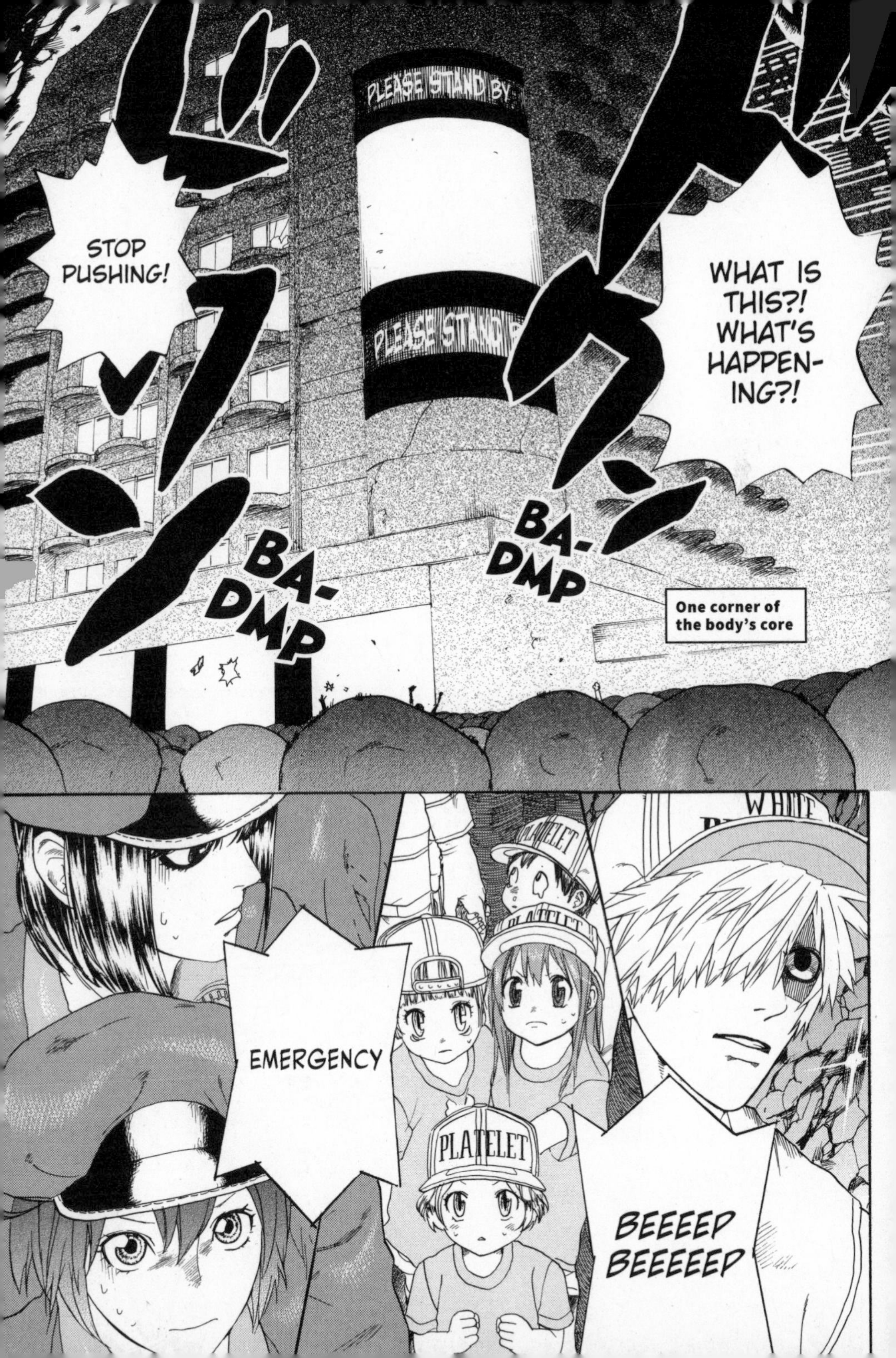
PLEASE STAND BY
WHAT IS THIS?! WHAT'S HAPPEN-ING?!
STOP PUSHING!
BA-DMP
BA-DMP
One corner of the body's core
BEEEEP BEEEEEP
PLATELET
PLATELET
PLATELET
EMERGENCY

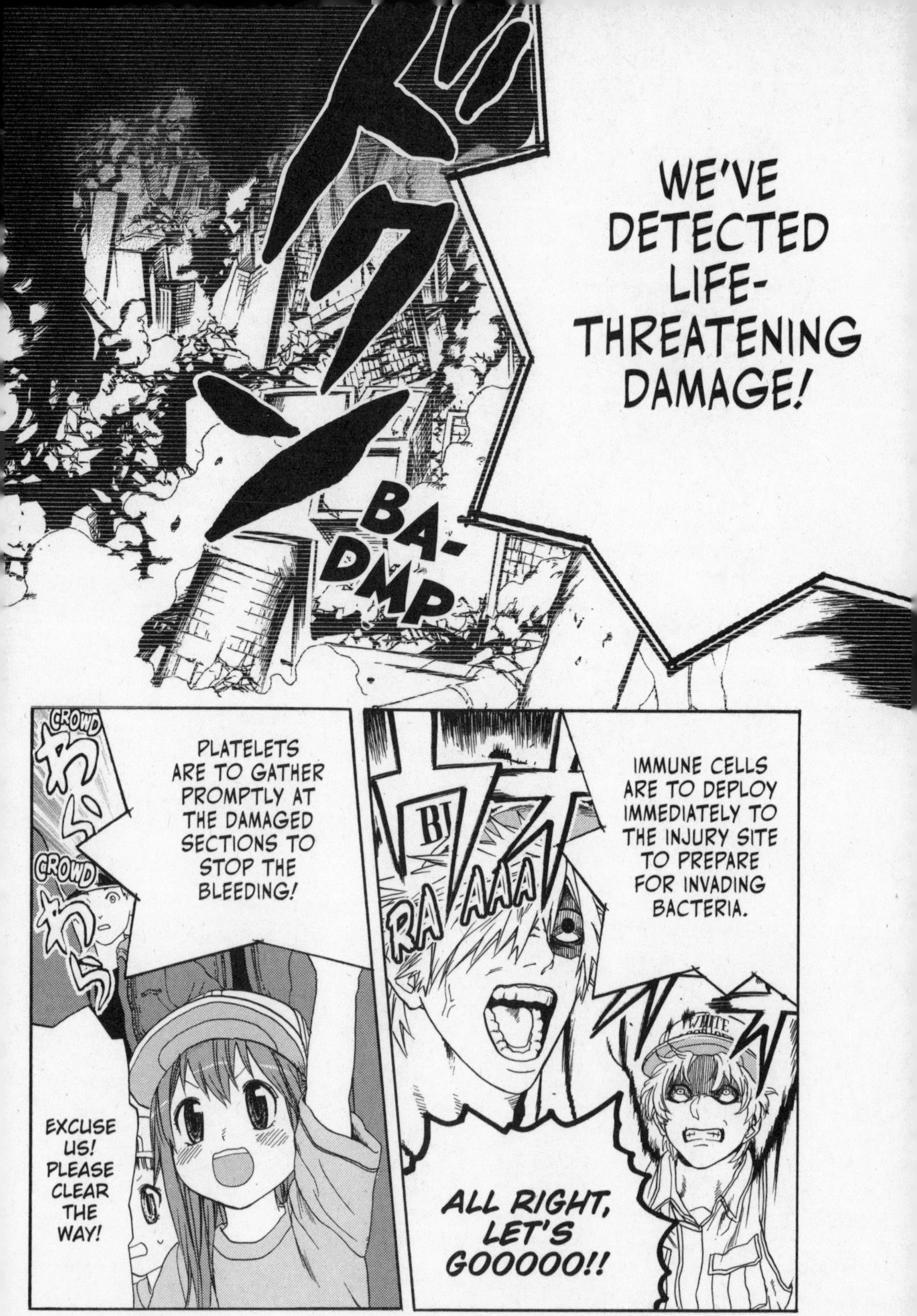

WE'VE DETECTED LIFE-THREATENING DAMAGE!
BA-DMP
IMMUNE CELLS ARE TO DEPLOY IMMEDIATELY TO THE INJURY SITE TO PREPARE FOR INVADING BACTERIA.
RAAAAA
ALL RIGHT, LET'S GOOOOO!!
PLATELETS ARE TO GATHER PROMPTLY AT THE DAMAGED SECTIONS TO STOP THE BLEEDING!
CROWD
CROWD
EXCUSE US! PLEASE CLEAR THE WAY!

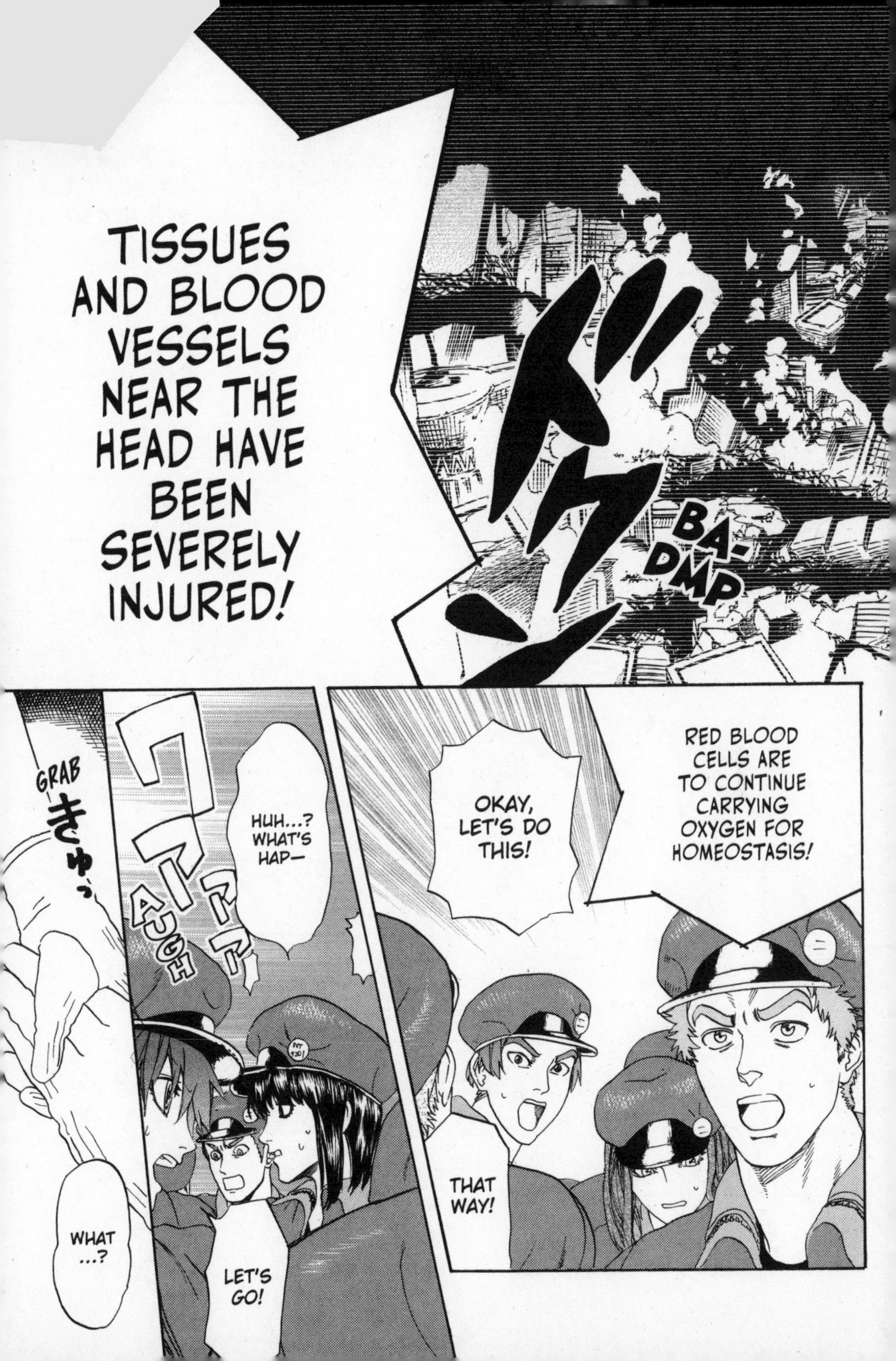
TISSUES AND BLOOD VESSELS NEAR THE HEAD HAVE BEEN SEVERELY INJURED!
BA-DMP
RED BLOOD CELLS ARE TO CONTINUE CARRYING OXYGEN FOR HOMEOSTASIS!
OKAY, LET'S DO THIS!
THAT WAY!
HUH...? WHAT'S HAP—
AUGH
GRAB
きゅっ
WHAT ...?
LET'S GO!

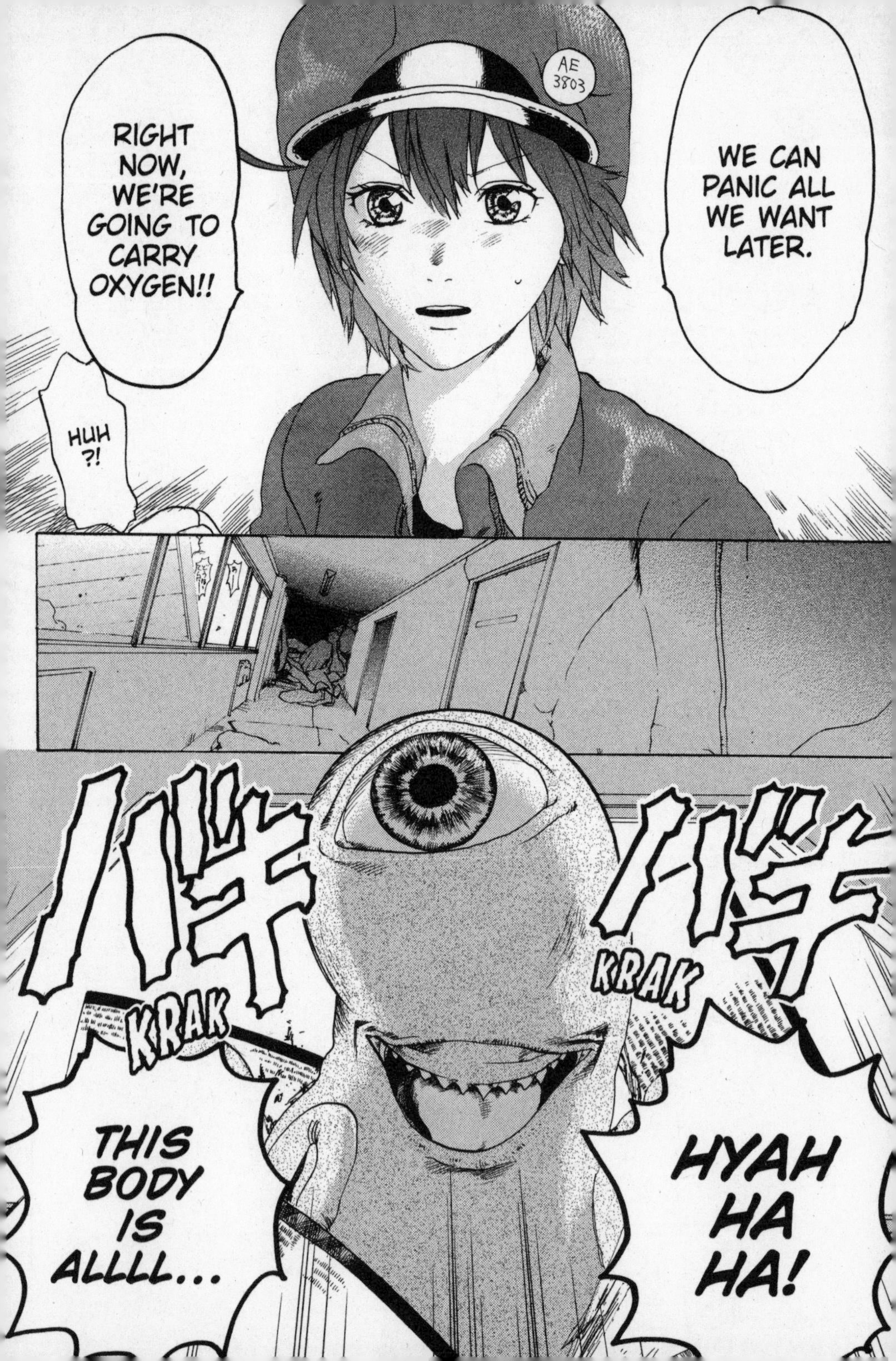
WE CAN PANIC ALL WE WANT LATER.
RIGHT NOW, WE'RE GOING TO CARRY OXYGEN!!
AE 3803
HUH ?!
バチ
KRAK
バチ
KRAK
HYAH HA HA HA!
THIS BODY IS ALLLL...

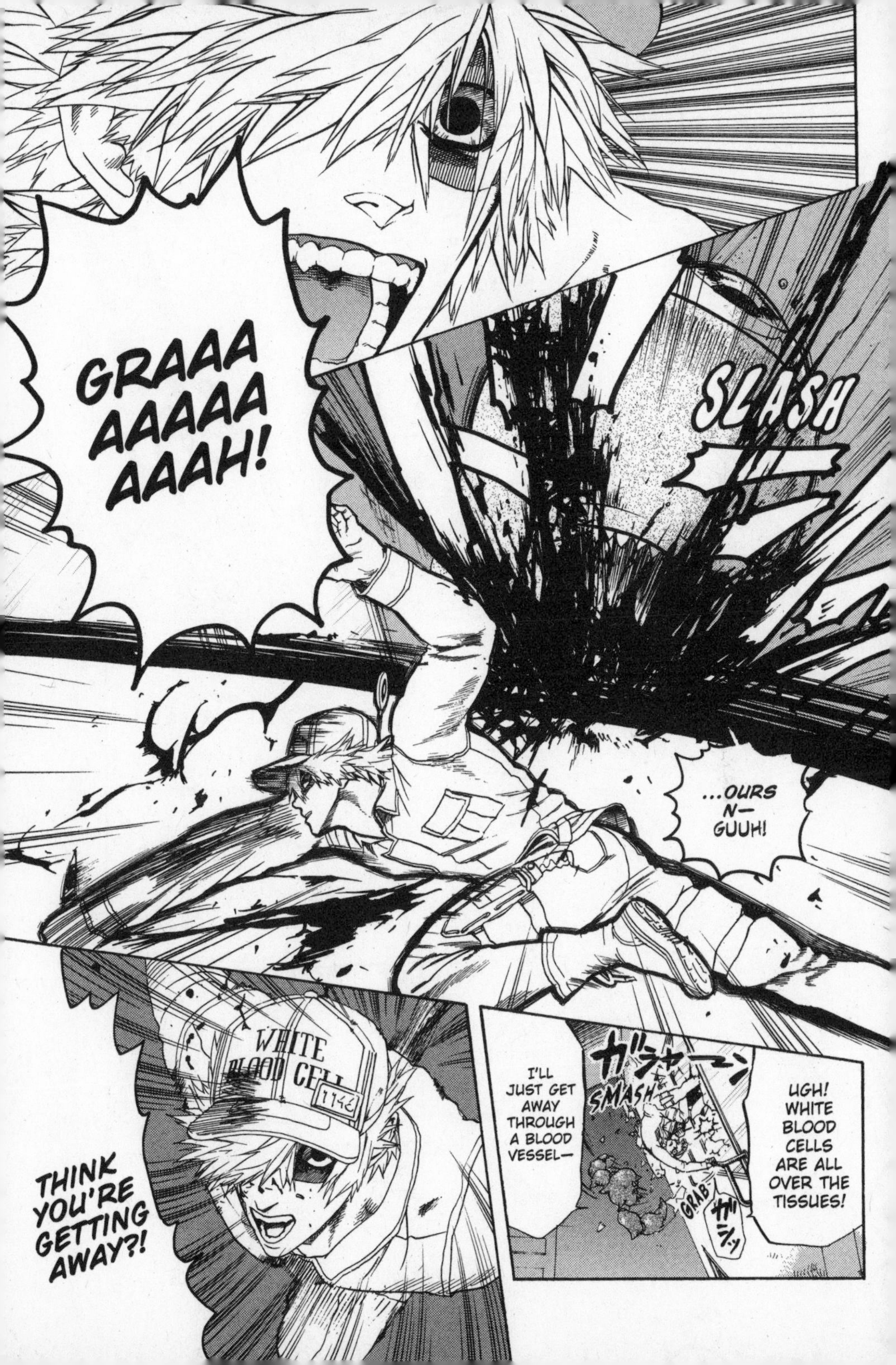

SLASH
GRAAA AAAAA AAAH!
...OURS N— GUUH!
UGH! WHITE BLOOD CELLS ARE ALL OVER THE TISSUES!
ガシャーン
SMASH
I'LL JUST GET AWAY THROUGH A BLOOD VESSEL—
GRAB
ガシッ
WHITE BLOOD CELL
1146
THINK YOU'RE GETTING AWAY?!

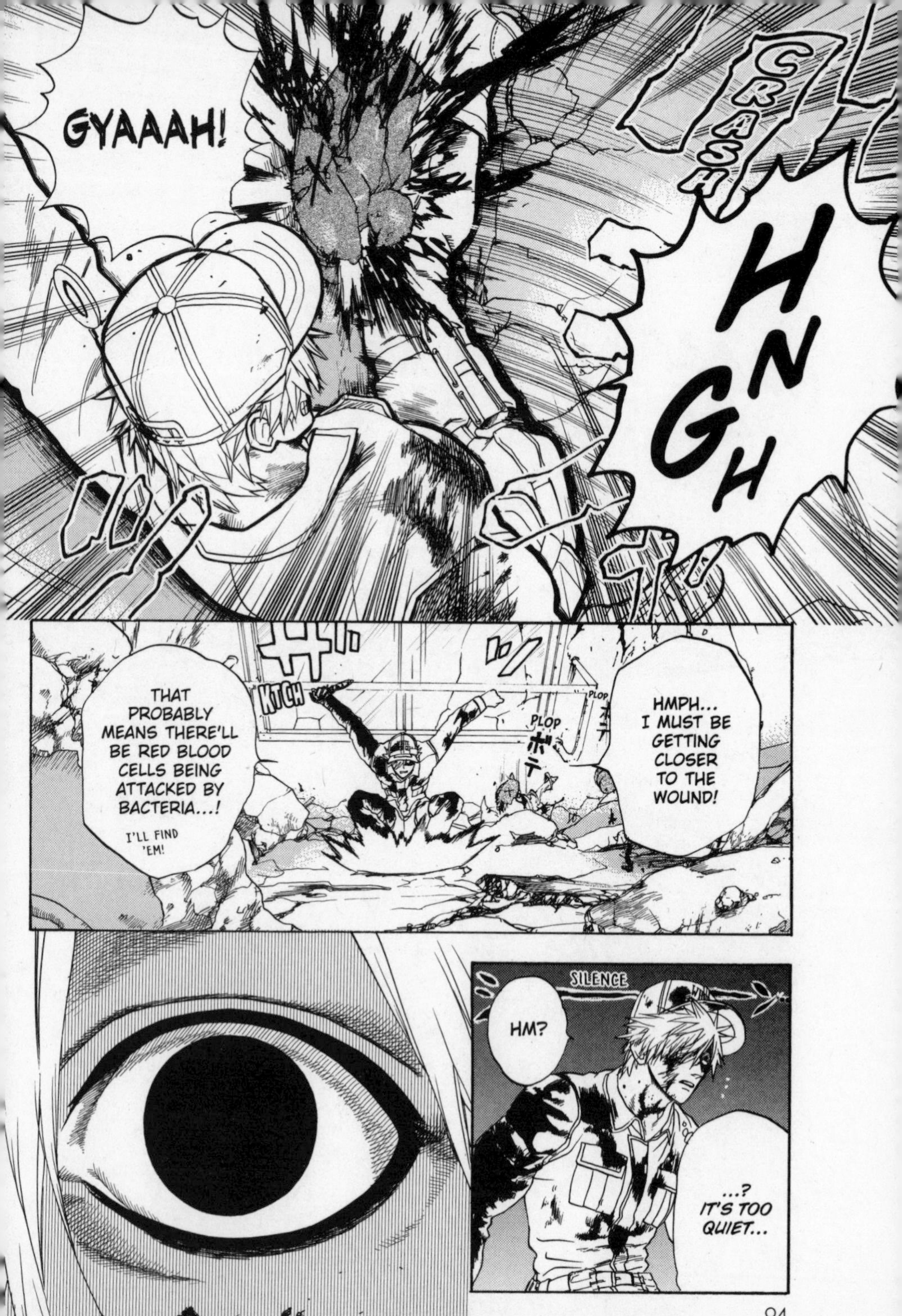
CRASH
HNGH
GYAAAH!
HMPH... I MUST BE GETTING CLOSER TO THE WOUND!
PLOP
PLOP
KTCH
THAT PROBABLY MEANS THERE'LL BE RED BLOOD CELLS BEING ATTACKED BY BACTERIA...!
I'LL FIND 'EM!
SILENCE
HM?
...? IT'S TOO QUIET...

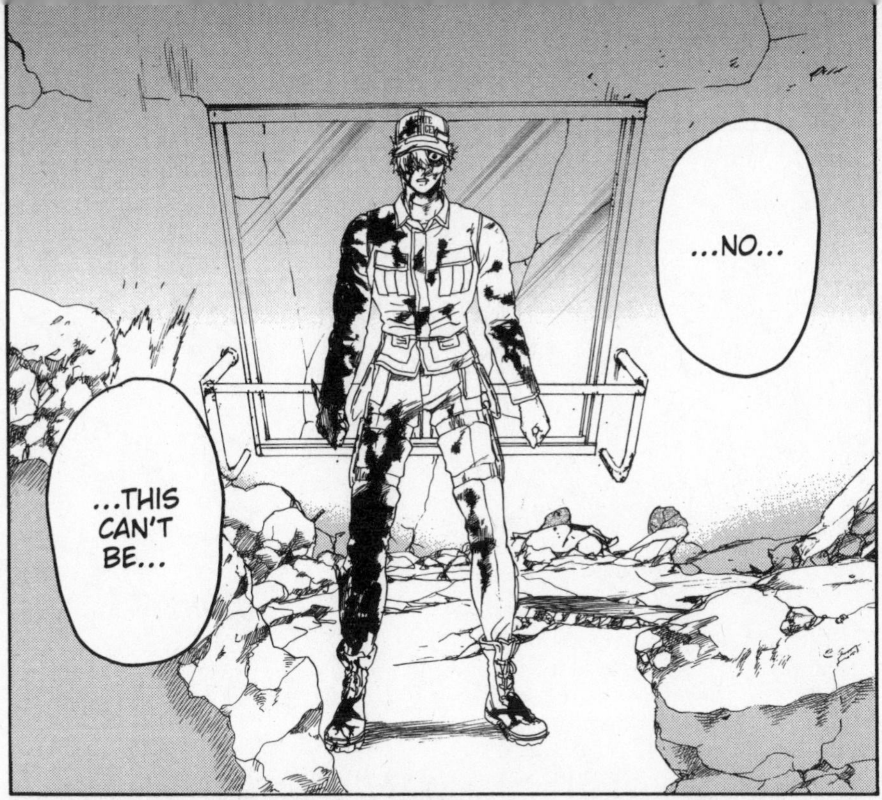
...NO...
...THIS CAN'T BE...

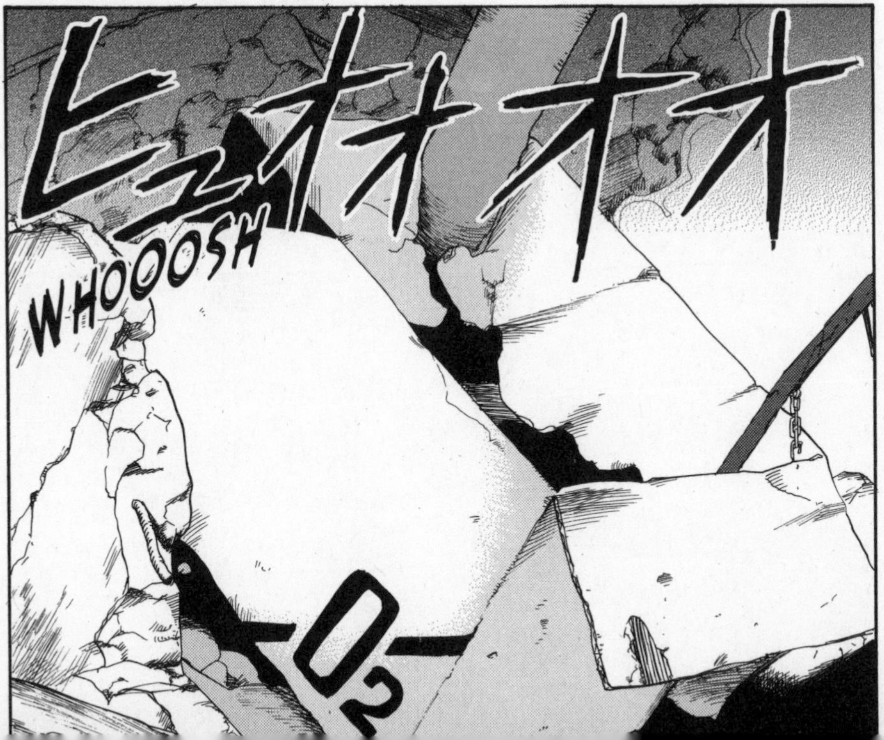
ヒュオオオ
WHOOOSH
O_2

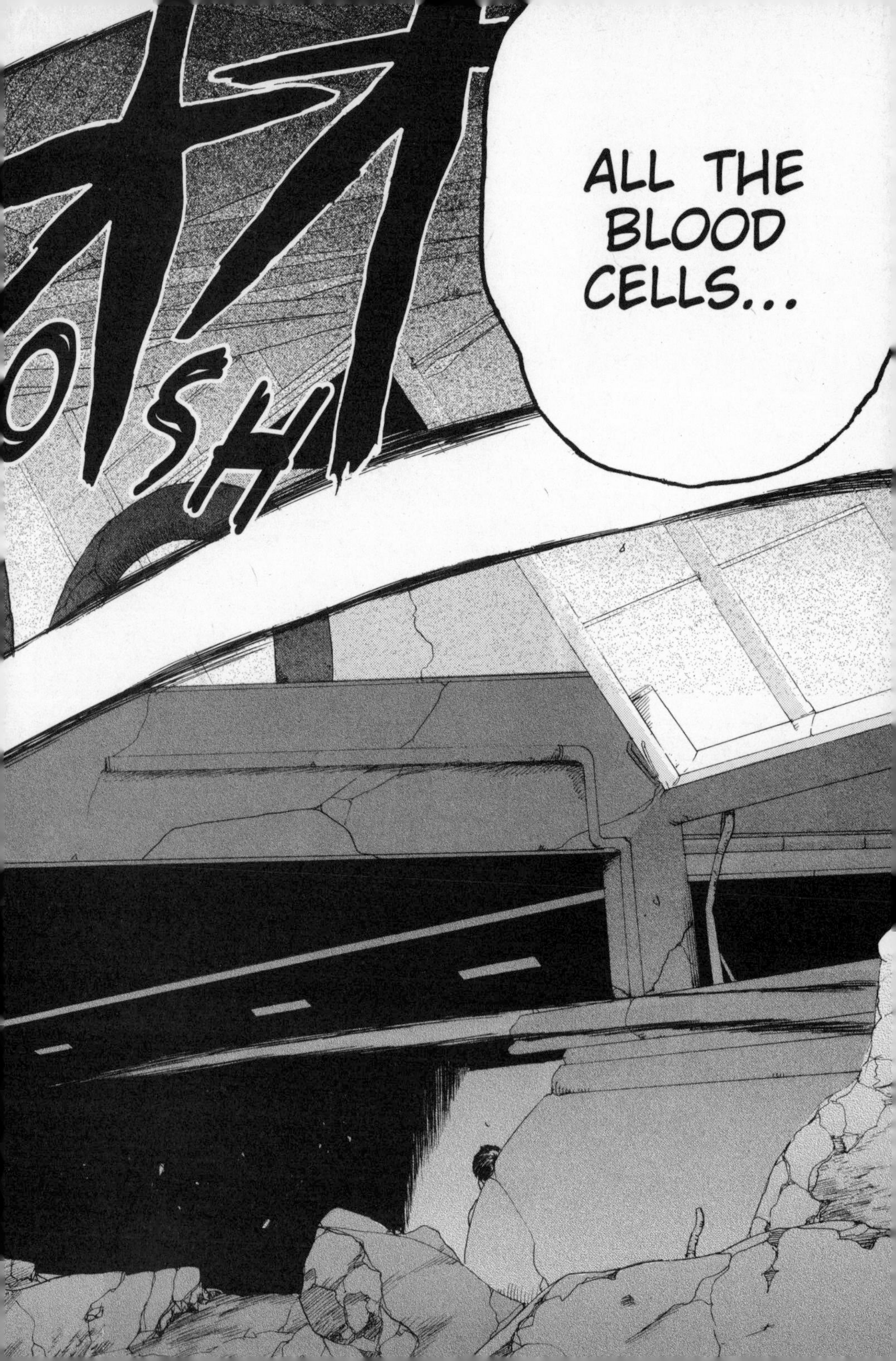
ALL THE BLOOD CELLS...
OSH

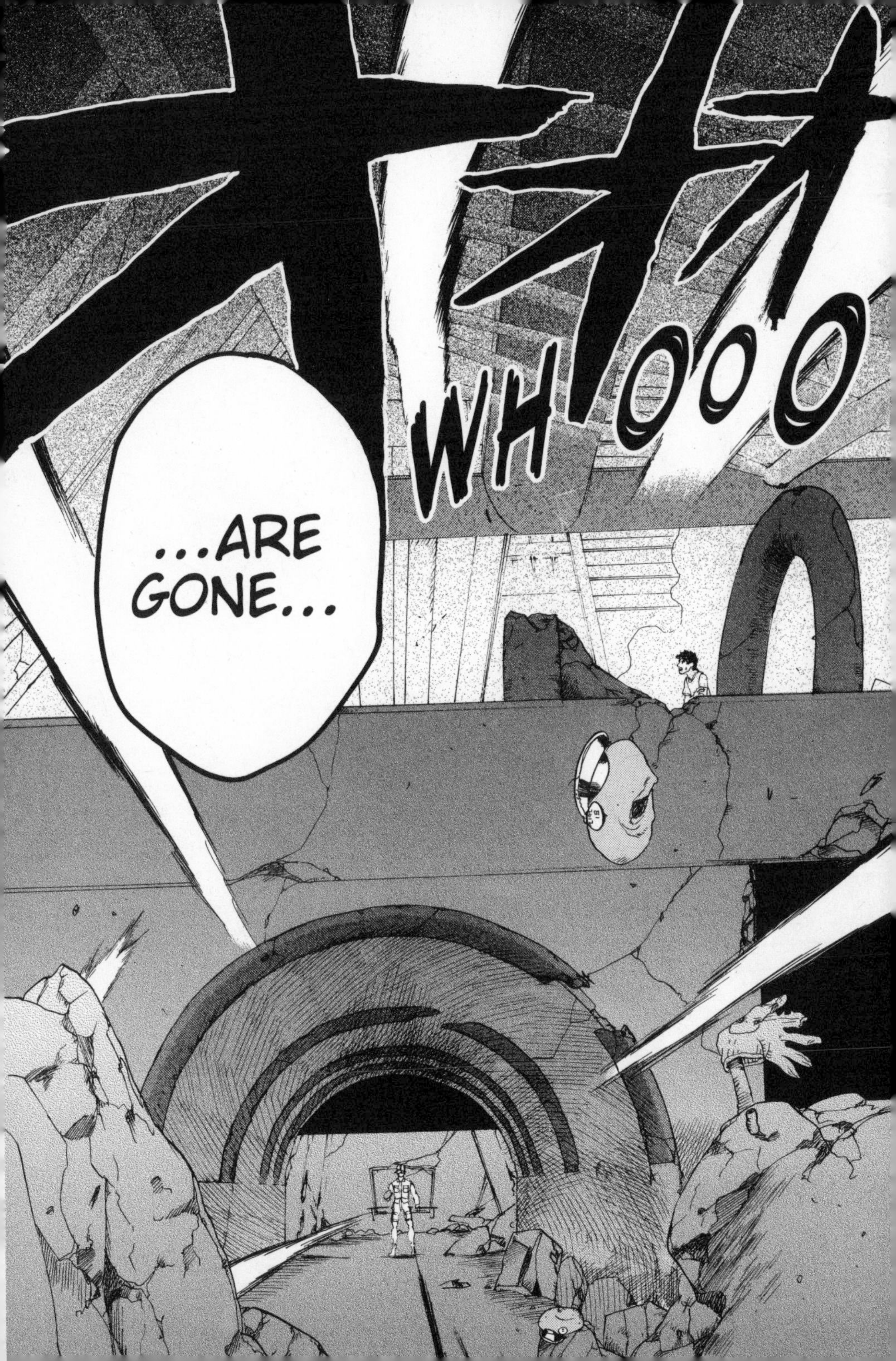
WHOOO
...ARE GONE...

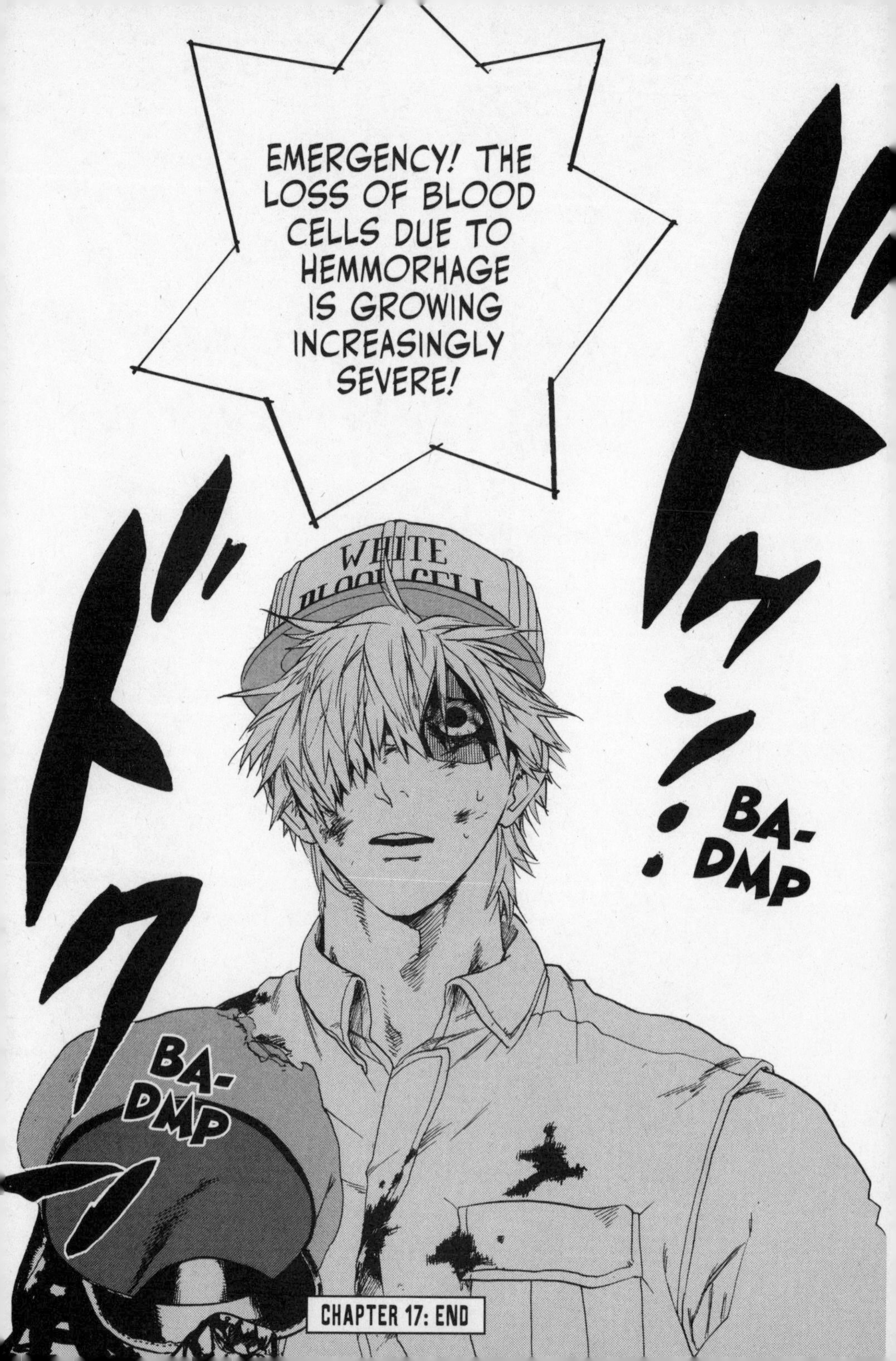
EMERGENCY! THE LOSS OF BLOOD CELLS DUE TO HEMMORHAGE IS GROWING INCREASINGLY SEVERE!
WHITE
BA-DMP
BA-DMP
CHAPTER 17: END

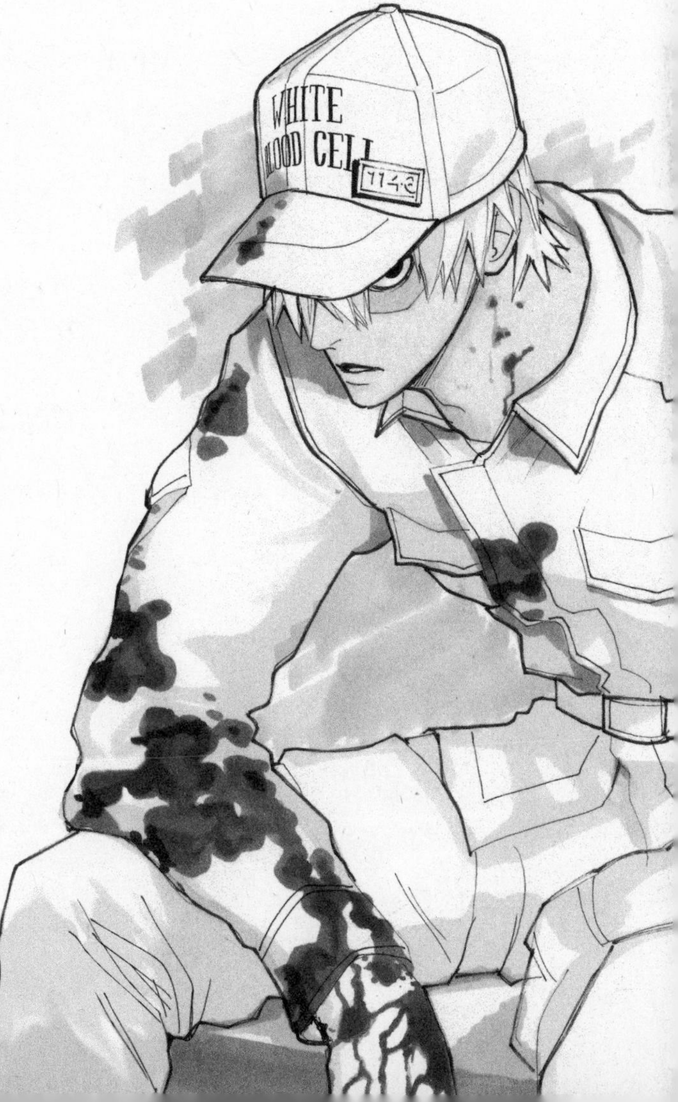
WHITE
BLOOD CELL
1146

Cells at Work!
はたらく細胞

CHAPTER 18: HYPOVOLEMIC SHOCK (PART III)

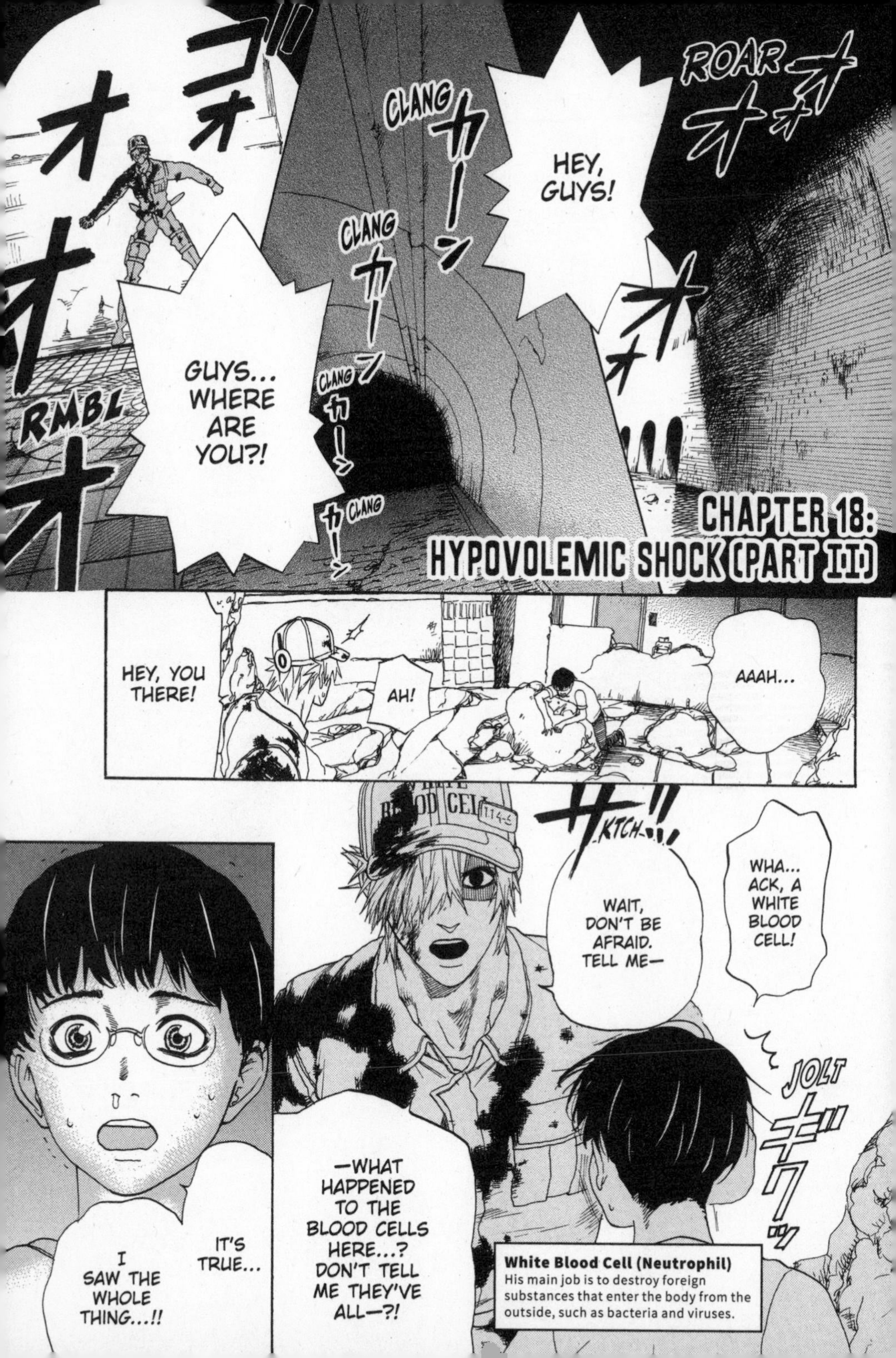
ROAR
HEY, GUYS!
CLANG
CLANG
CLANG
CLANG
GUYS... WHERE ARE YOU?!
RMBL
AAAH...
AH!
HEY, YOU THERE!
KTCH!!
WHA... ACK, A WHITE BLOOD CELL!
WAIT, DON'T BE AFRAID. TELL ME—
JOLT
—WHAT HAPPENED TO THE BLOOD CELLS HERE...? DON'T TELL ME THEY'VE ALL—?!
IT'S TRUE...
I SAW THE WHOLE THING...!!
White Blood Cell (Neutrophil)
His main job is to destroy foreign substances that enter the body from the outside, such as bacteria and viruses.

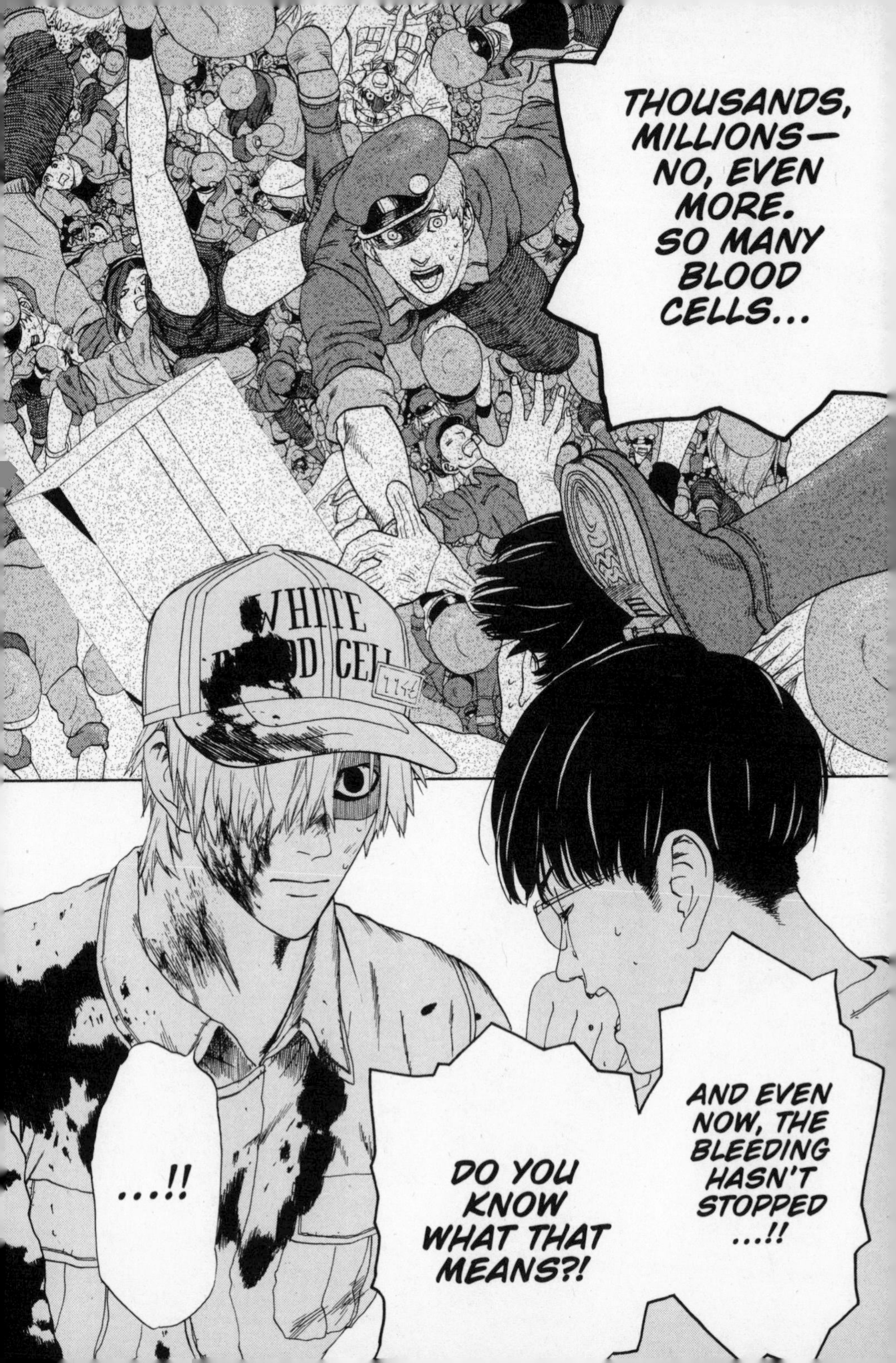
THOUSANDS, MILLIONS— NO, EVEN MORE. SO MANY BLOOD CELLS...
WHITE
AND EVEN NOW, THE BLEEDING HASN'T STOPPED ...!!
DO YOU KNOW WHAT THAT MEANS?!
...!!

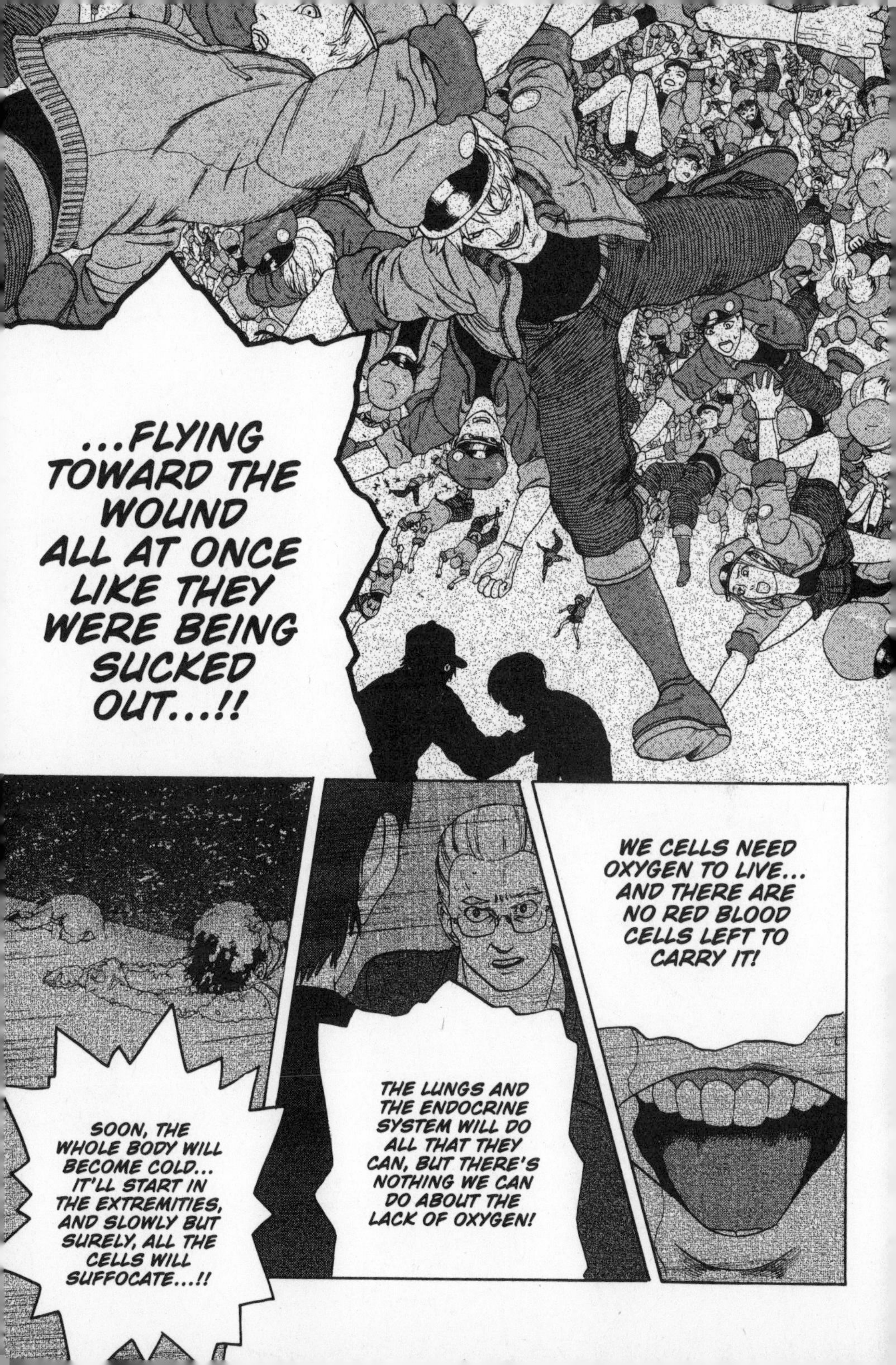
...FLYING TOWARD THE WOUND ALL AT ONCE LIKE THEY WERE BEING SUCKED OUT...!!
WE CELLS NEED OXYGEN TO LIVE... AND THERE ARE NO RED BLOOD CELLS LEFT TO CARRY IT!
THE LUNGS AND THE ENDOCRINE SYSTEM WILL DO ALL THAT THEY CAN, BUT THERE'S NOTHING WE CAN DO ABOUT THE LACK OF OXYGEN!
SOON, THE WHOLE BODY WILL BECOME COLD... IT'LL START IN THE EXTREMITIES, AND SLOWLY BUT SURELY, ALL THE CELLS WILL SUFFOCATE...!!

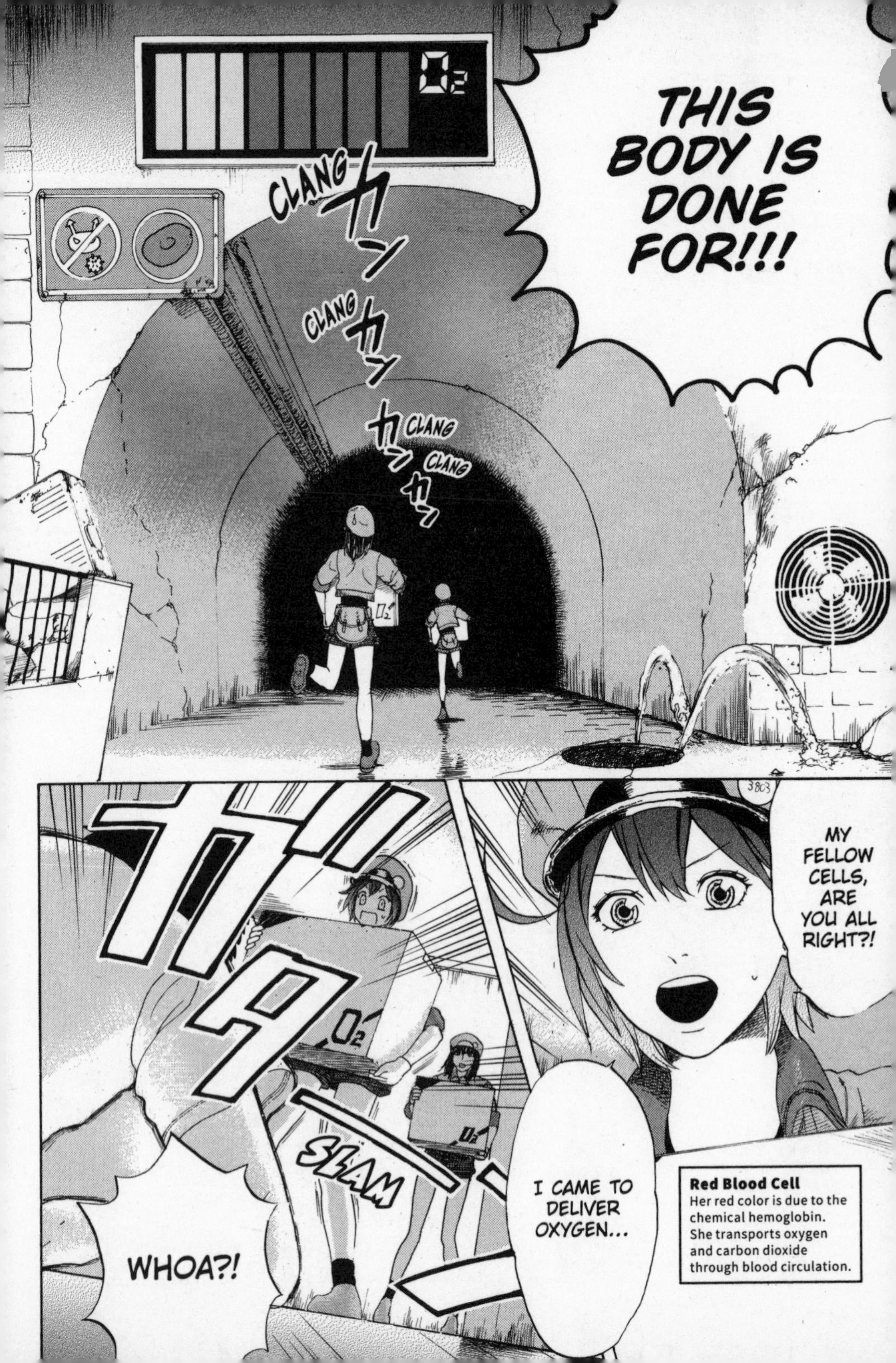
THIS BODY IS DONE FOR!!!
CLANG
CLANG
CLANG
CLANG
MY FELLOW CELLS, ARE YOU ALL RIGHT?!
I CAME TO DELIVER OXYGEN...
Red Blood Cell
Her red color is due to the chemical hemoglobin. She transports oxygen and carbon dioxide through blood circulation.
SLAM
WHOA?!

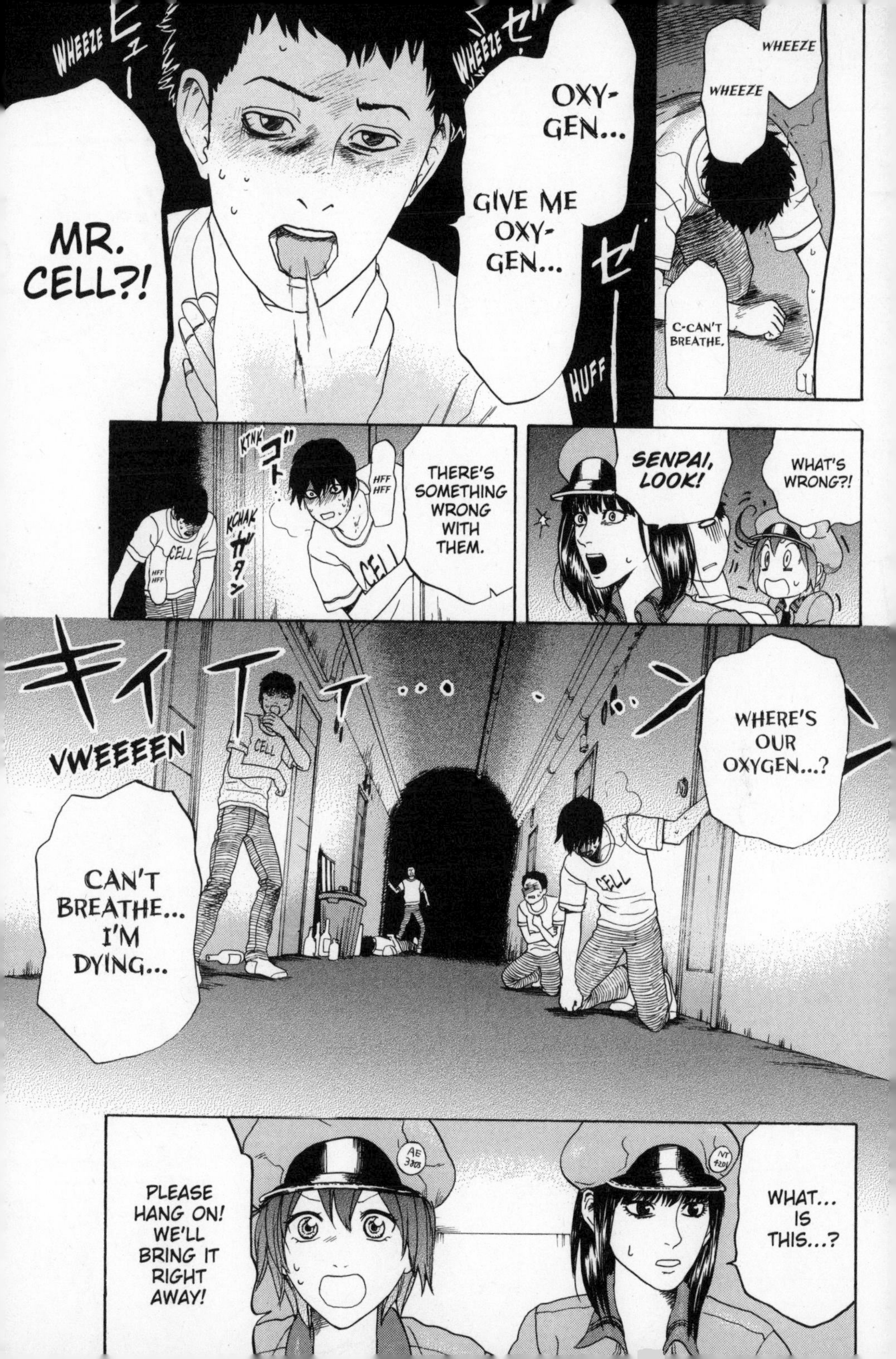
WHEEZE
WHEEZE
C-CAN'T BREATHE.
WHEEZE ゼ
OXY-GEN...
GIVE ME OXY-GEN...
ゼ
HUFF
WHEEZE ヒュー
MR. CELL?!
WHAT'S WRONG?!
SENPAI, LOOK!
THERE'S SOMETHING WRONG WITH THEM.
HFF HFF
KTNK ゴト
KCHAK ガタン
HFF HFF
WHERE'S OUR OXYGEN...?
キイイ・・・・ン
VWEEEEEN
CAN'T BREATHE... I'M DYING...
NT 4201
WHAT... IS THIS...?
AE 3803
PLEASE HANG ON! WE'LL BRING IT RIGHT AWAY!

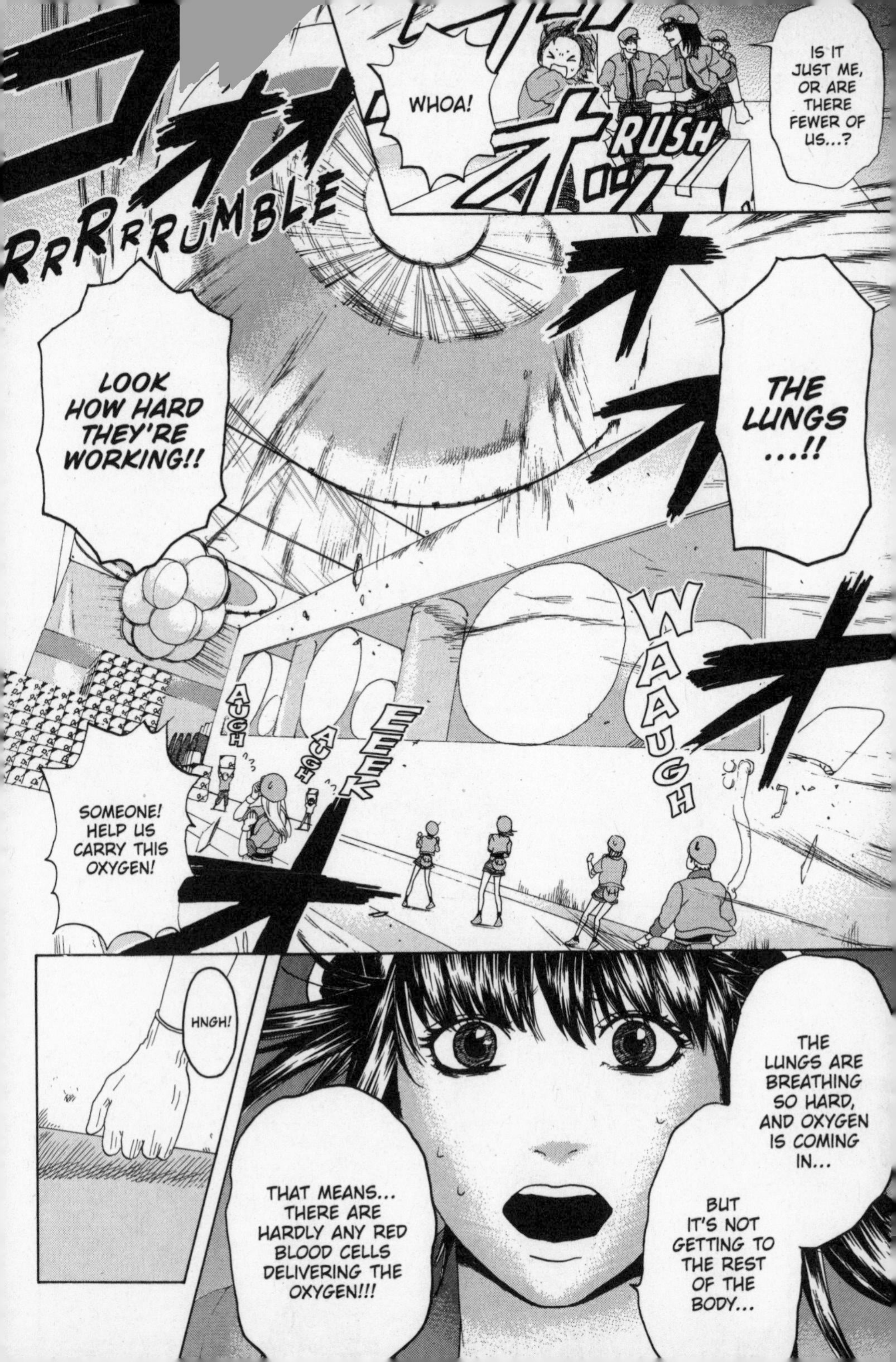
IS IT JUST ME, OR ARE THERE FEWER OF US...?
RUSH
WHOA!
RRRRRUMBLE
THE LUNGS...!!
LOOK HOW HARD THEY'RE WORKING!!
WAAAUGH
EEEK
AUGH
AUGH
SOMEONE! HELP US CARRY THIS OXYGEN!
THE LUNGS ARE BREATHING SO HARD, AND OXYGEN IS COMING IN...
BUT IT'S NOT GETTING TO THE REST OF THE BODY...
THAT MEANS... THERE ARE HARDLY ANY RED BLOOD CELLS DELIVERING THE OXYGEN!!!
HNGH!

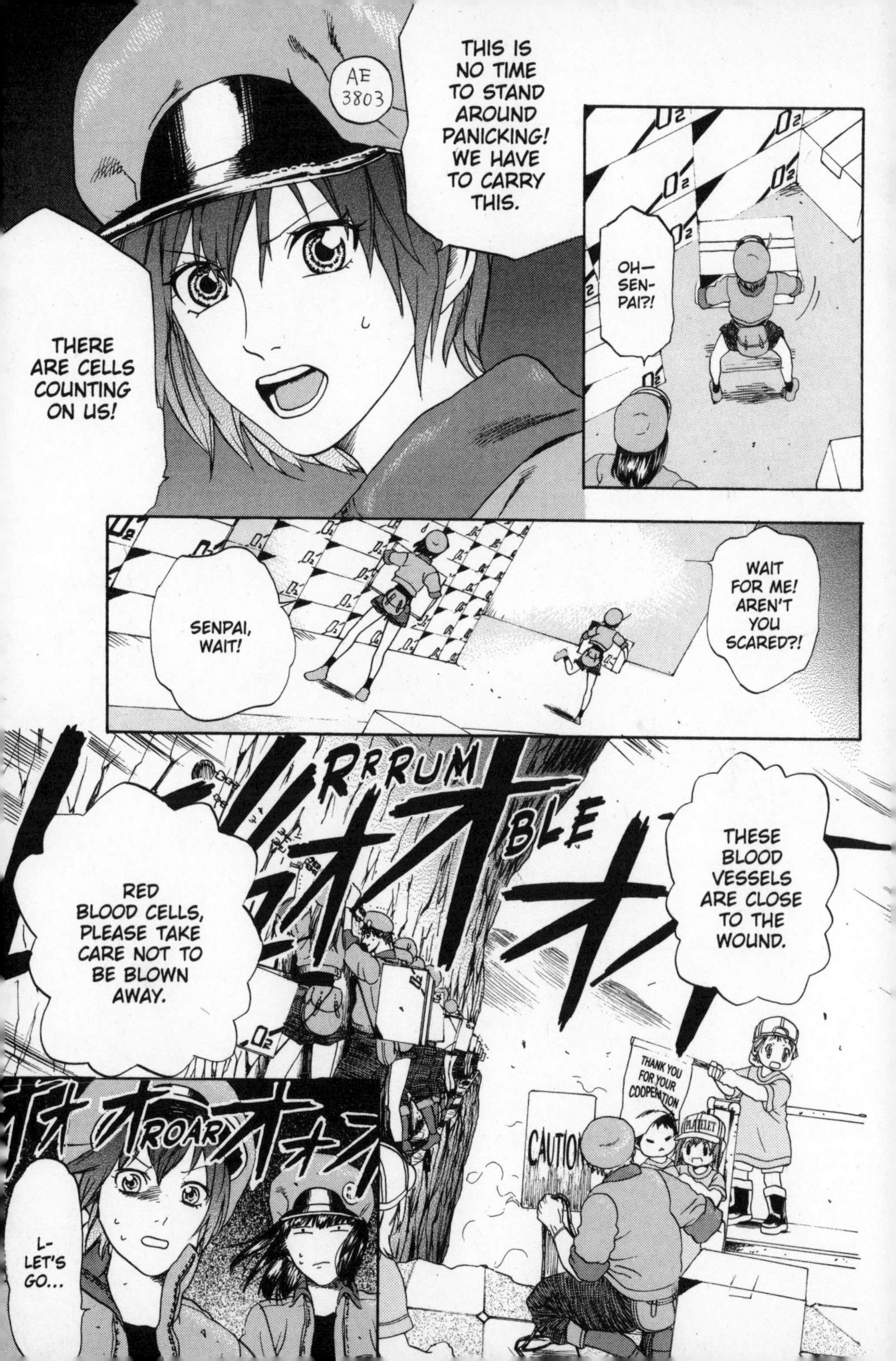
OH—
SENPAI?!
AE
3803
THIS IS NO TIME TO STAND AROUND PANICKING! WE HAVE TO CARRY THIS.
THERE ARE CELLS COUNTING ON US!
WAIT FOR ME! AREN'T YOU SCARED?!
SENPAI, WAIT!
RRRUMBLE
THESE BLOOD VESSELS ARE CLOSE TO THE WOUND.
RED BLOOD CELLS, PLEASE TAKE CARE NOT TO BE BLOWN AWAY.
THANK YOU FOR YOUR COOPERATION
PLATELET
CAUTIO
ROAR
L- LET'S GO...

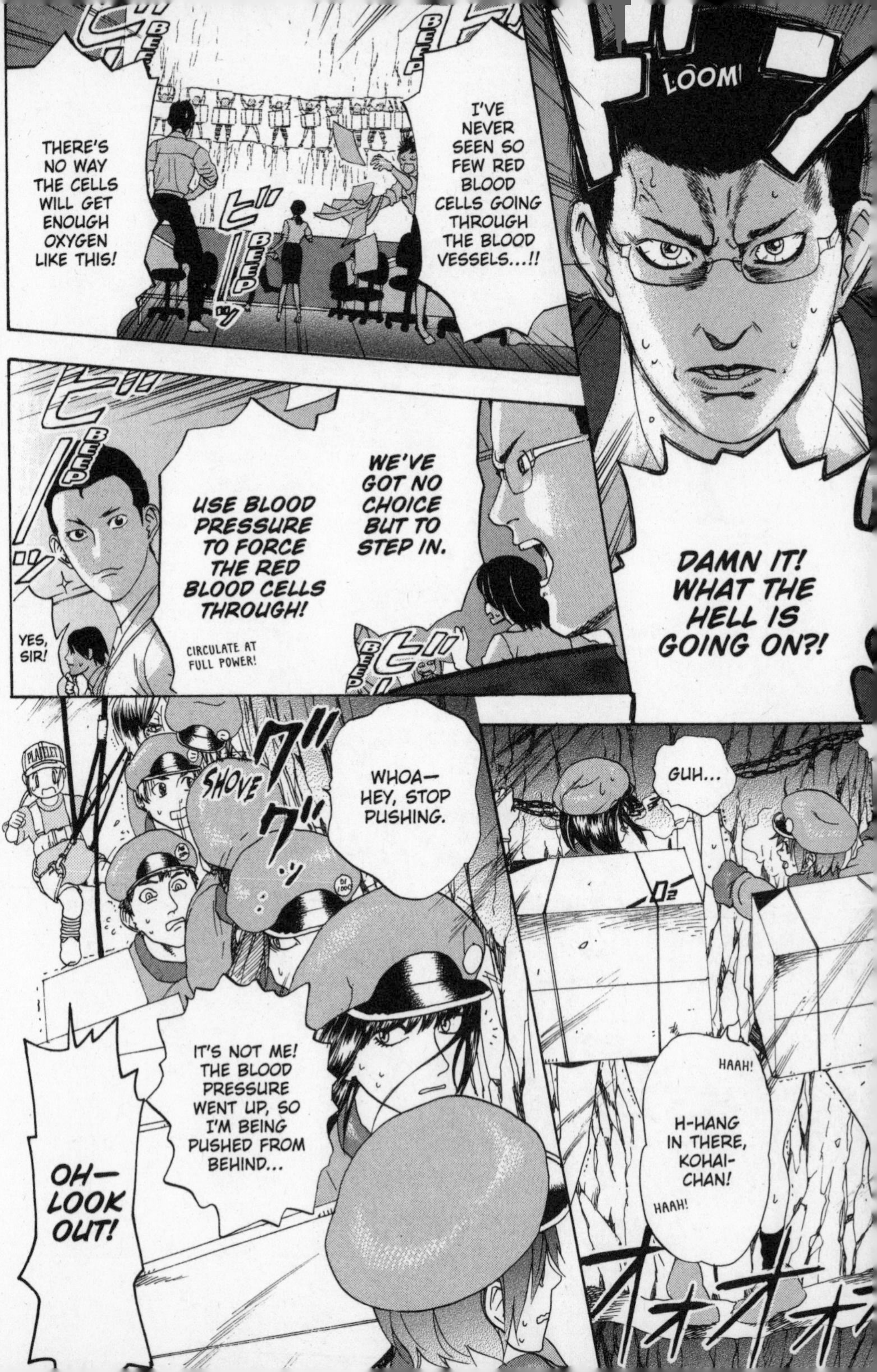

LOOM
DAMN IT! WHAT THE HELL IS GOING ON?!
BEEP
BEEP
I'VE NEVER SEEN SO FEW RED BLOOD CELLS GOING THROUGH THE BLOOD VESSELS...!!
THERE'S NO WAY THE CELLS WILL GET ENOUGH OXYGEN LIKE THIS!
BEEP
BEEP
WE'VE GOT NO CHOICE BUT TO STEP IN.
USE BLOOD PRESSURE TO FORCE THE RED BLOOD CELLS THROUGH!
BEEP
CIRCULATE AT FULL POWER!
YES, SIR!
GUH...
HAAH!
H-HANG IN THERE, KOHAI-CHAN!
HAAH!
WHOA— HEY, STOP PUSHING.
SHOVE
IT'S NOT ME! THE BLOOD PRESSURE WENT UP, SO I'M BEING PUSHED FROM BEHIND...
OH— LOOK OUT!

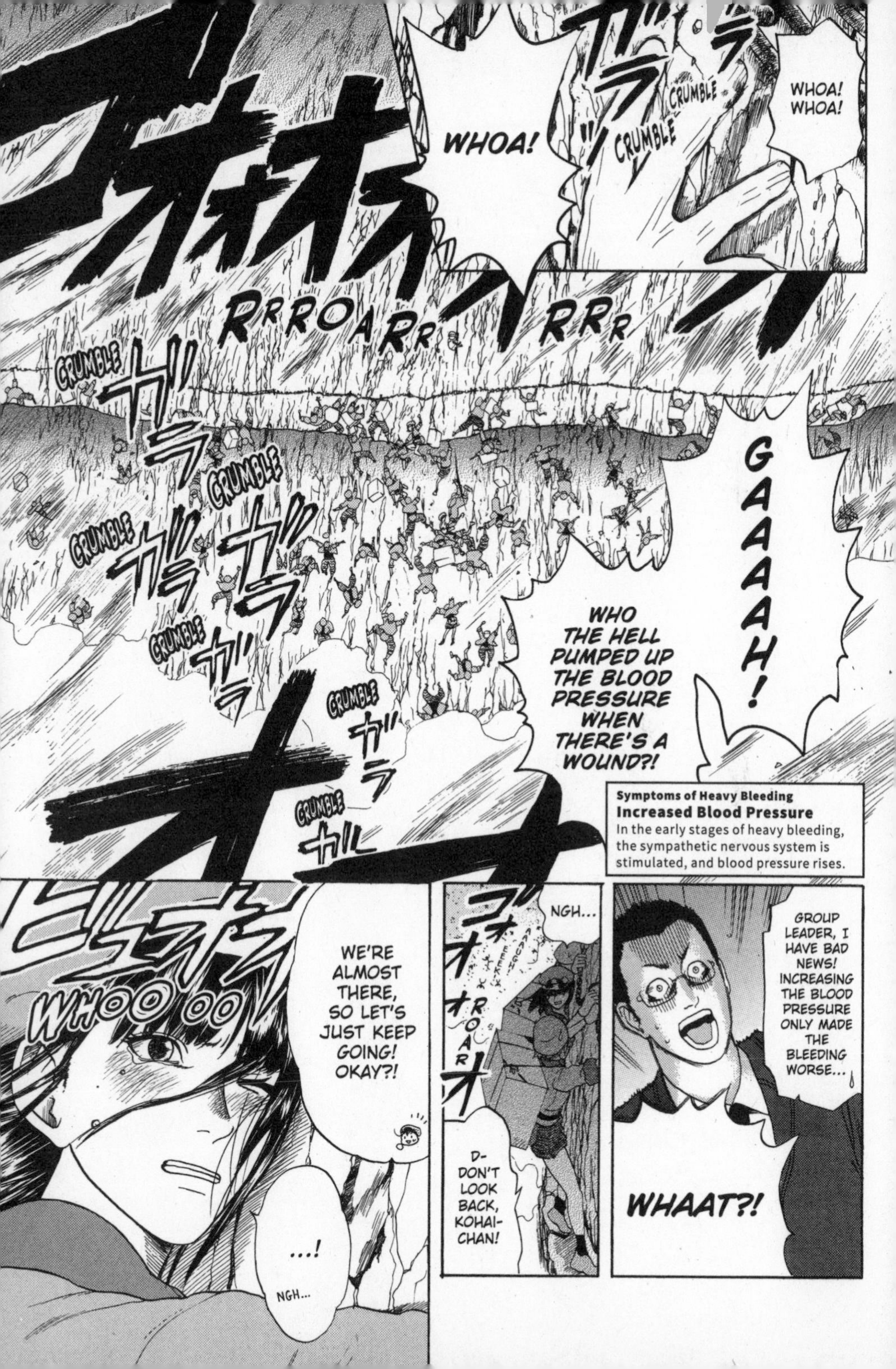
WHOA! WHOA!
CRUMBLE
CRUMBLE
WHOA!
RRROARRR RRRR
GAAAAAH!
WHO THE HELL PUMPED UP THE BLOOD PRESSURE WHEN THERE'S A WOUND?!
CRUMBLE
CRUMBLE
CRUMBLE
CRUMBLE
CRUMBLE
CRUMBLE
Symptoms of Heavy Bleeding
Increased Blood Pressure
In the early stages of heavy bleeding, the sympathetic nervous system is stimulated, and blood pressure rises.
GROUP LEADER, I HAVE BAD NEWS! INCREASING THE BLOOD PRESSURE ONLY MADE THE BLEEDING WORSE...
WHAAT?!
NGH...
ROAR
D-DON'T LOOK BACK, KOHAI-CHAN!
WHOOOOO
WE'RE ALMOST THERE, SO LET'S JUST KEEP GOING! OKAY?!
...!
NGH...

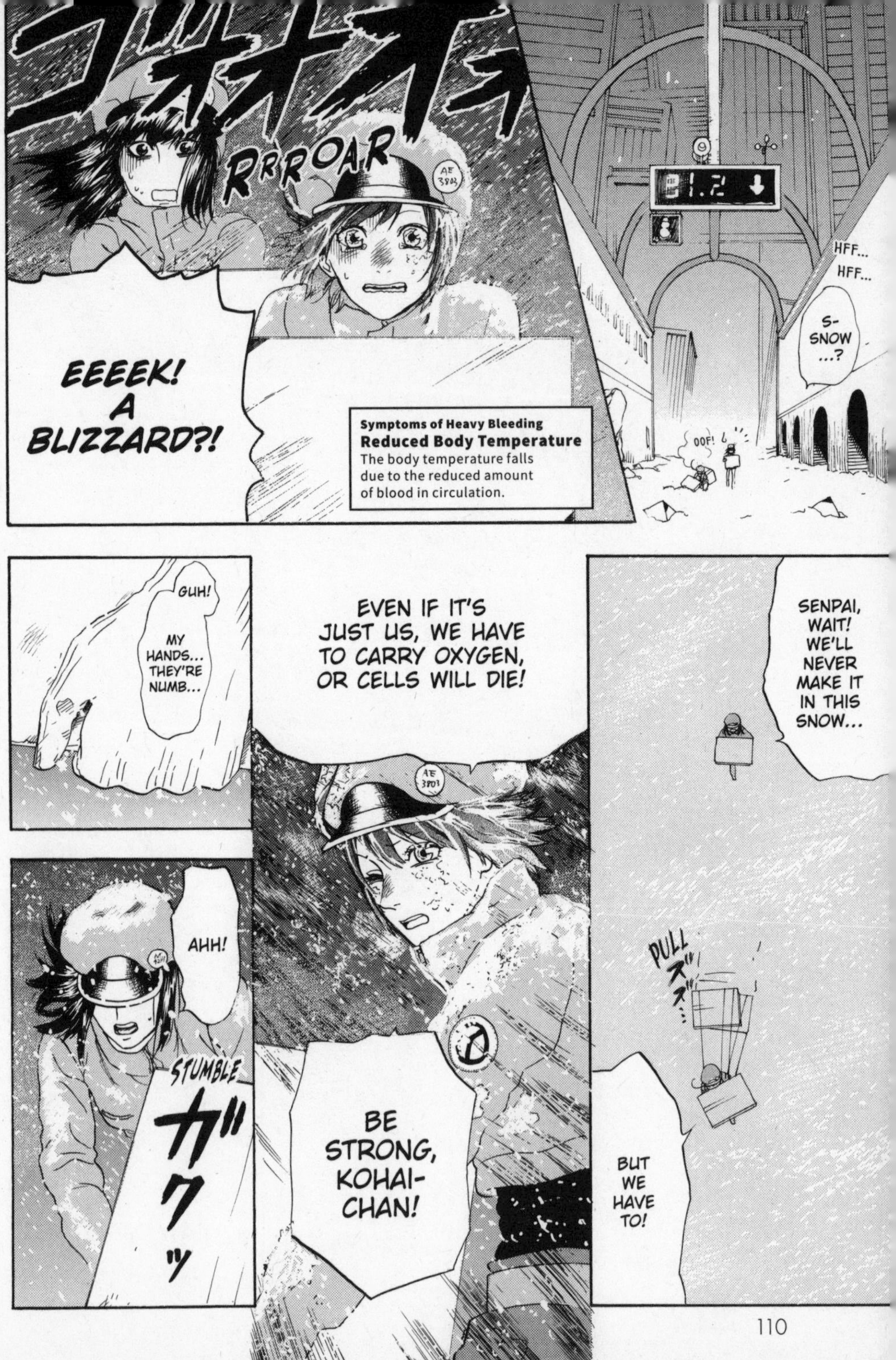
HFF...
HFF...
S-SNOW...?
OOF!
RRROAR
EEEEK! A BLIZZARD?!
Symptoms of Heavy Bleeding
Reduced Body Temperature
The body temperature falls due to the reduced amount of blood in circulation.
SENPAI, WAIT! WE'LL NEVER MAKE IT IN THIS SNOW...
PULL
BUT WE HAVE TO!
EVEN IF IT'S JUST US, WE HAVE TO CARRY OXYGEN, OR CELLS WILL DIE!
BE STRONG, KOHAI-CHAN!
GUH!
MY HANDS... THEY'RE NUMB...
AHH!
STUMBLE

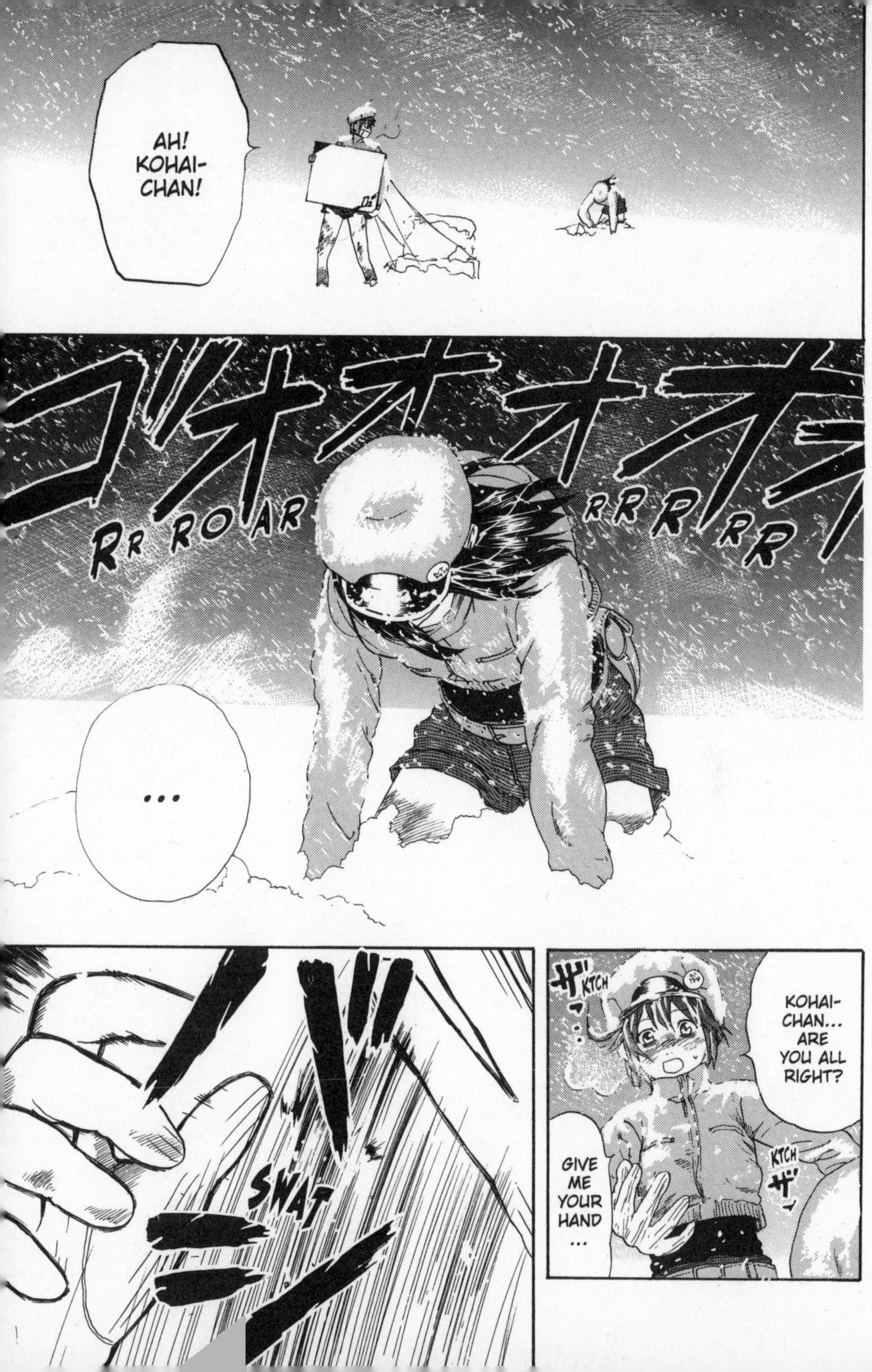
AH! KOHAI-CHAN!
RR ROAR RRRRRRR
...
KTCH
KOHAI-CHAN... ARE YOU ALL RIGHT?
GIVE ME YOUR HAND ...
KTCH
SWAT

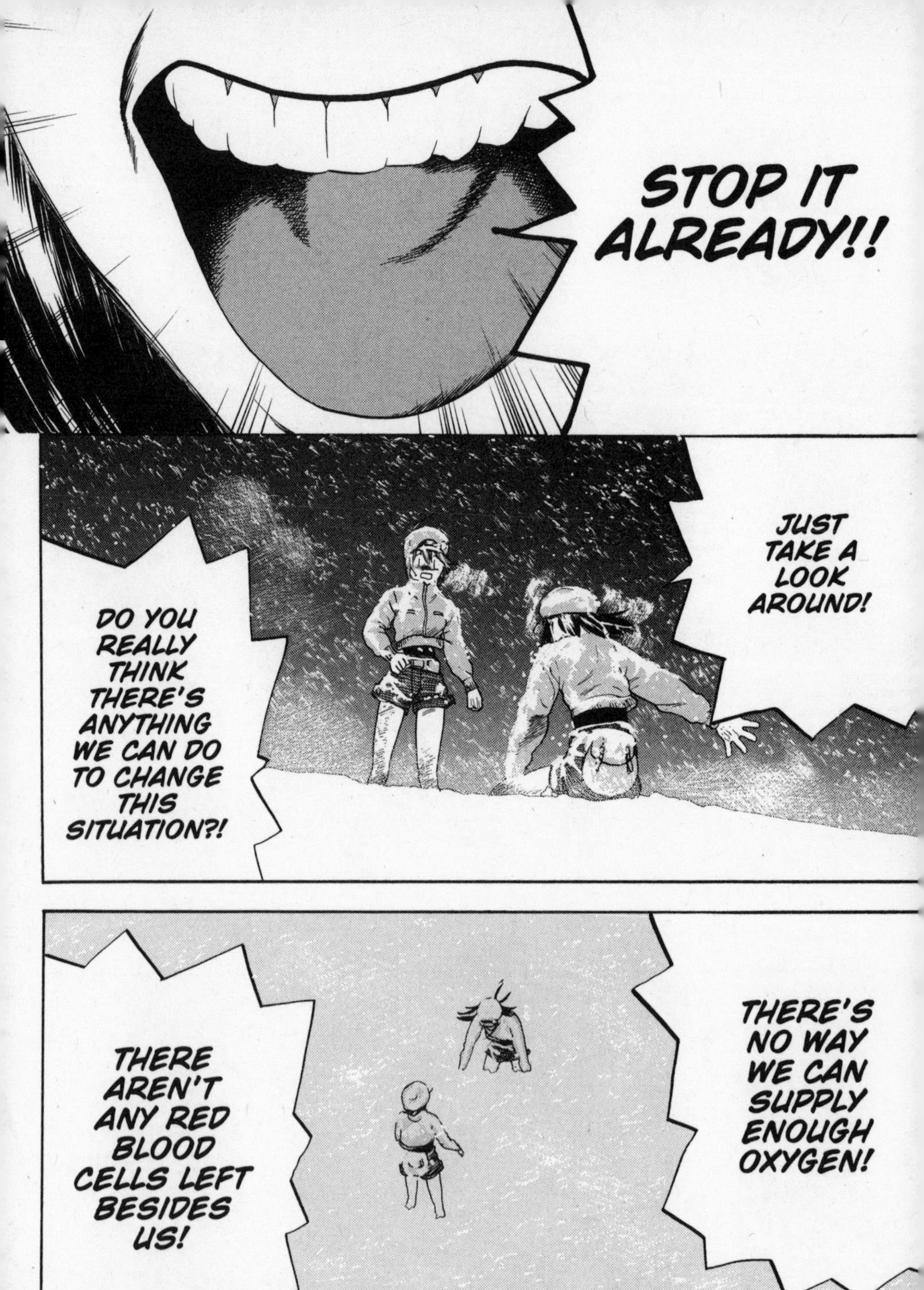
STOP IT ALREADY!!
JUST TAKE A LOOK AROUND!
DO YOU REALLY THINK THERE'S ANYTHING WE CAN DO TO CHANGE THIS SITUATION?!
THERE'S NO WAY WE CAN SUPPLY ENOUGH OXYGEN!
THERE AREN'T ANY RED BLOOD CELLS LEFT BESIDES US!

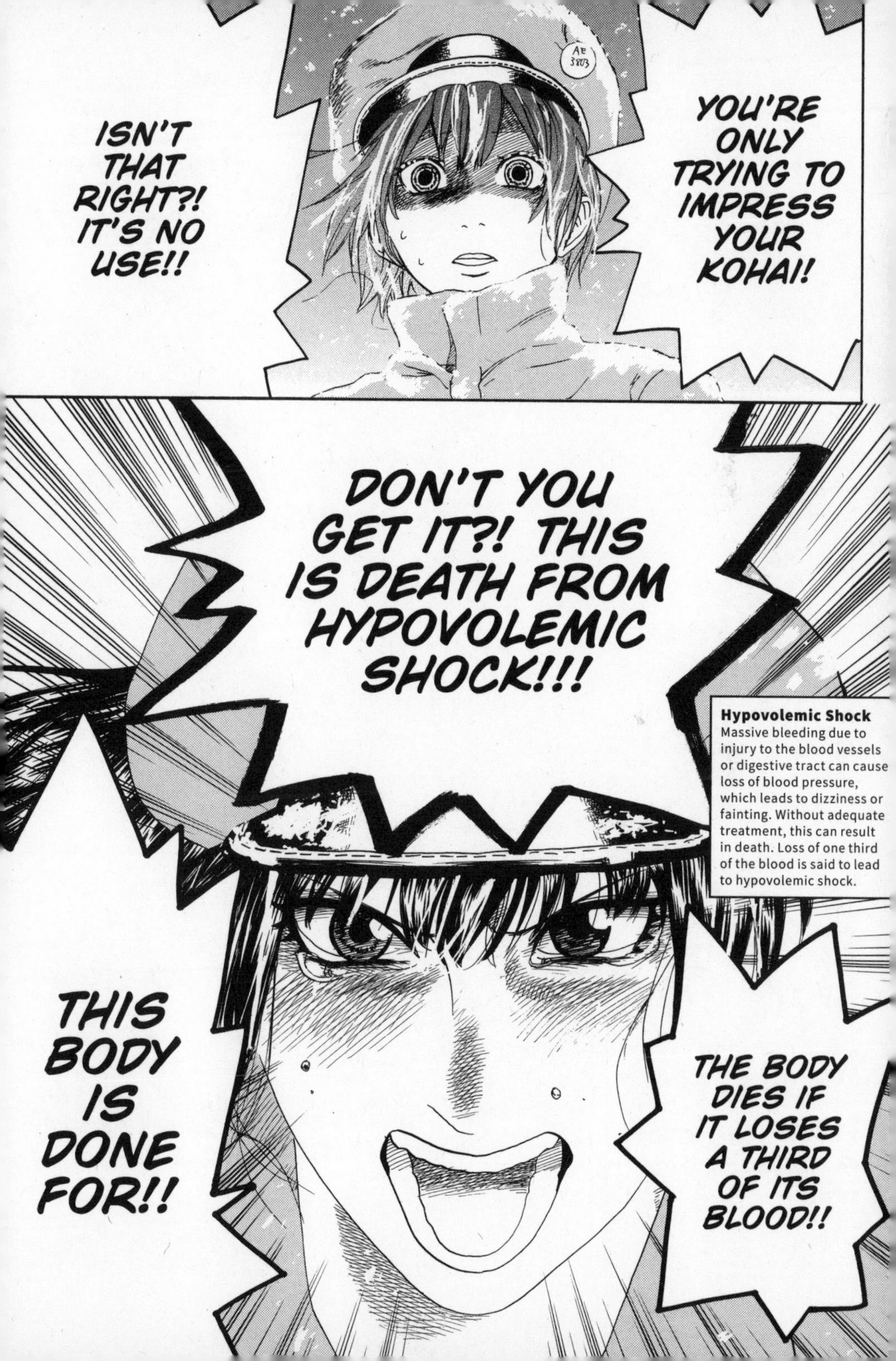
YOU'RE ONLY TRYING TO IMPRESS YOUR KOHAI!
ISN'T THAT RIGHT?! IT'S NO USE!!
DON'T YOU GET IT?! THIS IS DEATH FROM HYPOVOLEMIC SHOCK!!!
Hypovolemic Shock
Massive bleeding due to injury to the blood vessels or digestive tract can cause loss of blood pressure, which leads to dizziness or fainting. Without adequate treatment, this can result in death. Loss of one third of the blood is said to lead to hypovolemic shock.
THE BODY DIES IF IT LOSES A THIRD OF ITS BLOOD!!
THIS BODY IS DONE FOR!!

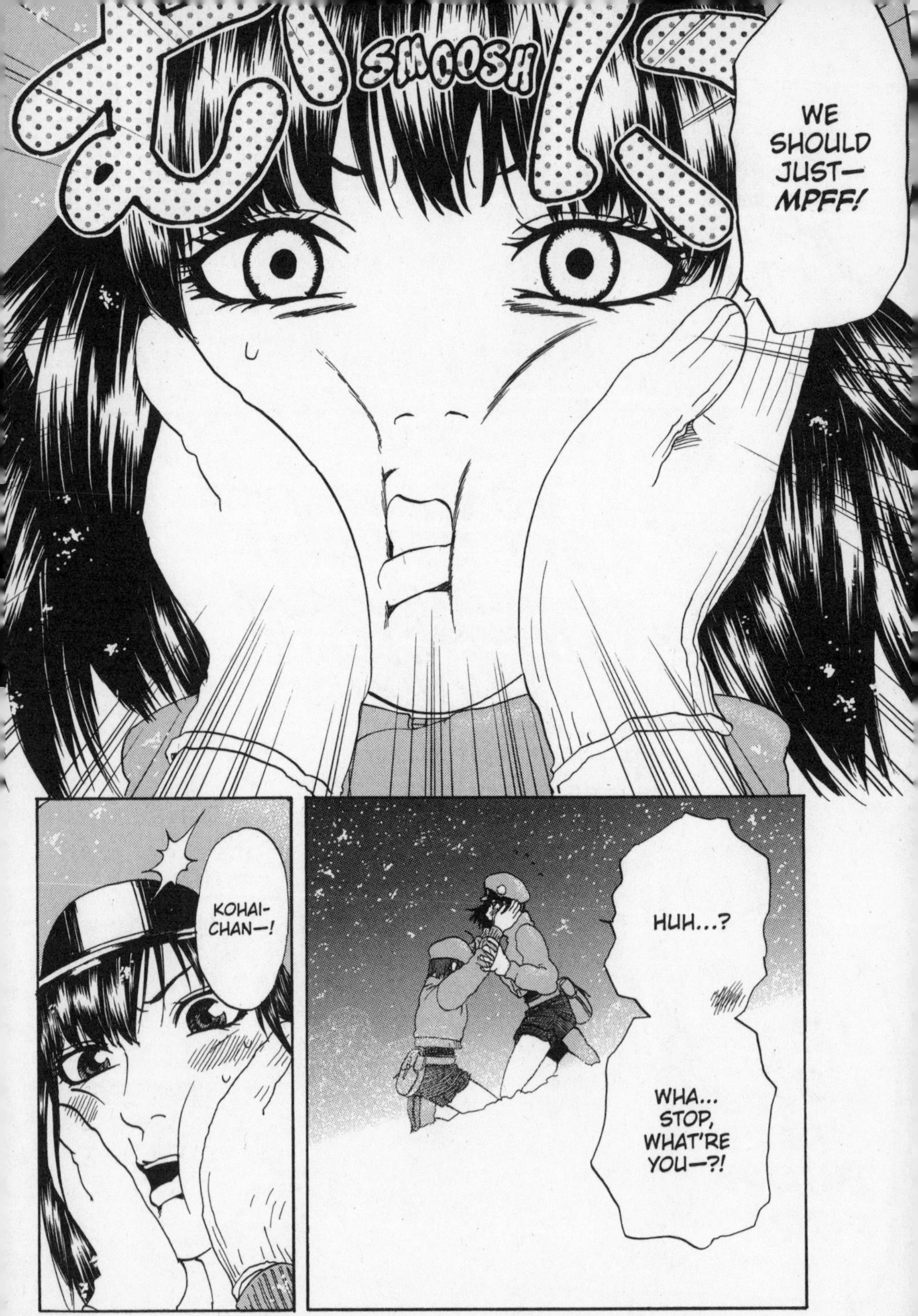
WE SHOULD JUST—MPFF!
SMOOSH
HUH...?
WHA... STOP, WHAT'RE YOU—?!
KOHAI-CHAN—!

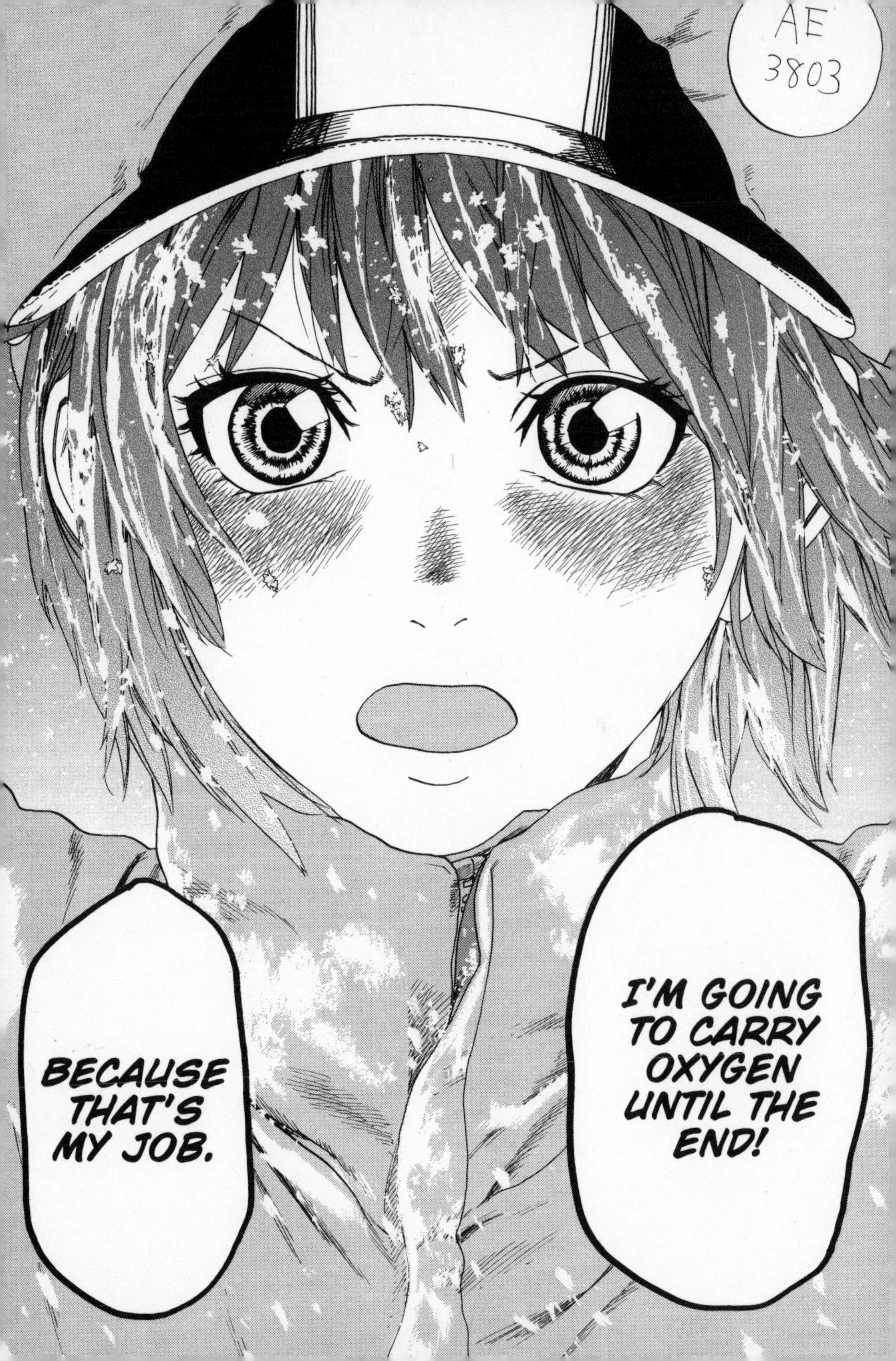
AE 3803
I'M GOING TO CARRY OXYGEN UNTIL THE END!
BECAUSE THAT'S MY JOB.

SENPAI,
WAIT...!
PLEASE—

STOP
THIS!

SEN-
PAI...

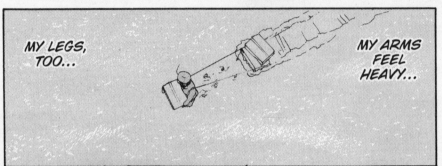

MY LEGS,
TOO...

MY ARMS
FEEL
HEAVY...

EVERYONE'S...
WAITING
FOR ME...

I HAVE TO...
DELIVER THIS
OXYGEN...

AS
SOON AS
I CAN...

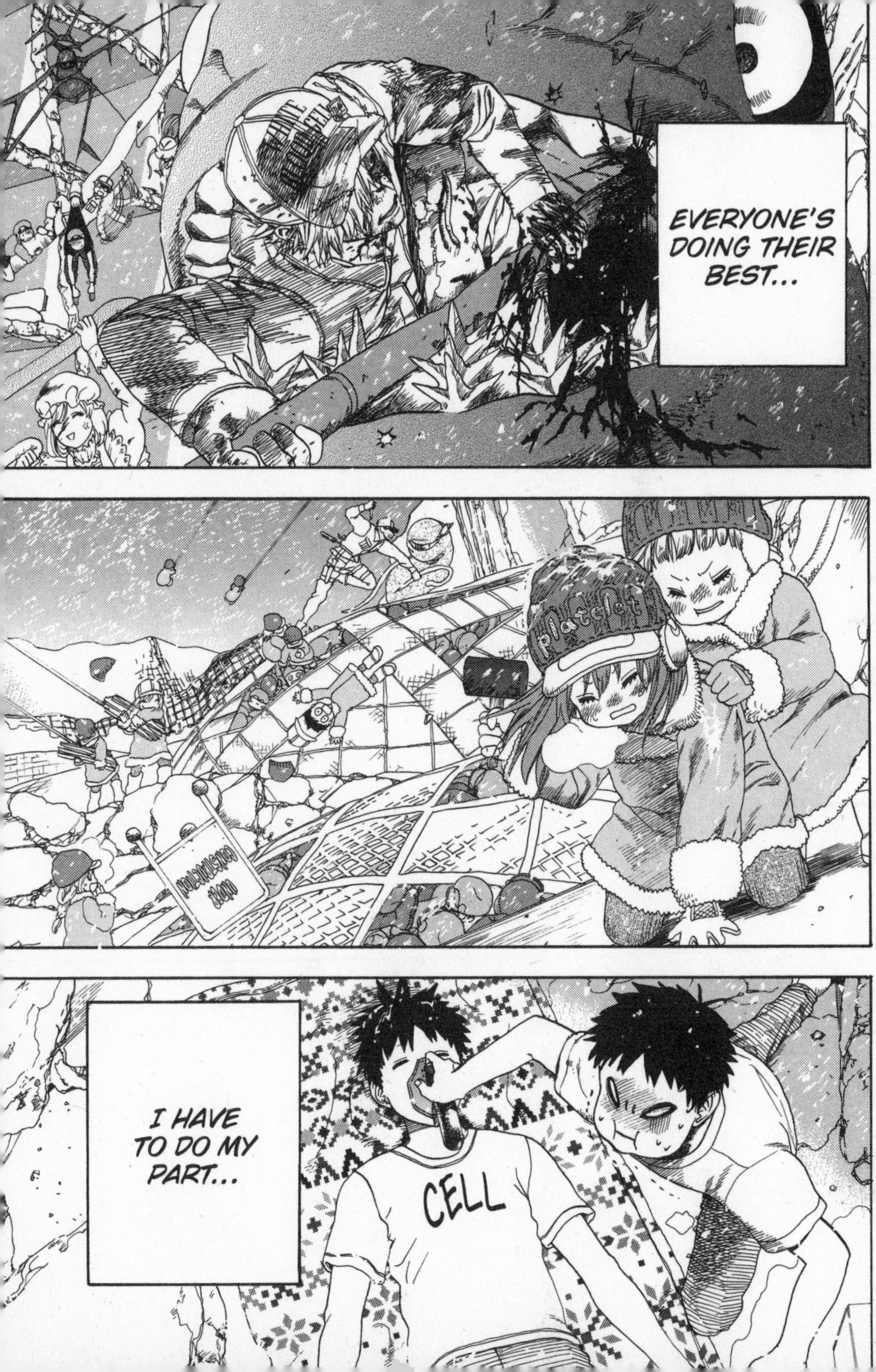
EVERYONE'S DOING THEIR BEST...
platelet
CONSTRUCTION ZONE
I HAVE TO DO MY PART...
CELL

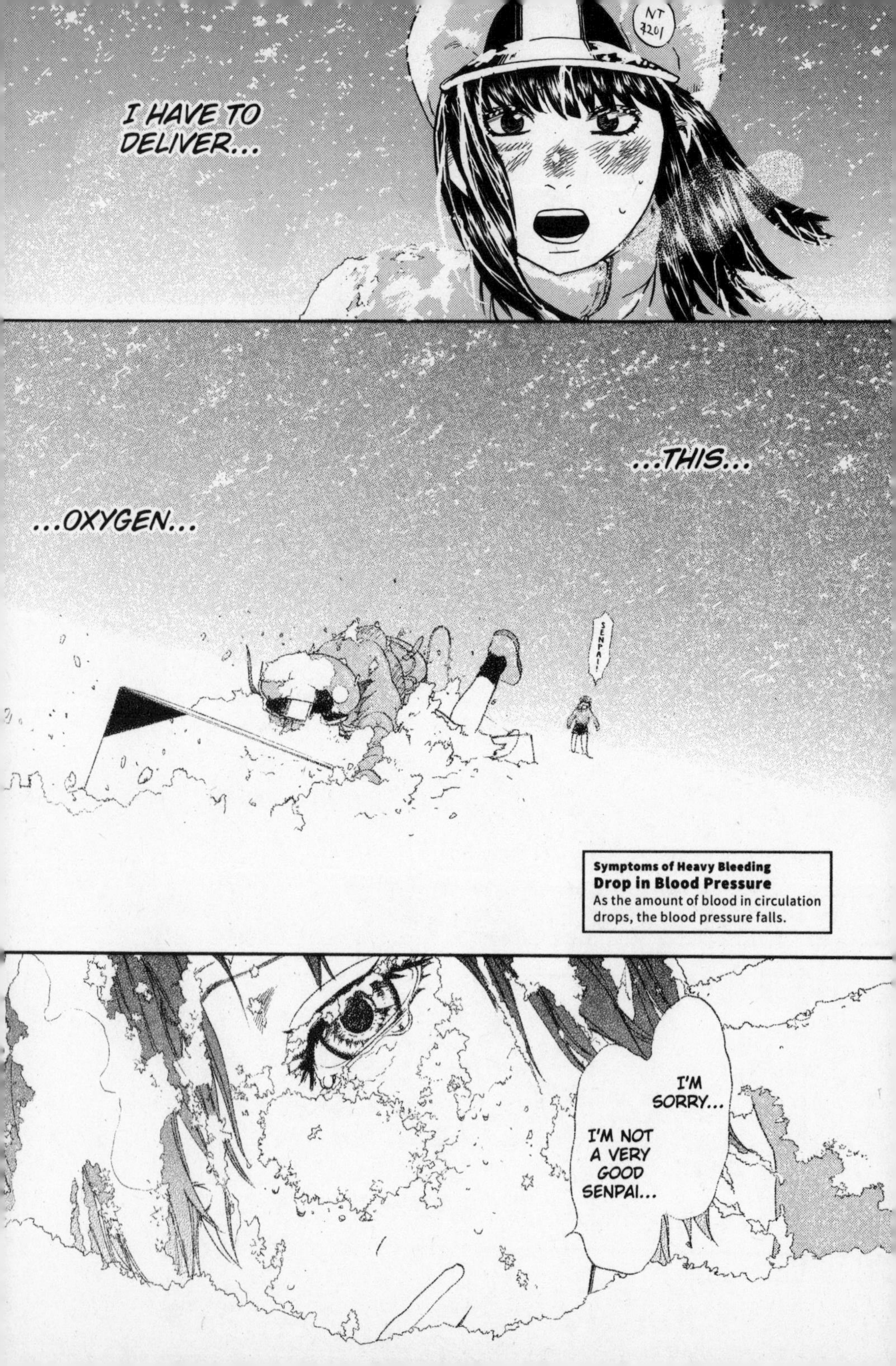
NT 7201
I HAVE TO DELIVER...
...THIS...
...OXYGEN...
SENPAI!
Symptoms of Heavy Bleeding
Drop in Blood Pressure
As the amount of blood in circulation drops, the blood pressure falls.
I'M SORRY...
I'M NOT A VERY GOOD SENPAI...

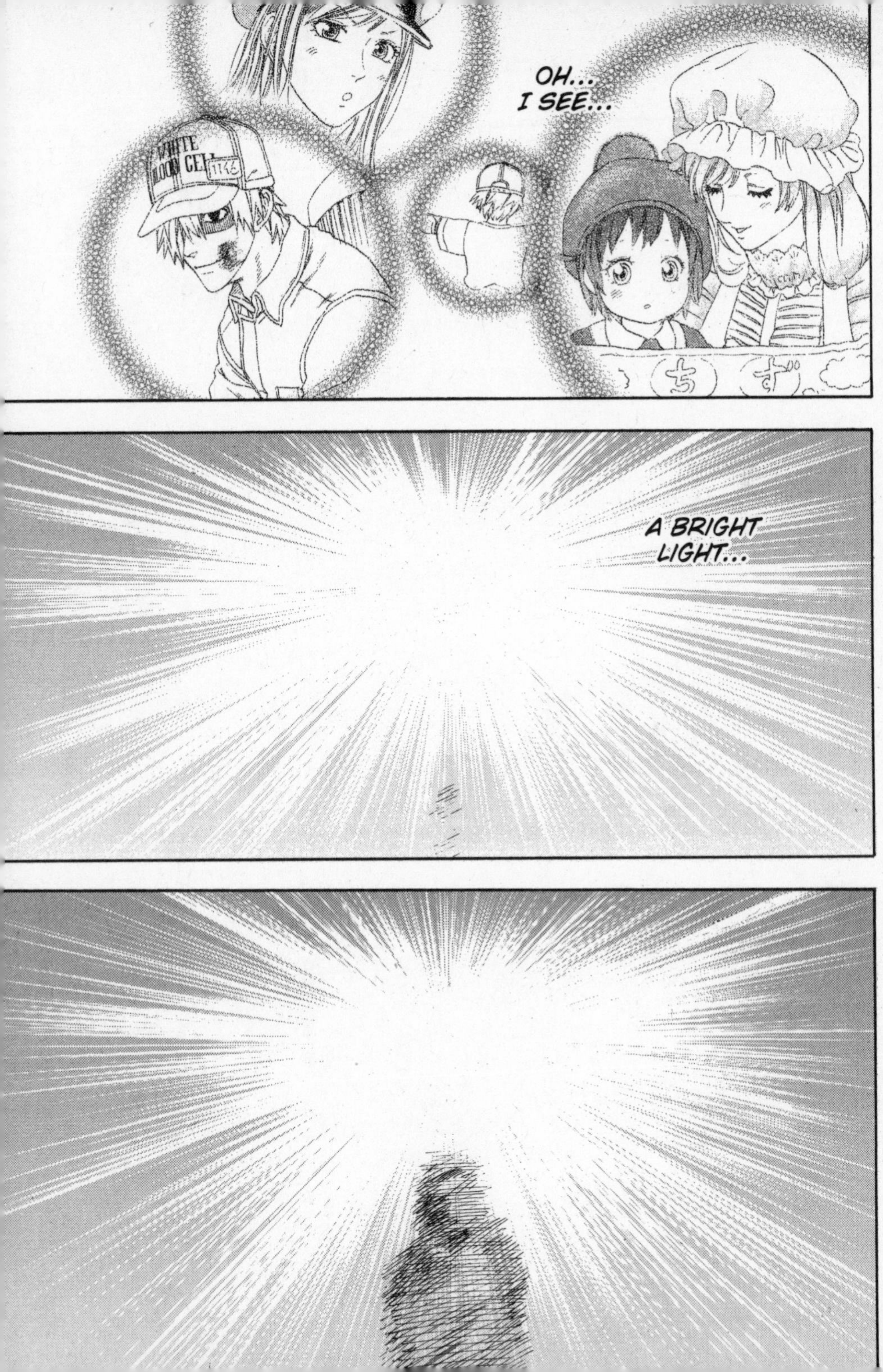
OH... I SEE...
A BRIGHT LIGHT...

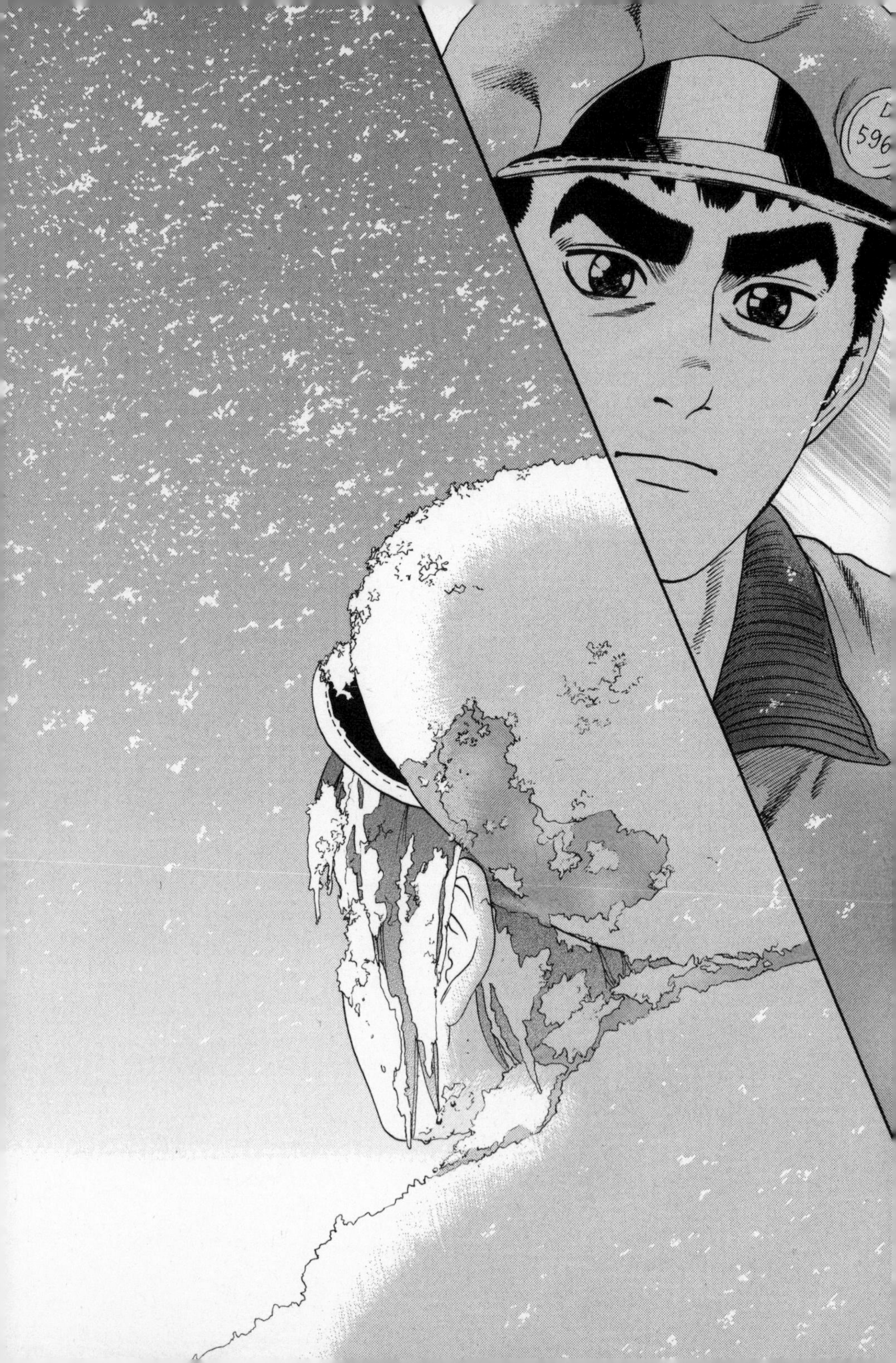
D
596

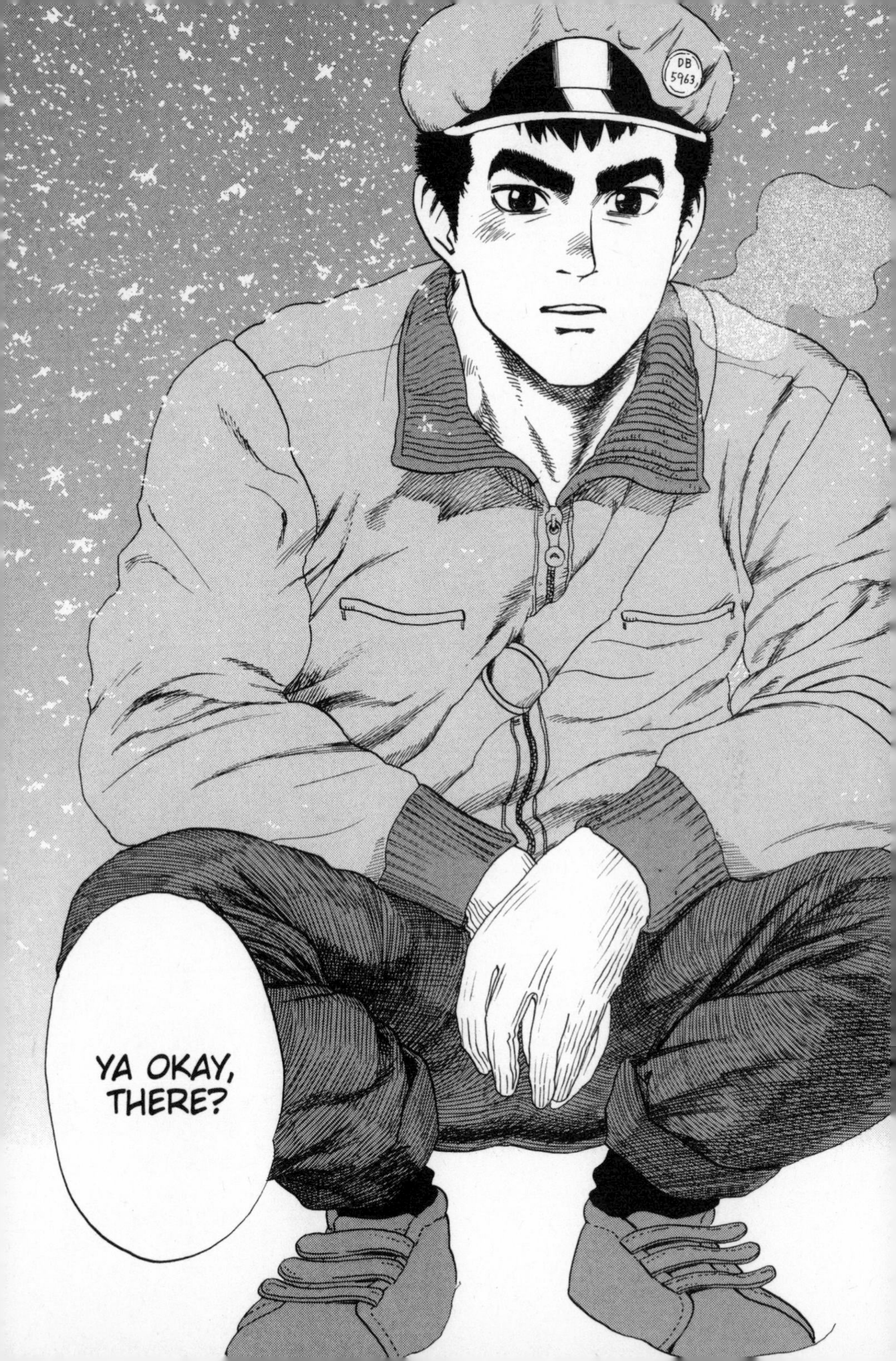
DB 5963
YA OKAY, THERE?

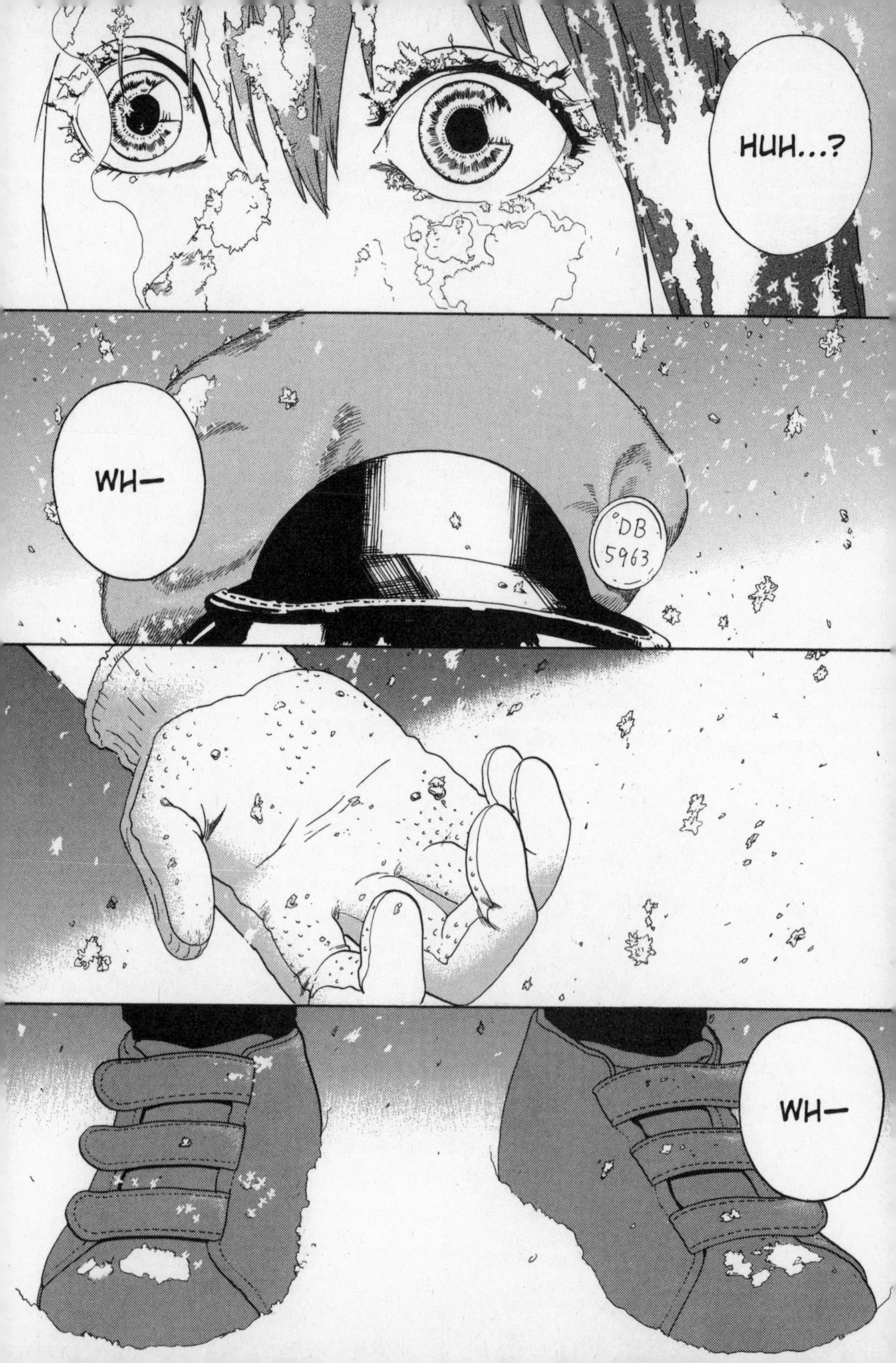
HUH...?
WH—
DB 5963
WH—

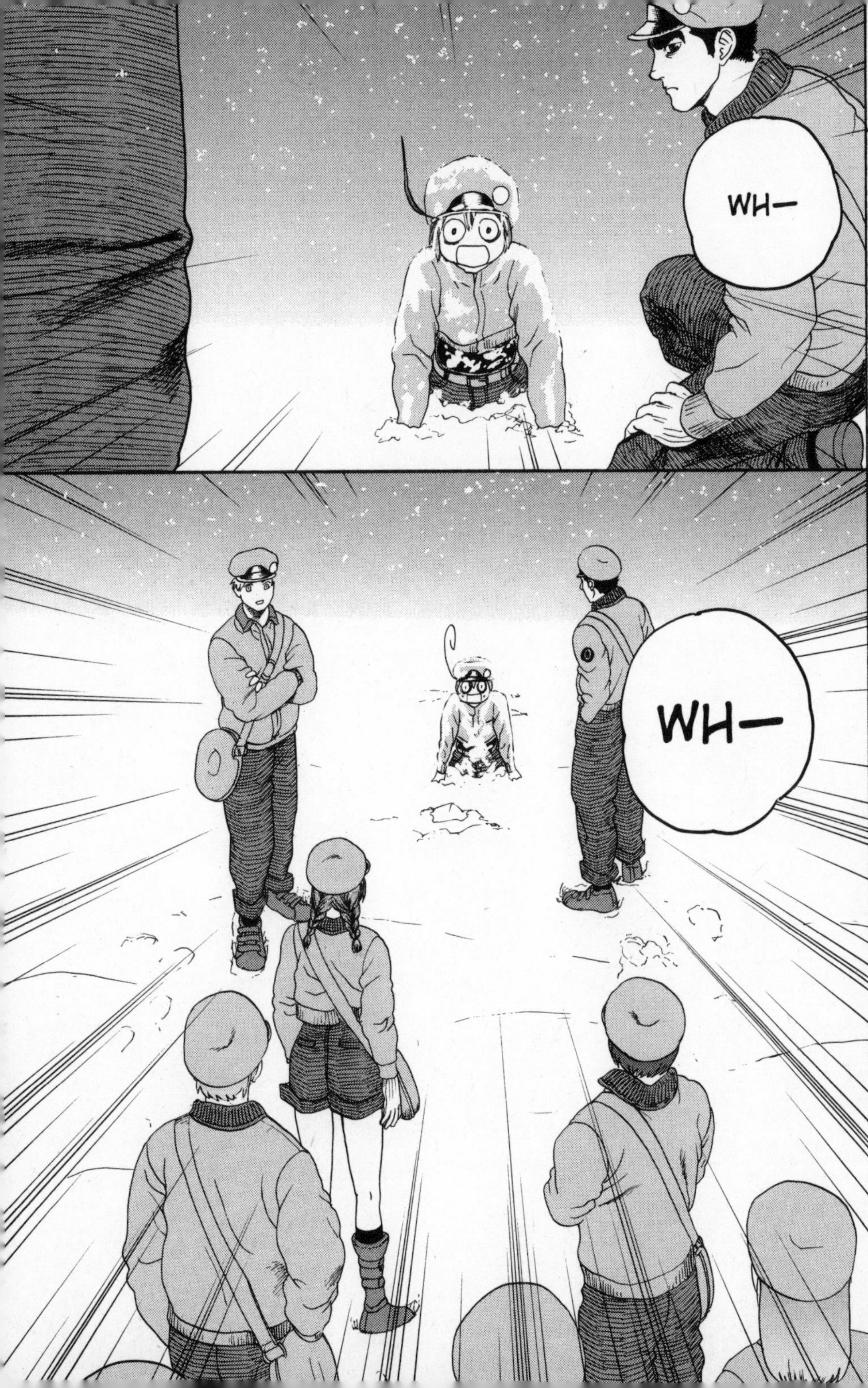
WH–
WH–

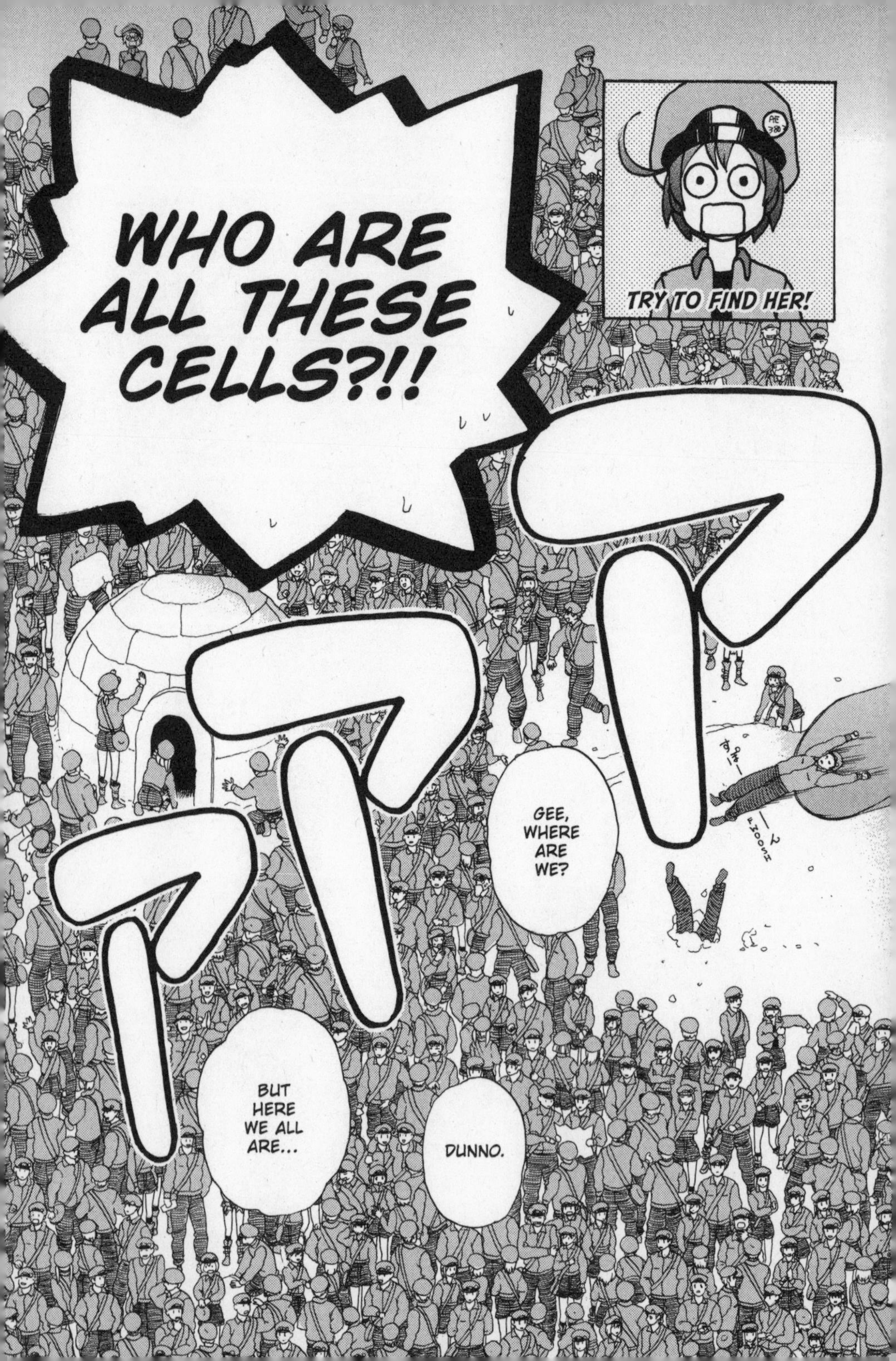

TRY TO FIND HER!
WHO ARE ALL THESE CELLS?!!
FWOOSH
GEE, WHERE ARE WE?
DUNNO.
BUT HERE WE ALL ARE...

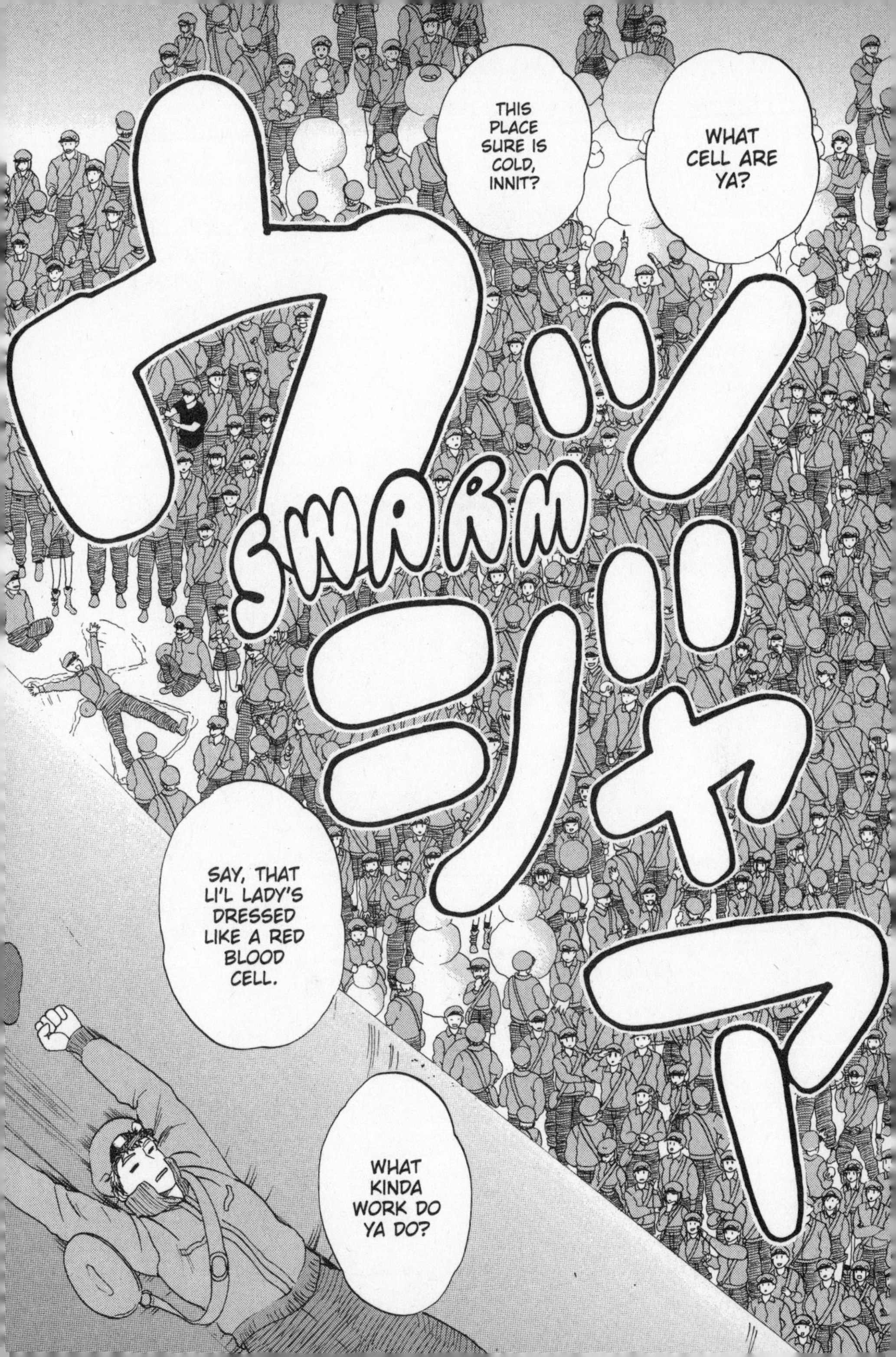
WHAT CELL ARE YA?
THIS PLACE SURE IS COLD, INNIT?
SWARM
SAY, THAT LI'L LADY'S DRESSED LIKE A RED BLOOD CELL.
WHAT KINDA WORK DO YA DO?

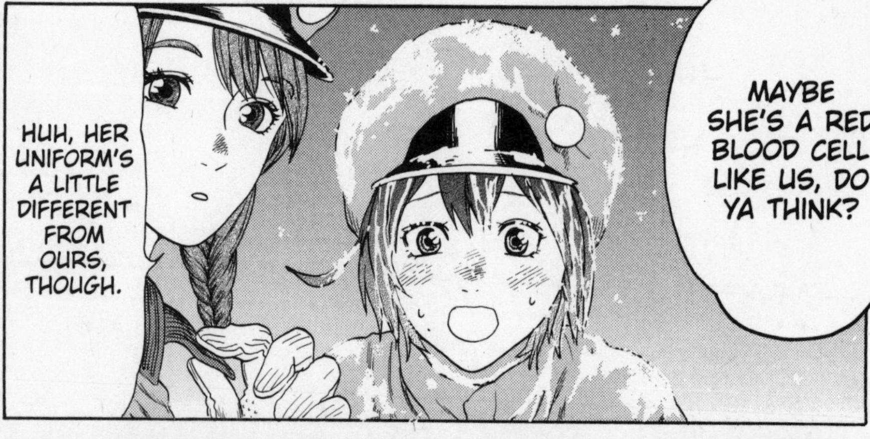
MAYBE SHE'S A RED BLOOD CELL LIKE US, DO YA THINK?
HUH, HER UNIFORM'S A LITTLE DIFFERENT FROM OURS, THOUGH.
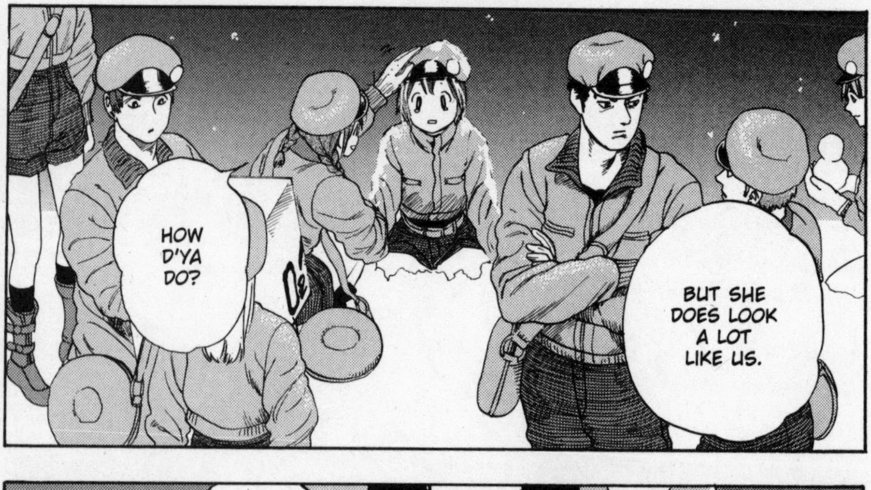
BUT SHE DOES LOOK A LOT LIKE US.
HOW D'YA DO?
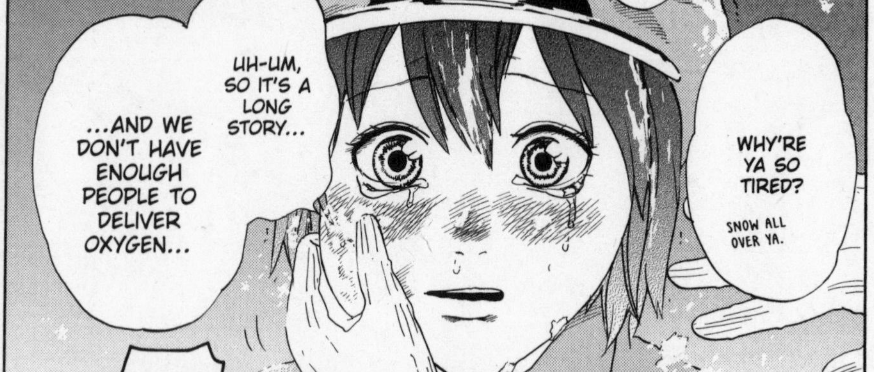
WHY'RE YA SO TIRED?
SNOW ALL OVER YA.
UH-UM, SO IT'S A LONG STORY...
...AND WE DON'T HAVE ENOUGH PEOPLE TO DELIVER OXYGEN...
WHAT?!

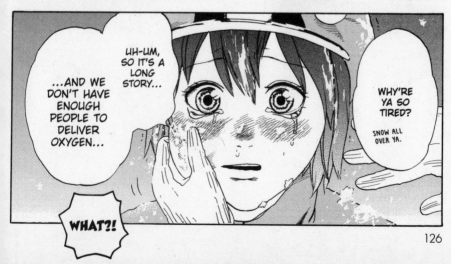

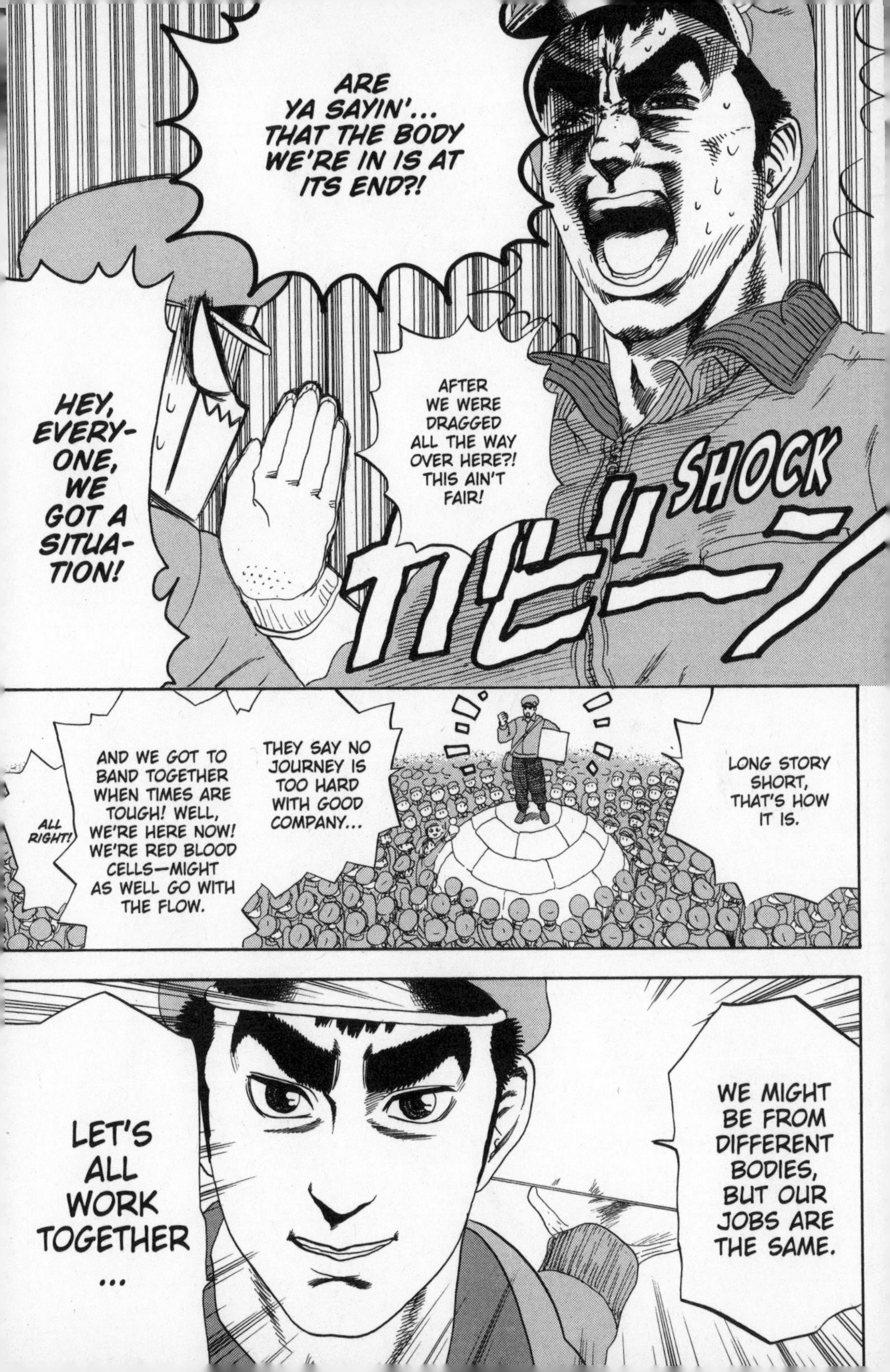
ARE YA SAYIN'... THAT THE BODY WE'RE IN IS AT ITS END?!
SHOCK
カビーン
AFTER WE WERE DRAGGED ALL THE WAY OVER HERE?! THIS AIN'T FAIR!
HEY, EVERY-ONE, WE GOT A SITUA-TION!
LONG STORY SHORT, THAT'S HOW IT IS.
THEY SAY NO JOURNEY IS TOO HARD WITH GOOD COMPANY...
AND WE GOT TO BAND TOGETHER WHEN TIMES ARE TOUGH! WELL, WE'RE HERE NOW! WE'RE RED BLOOD CELLS—MIGHT AS WELL GO WITH THE FLOW.
ALL RIGHT!
WE MIGHT BE FROM DIFFERENT BODIES, BUT OUR JOBS ARE THE SAME.
LET'S ALL WORK TOGETHER ...

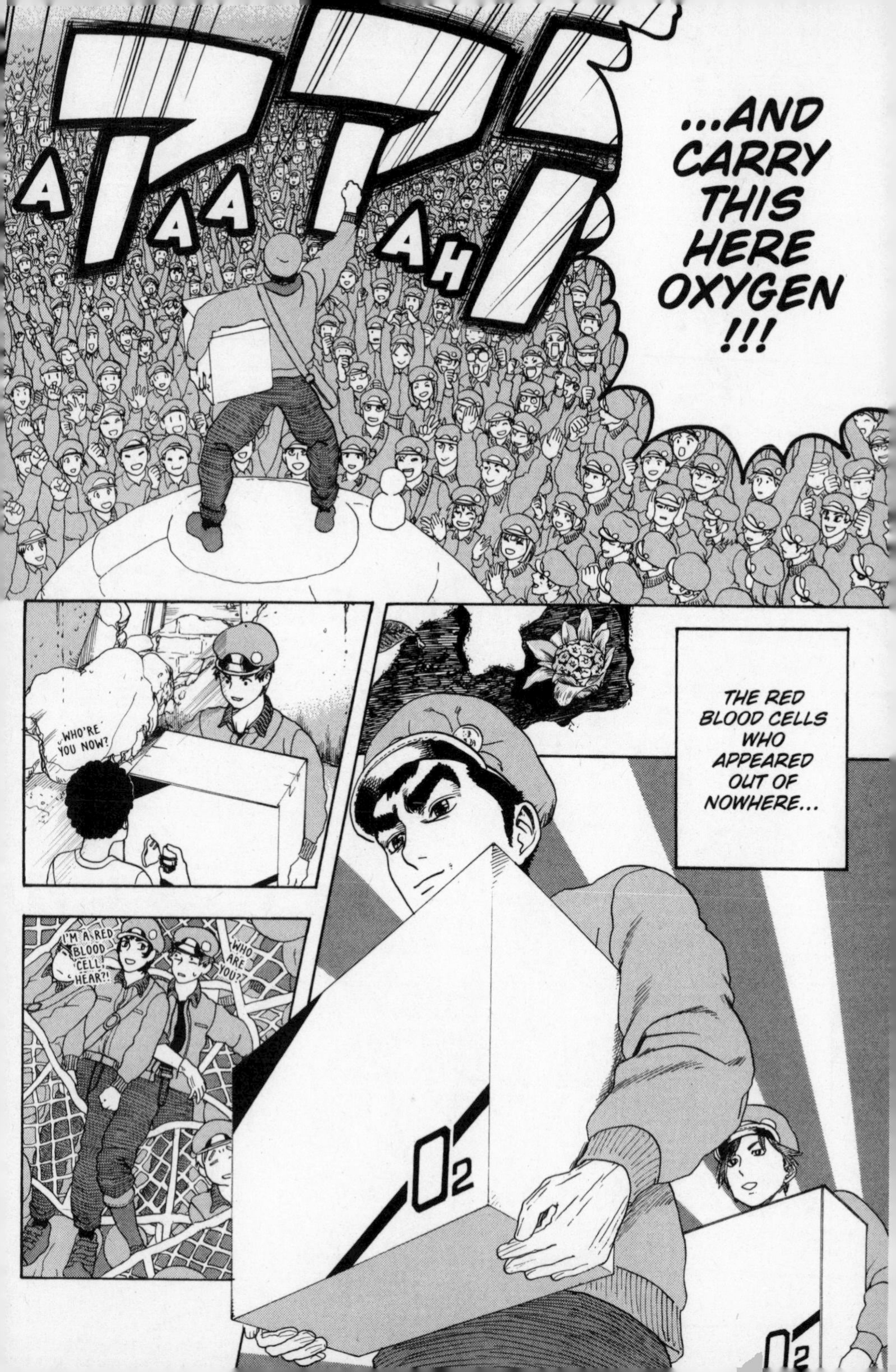
...AND CARRY THIS HERE OXYGEN!!!
AAAAH
THE RED BLOOD CELLS WHO APPEARED OUT OF NOWHERE...
WHO'RE YOU NOW?
WHO ARE YOU?
I'M A RED BLOOD CELL, HEAR?!

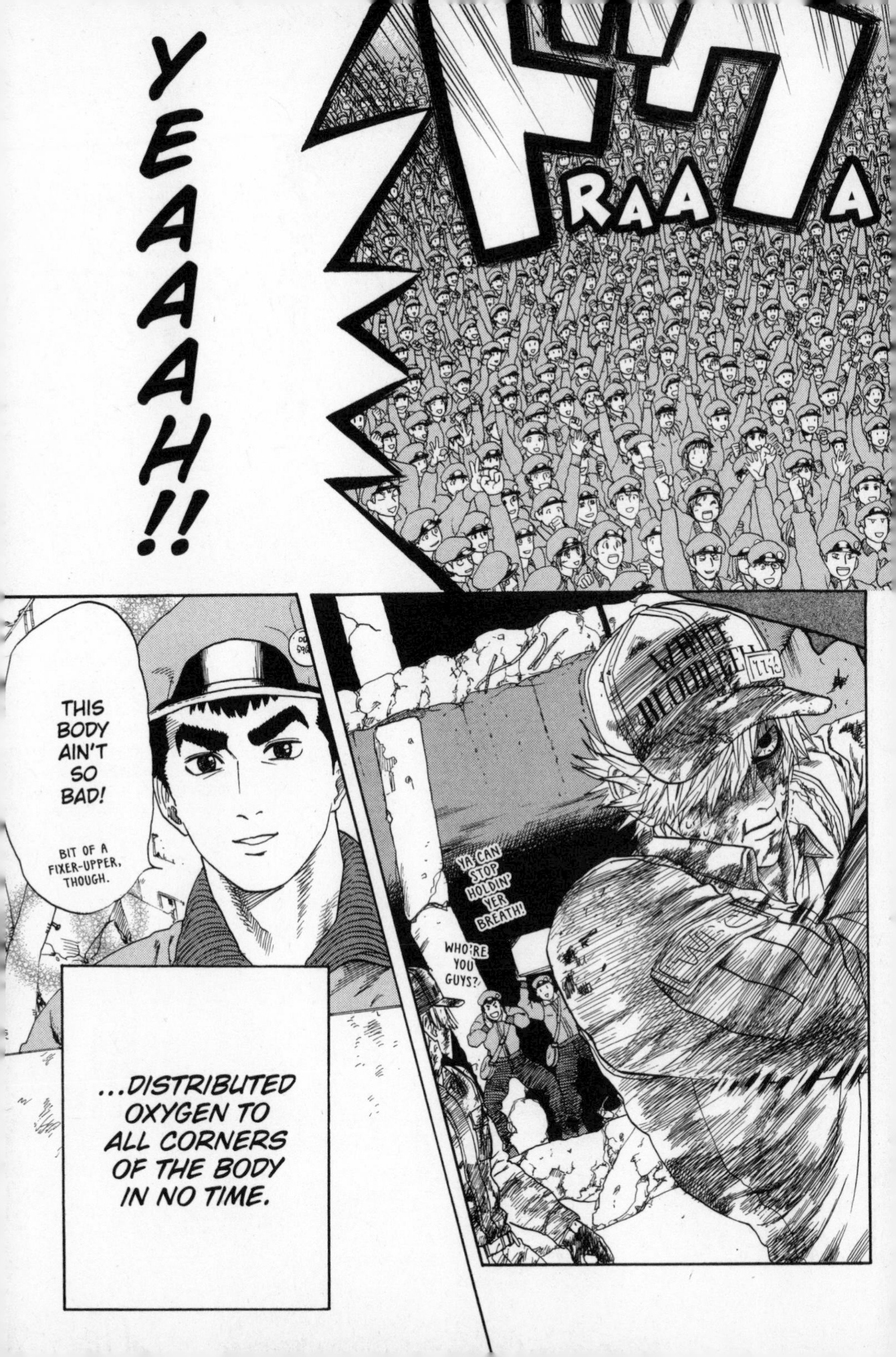
RAA A
YEAAAAH!!
YA CAN STOP HOLDIN' YER BREATH!
WHO'RE YOU GUYS?
THIS BODY AIN'T SO BAD!
BIT OF A FIXER-UPPER, THOUGH.
...DISTRIBUTED OXYGEN TO ALL CORNERS OF THE BODY IN NO TIME.

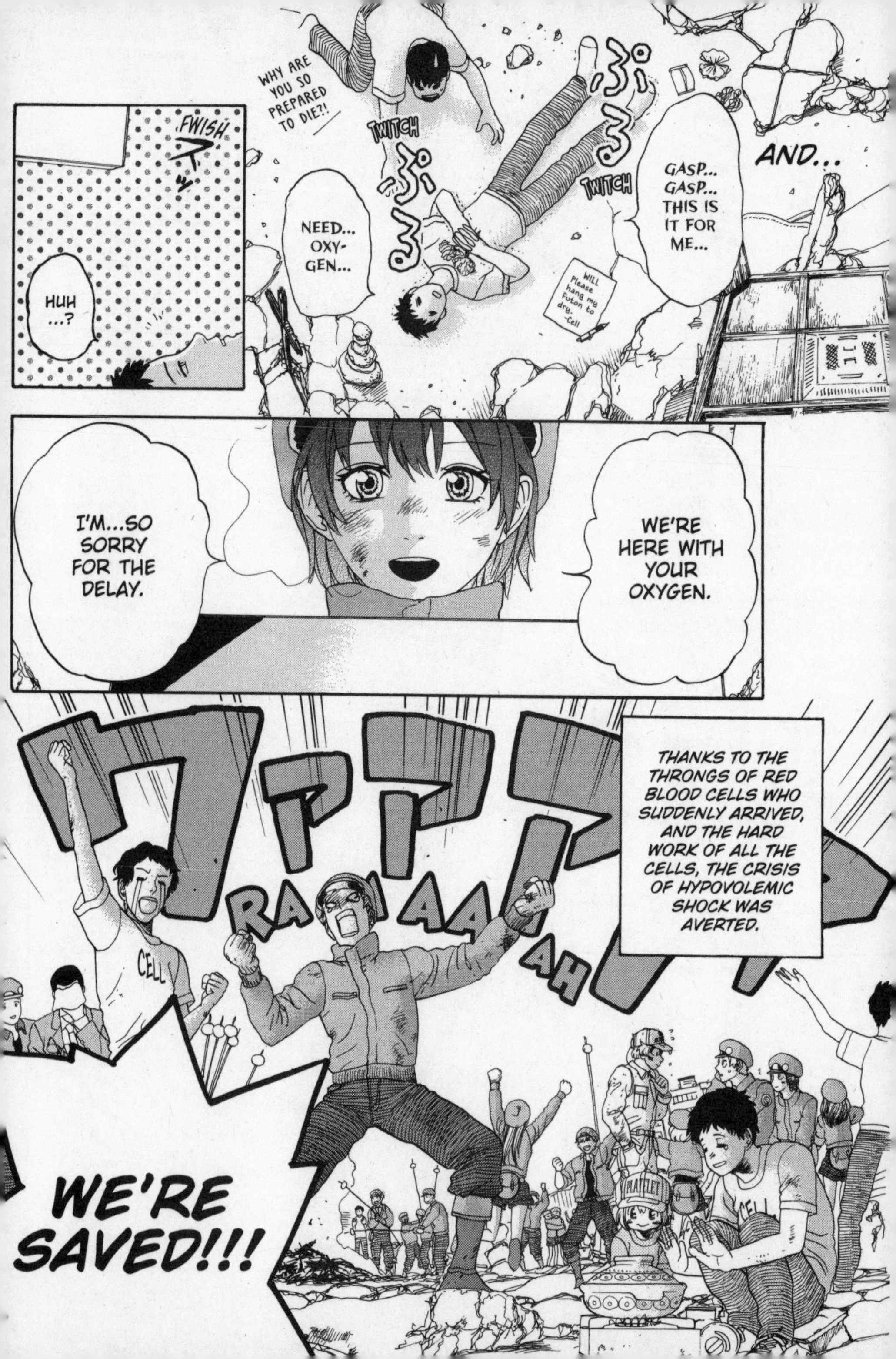
AND...
GASP... GASP... THIS IS IT FOR ME...
WILL Please hang my futon to dry. -Cell
TWITCH
NEED... OXY-GEN...
TWITCH
WHY ARE YOU SO PREPARED TO DIE?!
FWISH
HUH ...?
WE'RE HERE WITH YOUR OXYGEN.
I'M...SO SORRY FOR THE DELAY.
THANKS TO THE THRONGS OF RED BLOOD CELLS WHO SUDDENLY ARRIVED, AND THE HARD WORK OF ALL THE CELLS, THE CRISIS OF HYPOVOLEMIC SHOCK WAS AVERTED.
RA
AA
AH
CELL
PLATELET
WE'RE SAVED!!!

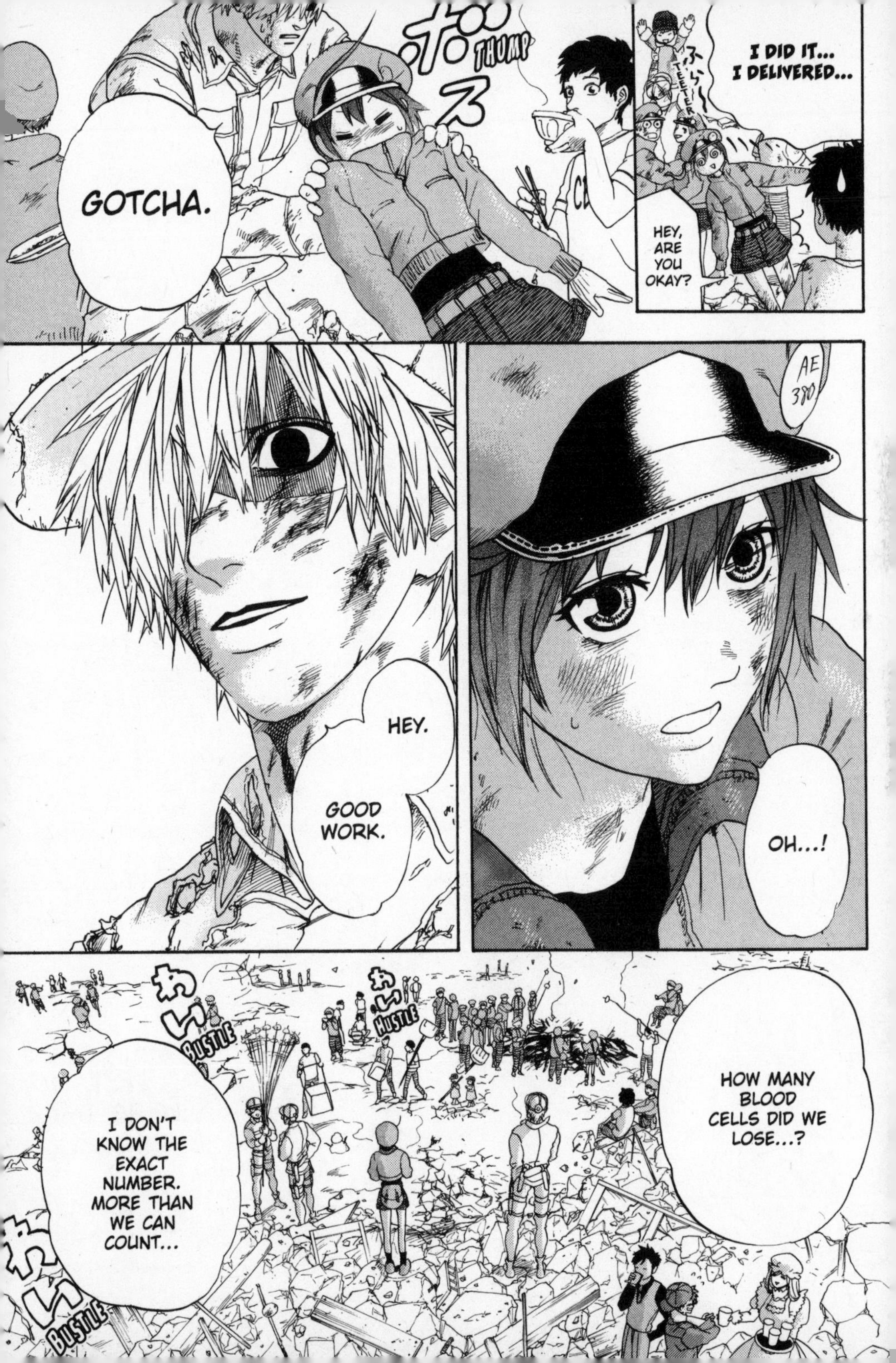
I DID IT... I DELIVERED...
ふら TEETER
HEY, ARE YOU OKAY?
THUMP
GOTCHA.
AE 380
OH...!
HEY.
GOOD WORK.
HOW MANY BLOOD CELLS DID WE LOSE...?
わい HUSTLE
わい BUSTLE
I DON'T KNOW THE EXACT NUMBER. MORE THAN WE CAN COUNT...
わい BUSTLE

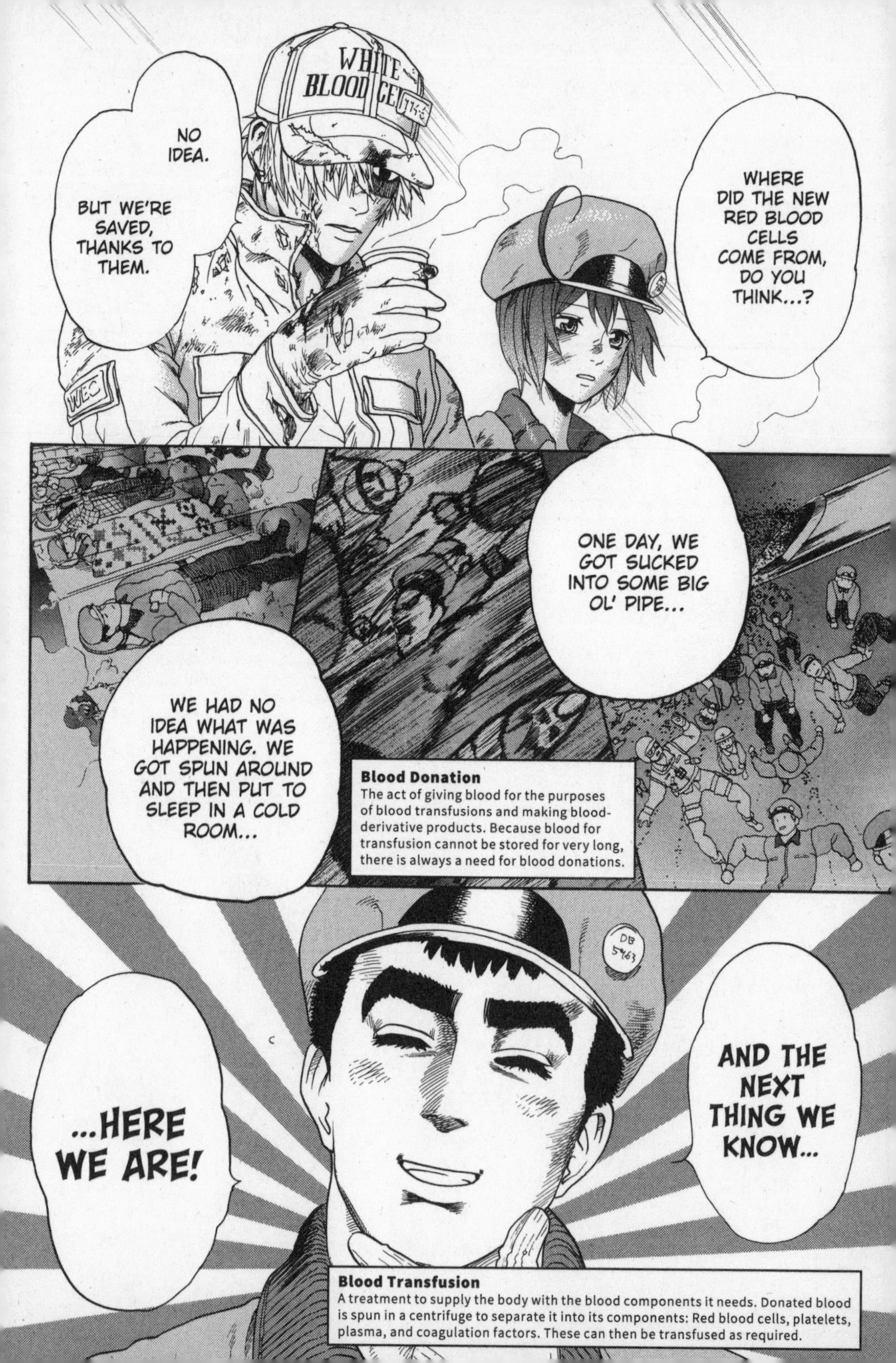
WHERE DID THE NEW RED BLOOD CELLS COME FROM, DO YOU THINK...?
NO IDEA.
BUT WE'RE SAVED, THANKS TO THEM.
ONE DAY, WE GOT SUCKED INTO SOME BIG OL' PIPE...
WE HAD NO IDEA WHAT WAS HAPPENING. WE GOT SPUN AROUND AND THEN PUT TO SLEEP IN A COLD ROOM...
Blood Donation
The act of giving blood for the purposes of blood transfusions and making blood-derivative products. Because blood for transfusion cannot be stored for very long, there is always a need for blood donations.
AND THE NEXT THING WE KNOW...
...HERE WE ARE!
Blood Transfusion
A treatment to supply the body with the blood components it needs. Donated blood is spun in a centrifuge to separate it into its components: Red blood cells, platelets, plasma, and coagulation factors. These can then be transfused as required.

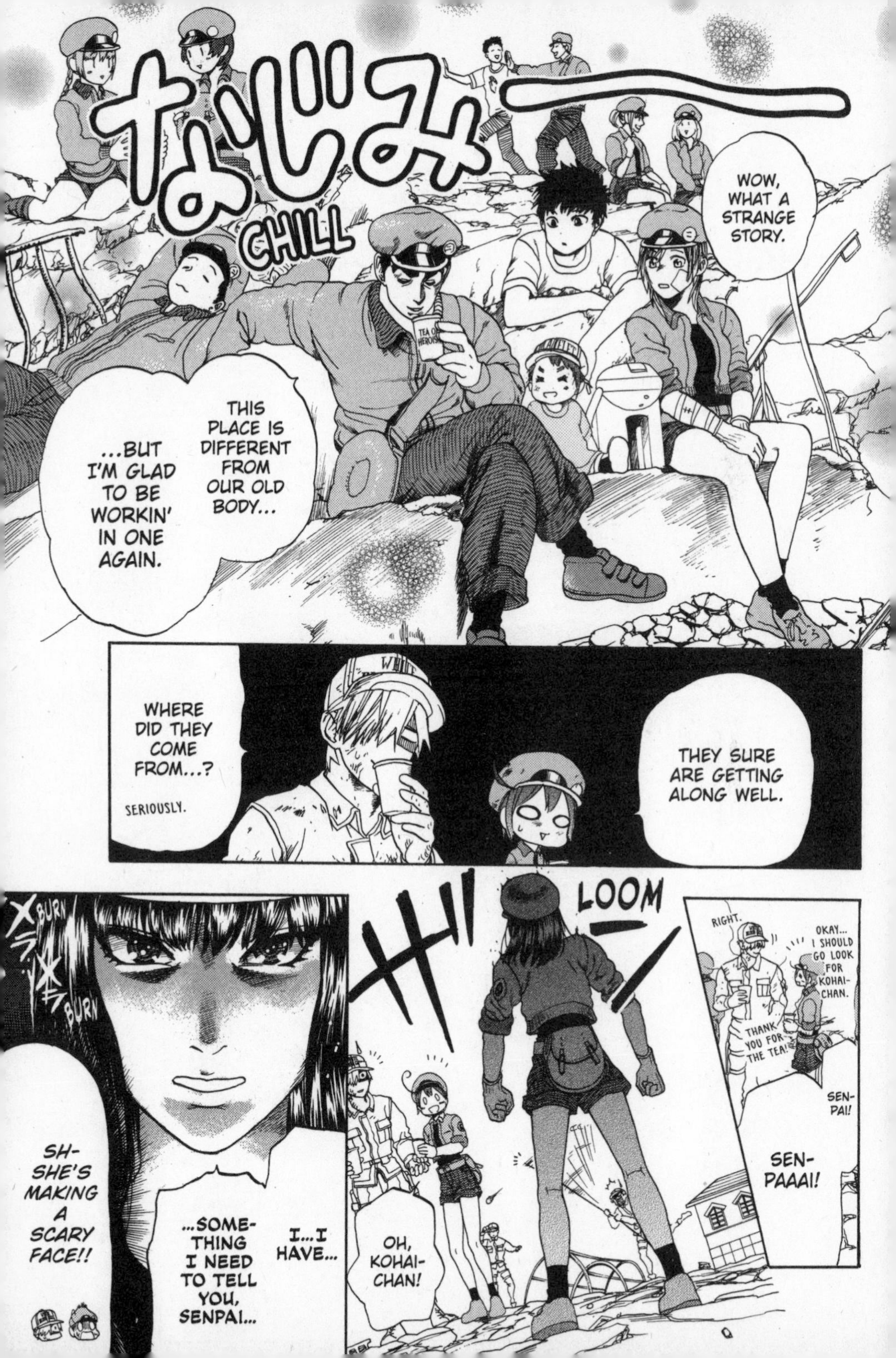
WOW, WHAT A STRANGE STORY.
なじみー
CHILL
THIS PLACE IS DIFFERENT FROM OUR OLD BODY...
...BUT I'M GLAD TO BE WORKIN' IN ONE AGAIN.
THEY SURE ARE GETTING ALONG WELL.
WHERE DID THEY COME FROM...?
SERIOUSLY.
RIGHT.
OKAY... I SHOULD GO LOOK FOR KOHAI-CHAN.
THANK YOU FOR THE TEA!
SEN-PAI!
SEN-PAAAI!
LOOM
OH, KOHAI-CHAN!
BURN
BURN
I...I HAVE...
...SOME-THING I NEED TO TELL YOU, SENPAI...
SH-SHE'S MAKING A SCARY FACE!!

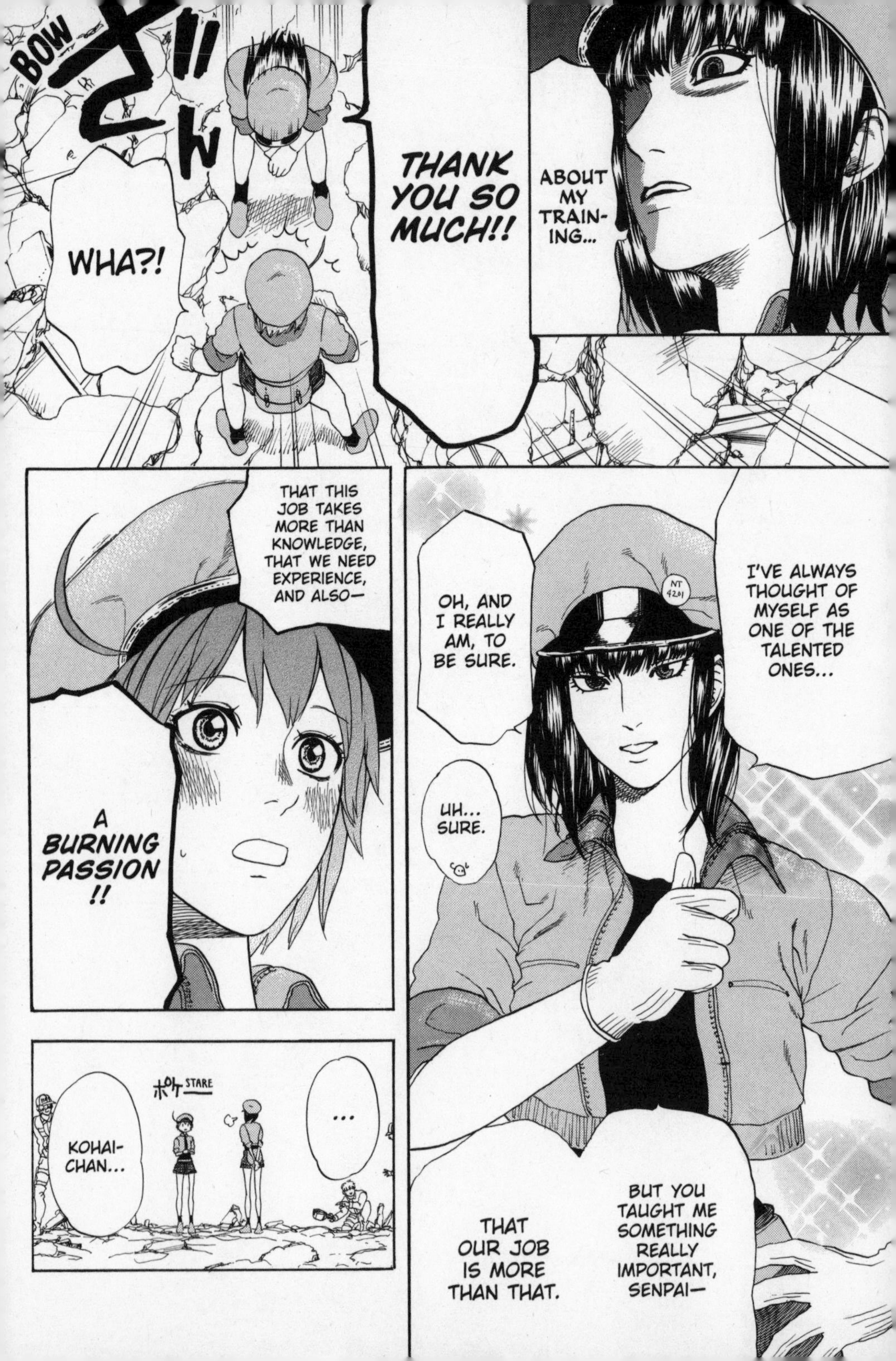
ABOUT MY TRAIN-ING...
THANK YOU SO MUCH!!
BOW
WHA?!
I'VE ALWAYS THOUGHT OF MYSELF AS ONE OF THE TALENTED ONES...
NT 4201
OH, AND I REALLY AM, TO BE SURE.
UH... SURE.
BUT YOU TAUGHT ME SOMETHING REALLY IMPORTANT, SENPAI—
THAT OUR JOB IS MORE THAN THAT.
THAT THIS JOB TAKES MORE THAN KNOWLEDGE, THAT WE NEED EXPERIENCE, AND ALSO—
A BURNING PASSION!!
...
STARE
KOHAI-CHAN...

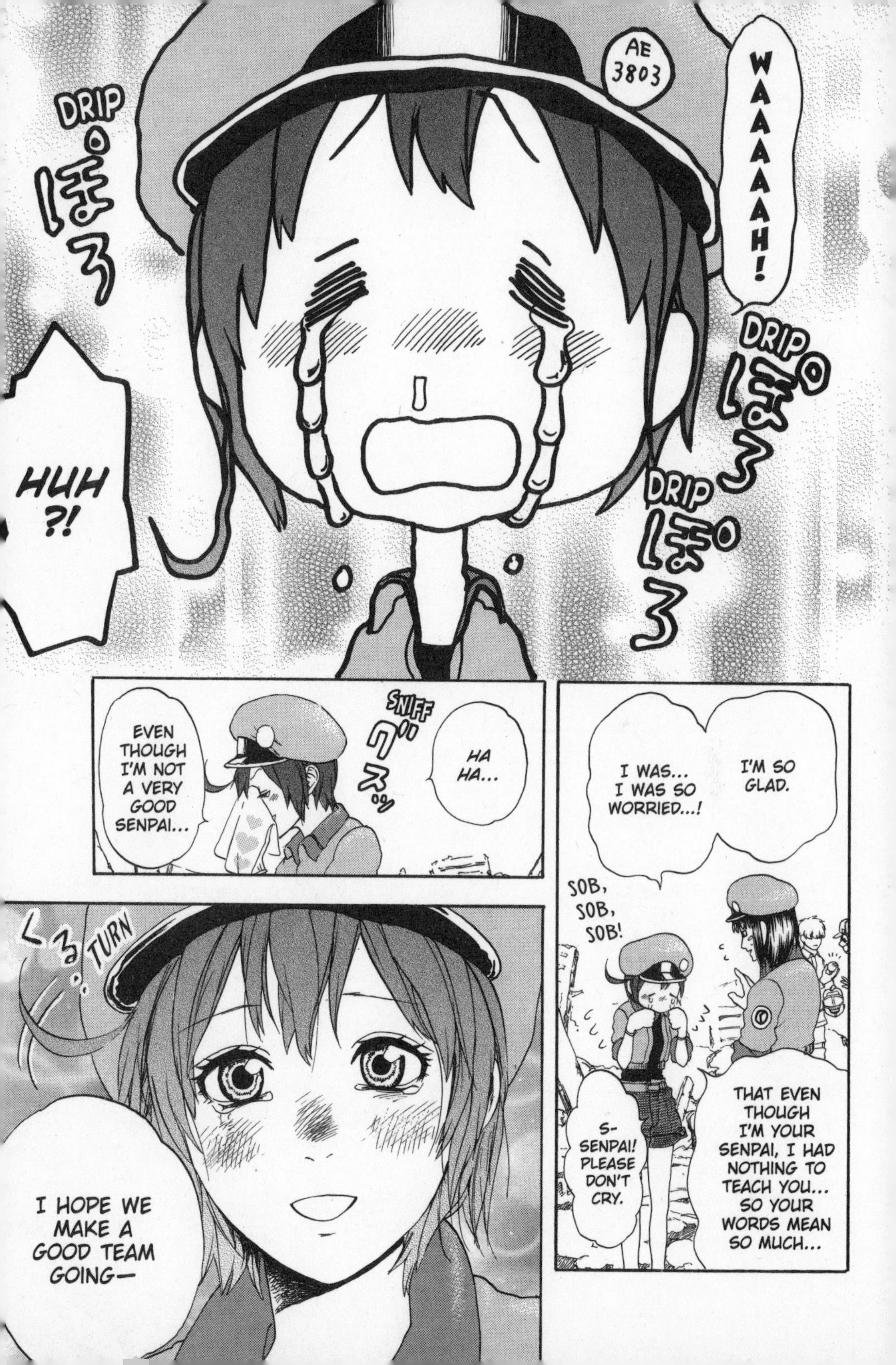
AE 3803
WAAAAAAH!
DRIP ぽろ
DRIP ぽろ
DRIP ぽろ
HUH ?!
I'M SO GLAD.
I WAS... I WAS SO WORRIED...!
SOB, SOB, SOB!
THAT EVEN THOUGH I'M YOUR SENPAI, I HAD NOTHING TO TEACH YOU... SO YOUR WORDS MEAN SO MUCH...
S-SENPAI! PLEASE DON'T CRY.
SNIFF グスッ
HA HA...
EVEN THOUGH I'M NOT A VERY GOOD SENPAI...
くる TURN
I HOPE WE MAKE A GOOD TEAM GOING—

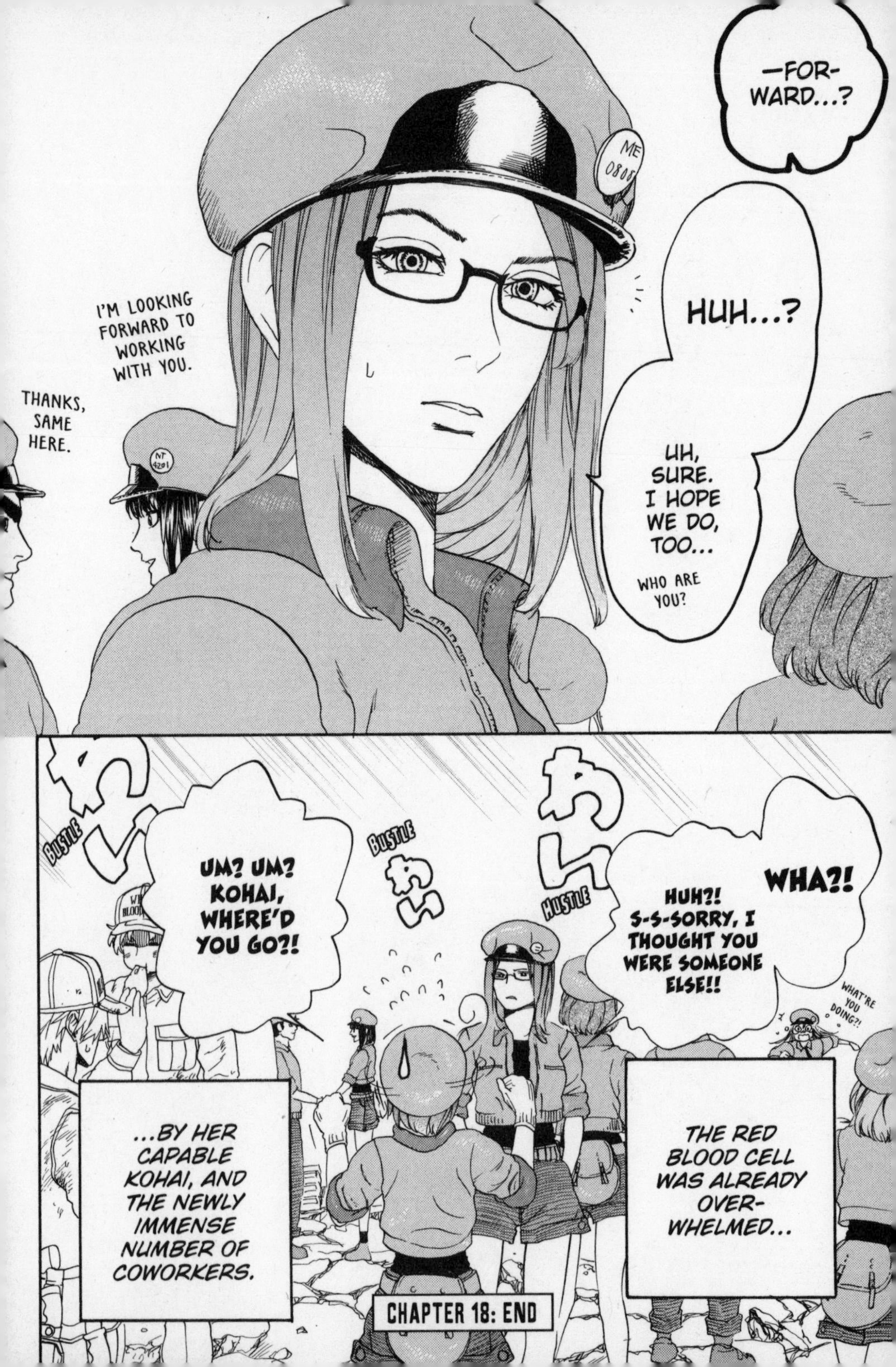
—FOR-WARD...?
HUH...?
UH, SURE. I HOPE WE DO, TOO...
WHO ARE YOU?
I'M LOOKING FORWARD TO WORKING WITH YOU.
THANKS, SAME HERE.
WHA?!
HUH?! S-S-SORRY, I THOUGHT YOU WERE SOMEONE ELSE!!
WHAT'RE YOU DOING?!
HUSTLE
BUSTLE
UM? UM? KOHAI, WHERE'D YOU GO?!
BUSTLE
THE RED BLOOD CELL WAS ALREADY OVER-WHELMED...
...BY HER CAPABLE KOHAI, AND THE NEWLY IMMENSE NUMBER OF COWORKERS.
CHAPTER 18: END

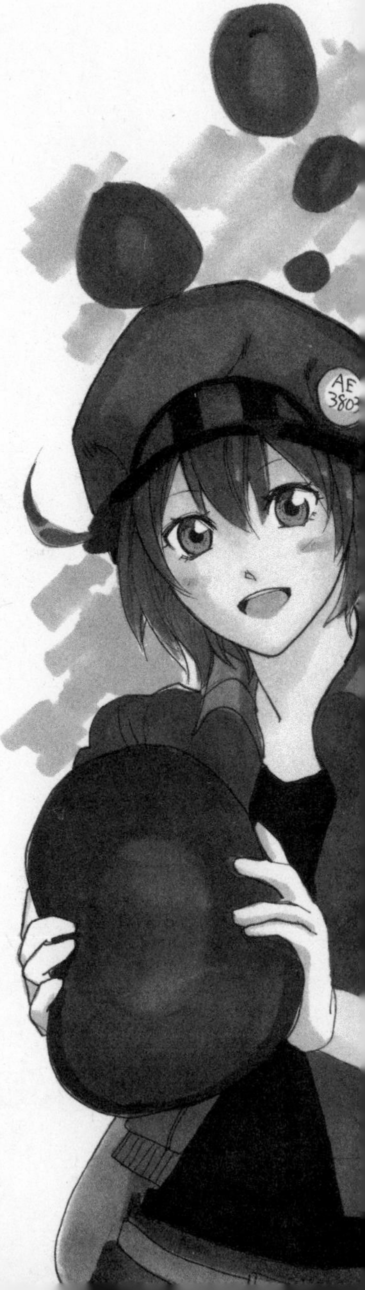
AE

Cells at Work!

はたらく細胞

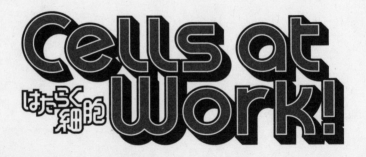

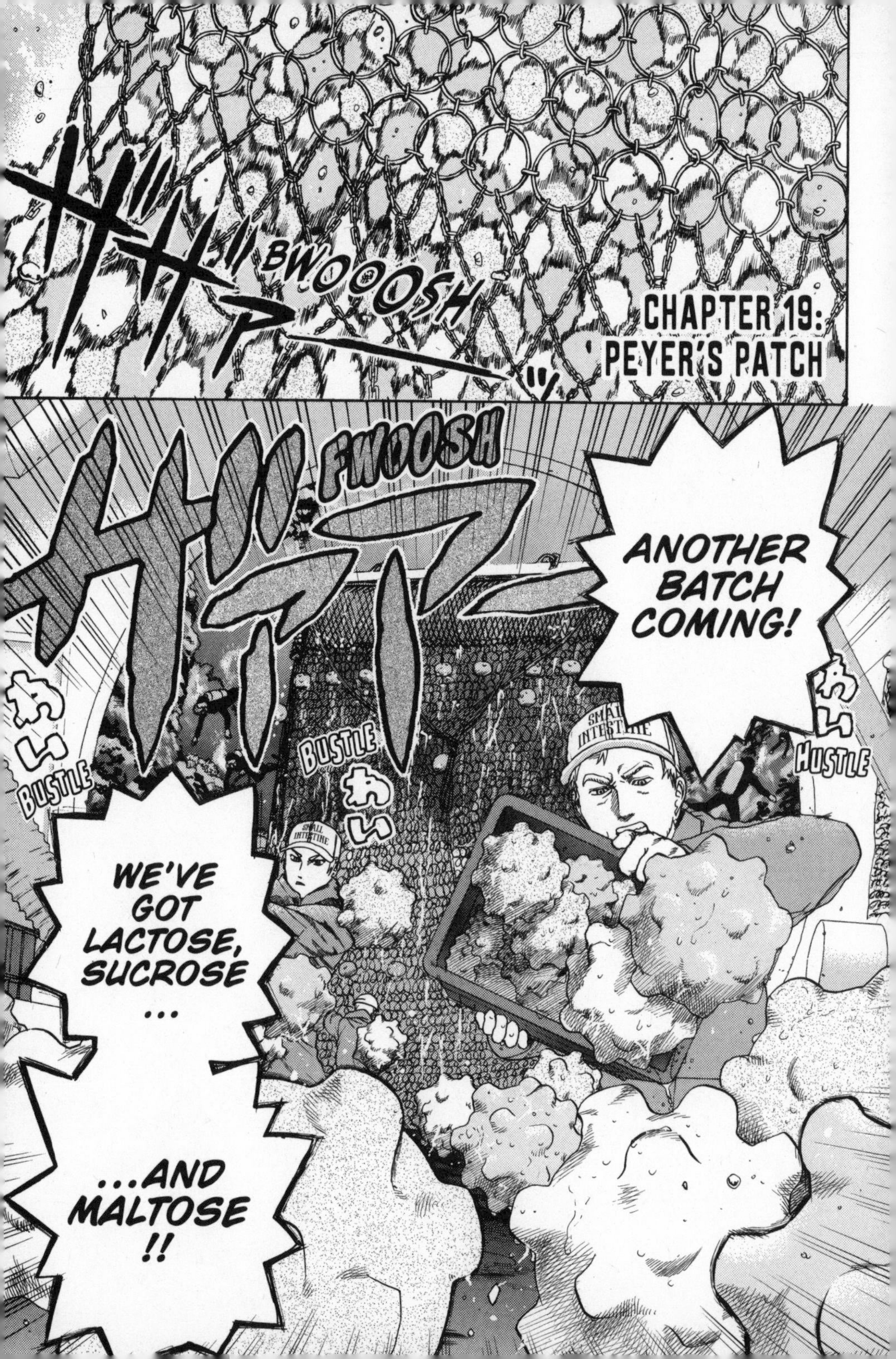
BWOOOSH
CHAPTER 19: PEYER'S PATCH
ANOTHER BATCH COMING!
わい
HUSTLE
FWOOSH
わい
BUSTLE
わい
BUSTLE
WE'VE GOT LACTOSE, SUCROSE ...
...AND MALTOSE !!

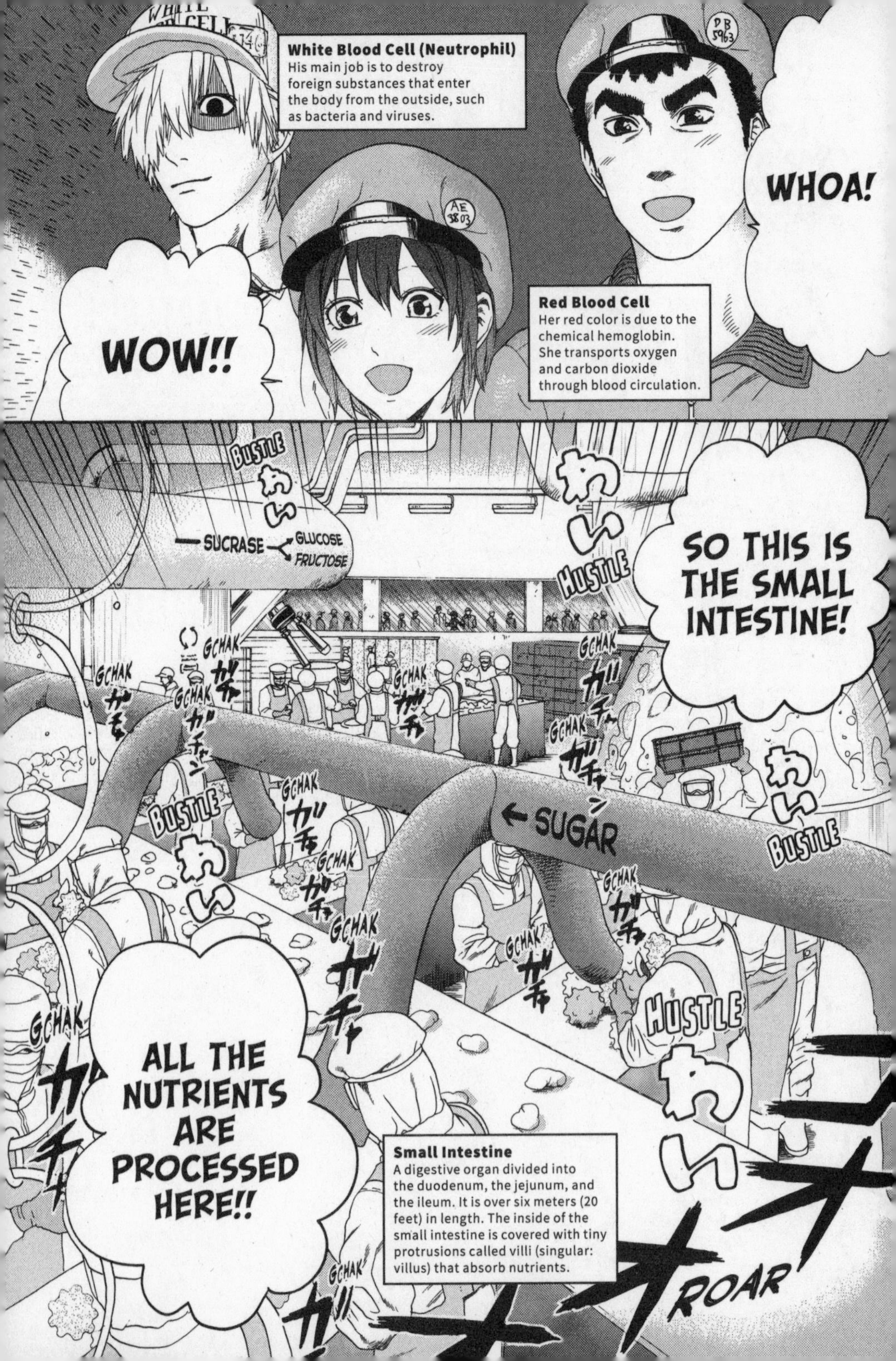

White Blood Cell (Neutrophil)
His main job is to destroy foreign substances that enter the body from the outside, such as bacteria and viruses.
WHOA!
Red Blood Cell
Her red color is due to the chemical hemoglobin. She transports oxygen and carbon dioxide through blood circulation.
WOW!!
SO THIS IS THE SMALL INTESTINE!
HUSTLE
BUSTLE
SUCRASE → GLUCOSE FRUCTOSE
GCHAK
← SUGAR
BUSTLE
HUSTLE
ALL THE NUTRIENTS ARE PROCESSED HERE!!
Small Intestine
A digestive organ divided into the duodenum, the jejunum, and the ileum. It is over six meters (20 feet) in length. The inside of the small intestine is covered with tiny protrusions called villi (singular: villus) that absorb nutrients.
ROAR

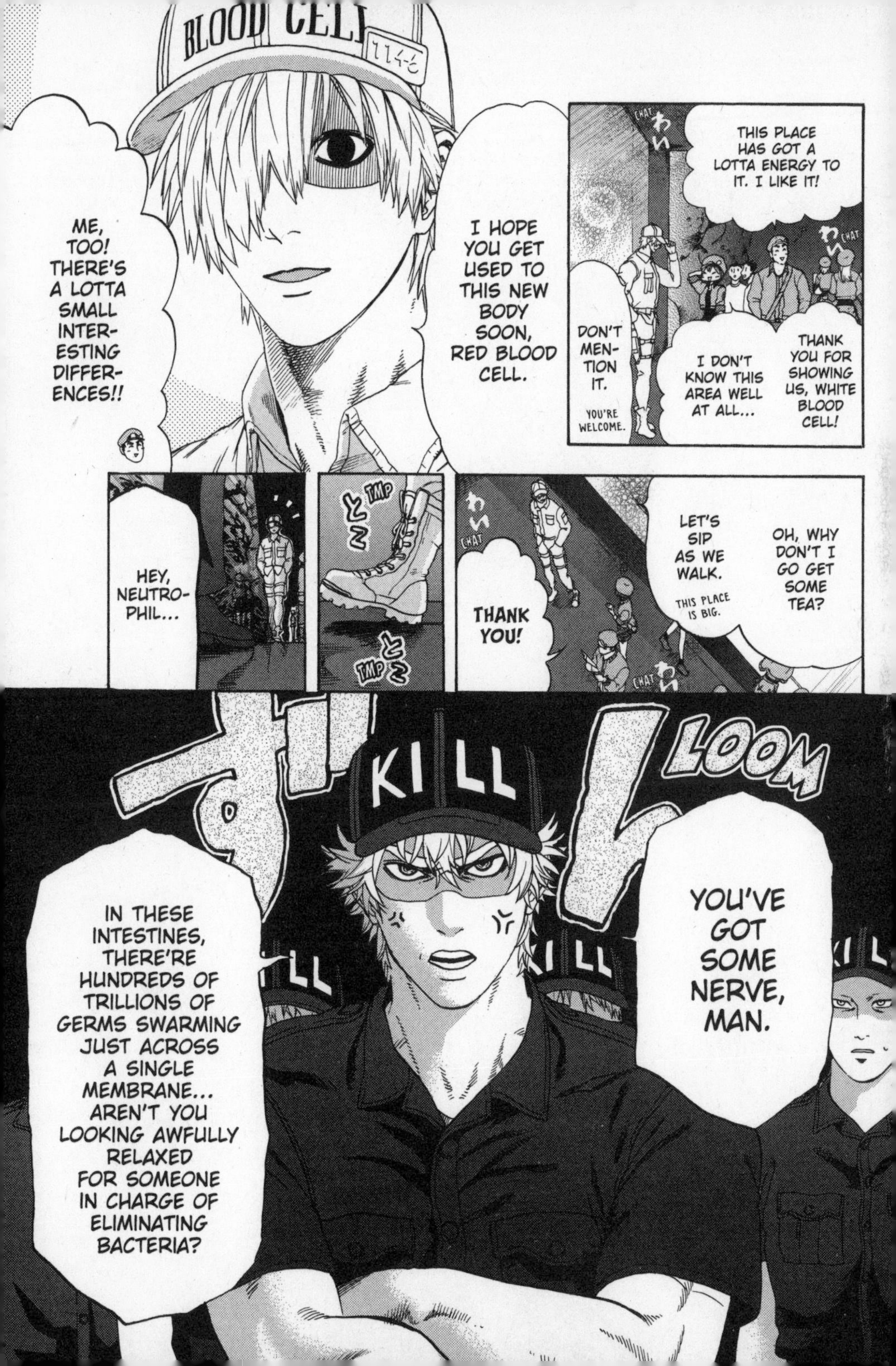
CHAT
THIS PLACE HAS GOT A LOTTA ENERGY TO IT. I LIKE IT!
CHAT
THANK YOU FOR SHOWING US, WHITE BLOOD CELL!
I DON'T KNOW THIS AREA WELL AT ALL...
DON'T MENTION IT.
YOU'RE WELCOME.
I HOPE YOU GET USED TO THIS NEW BODY SOON, RED BLOOD CELL.
ME, TOO! THERE'S A LOTTA SMALL INTER-ESTING DIFFER-ENCES!!
OH, WHY DON'T I GO GET SOME TEA?
LET'S SIP AS WE WALK.
THIS PLACE IS BIG.
CHAT
THANK YOU!
CHAT
TMP
TMP
HEY, NEUTRO-PHIL...
LOOM
YOU'VE GOT SOME NERVE, MAN.
IN THESE INTESTINES, THERE'RE HUNDREDS OF TRILLIONS OF GERMS SWARMING JUST ACROSS A SINGLE MEMBRANE... AREN'T YOU LOOKING AWFULLY RELAXED FOR SOMEONE IN CHARGE OF ELIMINATING BACTERIA?

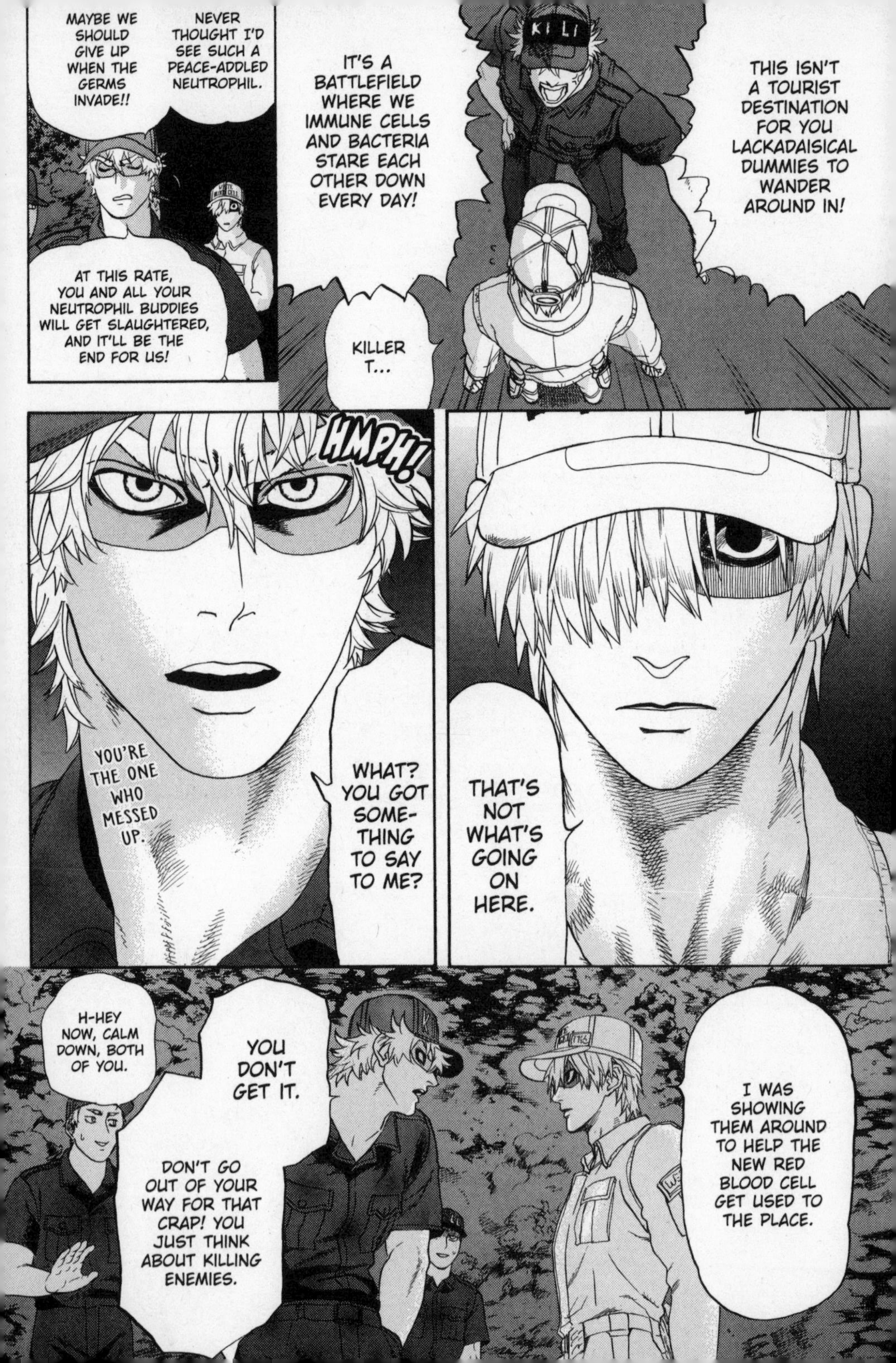
THIS ISN'T A TOURIST DESTINATION FOR YOU LACKADAISICAL DUMMIES TO WANDER AROUND IN!
IT'S A BATTLEFIELD WHERE WE IMMUNE CELLS AND BACTERIA STARE EACH OTHER DOWN EVERY DAY!
KILLER T...
NEVER THOUGHT I'D SEE SUCH A PEACE-ADDLED NEUTROPHIL.
MAYBE WE SHOULD GIVE UP WHEN THE GERMS INVADE!!
AT THIS RATE, YOU AND ALL YOUR NEUTROPHIL BUDDIES WILL GET SLAUGHTERED, AND IT'LL BE THE END FOR US!
THAT'S NOT WHAT'S GOING ON HERE.
HMPH!
WHAT? YOU GOT SOME-THING TO SAY TO ME?
YOU'RE THE ONE WHO MESSED UP.
I WAS SHOWING THEM AROUND TO HELP THE NEW RED BLOOD CELL GET USED TO THE PLACE.
YOU DON'T GET IT.
DON'T GO OUT OF YOUR WAY FOR THAT CRAP! YOU JUST THINK ABOUT KILLING ENEMIES.
H-HEY NOW, CALM DOWN, BOTH OF YOU.

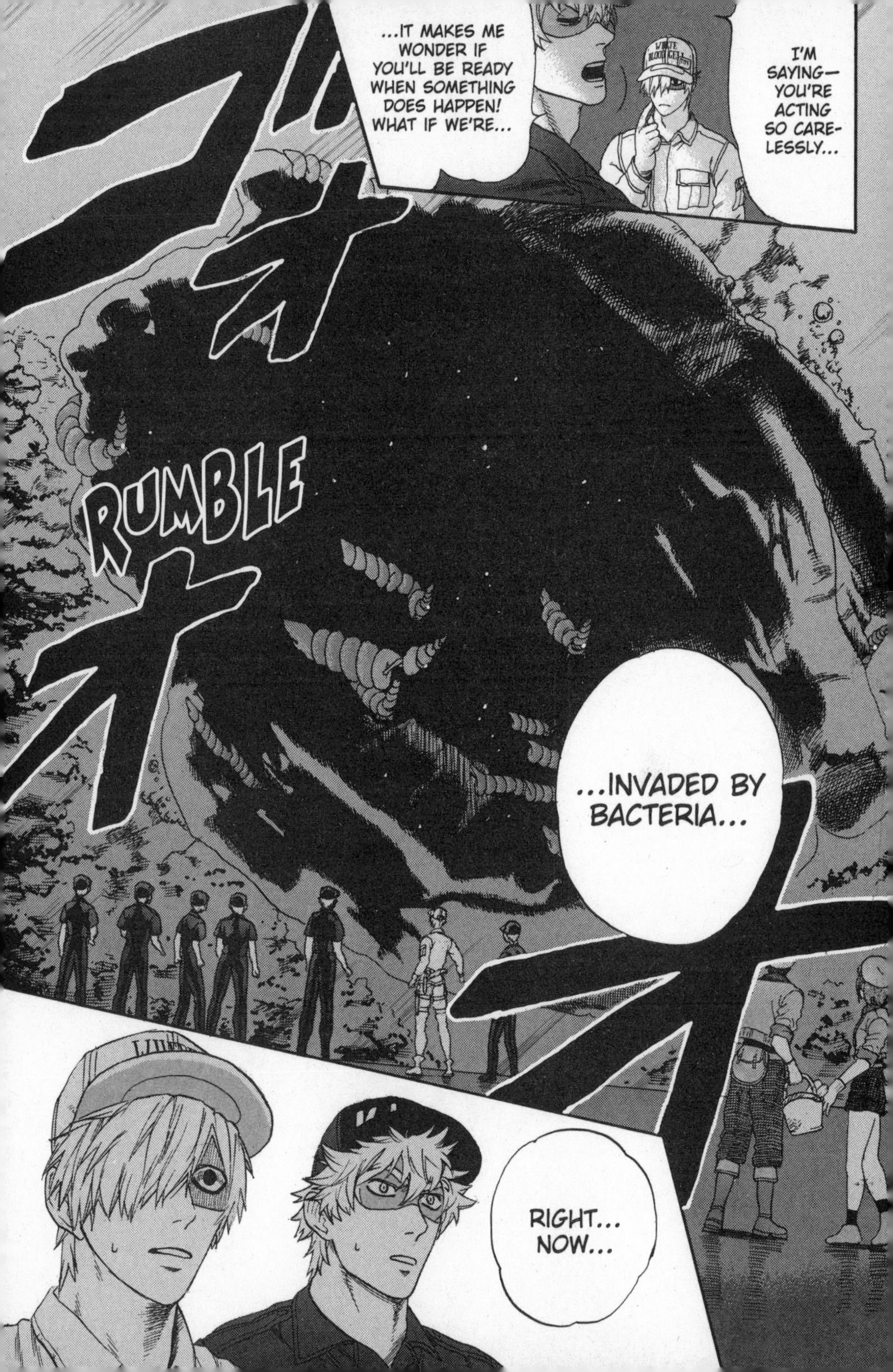
I'M SAYING—YOU'RE ACTING SO CARE-LESSLY...
...IT MAKES ME WONDER IF YOU'LL BE READY WHEN SOMETHING DOES HAPPEN! WHAT IF WE'RE...
RUMBLE
...INVADED BY BACTERIA...
RIGHT... NOW...

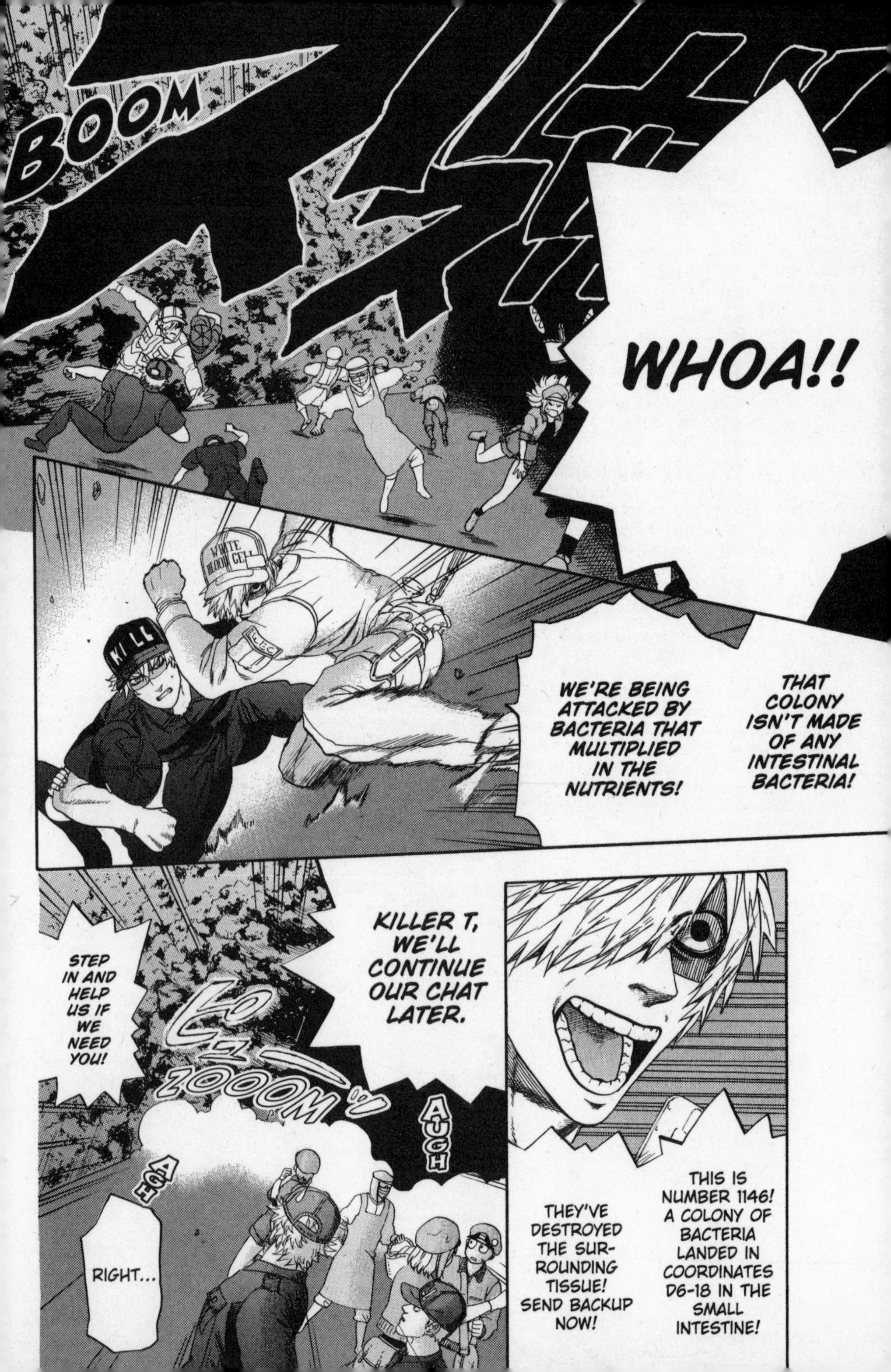
BOOM
WHOA!!
THAT COLONY ISN'T MADE OF ANY INTESTINAL BACTERIA!
WE'RE BEING ATTACKED BY BACTERIA THAT MULTIPLIED IN THE NUTRIENTS!
THIS IS NUMBER 1146! A COLONY OF BACTERIA LANDED IN COORDINATES D6-18 IN THE SMALL INTESTINE!
THEY'VE DESTROYED THE SUR-ROUNDING TISSUE! SEND BACKUP NOW!
KILLER T, WE'LL CONTINUE OUR CHAT LATER.
STEP IN AND HELP US IF WE NEED YOU!
ZOOOM
AUGH
AGH
RIGHT...

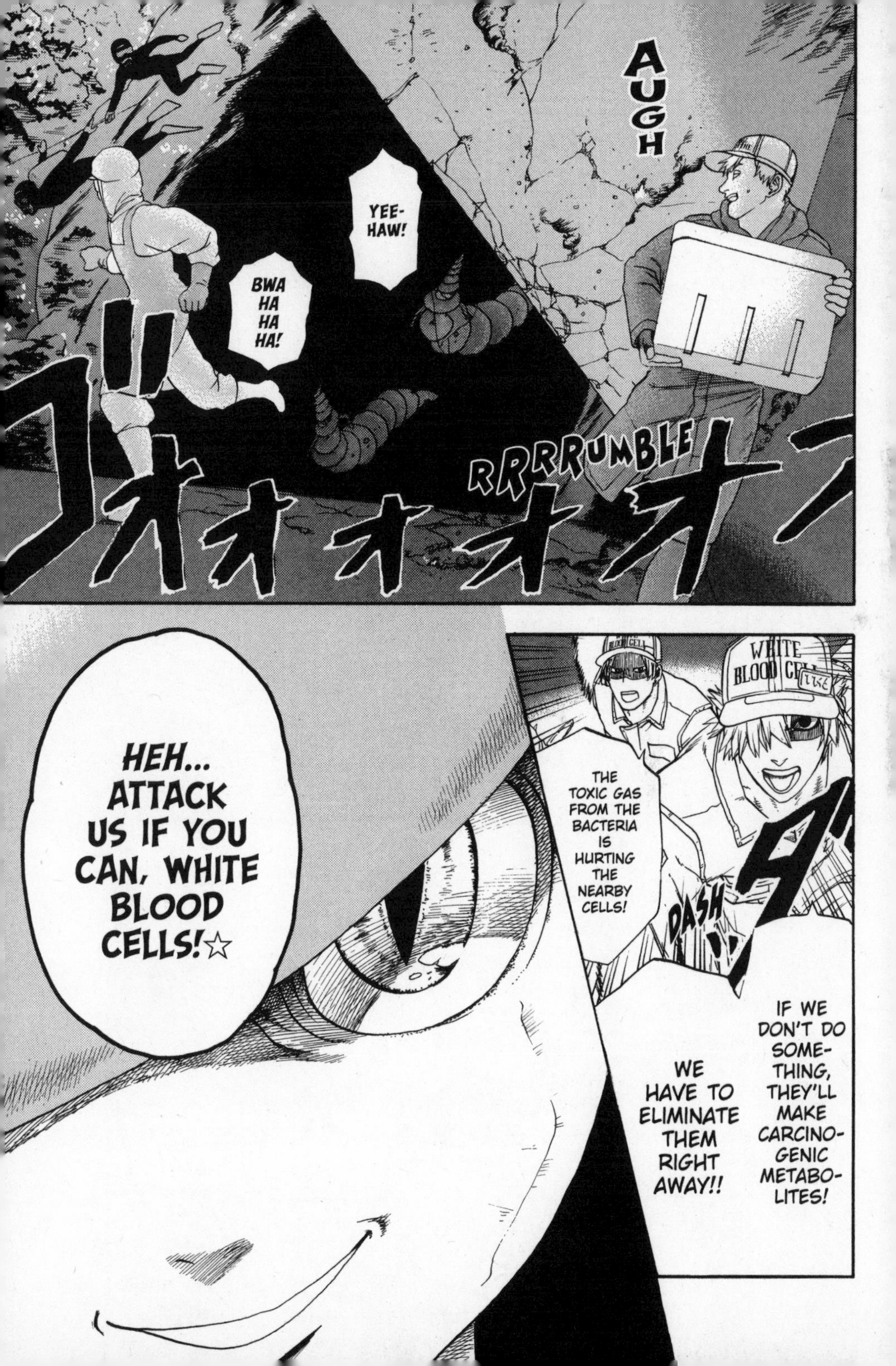
AUGH
YEE-HAW!
BWA HA HA HA!
RRRRUMBLE
THE TOXIC GAS FROM THE BACTERIA IS HURTING THE NEARBY CELLS!
DASH
IF WE DON'T DO SOME-THING, THEY'LL MAKE CARCINO-GENIC METABO-LITES!
WE HAVE TO ELIMINATE THEM RIGHT AWAY!!
HEH... ATTACK US IF YOU CAN, WHITE BLOOD CELLS!☆

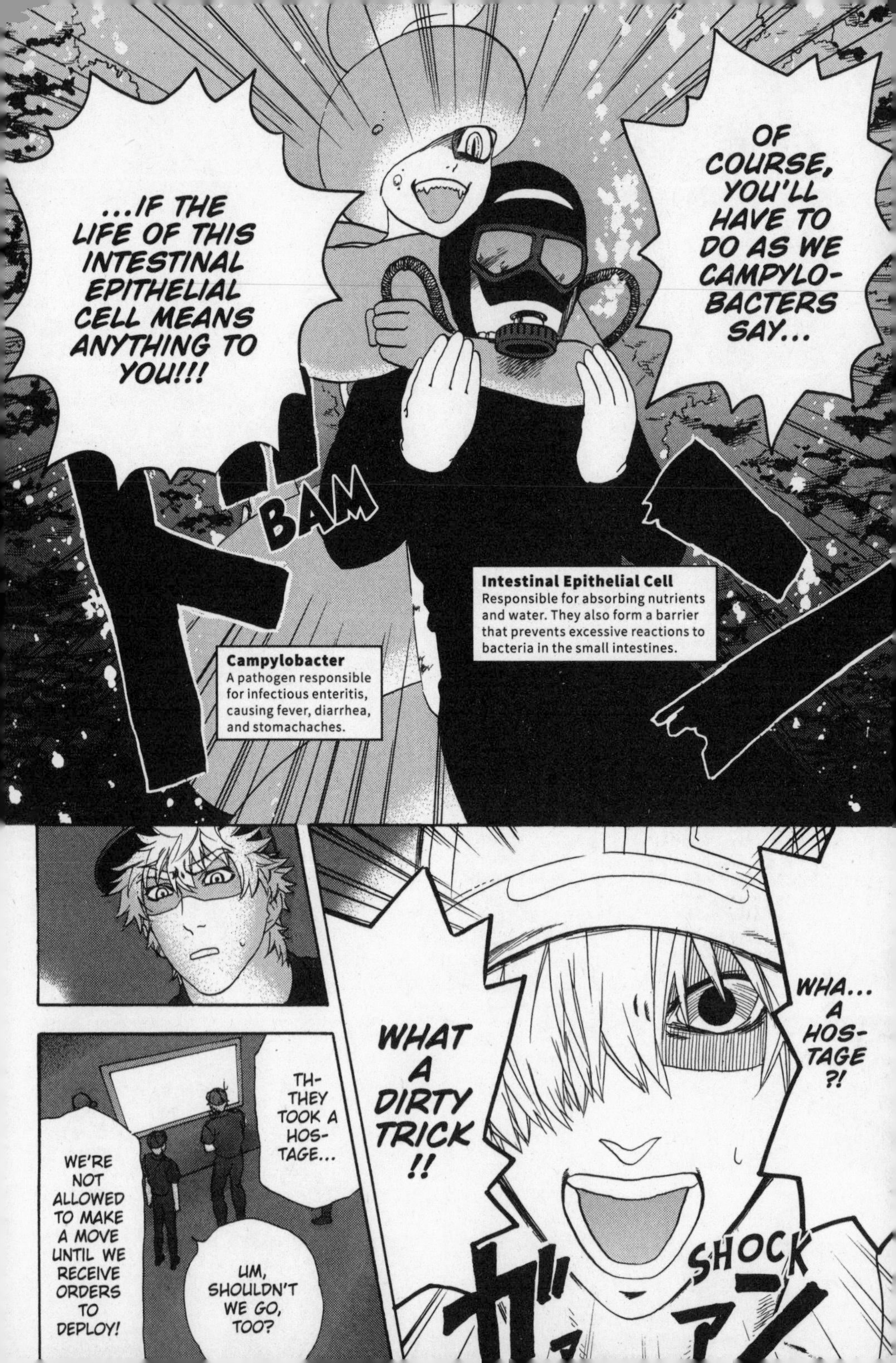
OF COURSE, YOU'LL HAVE TO DO AS WE CAMPYLOBACTERS SAY...
...IF THE LIFE OF THIS INTESTINAL EPITHELIAL CELL MEANS ANYTHING TO YOU!!!
BAM
Intestinal Epithelial Cell
Responsible for absorbing nutrients and water. They also form a barrier that prevents excessive reactions to bacteria in the small intestines.
Campylobacter
A pathogen responsible for infectious enteritis, causing fever, diarrhea, and stomachaches.
WHA... A HOSTAGE?!
WHAT A DIRTY TRICK!!
SHOCK
TH-THEY TOOK A HOSTAGE...
UM, SHOULDN'T WE GO, TOO?
WE'RE NOT ALLOWED TO MAKE A MOVE UNTIL WE RECEIVE ORDERS TO DEPLOY!

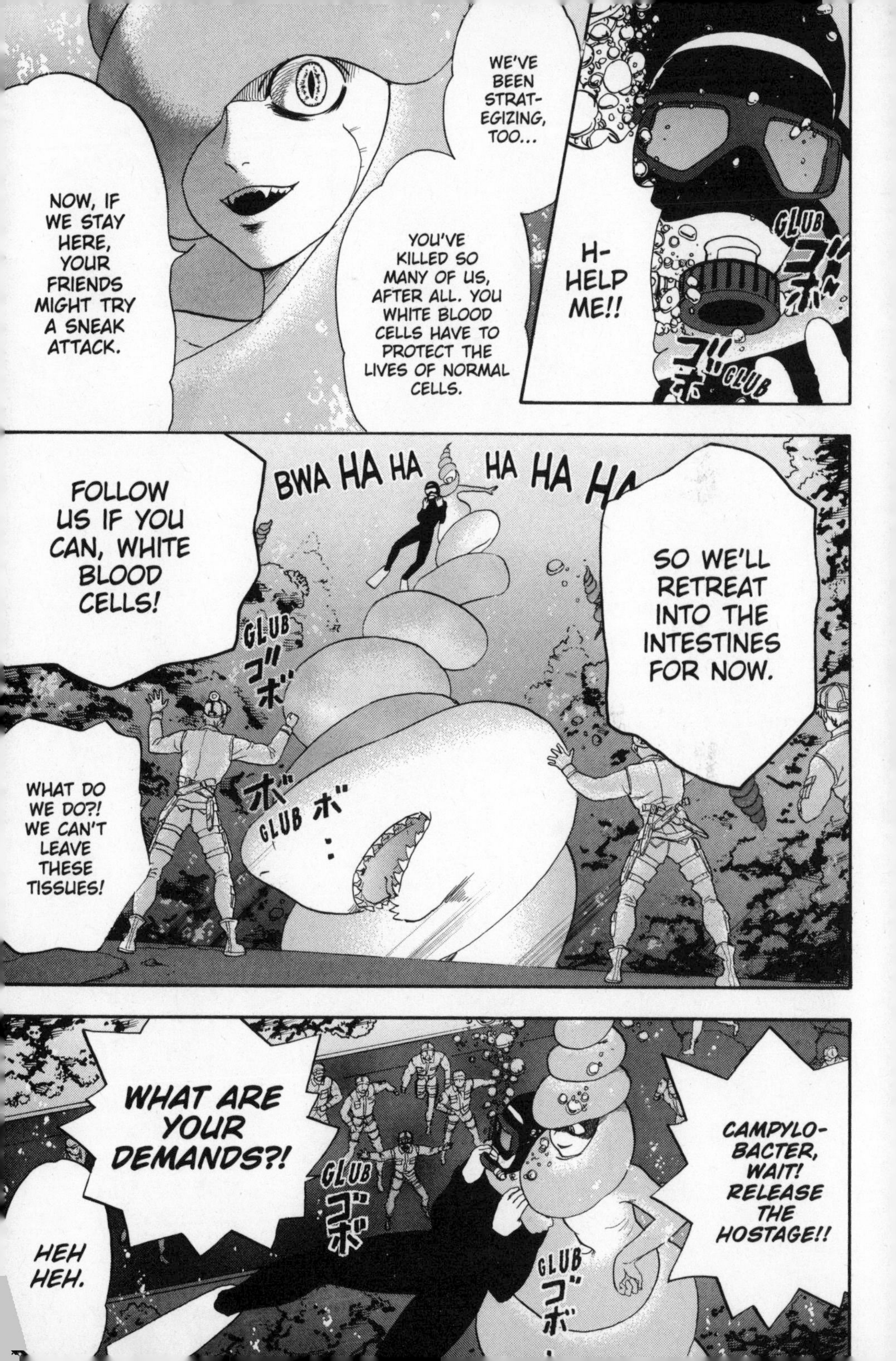

H- HELP ME!!
GLUB
GLUB
WE'VE BEEN STRAT-EGIZING, TOO...
YOU'VE KILLED SO MANY OF US, AFTER ALL. YOU WHITE BLOOD CELLS HAVE TO PROTECT THE LIVES OF NORMAL CELLS.
NOW, IF WE STAY HERE, YOUR FRIENDS MIGHT TRY A SNEAK ATTACK.
SO WE'LL RETREAT INTO THE INTESTINES FOR NOW.
BWA HA HA HA HA HA
FOLLOW US IF YOU CAN, WHITE BLOOD CELLS!
GLUB
GLUB
WHAT DO WE DO?! WE CAN'T LEAVE THESE TISSUES!
CAMPYLO-BACTER, WAIT! RELEASE THE HOSTAGE!!
GLUB
WHAT ARE YOUR DEMANDS?!
GLUB
HEH HEH.

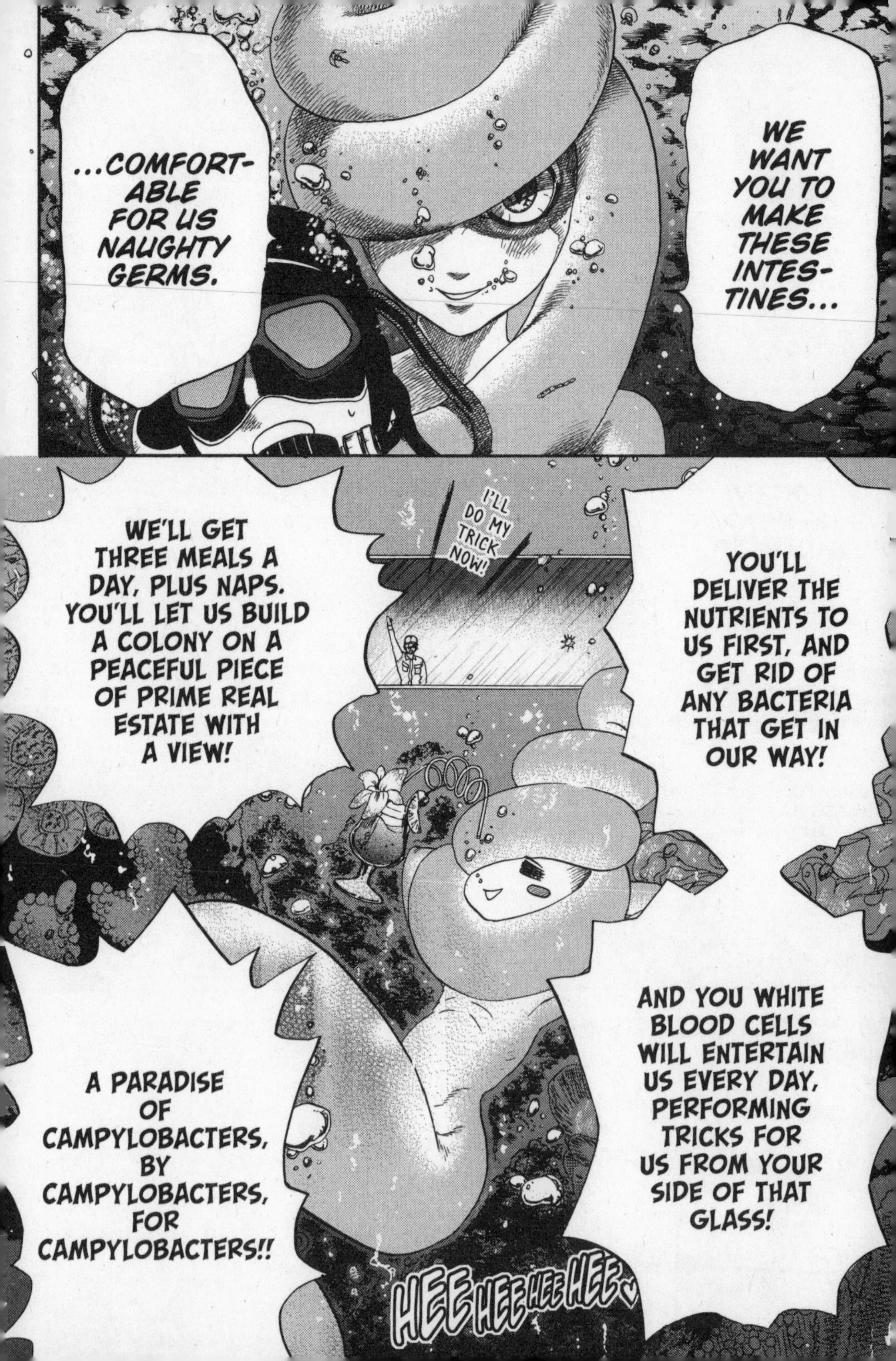

WE WANT YOU TO MAKE THESE INTES-TINES...
...COMFORT-ABLE FOR US NAUGHTY GERMS.
YOU'LL DELIVER THE NUTRIENTS TO US FIRST, AND GET RID OF ANY BACTERIA THAT GET IN OUR WAY!
I'LL DO MY TRICK NOW!
WE'LL GET THREE MEALS A DAY, PLUS NAPS. YOU'LL LET US BUILD A COLONY ON A PEACEFUL PIECE OF PRIME REAL ESTATE WITH A VIEW!
AND YOU WHITE BLOOD CELLS WILL ENTERTAIN US EVERY DAY, PERFORMING TRICKS FOR US FROM YOUR SIDE OF THAT GLASS!
A PARADISE OF CAMPYLOBACTERS, BY CAMPYLOBACTERS, FOR CAMPYLOBACTERS!!
HEE HEE HEE HEE♡

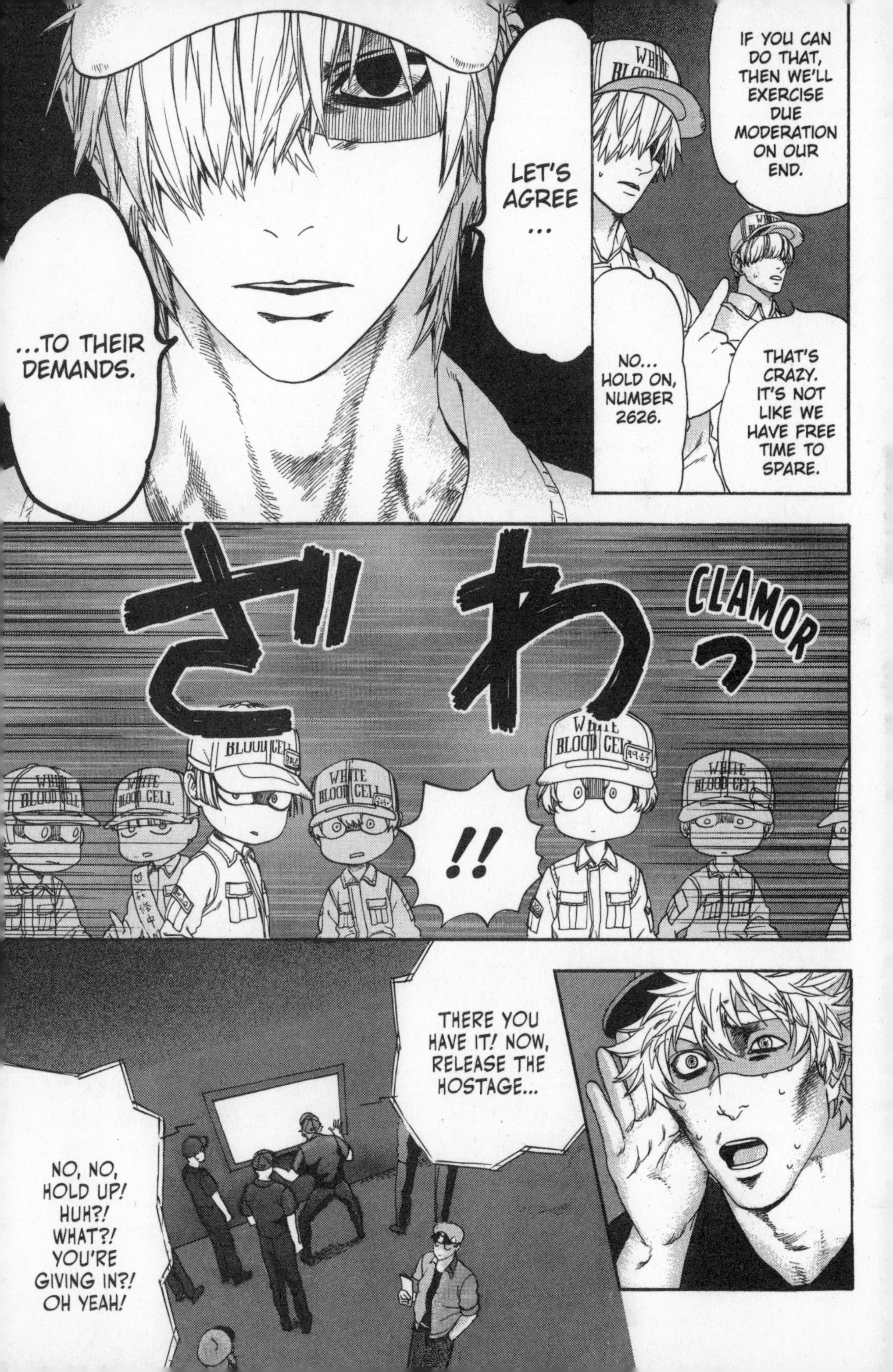
IF YOU CAN DO THAT, THEN WE'LL EXERCISE DUE MODERATION ON OUR END.
THAT'S CRAZY. IT'S NOT LIKE WE HAVE FREE TIME TO SPARE.
NO... HOLD ON, NUMBER 2626.
LET'S AGREE ...
...TO THEIR DEMANDS.
さわっ
CLAMOR
!!
THERE YOU HAVE IT! NOW, RELEASE THE HOSTAGE...
NO, NO, HOLD UP! HUH?! WHAT?! YOU'RE GIVING IN?! OH YEAH!

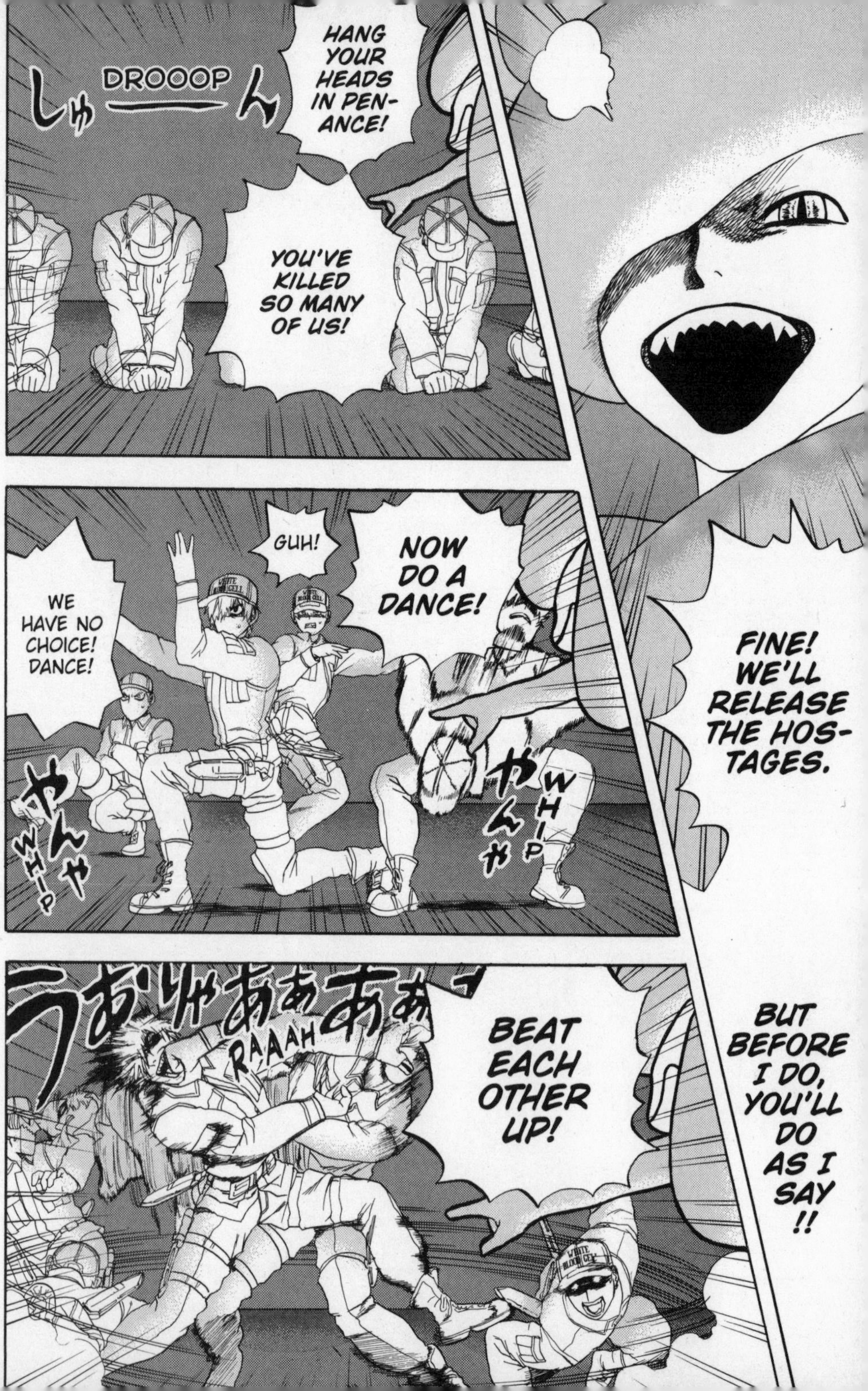

FINE! WE'LL RELEASE THE HOSTAGES.
BUT BEFORE I DO, YOU'LL DO AS I SAY!!
HANG YOUR HEADS IN PENANCE!
しゅーーん
DROOOP
YOU'VE KILLED SO MANY OF US!
NOW DO A DANCE!
GUH!
WE HAVE NO CHOICE! DANCE!
やんや
WHIP
やんや
WHIP
BEAT EACH OTHER UP!
うおりゃあああああ
RAAAH

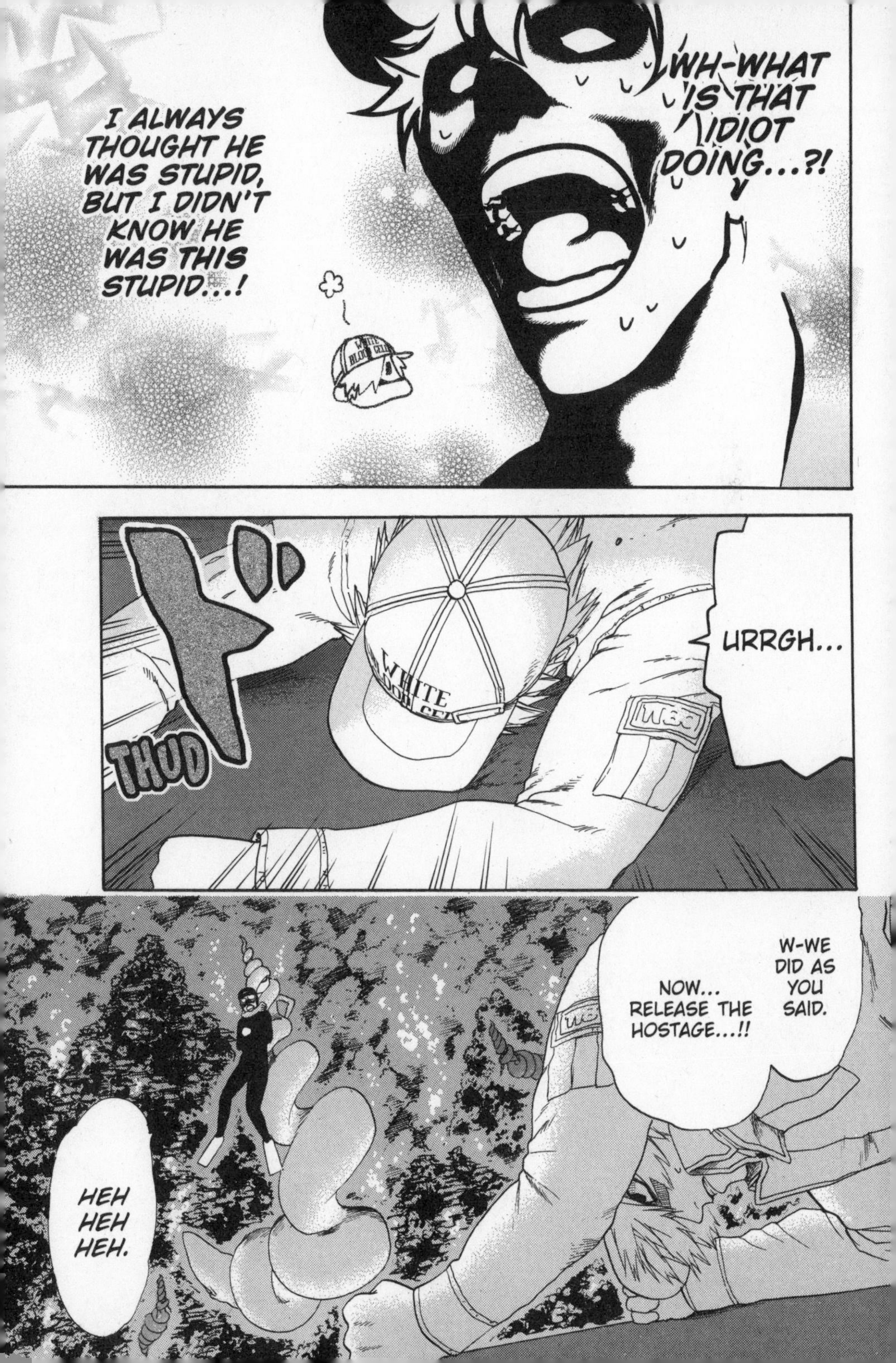
WH-WHAT IS THAT IDIOT DOING...?!
I ALWAYS THOUGHT HE WAS STUPID, BUT I DIDN'T KNOW HE WAS THIS STUPID...!
URRGH...
THUD
W-WE DID AS YOU SAID.
NOW... RELEASE THE HOSTAGE...!!
HEH HEH HEH.

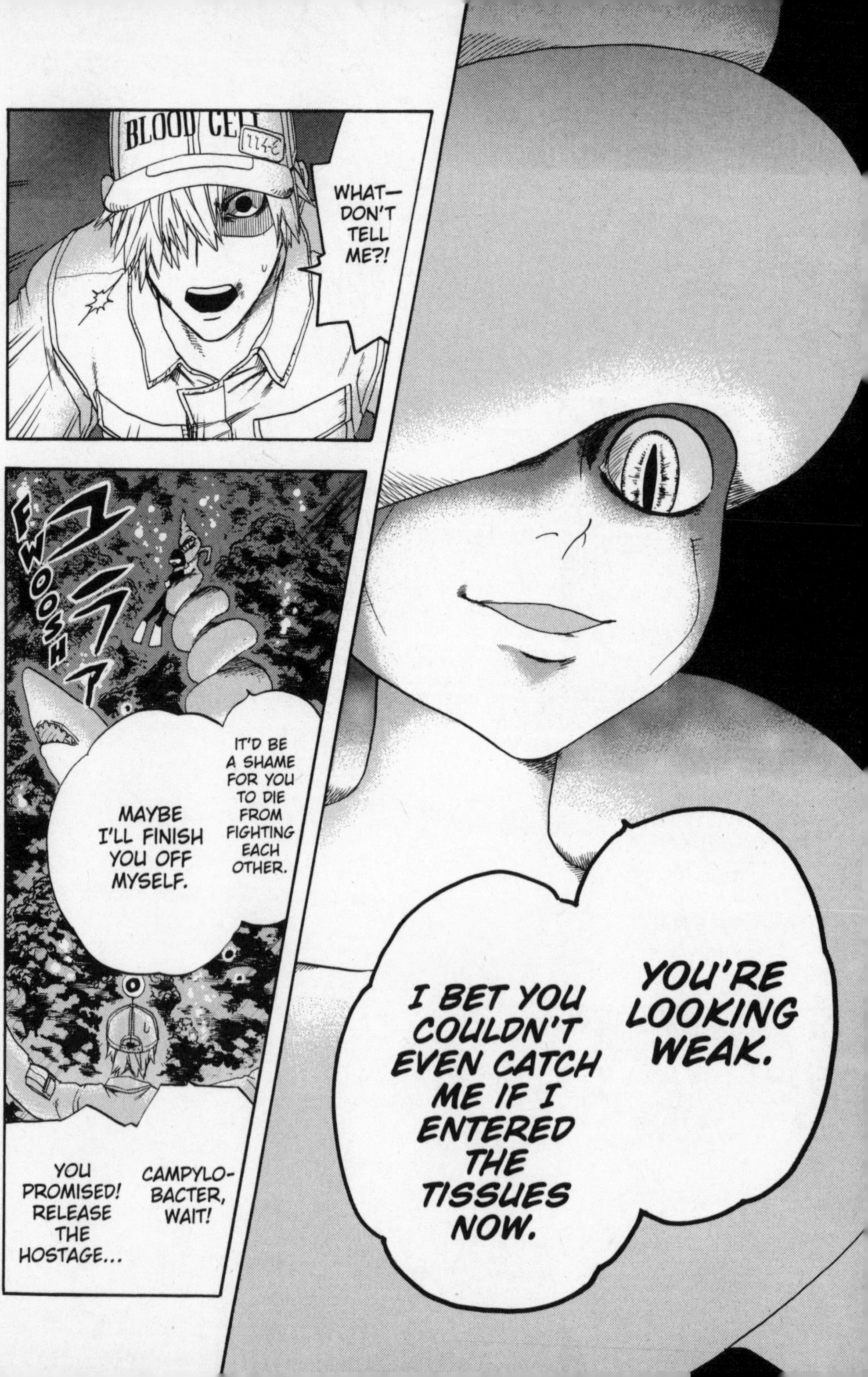
YOU'RE LOOKING WEAK.
I BET YOU COULDN'T EVEN CATCH ME IF I ENTERED THE TISSUES NOW.
WHAT— DON'T TELL ME?!
FWOOSH
IT'D BE A SHAME FOR YOU TO DIE FROM FIGHTING EACH OTHER.
MAYBE I'LL FINISH YOU OFF MYSELF.
CAMPYLO-BACTER, WAIT!
YOU PROMISED! RELEASE THE HOSTAGE...

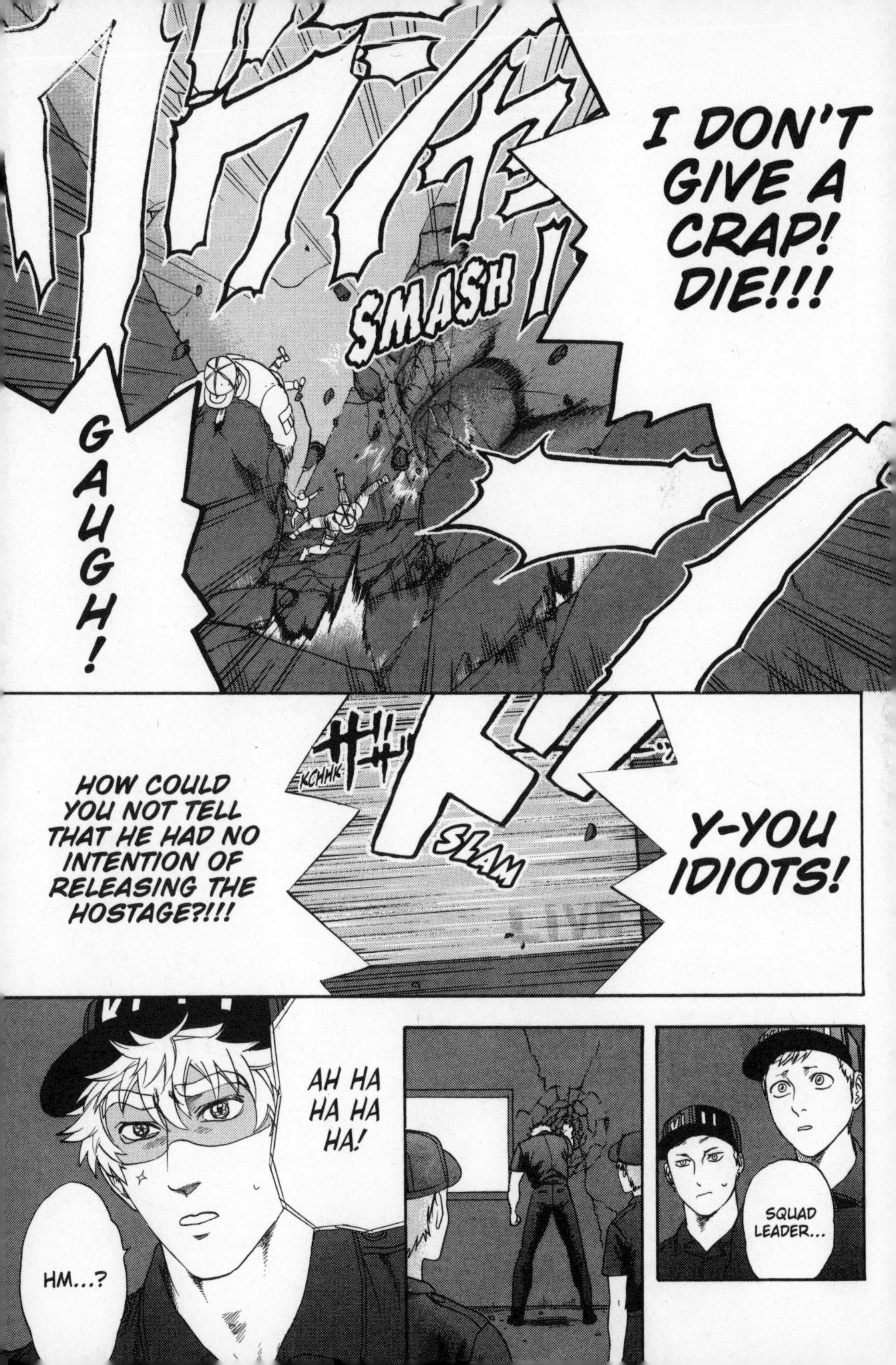
I DON'T GIVE A CRAP! DIE!!!
SMASH
GAUGH!
Y-YOU IDIOTS!
SLAM
KCHHK
HOW COULD YOU NOT TELL THAT HE HAD NO INTENTION OF RELEASING THE HOSTAGE?!!!
SQUAD LEADER...
AH HA HA HA HA!
HM...?

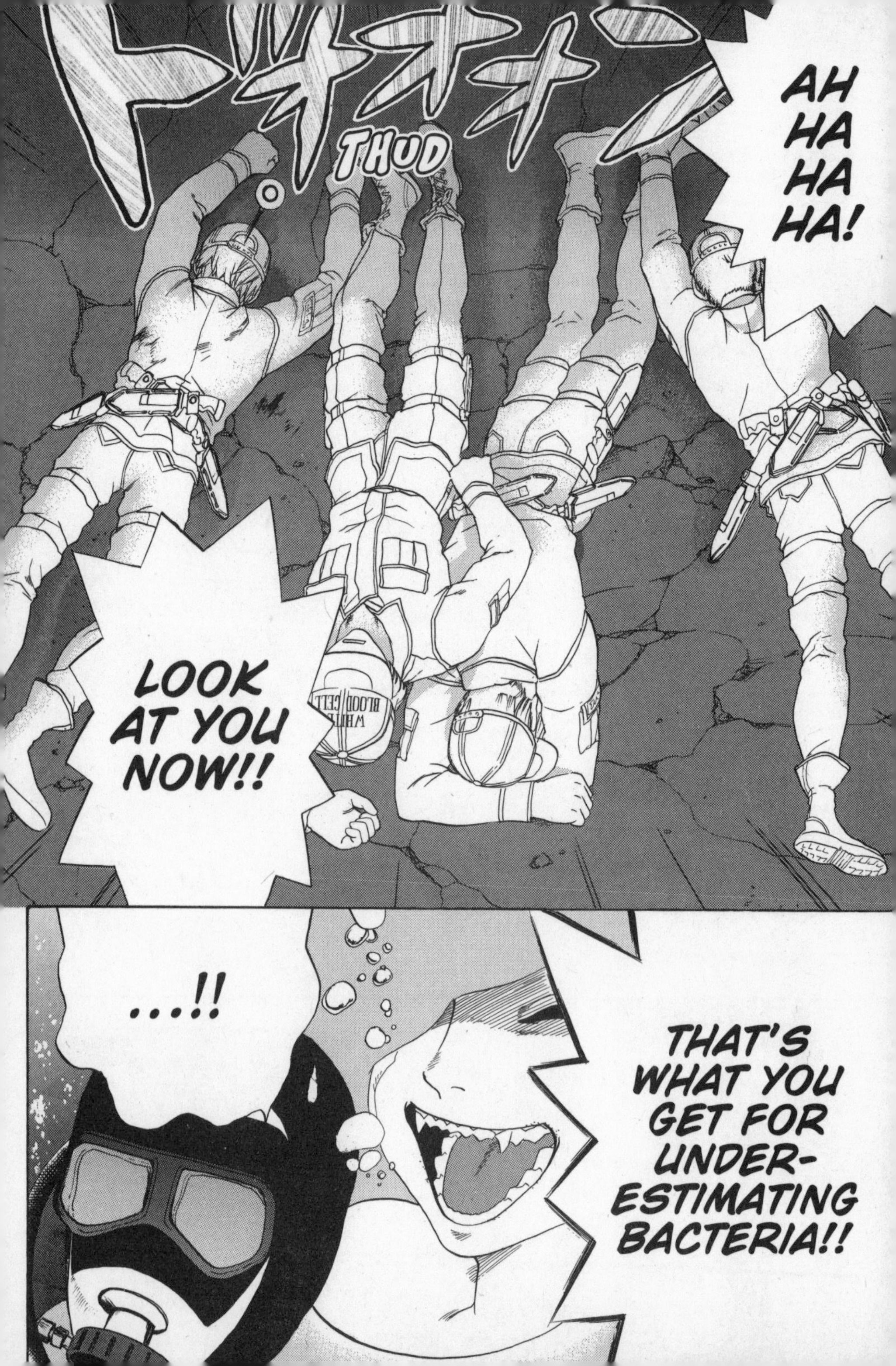
AH HA HA HA!
THUD
LOOK AT YOU NOW!!
THAT'S WHAT YOU GET FOR UNDER-ESTIMATING BACTERIA!!
...!!

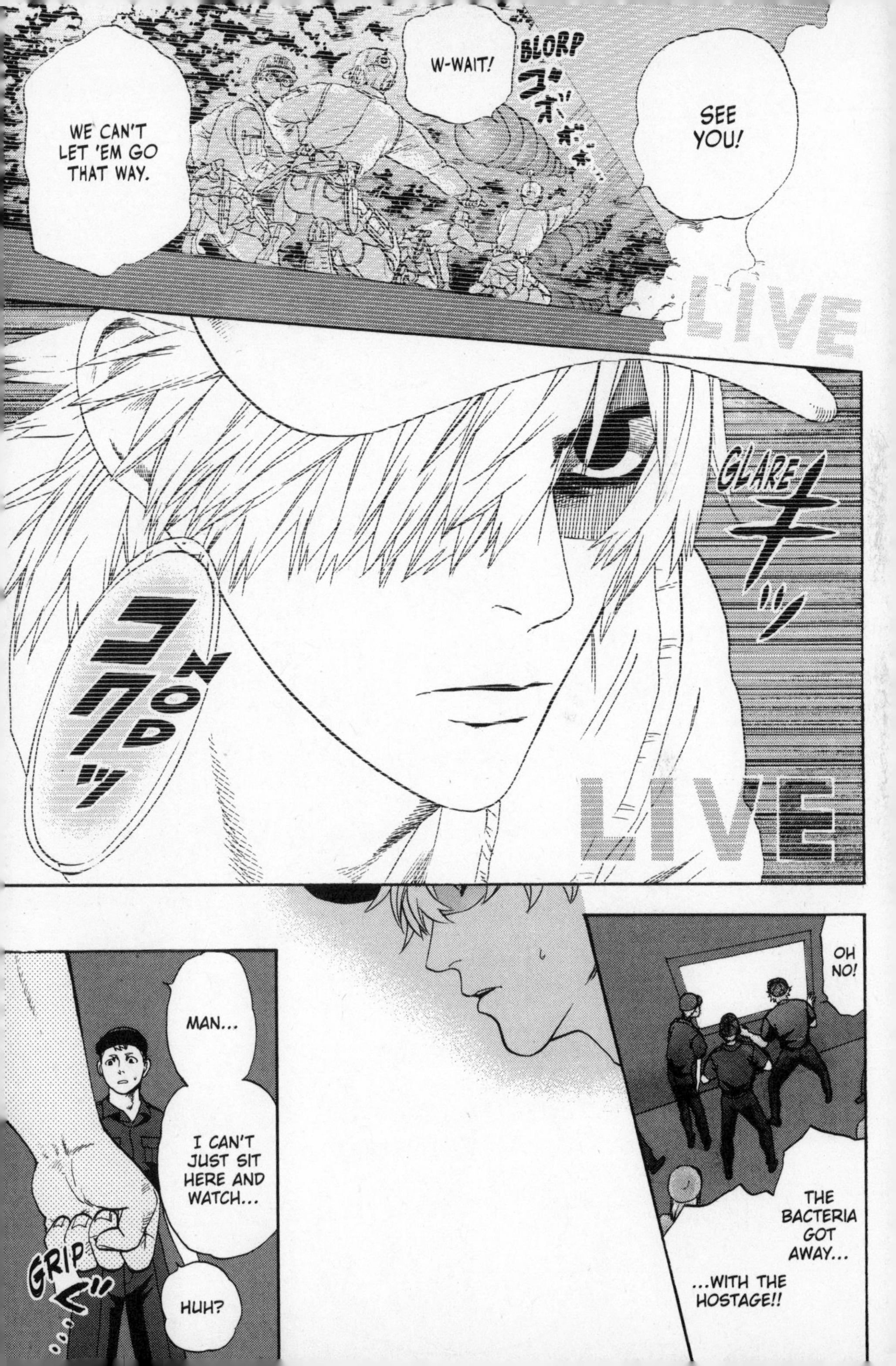

SEE YOU!
BLORP
W-WAIT!
WE CAN'T LET 'EM GO THAT WAY.
LIVE
GLARE
キッ
LIVE
NOD
コクッ
OH NO!
THE BACTERIA GOT AWAY...
...WITH THE HOSTAGE!!
MAN...
I CAN'T JUST SIT HERE AND WATCH...
HUH?
GRIP

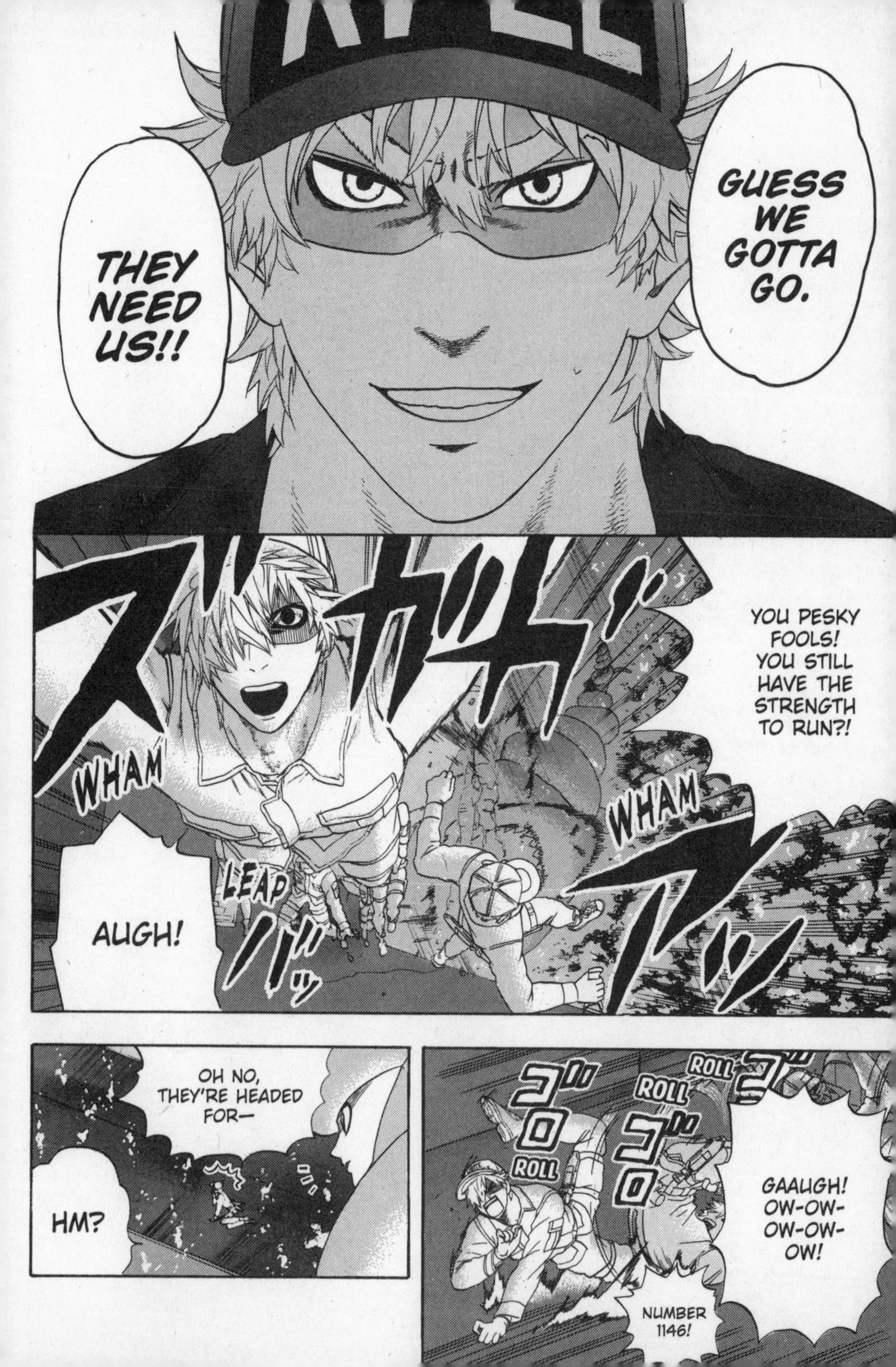
GUESS WE GOTTA GO.
THEY NEED US!!
YOU PESKY FOOLS! YOU STILL HAVE THE STRENGTH TO RUN?!
WHAM
WHAM
LEAP
AUGH!
ROLL
ROLL
ROLL
GAAUGH! OW-OW-OW-OW-OW!
NUMBER 1146!
OH NO, THEY'RE HEADED FOR—
HM?

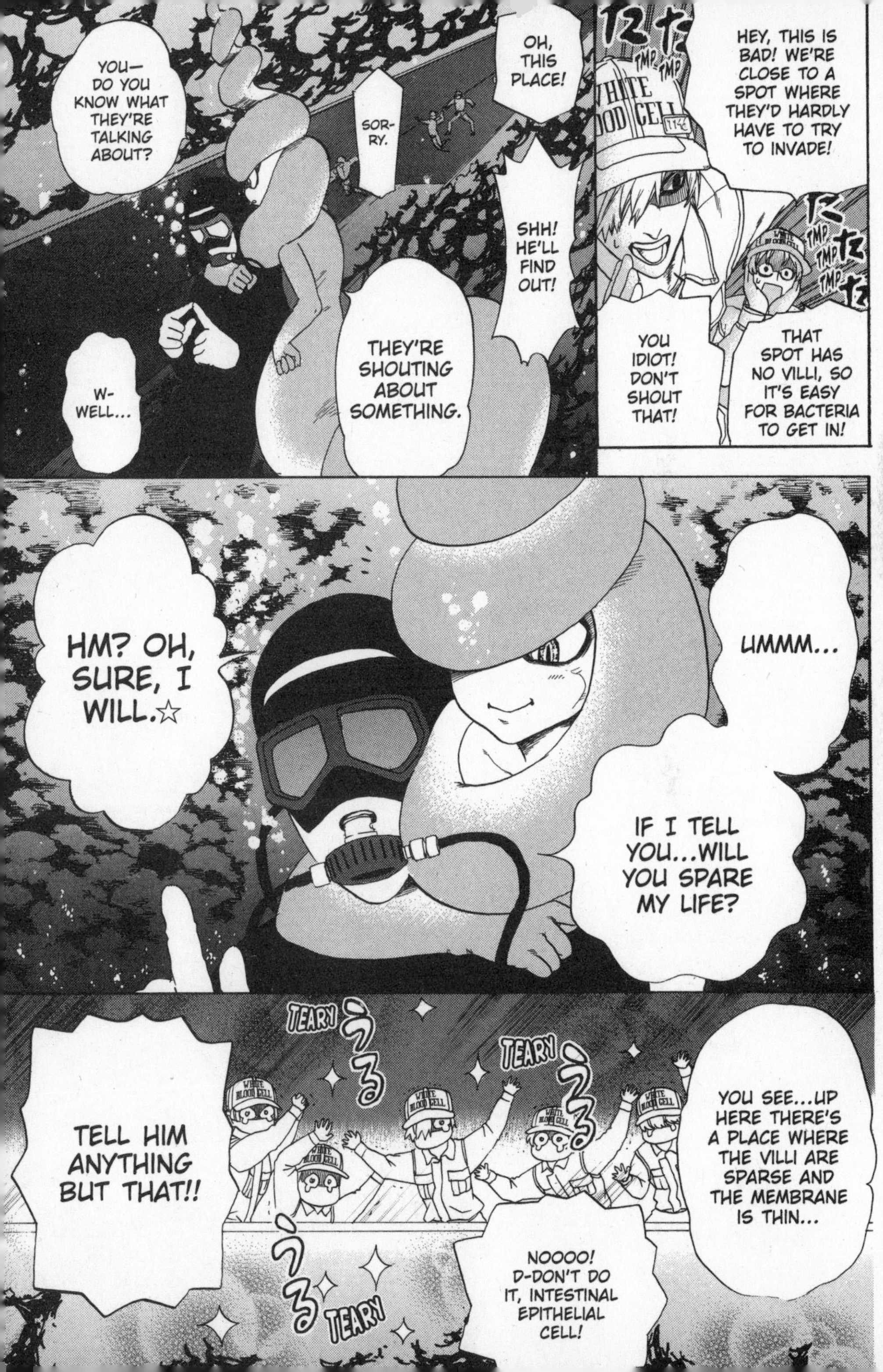
TMP TMP
HEY, THIS IS BAD! WE'RE CLOSE TO A SPOT WHERE THEY'D HARDLY HAVE TO TRY TO INVADE!
TMP TMP TMP
THAT SPOT HAS NO VILLI, SO IT'S EASY FOR BACTERIA TO GET IN!
YOU IDIOT! DON'T SHOUT THAT!
OH, THIS PLACE!
SOR-RY.
SHH! HE'LL FIND OUT!
YOU— DO YOU KNOW WHAT THEY'RE TALKING ABOUT?
THEY'RE SHOUTING ABOUT SOMETHING.
W-WELL...
UMMM...
IF I TELL YOU...WILL YOU SPARE MY LIFE?
HM? OH, SURE, I WILL.☆
YOU SEE...UP HERE THERE'S A PLACE WHERE THE VILLI ARE SPARSE AND THE MEMBRANE IS THIN...
TEARY
TEARY
NOOOO! D-DON'T DO IT, INTESTINAL EPITHELIAL CELL!
TEARY
TELL HIM ANYTHING BUT THAT!!

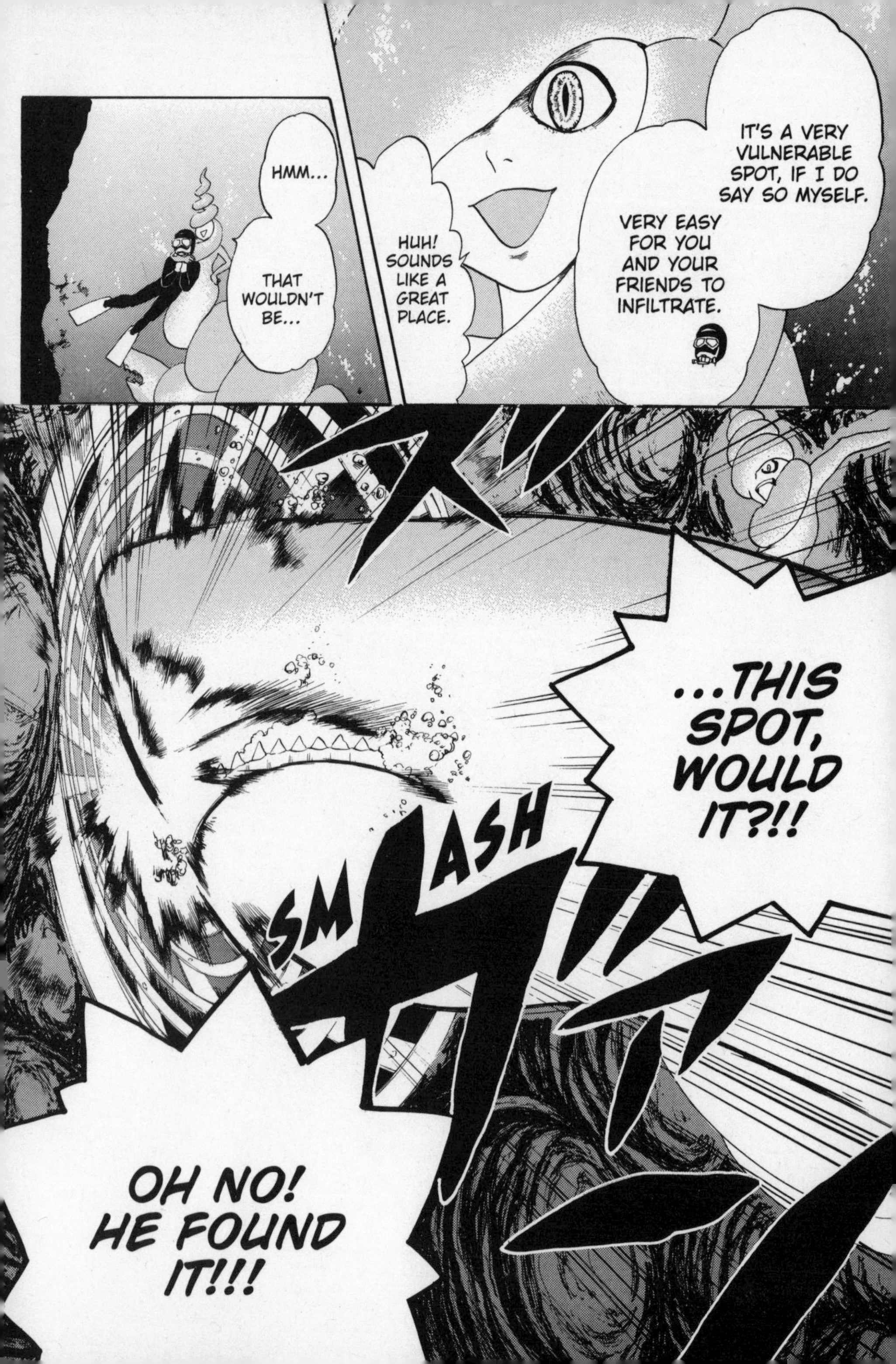
IT'S A VERY VULNERABLE SPOT, IF I DO SAY SO MYSELF.
VERY EASY FOR YOU AND YOUR FRIENDS TO INFILTRATE.
HUH! SOUNDS LIKE A GREAT PLACE.
HMM...
THAT WOULDN'T BE...
...THIS SPOT, WOULD IT?!!
SMASH
OH NO! HE FOUND IT!!!

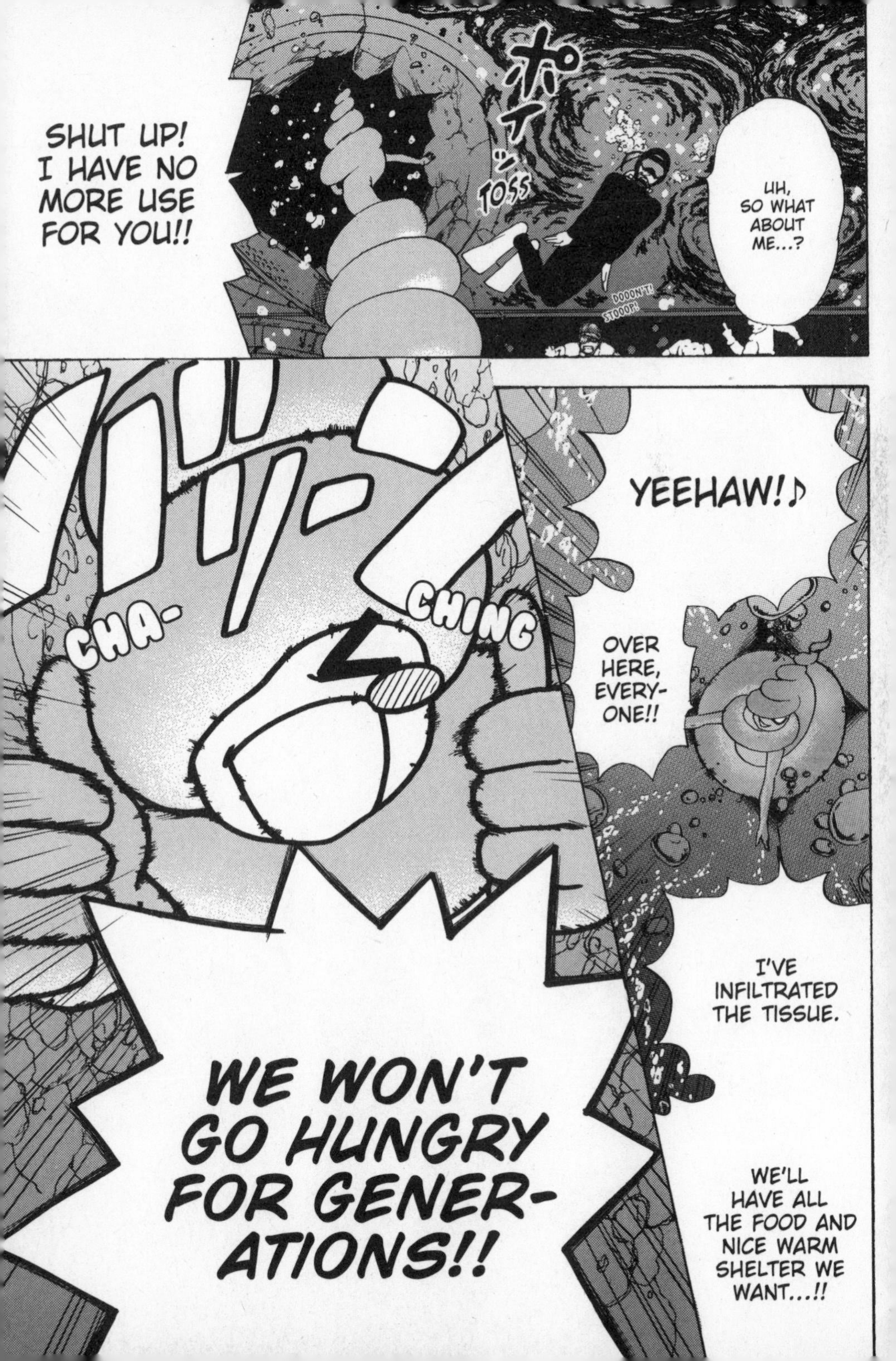
UH, SO WHAT ABOUT ME...?
ポイッ
TOSS
DOOON'T! STOOOP!
SHUT UP! I HAVE NO MORE USE FOR YOU!!
YEEHAW!♪
OVER HERE, EVERY-ONE!!
I'VE INFILTRATED THE TISSUE.
WE'LL HAVE ALL THE FOOD AND NICE WARM SHELTER WE WANT...!!
CHA-CHING
WE WON'T GO HUNGRY FOR GENER-ATIONS!!

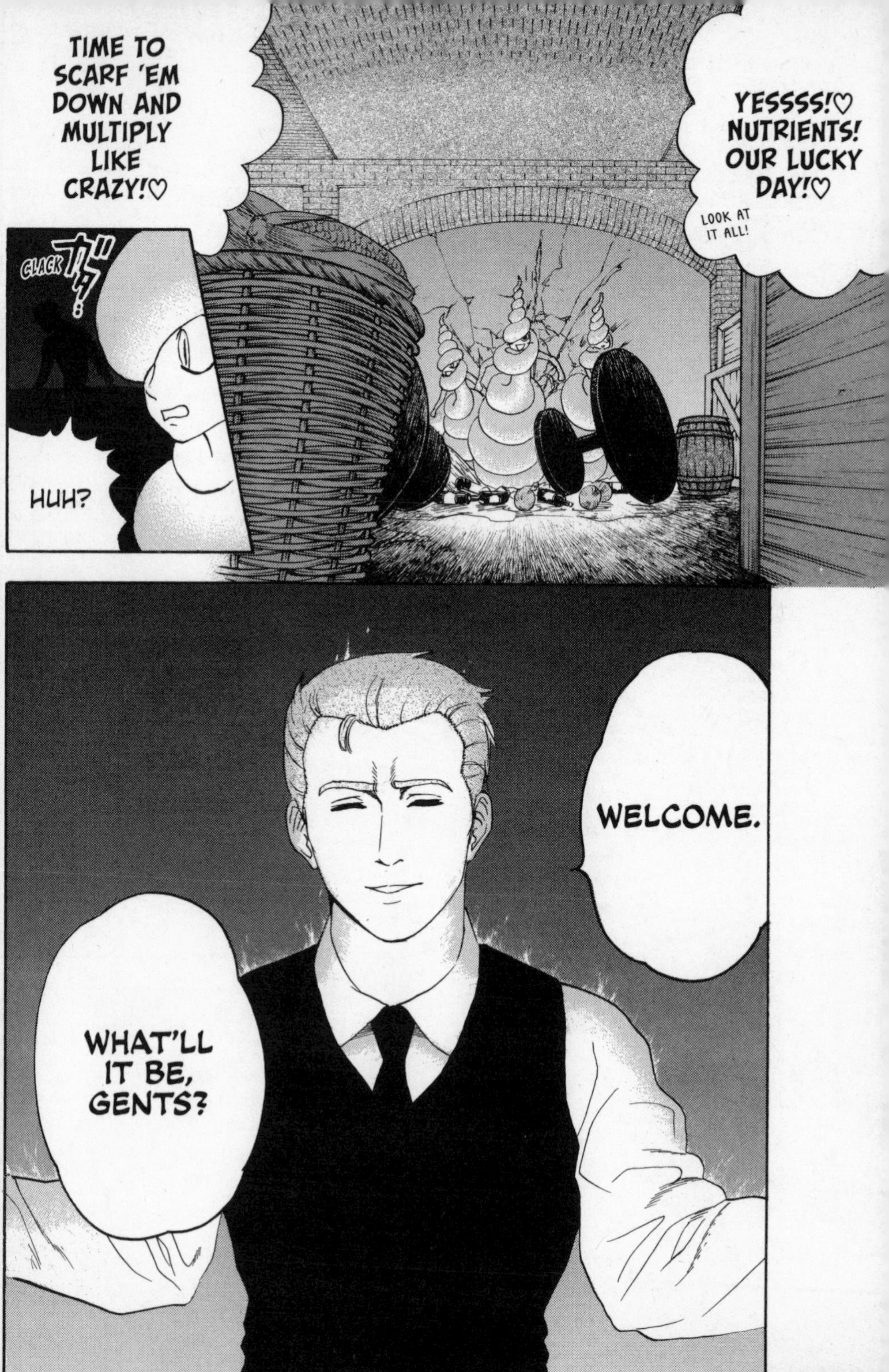
YESSSS!♡ NUTRIENTS! OUR LUCKY DAY!♡
LOOK AT IT ALL!
TIME TO SCARF 'EM DOWN AND MULTIPLY LIKE CRAZY!♡
CLACK
HUH?
WELCOME.
WHAT'LL IT BE, GENTS?

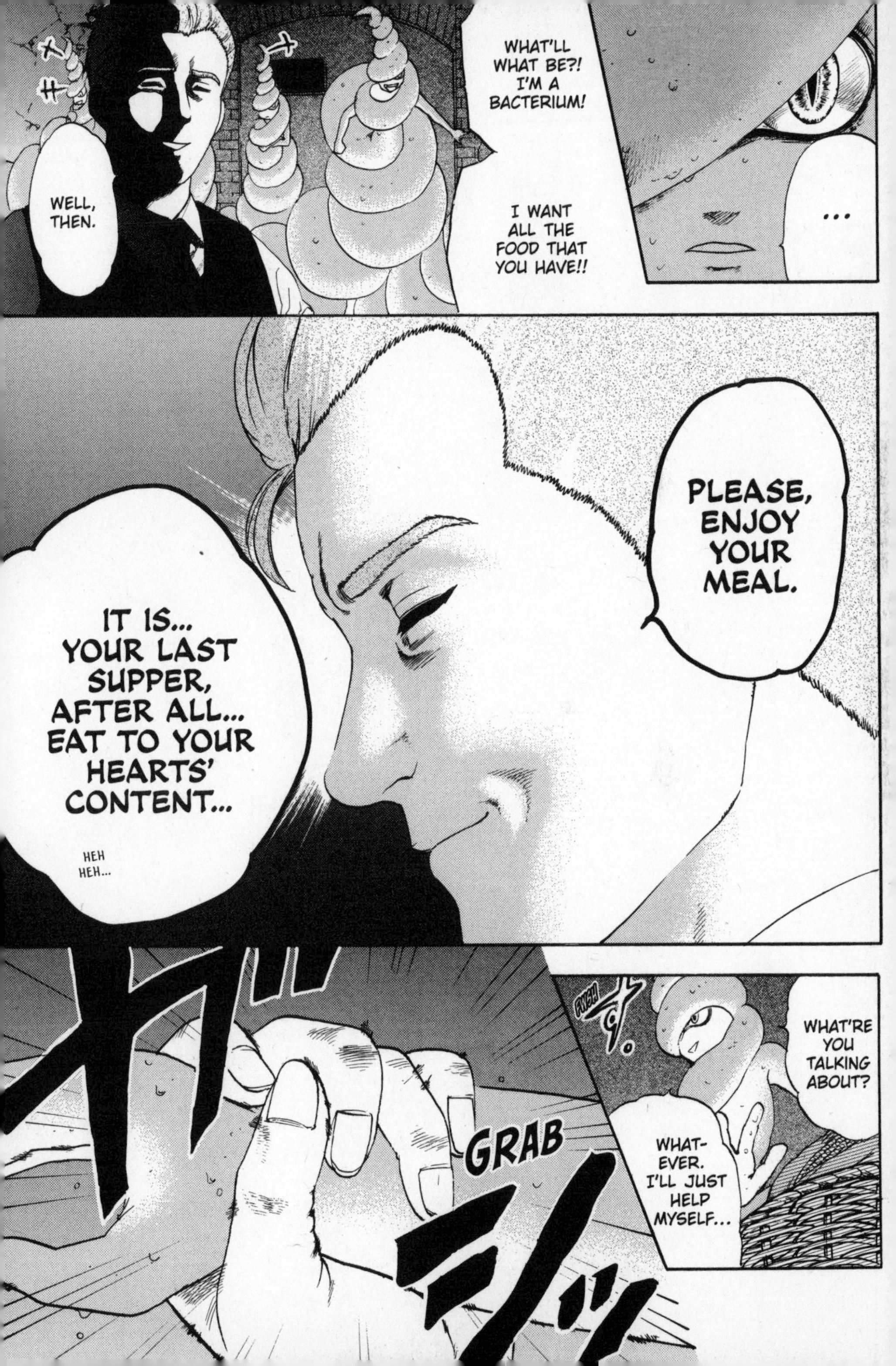
...
WHAT'LL WHAT BE?! I'M A BACTERIUM!
I WANT ALL THE FOOD THAT YOU HAVE!!
WELL, THEN.
PLEASE, ENJOY YOUR MEAL.
IT IS... YOUR LAST SUPPER, AFTER ALL... EAT TO YOUR HEARTS' CONTENT...
HEH HEH...
FWSH
WHAT'RE YOU TALKING ABOUT?
WHAT-EVER. I'LL JUST HELP MYSELF...
GRAB

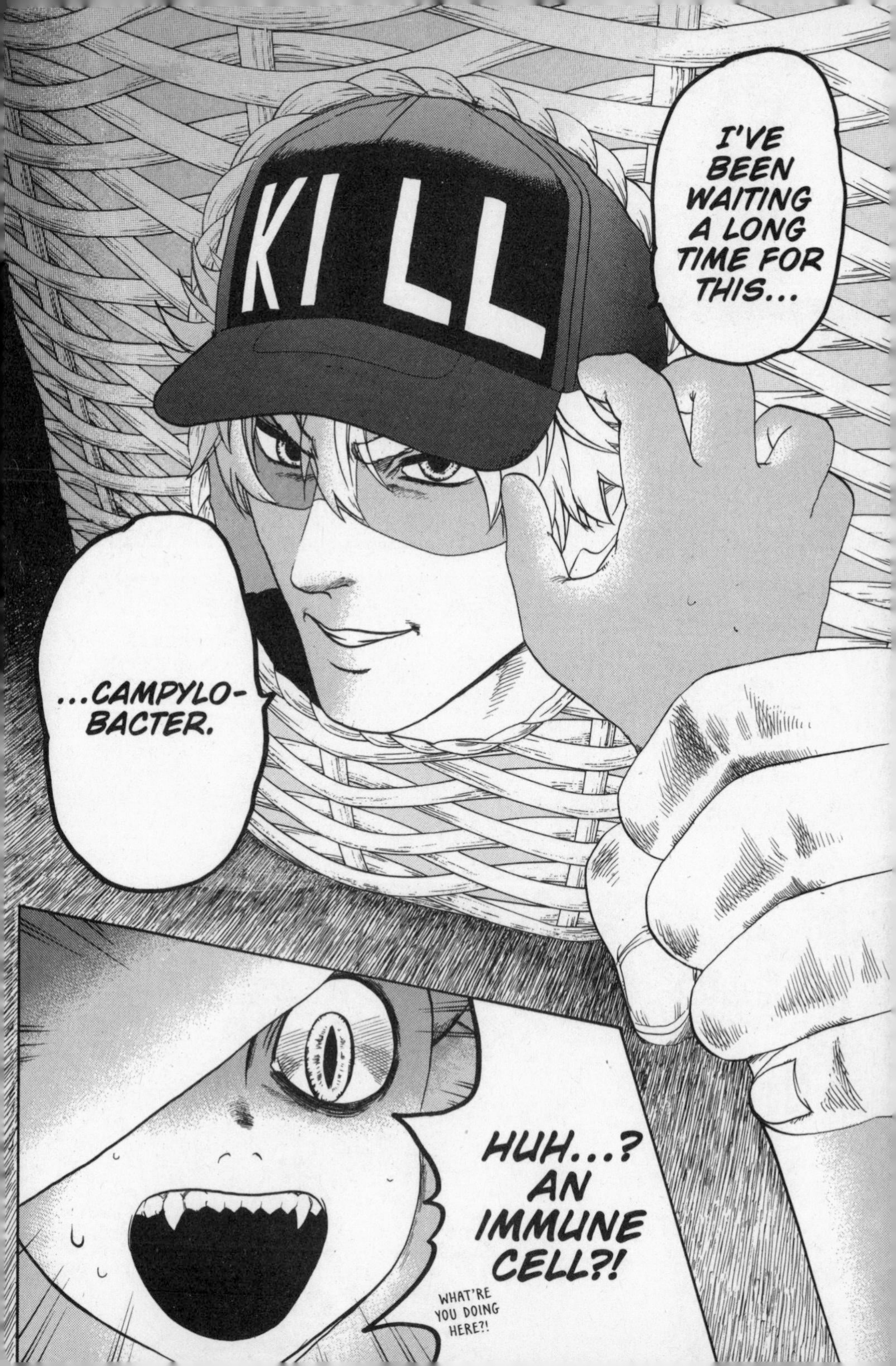
KILL
I'VE BEEN WAITING A LONG TIME FOR THIS...
...CAMPYLO-BACTER.
HUH...? AN IMMUNE CELL?!
WHAT'RE YOU DOING HERE?!

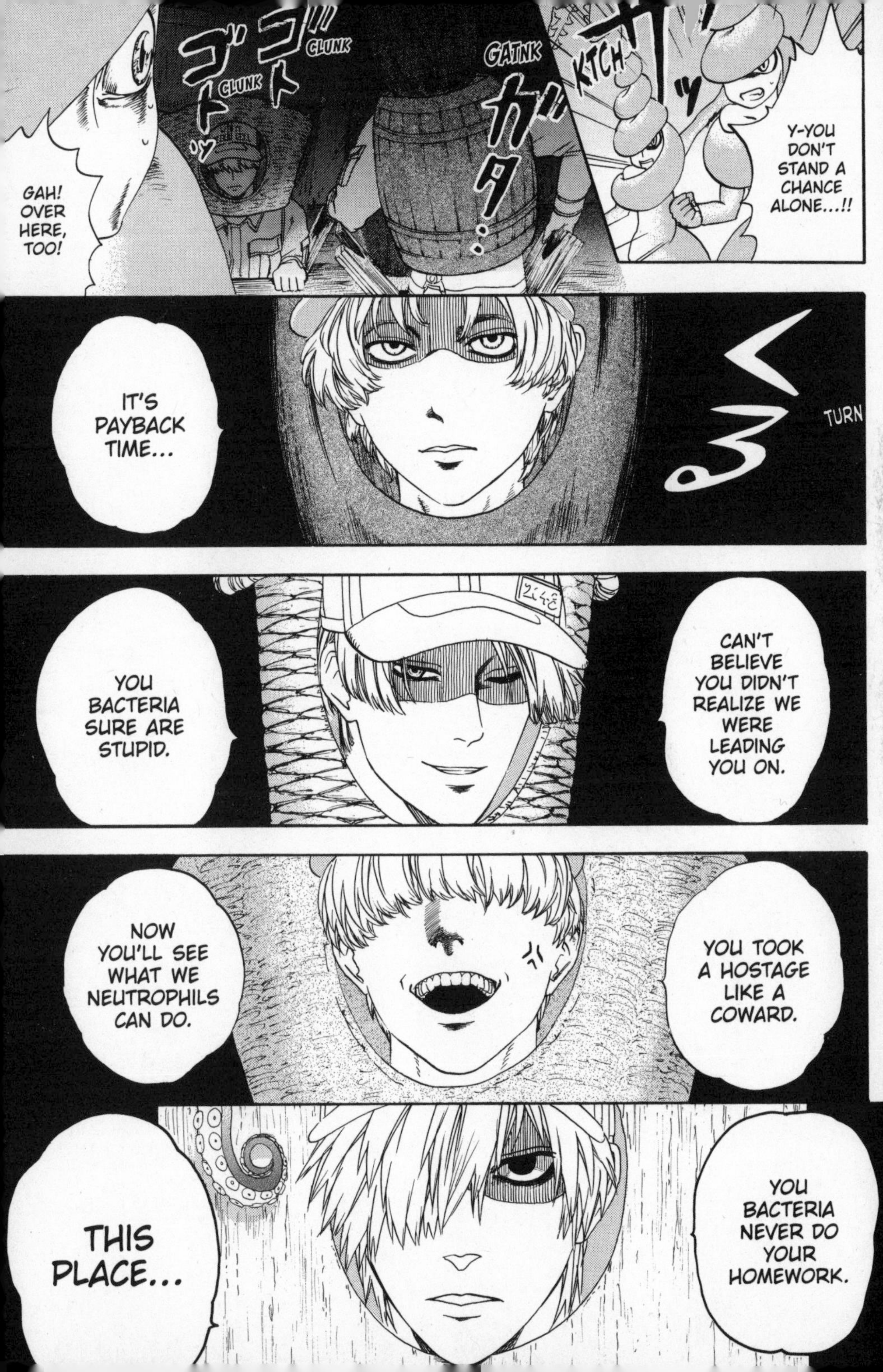
KTCH
Y-YOU DON'T STAND A CHANCE ALONE...!!
GATNK
CLUNK
CLUNK
GAH! OVER HERE, TOO!
TURN
IT'S PAYBACK TIME...
CAN'T BELIEVE YOU DIDN'T REALIZE WE WERE LEADING YOU ON.
YOU BACTERIA SURE ARE STUPID.
YOU TOOK A HOSTAGE LIKE A COWARD.
NOW YOU'LL SEE WHAT WE NEUTROPHILS CAN DO.
YOU BACTERIA NEVER DO YOUR HOMEWORK.
THIS PLACE...

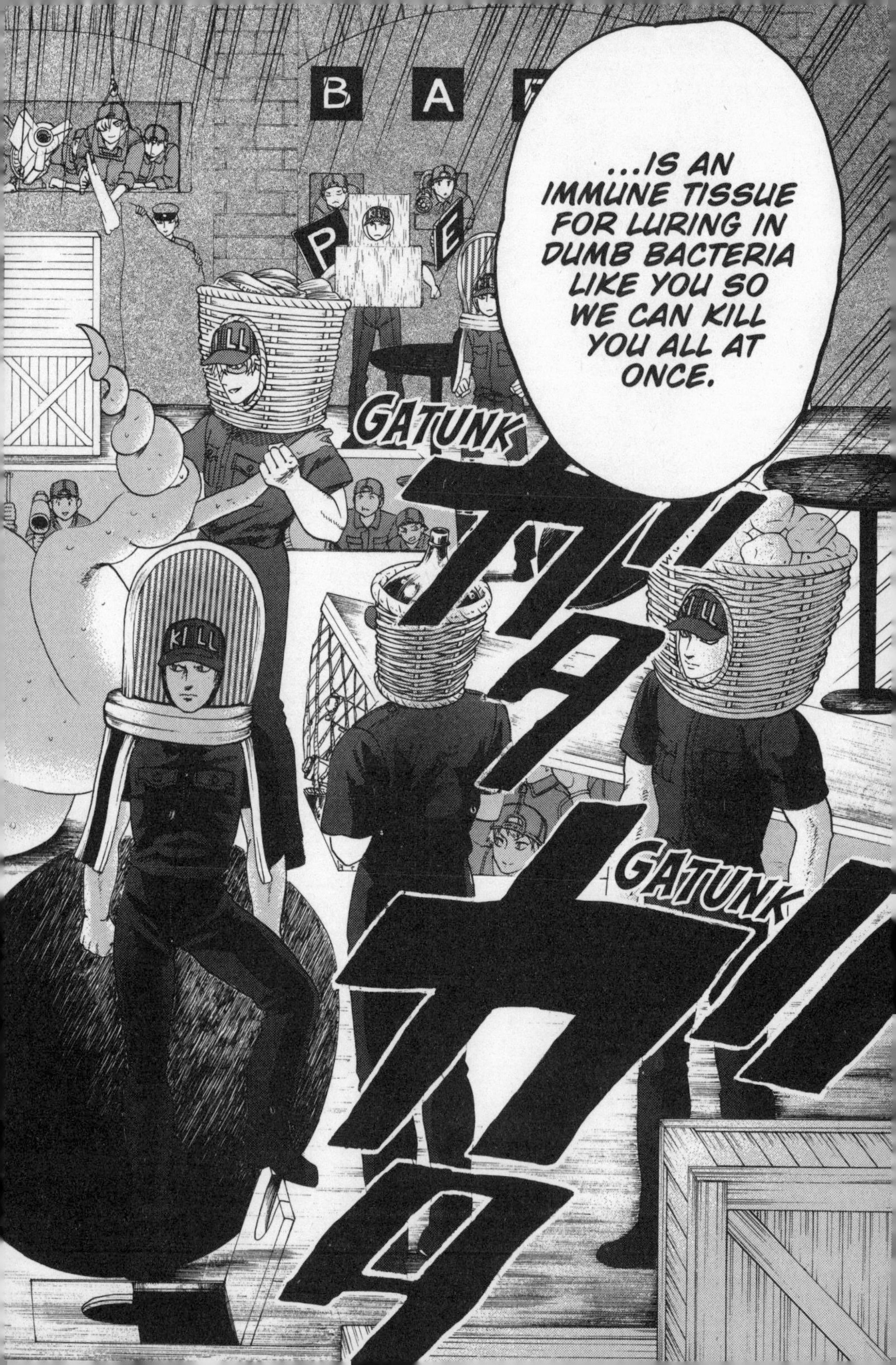
...IS AN IMMUNE TISSUE FOR LURING IN DUMB BACTERIA LIKE YOU SO WE CAN KILL YOU ALL AT ONCE.
GATUNK
GATUNK

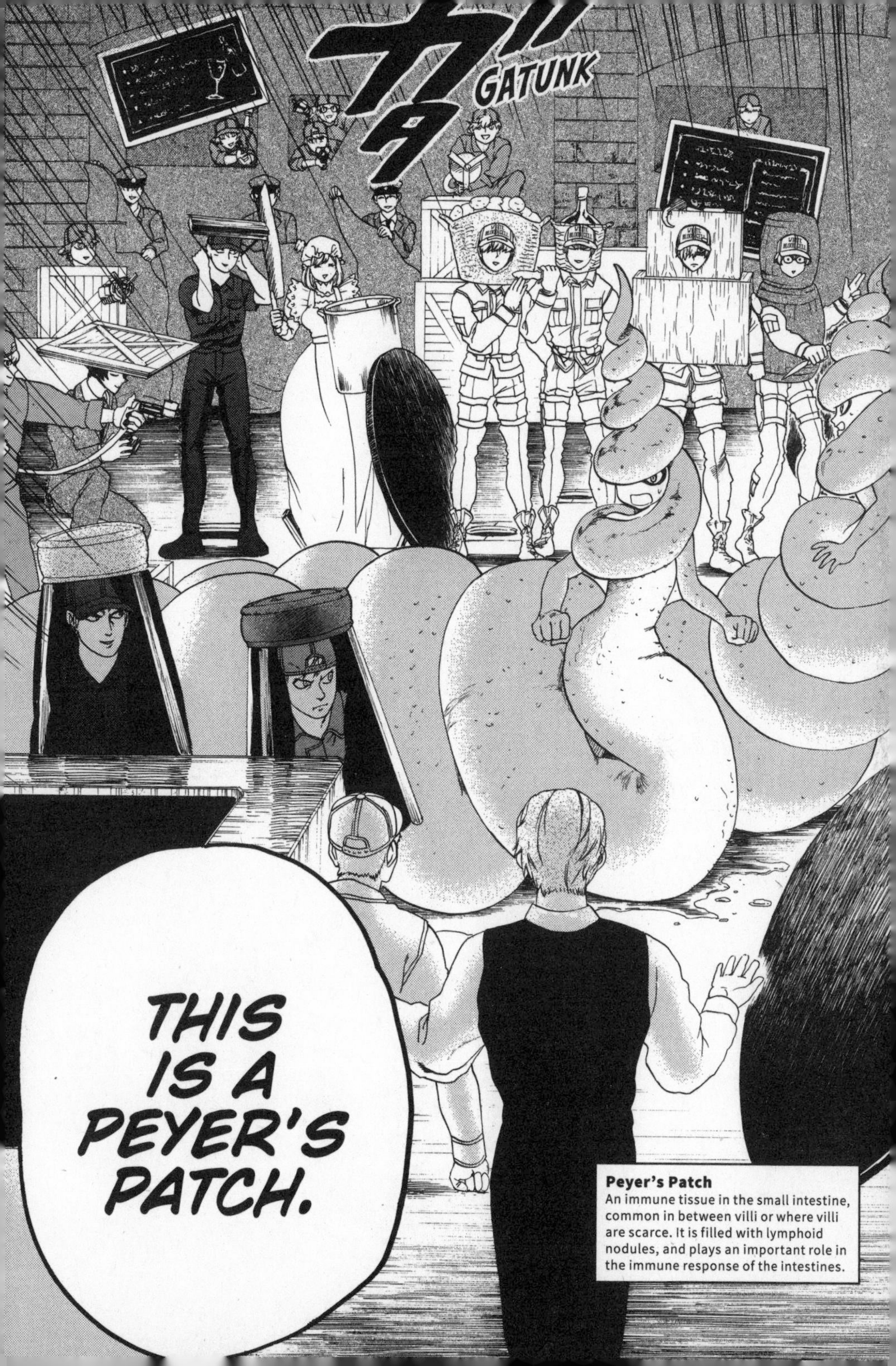
ガタ
GATUNK
THIS IS A PEYER'S PATCH.

Peyer's Patch
An immune tissue in the small intestine, common in between villi or where villi are scarce. It is filled with lymphoid nodules, and plays an important role in the immune response of the intestines.

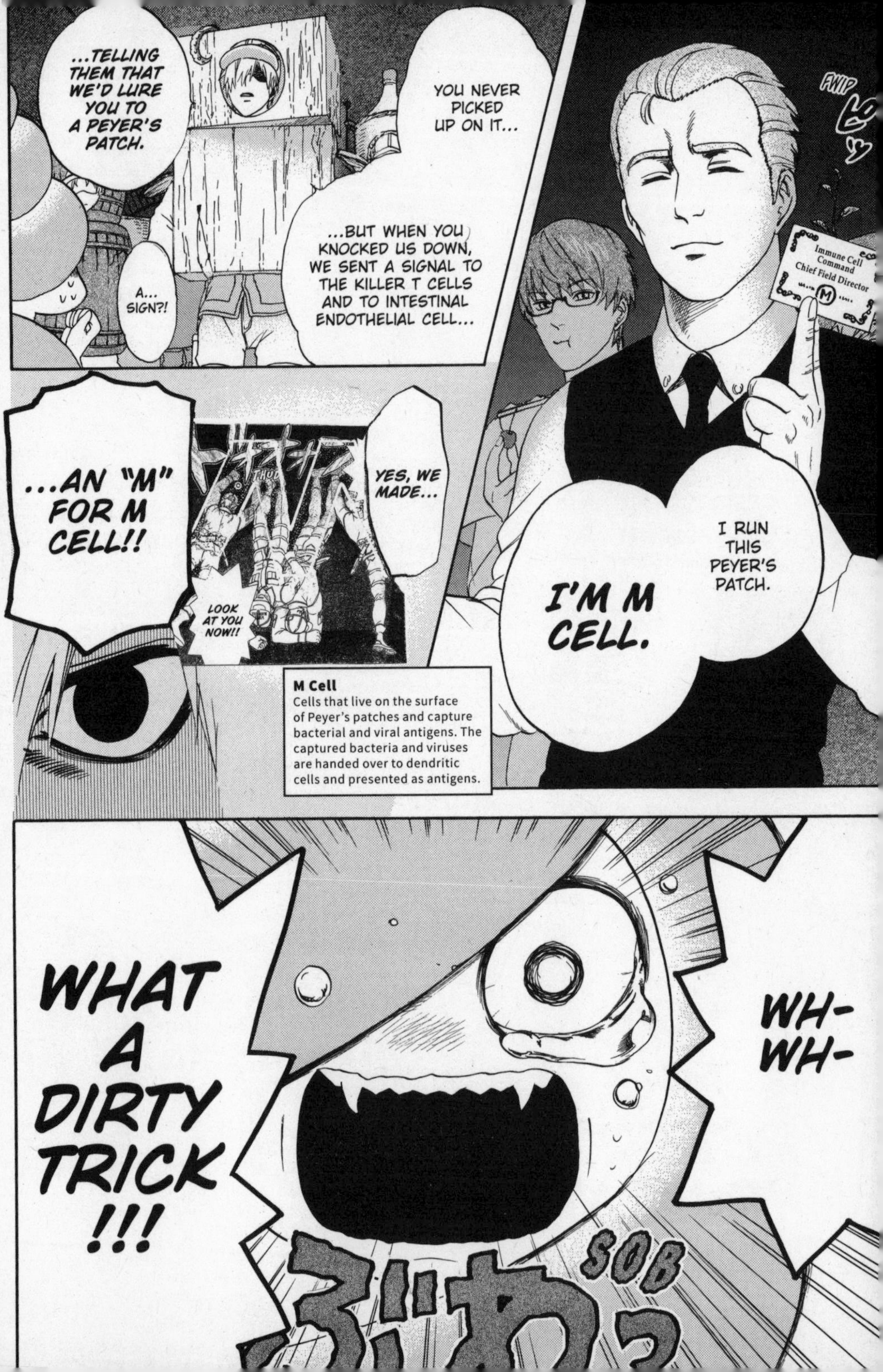
FWIP
Immune Cell Command
Chief Field Director
M
I RUN THIS PEYER'S PATCH.
I'M M CELL.
YOU NEVER PICKED UP ON IT...
...BUT WHEN YOU KNOCKED US DOWN, WE SENT A SIGNAL TO THE KILLER T CELLS AND TO INTESTINAL ENDOTHELIAL CELL...
...TELLING THEM THAT WE'D LURE YOU TO A PEYER'S PATCH.
A... SIGN?!
YES, WE MADE...
THUD
LOOK AT YOU NOW!!
...AN "M" FOR M CELL!!
M Cell
Cells that live on the surface of Peyer's patches and capture bacterial and viral antigens. The captured bacteria and viruses are handed over to dendritic cells and presented as antigens.
WH- WH-
WHAT A DIRTY TRICK!!!
SOB

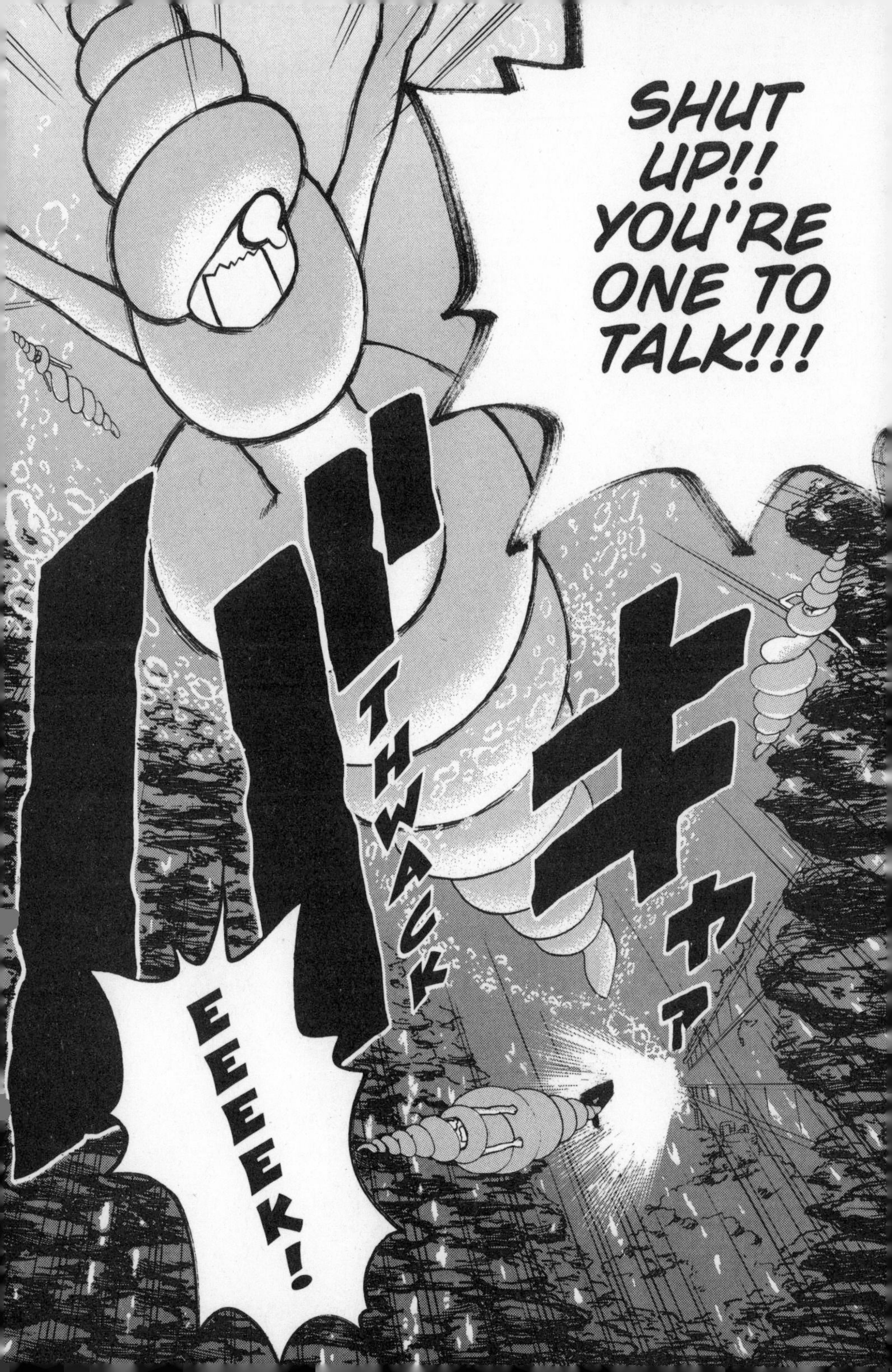
SHUT UP!! YOU'RE ONE TO TALK!!!
THWACK
EEEEEK!

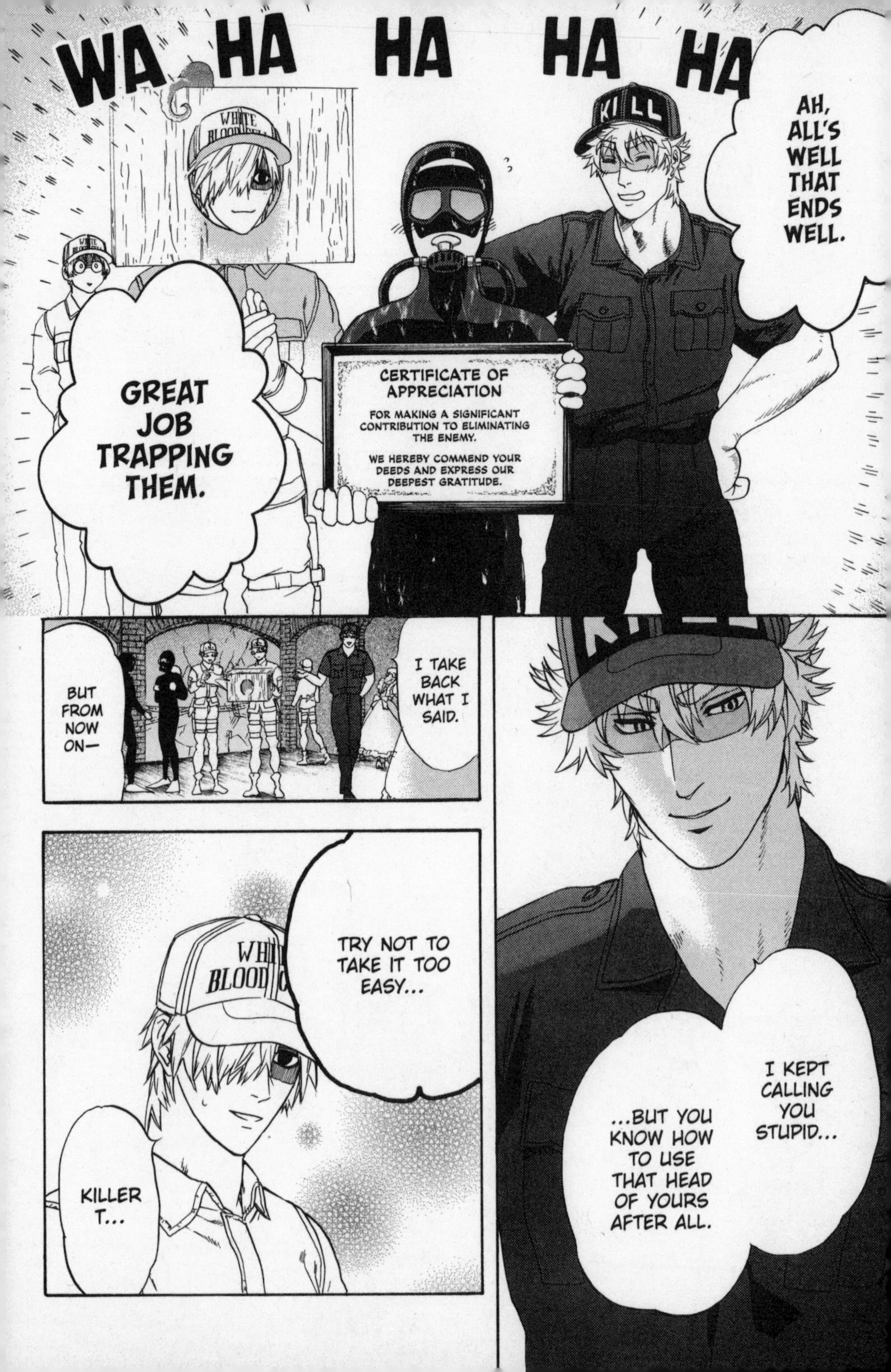
WA HA HA HA HA
AH, ALL'S WELL THAT ENDS WELL.
CERTIFICATE OF APPRECIATION
FOR MAKING A SIGNIFICANT CONTRIBUTION TO ELIMINATING THE ENEMY.
WE HEREBY COMMEND YOUR DEEDS AND EXPRESS OUR DEEPEST GRATITUDE.
GREAT JOB TRAPPING THEM.
I KEPT CALLING YOU STUPID...
...BUT YOU KNOW HOW TO USE THAT HEAD OF YOURS AFTER ALL.
I TAKE BACK WHAT I SAID.
BUT FROM NOW ON—
TRY NOT TO TAKE IT TOO EASY...
KILLER T...

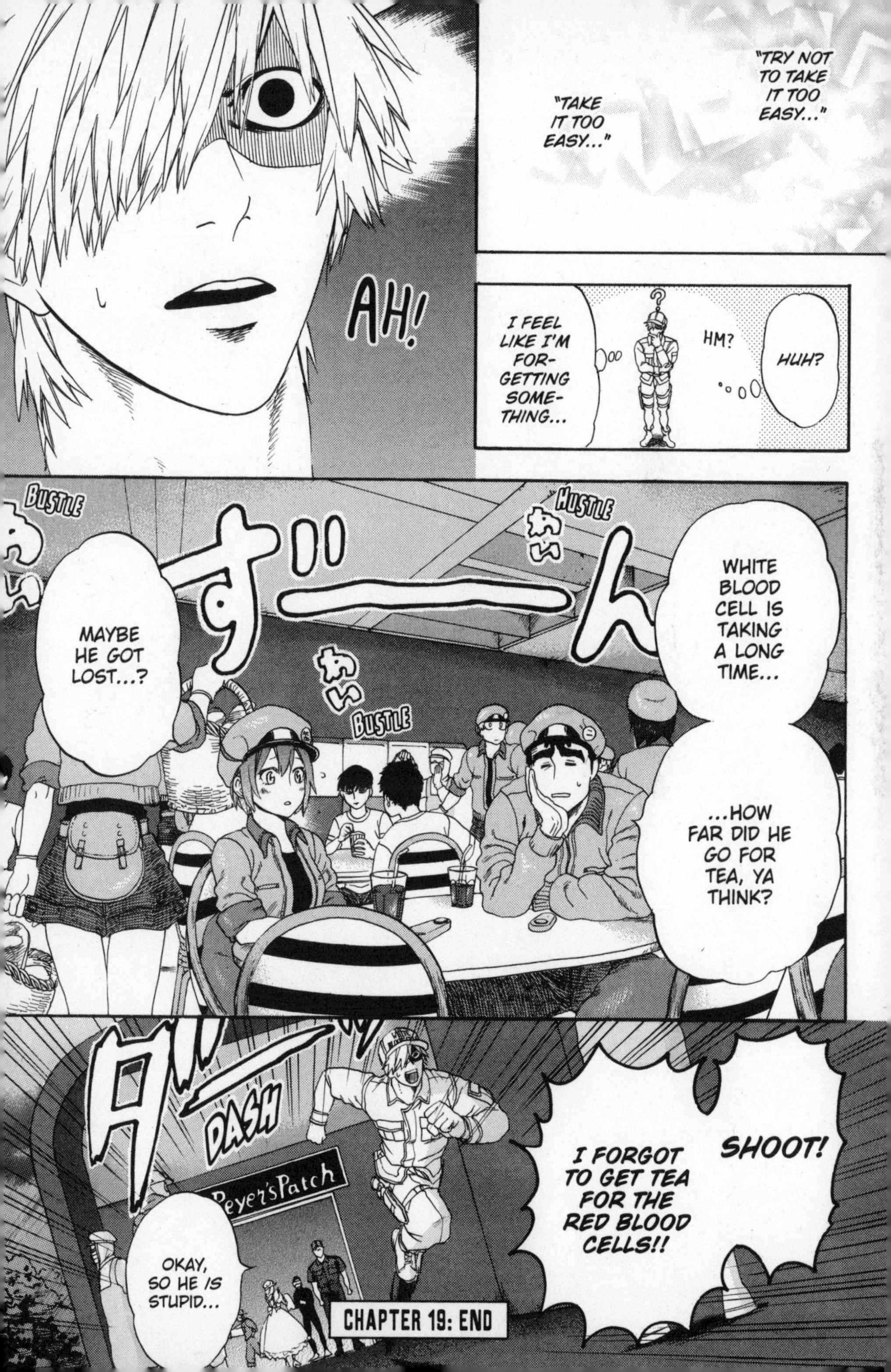
"TRY NOT TO TAKE IT TOO EASY..."
"TAKE IT TOO EASY..."
HUH?
HM?
I FEEL LIKE I'M FOR-GETTING SOME-THING...
AH!
HUSTLE
BUSTLE
WHITE BLOOD CELL IS TAKING A LONG TIME...
...HOW FAR DID HE GO FOR TEA, YA THINK?
BUSTLE
MAYBE HE GOT LOST...?
SHOOT!
I FORGOT TO GET TEA FOR THE RED BLOOD CELLS!!
DASH
Peyer's Patch
OKAY, SO HE IS STUPID...
CHAPTER 19: END

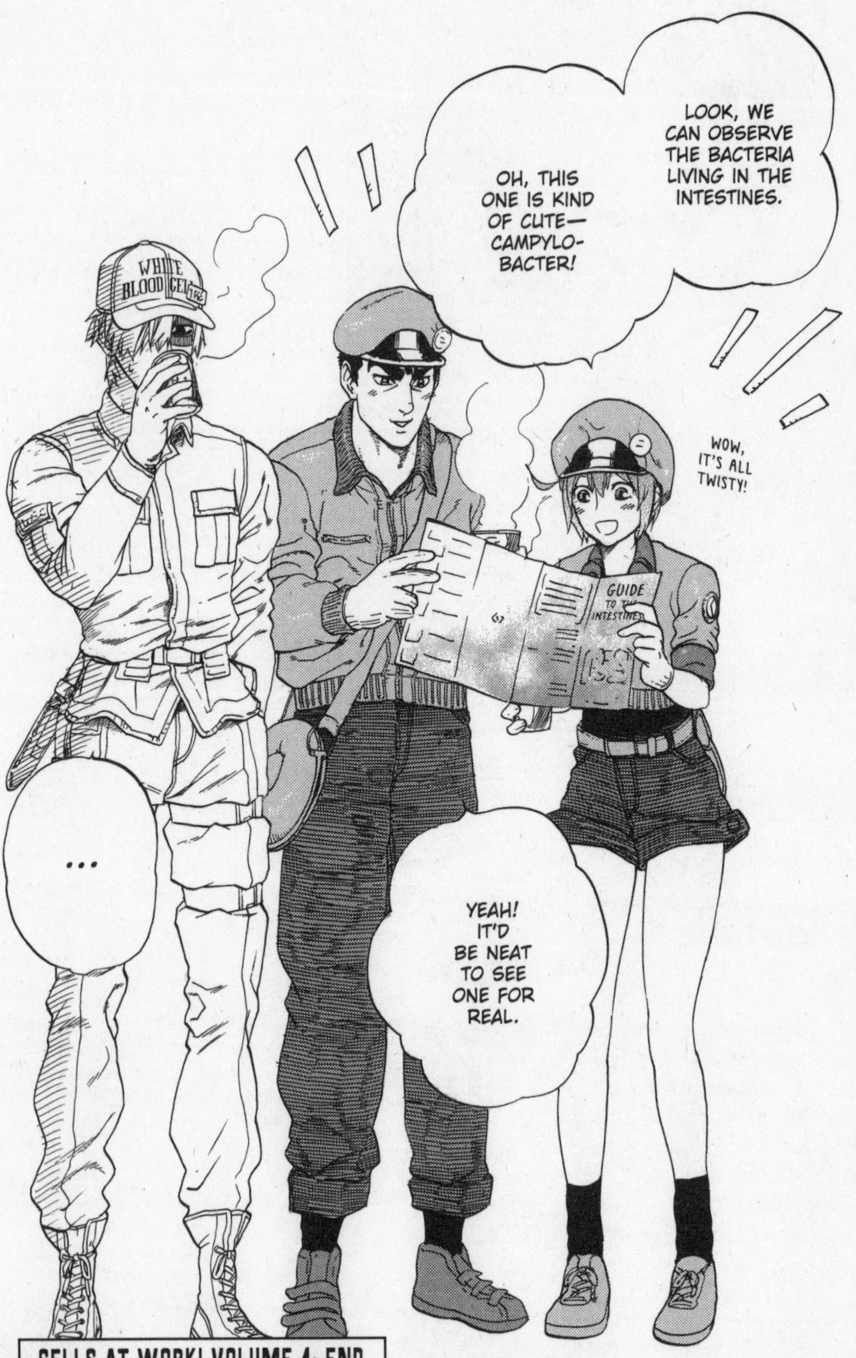
LOOK, WE CAN OBSERVE THE BACTERIA LIVING IN THE INTESTINES.
OH, THIS ONE IS KIND OF CUTE— CAMPYLO-BACTER!
WOW, IT'S ALL TWISTY!
YEAH! IT'D BE NEAT TO SEE ONE FOR REAL.
...

CELLS AT WORK! VOLUME 4: END

Medical Editor: Tomoyuki Harada

TRANSLATION NOTES

I AM THE SENPAI!!
SNAP
RIGHT.
HUSTLE
?
I'M YOUR KOHAI, RIGHT...?

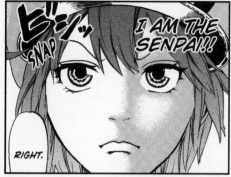

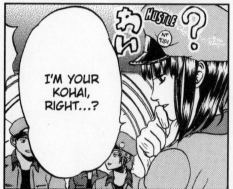

Senpai and Kohai

Page 68

The Japanese word "*senpai*" roughly translates to "upperclassman" or "senior." While it is used by students to refer to their older peers, it is not necessarily an academic term, and can be used to refer to anyone in a given situation who's more experienced than the speaker but not necessarily in a position of authority over them, as opposed to a teacher or a boss, who would not be considered a *senpai*.

"*Kohai*," meanwhile, refers the the opposite—someone who is junior or less experienced. An underclassman at a school would be an upperclassman's *kohai*, and a newly hired employee would likewise be their more experienced colleagues' *kohai*.

Senpai are generally obliged to look out for their *kohai*, while *kohai* are expected to respect their *senpai*.

Ora ora ora!

Page 71

White Blood Cell's exclamation as he tears into the bacterium is an expression of macho self-aggrandizement that may derive from the words "ore da," which are a particularly brash and masculine way of saying "it's me!"

However, the phrase has become best known for being a recurring catchphrase in *JoJo's Bizzarre Adventure,* Hirohiko Araki's long-running manga series, where (as it is here) it's shouted during an attack, typically with many more than the three repetitions White Blood Cell uses here.

ORA ORA ORA!

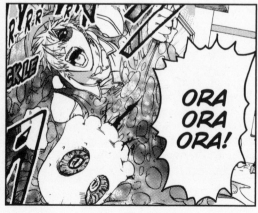

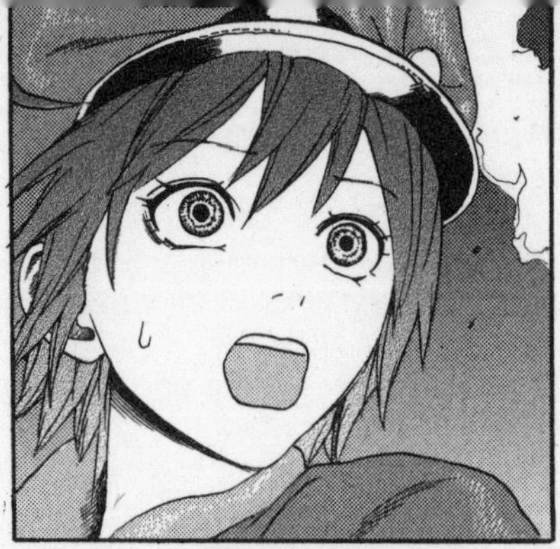

Kohai-chan

Page 85

In Japanese the suffix "*-chan*" is a diminutive honorific that denotes affection as well as implying a certain degree of social seniority on the part of the speaker. Like most honorifics in Japan, it would typically be used in conjunction with a proper name.

Red Blood Cell's usage of *-chan* with the term *kohai* is as charmingly eccentric (and slightly airheaded) as you might expect it to be.

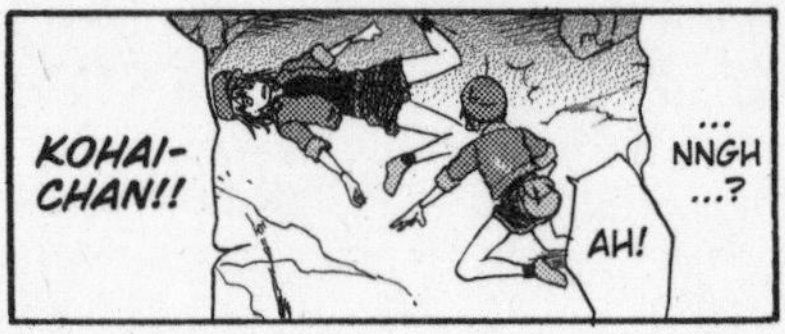
...NNGH...?
AH!
KOHAI-CHAN!!

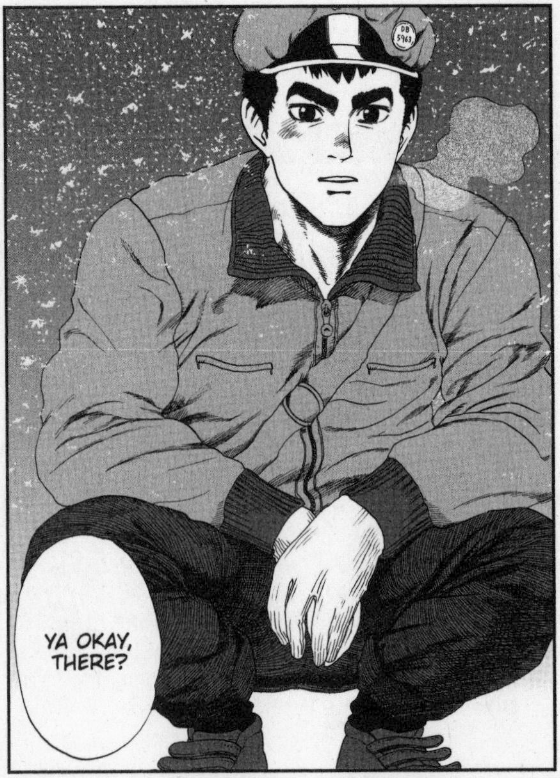
YA OKAY, THERE?

Kansai dialect

Page 109

The transfused red blood cells that save the day are immediately identifiable as unusual because of their speech. Starting with the very first line, they use the dialect of the Kansai region of Western Japan—an area which includes Osaka, Kyoto, and Kobe. *Kansai-ben*, as it's known in Japanese, is strongly associated with the heartily mercantile culture of Osaka, and is typically thought to sound earthier and jauntier than standard Tokyo-area Japanese.

Cells at Work!

はたらく細胞

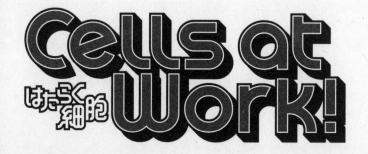

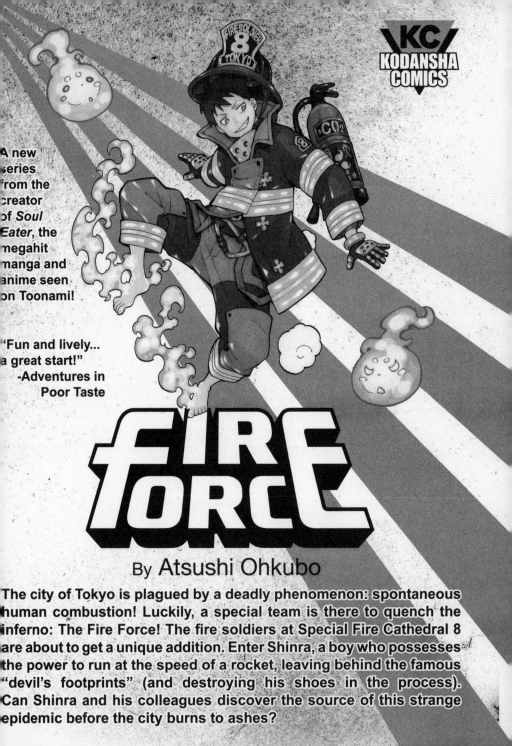

KC
KODANSHA
COMICS

A new series from the creator of *Soul Eater*, the megahit manga and anime seen on Toonami!

"Fun and lively... a great start!"
-Adventures in Poor Taste

FIRE FORCE

By Atsushi Ohkubo

The city of Tokyo is plagued by a deadly phenomenon: spontaneous human combustion! Luckily, a special team is there to quench the inferno: The Fire Force! The fire soldiers at Special Fire Cathedral 8 are about to get a unique addition. Enter Shinra, a boy who possesses the power to run at the speed of a rocket, leaving behind the famous "devil's footprints" (and destroying his shoes in the process). Can Shinra and his colleagues discover the source of this strange epidemic before the city burns to ashes?

"I'm pleasantly surprised to find modern shojo using cross-dressing as a dramatic device to deliver social commentary... Recommended."

-Otaku USA Magazine

The prince in his dark days

By Hico Yamanaka

A drunkard for a father, a household of poverty... For 17-year-old Atsuko, misfortune is all she knows and believes in. Until one day, a chance encounter with Itaru–the wealthy heir of a huge corporation–changes everything. The two look identical, uncannily so. When Itaru curiously goes missing, Atsuko is roped into being his stand-in. There, in his shoes, Atsuko must parade like a prince in a palace. She encounters many new experiences, but at what cost…?

Based on the critically acclaimed classic horror manga

The first new *Parasyte* manga in over 20 years!

NEO PARASYTE f

BY ASUMIKO NAKAMURA, EMA TOYAMA, MIKI RINNO, LALAKO KOJIMA, KAORI YUKI, BANKO KUZE, YUUKI OBATA, KASHIO, YUI KUROE, ASIA WATANABE, MIKIMAKI, HIKARU SURUGA, HAJIME SHINJO, RENJURO KINDAICHI, AND YURI NARUSHIMA

A collection of chilling new *Parasyte* stories from Japan's top shojo artists!

Parasites: shape-shifting aliens whose only purpose is to assimilate with and consume the human race... but do these monsters have a different side? A parasite becomes a prince to save his romance-obsessed female host from a dangerous stalker. Another hosts a cooking show, in which the real monsters are revealed. These and 13 more stories, from some of the greatest shojo manga artists alive today, together make up a chilling, funny, and entertaining tribute to one of manga's horror classics!

KC KODANSHA COMICS

KC
KODANSHA COMICS

New action series from Takei Hiroyuki, creator of the classic shonen franchise Shaman King!

In medieval Japan, a bell hanging on the collar is a sign that a cat has a master. Norachiyo's bell hangs from his katana sheath, but he is nonetheless a stray — a ronin. This one-eyed cat samurai travels across a dishonest world, cutting through pretense and deception with his blade.

NEKOGAHARA

STRAY CAT SAMURAI

By
Hiroyuki Takei

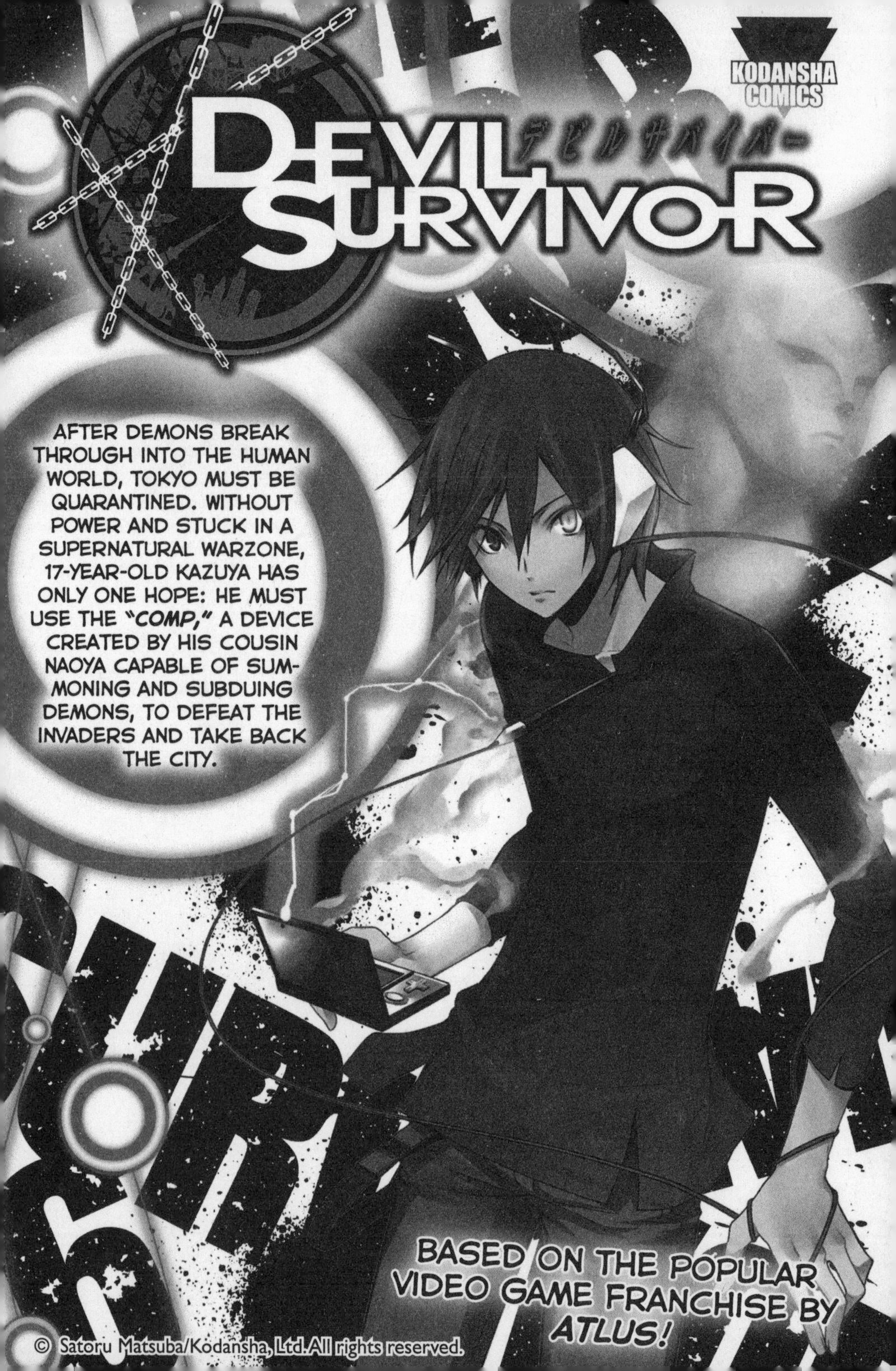
KODANSHA COMICS
DEVIL SURVIVOR
デビルサバイバー
AFTER DEMONS BREAK THROUGH INTO THE HUMAN WORLD, TOKYO MUST BE QUARANTINED. WITHOUT POWER AND STUCK IN A SUPERNATURAL WARZONE, 17-YEAR-OLD KAZUYA HAS ONLY ONE HOPE: HE MUST USE THE "COMP," A DEVICE CREATED BY HIS COUSIN NAOYA CAPABLE OF SUMMONING AND SUBDUING DEMONS, TO DEFEAT THE INVADERS AND TAKE BACK THE CITY.
BASED ON THE POPULAR VIDEO GAME FRANCHISE BY ATLUS!
© Satoru Matsuba/Kodansha, Ltd. All rights reserved.

"This series never fails to put a smile on my face."
-Dramatic Reviews

"A very funny look at what happens when two strange and strangely well-suited people try to navigate the thorny path to true love together."

-Anime News Network

My Little Monster

OPPOSITES ATTRACT...MAYBE?

Haru Yoshida is feared as an unstable and violent "monster." Mizutani Shizuku is a grade-obsessed student with no friends. Fate brings these two together to form the most unlikely pair. Haru firmly believes he's in love with Mizutani and she firmly believes he's insane.

KC
KODANSHA
COMICS

A Kodansha Comics Trade Paperback Original.

Published in the United States by Kodansha Comics,
an imprint of Kodansha USA Publishing, LLC, New York.

Publication rights for this English edition arranged through Kodansha Ltd., Tokyo.

First published in Japan in 2016 by Kodansha Ltd., Tokyo, as *Hataraku Saibou* volume 4.

ISBN 978-1-63236-391-6

Printed in the United States of America.

www.kodanshacomics.com

9 8 7 6 5 4 3

Translation: Yamato Tanaka
Lettering: Abigail Blackman
Editing: Paul Starr
Kodansha Comics edition cover design: Phil Balsman